MY FATHER'S WATCH

Patrick Maguire and Carlo Gébler

MY
FATHER'S
WATCH

The Story of a Child
Prisoner in 70s Britain

FOURTH ESTATE • *London*

First published in Great Britain in 2008 by
Fourth Estate
An imprint of HarperCollins*Publishers*
77–85 Fulham Palace Road
London W6 8JB
www.4thestate.co.uk

Visit our authors' blog: www.fifthestate.co.uk

1

A catalogue record for this book is
available from the British Library

HB ISBN 978-0-00-724213-9
TPB ISBN 978-0-00-728076-6

Typeset in Minion by Palimpsest Book Production Limited,
Grangemouth, Stirlingshire

Printed in Great Britain by Clays Ltd, St Ives plc

Mixed Sources
Product group from well-managed
forests and other controlled sources
www.fsc.org Cert no. SW-COC-1806
© 1996 Forest Stewardship Council
FSC

FSC is a non-profit international organisation established to promote the
responsible management of the world's forests. Products carrying the FSC
label are independently certified to assure consumers that they come
from forests that are managed to meet the social, economic and
ecological needs of present and future generations.

Find out more about HarperCollins and the environment at
www.harpercollins.co.uk/green

For Anniebow

As for those who wouldn't believe, didn't believe, and don't believe – bollocks.

Patrick Maguire

CONTENTS

PREFATORY NOTE

Some names have been changed in the text to protect the identity of those who would not wish to be identified.

Carlo Gébler and Patrick Maguire

OVERTURE

I was a boy, eight, maybe nine. It was evening and Dad came in from the pub. He smelt of beer and cigarette smoke, had shiny eyes and moved funny.

He lay on the settee. I crept up and stared at his watch. The face was white in the centre, black around the edge, and all the numbers were gold. The strap was the expanding sort, little silver-coloured pieces that hinged and fitted tightly around his big wrist. I was sure the strap must hurt where it caught the hairs on his arm but he never said anything about that.

He had bought the watch when he was stationed in Egypt with the Royal Inniskilling Fusiliers from a man on a camel. That was his story anyway, and I believed him. He was eighteen, it was nineteen fifty-something, and for a boy from Belfast to get a good watch like that then, it was a big deal. He always said the watch would be mine one day, and though he never said when exactly that would happen, I believed this too.

I bent down and got my ear near the casing. I heard tick, tick, tick, and behind this Dad's regular breathing.

Now I wanted to wear the watch like I had many times before. Often, when he came home from work he'd say, 'Here, look after my watch,' and give it to me. Or if he'd had a drink, he'd take it off before he stretched out on the settee and I'd put it on. Or if he made it up the stairs, he'd leave it on the bedside table and I'd get it from there. In the morning, he didn't have to look far for it. He'd call, 'Son,' – he called me Son or very occasionally Patrick, never Paddy – and I'd come running with it.

I began to tug it off. Dad opened an eye and squinted up at me. 'Do you want it?' he said.

'Can I?'

He took it off and handed it to me.

I slipped it over my left hand and pushed it up towards my shoulder. Now I could be sure it wouldn't fall off.

Dad closed his eye. I strutted off.

'Son,' Dad called.

I came running.

'Watch needs winding,' he said. He pulled it off. 'Only twelve times now.'

I'd done this before. 'One, two, three . . .' I counted, turning the little wheel on the side, hearing first the watch coming back to life, and then the tick going faster and faster.

'. . . twelve,' I shouted.

'Well done, son. You're a good lad.' He rubbed the top of my head, then turned and left.

It was evening. Dad came home. He was working as a security guard in a toy factory. 'Son,' he called.

I ran up. He was in his guard's uniform and he had a couple of interesting boxes under his arms, each six or seven inches high, and each holding – I could guess this – a toy, probably an action figure.

'Here,' said Dad.

I took them, and as I saw what they were, my heart raced and I felt giddy. In one box the Lone Ranger sat on his horse and in the other was his faithful Indian assistant, Tonto. The figures came with all the extras – lassos, guns, holsters, a feathered headdress – and each box was decorated with pictures of the American west.

'Oh, thanks, Dad.'

Mum appeared. 'Did you pay for them?'

'Yes,' said Dad, winking at me. 'I paid for them.'

I set the figures free, nudged the settee from against the wall and squeezed into the space behind. Now, in my mind, I made the Rocky Mountains and sent my figures off on great adventures.

As Anne-Marie got older, she started playing there. Dad would pin a blanket to the wall and hang the rest of it over the settee to make her a house, and I took the Lone Ranger and Tonto on adventures in other parts of our home.

I was on the settee watching TV.

'Here, son.' Dad handed me his tobacco pouch, the one we'd given him for Father's Day, leather, dark brown, shaped like an envelope, fastened with a popper, plus a packet of Old Holborn. 'Can you do the business for me?'

'Oh, yes,' I said. I liked this job.

I sat at the table. I undid the foil round the tobacco and the smell came up, rich and dark. I broke off a piece and started to tease it into a pile of loose threads that Dad could roll into cigarettes. I shredded the whole lot and the heap was several times bigger than the block had been. I opened the pouch and tipped everything in. Then I closed the popper. It made a nice ping. 'Dad, I done it,' I shouted. I gave him his pouch.

'Well done, son,' he said, and gave the top of my head a little rub, like he always did when he was pleased with me.

Seven years later, Court Two, the Old Bailey. The place smelt of dust and old wood, dry leather and radiator paint.

I was in the dock behind my dad. I leant forward on my chair, balancing on the two front legs, and tapped his right shoulder. 'What time is it?'

He looked at his watch. He'd had it with him on remand so I'd hardly seen it for months except on visits when he'd take it off and give it to me to hold. He turned his head a bit and, from the corner of his mouth, he told me.

The trial started. Every now and again I would ask Dad the time. After the third or fourth time he looked right and nodded instead of answering.

I looked in the same direction. On the wall, below the public gallery, I saw an indoor clock. It was no good to me. Even though I was fourteen I couldn't read the time. I couldn't tell Dad that. It would have been humiliating.

The court voices droned on. I did try to listen but I couldn't understand what they were saying. I got bored, then very bored and then, because there was nothing else to do, I began teaching myself to read the time, using the big clock. It took a day or two and then I had it, and once I had it, well, I couldn't stop myself. 'It's ten thirty . . . It's twelve forty-five . . . It's two twenty.' I drove everyone mad with my announcements.

On Thursday, 4 March 1976, a few weeks short of my fifteenth birthday, just before half twelve, the jury delivered their verdicts.

Unanimously, on the charge of unlawful possession of nitro-glycerine, they found my parents Anne and Paddy Maguire, my brother Vincent Maguire, my uncle by marriage Giuseppe Conlon, my mother's brother Sean Smyth and our old family friend Pat O'Neil guilty. By a majority of eleven to one, I was found guilty too. We all got jail, lots of it.

A few minutes later, in a holding cell under the court, Dad gave me his wristwatch. He'd always said it would be mine one day and now it was.

That evening, in Reception at Ashford, I asked the screw if I could keep it. He said, no, I didn't need to know the time because I wasn't fucking going anywhere for the next four years, was I?

I started the sentence. The screw was right. I didn't need to know the time. I just had to do it and no watch could help with that.

At the end of my sentence, the watch came back to me. I took it to London and put it away. It was no longer just a watch. It was the only thing left of the life I'd had before I went to jail.

PART ONE

1

Mum was from West Belfast, the Lower Falls, Abyssinia Street. Her maiden name was Anne Smyth. She was Catholic. After school, she worked in a mill. Her first and only boyfriend, my dad, also from Belfast, also a Catholic, was a soldier. He enlisted in the Irish Army in 1952, deserted about eighteen months later, crossed the border into Northern Ireland and joined the Royal Inniskilling Fusiliers. He served with them in Egypt and Cyprus. He was demobbed in 1956, and the following year he and Mum got married in St Peter's Pro-cathedral in Belfast, Mum's parish church. The date was 26 September 1957.

After the ceremony, there was a reception. Then Mum and Dad went down to the docks and caught the boat for England. People would do that in those days: they would marry and go straight to England.

That night Mum and Dad got to London. They went to my aunt Teasy's. She was Granny Smyth's sister. She lived in Kennington in south London. Mum and Dad's plan was to live and work in London, save up enough money for a deposit on a house in Belfast, then come home. That was the plan but they only got as far as the living and working in London part.

The following morning Dad took Mum to their new home. It was a bedsit in Lanark Road, Maida Vale – one room with a shared cooker on the landing. Mum burst into tears. Granny and Grandpa Smyth's small house in Belfast, which she'd left behind, was better than this. My father said it wasn't for ever. He promised that in time they would move on to a better flat.

And, after a couple of months, they did. Mum got a basement flat at 99 Randolph Avenue, also in Maida Vale. The rent was three pounds ten shillings a week, and it had a garden.

On the eighth of the eighth 1958 my brother Vincent was born in St Mary's Hospital on the Harrow Road. Mum was warned not to have another baby too soon, but she did. In 1959 John was born. In the same year Dad, through his contacts at the British Legion, got a job with the North Thames Gas Board as a fitter.

In the summer of 1960, Mum took her two boys to Belfast for a holiday with her parents. She didn't feel very well. She told Granny Smyth she thought she was pregnant, and she was. Granny Smyth decided her daughter couldn't go back to a one-bedroom flat in London and have the baby there. She must have it in Belfast.

Mum phoned Dad in London. Dad agreed. In the meantime, he said, he would try to find a bigger flat. He got nowhere.

When she was six months pregnant, Mum left Vincent and John with Granny Smyth and went back to London to help Dad find somewhere bigger. She had no more luck than he had. A housing association advised her to move into a halfway house with the children. She wouldn't. She went home to Belfast.

A bit later Dad followed. He knew Mum wanted to stay in Belfast, now she had two sons and a third child on the way. Through his army contacts, he was offered a job at Thiepval Barracks in Holywood outside Belfast. He had lived there when he was a soldier. He was also offered work by the post office, stringing wires between telegraph poles. The trouble was, he couldn't settle. He didn't want to be in Belfast. London was his home now – or it was where he felt at home, anyway. After a few weeks, he went back. Mum stayed behind with my two brothers.

I was born in the Royal Victoria Hospital on 22 March 1961. My mum wanted to call me Gary or Kevin. Granny Smyth wouldn't hear of it. She said that as I was due on St Patrick's Day, March 17, I'd come with my name attached, even though I was a few days late. Also, Patrick was my dad's name. He agreed with Granny Smyth, so Patrick I became, second name Joseph. Mum said later my name was about the only thing he and Granny Smyth ever agreed on.

Mum and her three sons went back to London in May. Dad had at last found us a new flat. It was on St Luke's Road, near the Portobello Road. The rent was six pounds a week so we took in a lodger, Pat O'Neil, a family friend. He had a folding bed in the sitting room.

Now we were settled, my parents started saving, and once there was enough we had a holiday, the first we ever took. We went to Margate. This was the summer of 1963: I was two.

The first morning, I toddled down the stairs of our B-and-B and went into the breakfast room. It was filled with sunshine and smelt of toast, grapefruit and marmalade. The family sat together at a table and tucked into a full English breakfast. A radio was playing somewhere in the background and the windows were open. The nets moved like flags with a light breeze that carried the scent of seaweed and salt. I was desperate to get out on the beach with my bucket and spade.

I got there, and didn't leave until evening. Every day that followed was the same. The highlight of the holiday was the huge rowing-boat-shaped hole that Dad dug in the sand.

Lots of photographs were taken – Mum kept them in a bag in her wardrobe. Once I could open the door, I loved to get them out. I loved to see the look on everyone's face, the look of a good time.

When we moved into our flat in St Luke's the landlady's husband was in prison. He got out after we'd been there two or three years and came with his wife to see what Mum had done with the flat. He took one look and decided she'd made it so nice he fancied moving back in. He offered to ask the Paddington Churches Housing Association if they could rehouse us.

Paddington Churches offered two places, and Mum chose a basement flat in Tavistock Crescent. It wasn't in good shape but the rent – just over two pounds a week – was a lot less than we were paying at St Luke's Road.

Our new home was in a large house with two families upstairs.

Our flat had a large front room and a kitchen with a manhole in the middle of the floor. One day, it rained heavily. Water thundered down in the street outside, surged along the gutter and poured through the grilles over the storm drains. Suddenly the manhole in the kitchen lifted and rainwater flooded into the kitchen. I jumped in and splashed around, even though it was dirty, brown, and smelt of drain and rotting food. Mum opened the back door and swept it out with a brush.

When the rain stopped and the water was gone, our kitchen floor was covered with bits of paper and leaves, twigs and grit. Mum had to mop it clean. This happened every time it rained heavily.

The flat had only one bedroom so we all slept in it. For us boys there were bunk beds. Vincent slept on top because he was the oldest. I shared the bottom with John. Mum and Dad had a double bed. Most mornings, when I woke up, that was where I found myself. In the night, I would toddle over or Mum would fetch me across.

There was a large garden at the back. Mum once tried to grow flowers, but with three children and a dog to look after, as well as keeping a home and going out to work, she had to give up. At the end were the railway lines running between Ladbroke Grove and Westbourne Park. I would watch the trains going up and down and wave to the people in the carriages. I played in the garden all the time. I liked to collect snails in the bucket Mum and Dad had bought me in Margate. Once I got into a neighbour's garden and took theirs. When the children there discovered what I'd done, they wanted their snails back. But I couldn't remember where I'd buried them.

2

It was June 1963. I was two and a quarter. Mum looked after a neighbour's children whose father – he was black – came from some city in the United States. This neighbour, I was told, had a friend, a very important person, who came from the same city and would soon be visiting our street. This VIP was coming to see someone across the road who wanted to open a club for children. We would be able to meet him because our neighbour and the VIP were old buddies and we knew our neighbour.

The day came. My mum got us ready and we went out into the street. There were people and photographers with cameras. Then a car swept up and a huge man with short curly black hair, shiny brown skin and very white teeth climbed out. There was a lot of shouting and cheering.

Everyone followed him inside a house. He went to the top of the room and the crowd was packed around him. He was talking and the crowd were clapping, and I felt Mum pushing me forward. Suddenly I was at the front, and then this big man had me in one arm and another little black boy in the other. He lifted us both on to his lap. 'Don't wet my knee or I'll sting your bum like a bee,' he said, and the crowd laughed.

I felt anxious. I looked for Mum. There she was, not far away, with Vincent and John beside her. A huge smile lit her face.

'White is white and black is black,' the man said. The crowd went wild now and there were blinding flashes as photographs were taken. The little black boy's eyes filled with tears and when he started to cry I began to cry too.

The next thing I remember, Mum was holding me in her arms and we were walking home.

Next week there was a photograph of me, the other boy and the man in the local paper. The text identified him as Cassius Clay, who was in England to fight the British heavyweight champion, Henry Cooper. They met on 18 June at Wembley. Clay had predicted victory in five rounds. In round four, Cooper surprised him and put him down, but at the start of the fifth, Clay came out fighting. He pummelled Cooper and opened a small cut over the Englishman's eye into a big gash that gushed blood. That was it. Clay was declared the winner.

We went to the circus. The juggling clowns impressed me most.

The next day, standing outside on our front door step, I noticed several empty milk bottles. Up they went. I held out my hands to catch them. Mum was in the kitchen. When she heard glass breaking she ran out to see what had happened.

I was taken to St Mary's Hospital, Praed Street, and stitched up.

We left the flat together, Mum, my brothers and me, and headed along Tavistock Crescent. We were going somewhere we loved and arrived a few minutes later. It was Portobello, a long, narrow, hilly street with market stalls on both sides, bustling and colourful. We knew that if we behaved well, Mum would buy us a treat. She always did.

We joined the stream of people moving between the stalls and let ourselves be carried along. Every now and again Mum would stop at a stall and buy what she wanted, fruit here, vegetables there. At the top end, near the Goldhawk Road, she met a friend. They got talking and she put down her shopping. Here was our chance.

We slipped away, my brothers and I, and ran to the special place we always visited. It was a block of flats with gardens surrounded by a big wall topped with a wire-mesh fence. Vincent was tall enough to see through the mesh, but John and I had to stand on tiptoe. It was worth it, though. The garden was filled with gnomes, hundreds of them. There was also a pond with stone rabbits, a tortoise and, right in the middle, a windmill. To me it looked like a helicopter that had crashed, head first, into the ground. I liked to imagine that the gnomes had shot it down.

I scrambled up on to the wall. I wanted to climb in, wrench the helicopter from the ground and carry it home. Several other children had the same idea and were up on the wall with me. We shoved and pushed, hoping to make a hole in the fence.

Suddenly the owner was rushing towards us. I jumped down. So did the others. The man stopped. Victory! He'd seen us off. He went inside. We swarmed back on to the wall. He came out again, ran right up to us this time and shouted through the fence. He was going to tell all our mums that we'd tried to get into his garden to steal his gnomes – and when the police caught us, he said, we'd be punished for what we'd tried to do.

I felt a hand grip my arm. It was Mum. 'What have I told you about climbing on that man's wall?' she said.

She always said that and I knew she would say it next time because we'd be back on that wall again. We couldn't keep off it.

It was another day and we were setting off for Portobello Market again, Mum, the brothers and I. We'd get a treat, said Mum, if we were good. On the other hand, she said if we ran off to look at the gnome garden, we wouldn't.

We shook our heads. We wouldn't be naughty. We wanted our treat, oh, yes.

In Portobello we followed Mum from one stall to another. She bought what she wanted and put the goods in her basket. It wasn't long before I started to lose patience. I hated shopping. When would I get my treat? Maybe she'd just promised so we'd be quiet and good, and once she was done she'd whisk us home without a treat. But Mum had never done anything like that before, had she? Never. But, oh, this was taking so long. Please, please, treat now, I thought. I can't go another step . . .

And then, wow, we were at the pet shop, my favourite.

A couple of children were at the door, waiting to go in. We'd have to wait for the ones inside to come out and make space for us, but that wasn't the end of the world. There was plenty to do out here.

The canopy to keep out the sun and rain was pulled forward with empty birdcages and small bags of hay hanging from the two iron arms that held it up. There was a gentle breeze blowing along Portobello and the cages were banging softly against each other. They made a lovely noise as they did.

I moved forward. In front of the shop, just below the window, there were wooden kennels and rabbit hutches. I climbed straight into a kennel and sat down. I fitted snugly.

I wriggled out and put my face to the window. There were two boxes behind the glass with kittens in one, puppies in the other. I tapped. Heads and ears went up. I tapped again. The puppies turned towards me, except one, stretched out in the wood shavings at the back. There was always one who wouldn't respond. I'd noticed that before. I admired it. That was the one, I decided, that I wanted. He was the dog for me.

'You see that puppy?' I said. I tugged at Mum's sleeve. 'The one lying stretched out. Do you see him?'

'Yes.'

'That's the one I want. Can I have him?'

'What are you on about?' said Mum. She launched into her set speech. We already had a dog and a budgie at home so we wouldn't be buying anything from this shop. We were here to look, and once we'd all had a look, we'd be going home without buying anything. Did I understand?

'Yes,' I said.

Some children came out, which meant there was room inside for the children in front and for us. I went round the coloured bowls, the trays, the bags of dog, cat and rabbit food stacked about the entrance, and in through the door.

Inside, the shop smelt of animal fur and fish food, wet sawdust and stinky wood shavings. Oh, I loved those smells. The walls were covered with cages, each with a bird whistling and singing, and at some cages kids had their fingers stuck through the bars, driving the birds inside mad.

I loved the birds, but I loved what was at the back more and ran there now. This space had black walls and was lined with fish tanks, the only light the little bulbs inside each one.

I ran to the first and peered in. The floor was carpeted with coloured stones, and dotted with rocks and plants with long green tendrils, and hanging there in the water, with bubbles flowing around them, were small purple fish with two huge frilly fans.

How great would it be, I thought, to be so small I could get inside and swim around with them? Or better still, to be a diver in there, dressed in an old-fashioned diving suit and heavy boots, a knife strapped to my leg. I'd get so close to the purple fish I'd reach out and touch them.

I moved to another tank; John was there. This one was full of goldfish. One had something trailing from near his tail.

'What is that?' I asked. 'Is it a baby?'

I wasn't to be so stupid, said John.

But if it wasn't a baby, what was it? John wouldn't say.

Whatever it was, it now detached from the goldfish and floated for a second before another goldfish zoomed up, swallowed it and then spat it out.

'He didn't like that, did he?' said John, and he laughed.

The penny dropped.

'Was that his number twos?'

I wasn't so stupid after all, said John.

In the next tank, the fish were red with yellow barbs dangling from their mouths . . .

Later, I heard Mum calling. We'd been in long enough, she said, it was time to go. I didn't want to go. But if I didn't, perhaps next time we were in Portobello Mum mightn't let us come here.

I pulled my face away from the tank I was staring into and ran to the front of the shop. A packet of budgie seed sat on top of Mum's basket. What was that for? We'd plenty at home, hadn't we? Almost a full packet.

The shopkeeper was smiling but he didn't look like he meant it. He couldn't wait for us to clear off. He didn't want three noisy boys trailing around his shop. Good old Mum. That was why she'd bought the budgie food – it had bought us the time we needed for a really good look.

Mum led me out of our flat and across the road. A beautiful motor-car was parked by the kerb. It was a Rolls-Royce and she said it belonged to Ringo Starr, one of the Beatles. They were shooting a scene for their new film, *A Hard Day's Night*, in Tavistock Road, just round the corner. In it, they ran past a burnt-out church that looked like a bombsite.

Next thing, we were with Ringo and he was signing the guitar Mum had brought with her that belonged to a neighbour, a boy who was mad about the Beatles. After he had signed, Ringo took his hat off and put it on me. It was white and had a peak.

Someone was shouting. It took us a moment or two to realize they were shouting at us. The flat was on fire. We had to go now, said Mum. I knew what that meant. What had just been given to me was about to be taken back.

I turned to run. I wanted to keep that hat. But Mum knew me too well. She caught hold of me before I'd gone a step. The hat was returned to its owner and Ringo explained that he'd worn the hat in all his scenes and he couldn't suddenly stop now, could he?

We hurried away, Mum pulling and me whining for my hat, and got home to see black smoke pouring out of a window and the front door. We went in. It was the kettle. Mum had forgotten she'd put it on to boil before we left.

As I got a bit older, I was able to play in the street. It was fun, and it was safe. This was still the sixties. I'd empty a bottle of water into the gutter and float lolly sticks along.

There was an adventure playground not far from our house, where all the children from the Crescent went. This was where I put on my first pair of boxing gloves. They were a sixteen-ounce pair. My opponent hammered me. It was a long time before I was tempted to put gloves on again.

For my fourth birthday I got a Batman costume, of mask, cape and belt. It was the first one in our street. To begin with I didn't like the mask. I couldn't see properly through the tiny eyeholes. But I got used to it and, the mask mastered, I would roam the street in my outfit (to which I added black wellington boots for the complete Batman look), climbing trees, jumping on and off walls and singing the Batman song. Some of the other children fancied the costume and tried to take it. I fought them off.

There was a sweet shop on the corner. One day I was with another boy, a little bit older, when I noticed that there was a small hole in the wooden trapdoors outside the shop. We looked through and saw empty boxes and a lot of paper underneath.

We went into the shop and each bought a box of matches. Outside, we lit the matches and dropped them one by one through the hole. Smoke began to come out. Now I'd gone and done it. What had seemed a good idea suddenly looked like a very bad one. I began to cry.

The shopkeeper rushed out. He got hold of the two of us and

shouted at us. People from the street ran up to see what was happening. I cried harder, but not so hard I couldn't hear the clang of the fire engine's bell as it drove up the street. Firemen jumped down, unrolled their hoses and squirted water. There was smoke and a smell of burning.

Mum appeared. She took me in her arms. My crying reached its height. 'I was just watching,' I said, between huge sobs.

The shopkeeper, who knew Mum, said nothing. He didn't need to. She knew I was the culprit. At home, I got a slap on the back of my legs.

As I got older, I would ask, 'Why was I born in Belfast when Vincent and John were born in London?' I was told this story.

It was a sunny Sunday afternoon. Mum and Dad were walking through woods near Belfast. They came to a gypsy caravan, the old kind with the rounded roof and tapering sides, horseshoe-shaped. I was chained to the wheel. An old man stood over me. I was his prisoner. Dad punched him on the nose. Mum got the chains off. They brought me home with them, first to Granny Smyth's house in Belfast, then to London. That was how I'd come into the family. I wasn't their son. I was a boy they'd found in a wood.

Later, Mum would also say, when I knew the story was just a story, how happy she was that at least one of her children had been born in Belfast. She loved the city. When the Troubles started, she was grateful she'd ended up in London – we might have had a terrible time in Belfast. Later still, when the Troubles arrived on our doorstep, Belfast suddenly looked as if it mightn't have been so bad, after all. If we'd stayed there, life wouldn't have turned out the way it did. It would have been very different for all of us.

3

In September 1965, when I was four and a half, I started at Colville Primary School, on Lonsdale Road, off Portobello. I told the story that I was found in the woods to some of the children in my class. I can't remember if they were impressed but at some point I know it was explained to me that it was just a story and I was actually born the same way as my brothers.

In the week leading up to 5 November, everyone in my class had to paint a picture of what they'd see on Bonfire Night. We used all the colours in the paint-pots, and then the teacher put our work on the walls. Suddenly my classroom was alive, with my own bit of Picasso lost in one big picture of madness.

I'm sure we were told Guy Fawkes was a Catholic, like my family. I'm sure we were told that when he put the barrels of gunpowder in the vault below the House of Lords his plan was to kill the Scottish Protestant King of England, James I, who was persecuting Catholics. I'm sure we were told that the betrayal of the plotters and the discovery of the gunpowder saved the Protestant monarch and his Parliament from destruction. And Bonfire Night celebrated that. But it went over my head. I didn't care about the history. I just wanted Bonfire Night to come on. I loved it.

Mum found some old clothes, a jumper, a shirt and a pair of trousers. Dad tied the trouser legs and the shirt cuffs with twine, then stuffed them with newspaper until the guy had a full, firm body. Then he found a brown-paper bag, stuffed that, too, and drew a face on the front. The head went on and, as a final touch, a hat was added.

Mum said we could go to the top of the street but no further. My two brothers and I put our guy in the wooden go-kart Dad had made for us earlier in the year and trundled him up the street. We stopped outside the pub, the Metropolitan, and sat on the steps. 'Penny for the guy,' we called, to the people who walked past and the customers who came in and out of the pub. Some threw us change, ha'pennies, pennies and threepenny bits, and if we were very lucky, the odd sixpence or shilling. Later, Dad came out with drinks and packets of crisps.

'You're not to go wandering off,' he said. He was holding the door open and I saw the inside of the pub. There were men along the bar or around tables, bottles and glasses filled with drink, a thick cloud of blue smoke drifting under the ceiling, and the warm smell of beer and fags and working men coming out to me.

'Yes, Dad.'

He went back in.

'Penny for the guy,' we hollered. 'Penny for the guy.' We kept it up until we were cold and went home.

The money we got that week, plus what Mum and Dad gave us, went on fireworks. Dad came home with them just as it was getting dark. We pulled on our coats and went into the garden, and the two families that lived above us came down bringing food, drink and more fireworks. There was a bonfire at the end built with wood we'd scavenged and our guy was on top, his head lolling sideways.

Dad got it going. The flames whooshed up and the guy caught fire. Then Dad lit the fireworks, and the sky above us was alive with sparkling colours, and the whizzes and bangs of rockets. The fire made our upturned faces hot and red.

After the excitement, Mum gave us sandwiches, cakes and drinks. We put potatoes on to bake in the hot embers. Suddenly a ghost jumped on to the wall separating our garden from next door. We screamed. The sheet came off and it was Dad, laughing. Later, when the potatoes were soft and their skins were black, we cut them in half, covered them with butter and scooped out the insides with spoons. The first mouthfuls burnt our tongues.

The following morning, as I walked to school, the air was full of the smell of burning. Charred sticks and the cardboard casings of spent fireworks lay everywhere. As we walked we started a game, me and a couple of lads from my school. How many dead rockets could you find lying about? The boy who found the most was the winner. I could only count up to ten so it wasn't me.

It was the late summer of 1966. I was five and a half. Vincent and John were in Belfast with Granny Smyth. I was at home with Mum. We left the flat in Tavistock Crescent and went to St John's Wood, to the hospital of St John and St Elizabeth. It was a private hospital and the nuns ran it, but they always had two non-paying patients. Mum was one. She was pregnant again.

The hospital had big wooden doors with a bell at the side. Mum pushed the button. I heard the ring inside. We waited. After a bit, one of the doors opened slowly, the hinges squeaking, and there was the nun who always let us in.

'Hello, Mrs Maguire, and how are you today?' she said. Then she patted my head. 'And how is little Patrick?' she said. 'Is he not an angel?'

Mum looked at me in a funny way. She wasn't going to argue with the nun but she wasn't going to agree with her either.

We went in. Mum had her check-up while I sat in a waiting room. Then it was time to go home. When we got back to the front hall, the nun who let us in was standing by the front door. Mum opened her purse. She took out a coin – it was a shilling or maybe a florin – and gave it to me. I put it through the slot in the collection box and heard it clink as it hit the bed of money underneath. I did this on every visit. I had been told the nun would give the money to God, and that in return I would get a sister.

And lo and behold, it happened. Anne-Marie was born on 7 October 1966. I became a staunch believer. When I helped Mum later with the baby, she said I was a good boy, and I always said, 'Mum, I paid for her, didn't I? Of course I'm going to help.'

4

It was 4 March 1967, a Saturday, and I was nearly seven. Pat O'Neil came round early and Mum made bacon sandwiches and tea for breakfast. When I'd eaten I put on my warmest coat. Mum pinned a QPR blue-and-white rosette to my lapel, wrapped a blue-and-white scarf round my neck and put a blue-and-white bobble hat on my head. She'd knitted the last two secretly, and until now I'd never seen them.

I left the house holding Dad's hand, with Vincent and John. Outside, I saw blue-and-white QPR banners strung up everywhere.

Today was the League Cup Final: QPR, in the third division, versus West Bromwich Albion, a first-division team who had won the cup last year.

We wandered down the road and into the Tavistock Hotel, the pub at the end where QPR supporters hung out. The men had pints, while we had crisps and pop. Two coaches appeared and we got on one. It was full of people laughing, singing and drinking beer. There were crates of the stuff in the gangway between the seats and to get down to the back, where the kids had to go, I had to be lifted over them.

The coach nosed slowly off. On the pavements, strangers waved and I waved back. We got to Wembley Stadium and piled out, complaining of hunger. Pat and Dad bought hot dogs and drinks, and we made our way into the ground and to the stands. I found a spot close to a low wall behind one of the goals with a lot of other kids in bobble hats and scarves. Dad was behind, talking to Pat and some others from the coach. Every now and again, as we waited for the match to start, I would turn round to make sure he was still there, and he would smile and ask me if I was all right, and I would nod and smile back at him before turning round again. The stand was noisy with shouting and singing and it was all very new to me as I'd never been to a game before. Then the shouting and singing got louder still, which made me turn to look for Dad. He put out his arms and lifted me on to his shoulders, where I was safe.

QPR won, three goals to two, before a crowd of nearly a hundred thousand.

One day in the summer that year a removals van pulled up outside our flat in Tavistock Crescent. Everything we owned was loaded into it.

'Get in the back,' Dad said to us boys.

Mum wasn't happy. She thought it was dangerous. Dad wondered how we would get to where we were going if we didn't hitch a ride in the van. It was either that or walk. Mum saw the sense in that, not that she would take a lift. She had the pram. What if a stray piece of furniture banged into my little sister during the journey?

We got in. Mum said to sit down while the lorry was moving. I sat and held my most precious possession, a tricycle with a tin bin on the back.

The ramp at the rear was raised and fastened. Now I couldn't see out. I stood up on something so I could. My brothers did likewise. The whole point of riding in the back of the van was to look out as it drove along. The driver, his mate and Dad got into the cab and I heard their doors close, clunk and clunk.

The engine came to life. The van trembled.

'Be careful,' Mum called, standing by the pram with Anne-Marie in it. 'Hold on tight.'

Off we went down Tavistock Crescent, we three boys in the back shouting and roaring. We waved at Mum. She waved back. We waved at the people in the street. They waved back. I saw the house with our flat getting smaller as we followed the curve of the road. I saw Mum with the pram, waving and calling after us to be careful, getting smaller too.

By the Underground station we turned into Great Western Road. Tavistock Crescent, Mum and the pram had vanished. We were on our way. I was extraordinarily excited. I was only travelling a few streets but I might as well have been going to a new continent.

We went over the bridge that crossed the Grand Union Canal and we came to the T-junction at the top of the Great Western Road. The driver turned left and we were on the Harrow Road, a high street of family shops and old businesses. It ran east–west, the canal on its south side and terraces of shops opposite, broken by the streets running north. Fernhead, Ashmore, Portnall and Bravington Roads, then First, Second, Third, Fourth, Fifth and Sixth Avenues.

We entered the Avenues, as we called it, or the Queens Park Estate, as it was officially known, which lay between the Harrow Road and Kilburn Lane. It wasn't a modern 1960s estate with tower blocks. It had been built before the First World War. The terraced houses were called cottages, and they were low, built of dark brick and had porches with pointy roofs.

The van drove on. We passed the streets that led off Third Avenue, Droop, Enbrook, Farrant and Ilbert. Now the driver slowed. The next one, Kilravock Street, was where our new council house was. It was another street of tiny houses with a tree outside every front door – as if they had been built in a park. (In the coming months John and I played a game out there. We'd both stand next to a tree, one on either side of the street, and throw a dart at the other one's tree. It was going well until my dart hit John right in the middle of his forehead.)

The driver stopped outside number seventy-nine, then dropped the ramp to let us out. When I got on to the pavement, I saw some of our new neighbours. They'd heard the van, with my brothers and me roaring, and had come out to look at us. I didn't like being the centre of attention – and I never got to like it.

The new house had two bedrooms and a garden that wasn't as big as the one we'd left behind. It didn't have as good a view either. Instead of railway tracks, there was nothing to see but other small gardens, like ours, with washing-lines hung with laundry. Dad strung one up for us soon after we moved in. Mum washed a few things by hand and put them on the line to dry. Then we were like everyone else.

As there was nothing in the garden I turned to the street for my amusement. I hauled out my tricycle and pedalled up and down the pavement. I wasn't yet ready to move out of sight of our house.

Now that we had moved, we had to go to a new school. On the other side of the Harrow Road, in Kensal Town, there was a Catholic one. Mum and Dad went to see the nuns, but when they heard we'd already been to a Church of England school, Colville Primary, they said we couldn't come. In that case, Mum decided, we should go to Queens Park Primary School, on the corner of Third Avenue and Droop Street. She met the headmaster, who told her he only had room for Vincent. John and I would have to attend a different school on the Harrow Road.

My mother wouldn't hear of it. She wanted us to stay together.

She had several cleaning jobs, and if we were at two different schools her life would become even more complicated than it already was. Since the school of her choice wouldn't have us, she decided to keep us at home until it would. We wouldn't miss much anyway. In a few weeks the summer term would end and then it was the holidays. She reckoned that by September, the headmaster of Queens Park Primary would have seen sense and we'd be in. So, we stayed at home. John and I were delighted. Though Mum and Dad both made us sit down and practise our reading and writing, we were free for the most part to ride about the street, me on my tricycle, John on his bike, and have a good time.

We set out from the house in Kilravock Street with towels and our swimming trunks. Mum had the pram with Anne-Marie at one end and our laundry at the other.

We went down Third Avenue to the Harrow Road and crossed. In front of us now was the Grand Union Canal, filled with black, dirty-looking water. The only way over was by a footbridge, known as Ha'penny Steps. It used to be a toll bridge, or so I was told, and you paid a ha'penny to use it. Now it was free.

We helped Mum carry the pram up the steps to the bridge. The sides were made of iron and the spars were painted deep green. On the other side, we helped her bump the pram down. We had reached our destination: the Harrow Road Baths. We went in and Mum paid the ticket lady. Then she went into the laundry while we ran to the changing rooms, got into our trunks and then into the pool. We had been before. We knew the place. We liked it.

The pool was long and deep, the water cold. It tasted of chlorine. In one corner, there was a room with a sunken square bath, the sort football players sit about in after a match, drinking champagne and singing. There were showerheads above it and we turned them on. Lovely hot water poured down. My brothers and I got in and splashed each other. The bath filled and water flowed over the sides, splashed across the floor and down the drains. Steam, thick and milky, almost like a fog, hung in the air so we didn't see the pool man when he came in – but we heard him when he told us to clear out and turned off the showers.

We ran out and jumped into the pool. We waited in the cold water until the pool man had gone. Now came our chance to do the really exciting thing but we had to be careful that he and the ticket lady didn't catch us. We got out, tore up the stairs and burst through the big doors at the top.

Now we were on the balcony that ran round the pool. Mum had said that in the past, when kids jumped, some had missed the water, hit the hard poolside and broken their ankles and wrists, their ribs and skulls. We were not to do it, she had said. But we had to do it. It was too exciting to pass up. Only we had to do it quickly before anyone could stop us.

I bolted to the front of the balcony and, without a second's hesitation, jumped over. Suddenly I was plunging down, screaming with terror and excitement. I hit the surface with a splash and down I sank through the cold water. My feet found the bottom, pushed, and up I came. My head broke the surface. I heard myself shouting and laughing at my daring, and I wanted to do it again, which I did, which we all did, not once but several times.

Later, Mum came to the poolside and called us. She was nearly ready, the laundry just about done.

We paid no attention as we larked about in the water.

'Come on,' Mum said, 'it's time to get out. Go and get dressed.'

We would, we promised, if we could have just another minute in the water.

'All right,' said Mum, 'but then you've got to get out and get dressed. Then I'll be back for you and we'll go home.'

We stayed in the water, squirting, fighting, throwing each other into the air. She came back a second time and we promised to get out. She came back a third time and we promised again, and this time, we said, we really meant it. She left and we stayed in the water. Then she came back and she said that if we didn't get out now there would be no treat on the way home.

We knew she meant it, so we got out and got dressed. Then we carried the pram up the steps, she pushed it over the bridge, and we carried it down the other side. There was a chip shop near where the bridge came out with steam on the windows. We went in. It smelt of vinegar and batter. Chips and crackling for the kids, fish and chips for Dad, then up Third Avenue towards home, Mum with the pram piled high with clean laundry, Anne-Marie somewhere in the middle, us eating. Lovely.

The headmaster of Queens Park Primary relented and said John and I could join Vincent at his school. Of my time as an infant there I remember the playground mostly, kicking a football, playing war games or chasing the girls.

When it came to learning, my memories are not nearly so rosy. Our early reading books featured Peter, Jane and Pat, their dog. To be named Pat, as I was, became a curse so I insisted on being called Paddy. Unfortunately the prime minister Harold Wilson's dog was called Paddy. That, though, was better than having the same name as the dog in our reading books.

Once I had mastered a few words (and they didn't come easy), I started to write little stories. We were taught to begin our compositions 'One day . . .' then add what happened after that. It was a system that worked well for me.

Time passed and came the day when the teacher stood in front of us.

'You start your stories "One day", don't you?'

'Yes, Miss,' we said. Of course we did. That was what we'd been taught.

'From now on you're going to stop writing "One day".'

Oh?

'Because that's for babies,' she said.

So, how were we to start our stories if not in the old babyish way? I waited, but there was no word from the teacher about the new way. I had lost something reliable and been given nothing new to hold on to.

In September 1968, I moved up from the infants' to the juniors' school. My handwriting was good – it was neat – but the only thing I could spell with confidence was my name. My reading was bad too. I had to attend special reading classes. The teacher would break down the words into their syllables but this put me off altogether. It made me think I couldn't manage a whole word and therefore I was stupid. I wasn't, but as a kid, in this situation, what else would you think?

'Now boys and girls,' said the teacher, a few days later, 'I want you to write something about what you did at the weekend.'

I wrote about playing in the park where I had gone as usual, and added a drawing of some trees, grass and me. I was always happy to do a bit of art: other than my handwriting it was the only thing I was good at.

'Patrick,' said the teacher, 'come up and show me your work, please.'

I carried my book to the desk. She took it and started to read. Her face was still for a moment. Then she scowled and, with her red correcting pencil, she circled a word.

'Look at this,' she said. 'Playing is not spelt p-a-l-y-i-n-g, is it?'

My face reddened and I wanted to turn and run. I always felt like that when I was scolded.

She went to the blackboard and chalked P-A-L-Y-I-N-G.

'This is how Patrick spelt "playing" and that's not right, is it?' she said. 'Can someone tell me how to spell it properly?'

'P-L-A-Y-I-N-G,' shouted a child.

'Thank you. And you should know that, Patrick,' she said. 'We've been over it enough times.'

I went back to my desk thinking, fuck this, they won't get any more out of me, and from then on I gave up. I won't say I went downhill from there because I don't think I'd even got on to the hill, but I wasn't going to do any more reading and writing because I was never going to give my teacher the chance to humiliate me like that again.

School became a punishment. I knew I was no good – or I believed I was no good – and nothing happened to change my mind, not even winning a prize. It was a book, *The Call of the Wild* by Jack London. The cover was very nice. I got it home, opened it and saw this:

CHAPTER I

Into the Primitive

Old longings nomadic leap,
Chafing at custom's chain;
Again from its brumal sleep.
Weakens the ferine strain

I couldn't make head or tail of it or any of the rest of the page. Someone at school had said I was given it so I wouldn't feel left out. Now I knew that was true.

A man came to the school to test the children's musical ability and somehow I was selected to learn the violin. I carried it to and from school every day and had a lesson once a week, but I had nothing to show for my pains, other than a sore neck. Mum was proud, though. She would say to people, 'My son Patrick plays the violin, you know.'

There was a man who used to come to our house – Dad, who was still a gas fitter, did private jobs for him – and he played the violin in the London Symphony Orchestra. When he came, I would run up the stairs and hide in my bedroom for fear that he would ask me to play a note or two. I didn't want to show myself up in front of Mum.

In the late autumn of 1969, when I was eight, preparations started for Christmas at the Queens Park Primary School. There was a band made up of the oldest juniors but each year a few younger children played with them. I was chosen and so was another kid who was also having violin lessons. He was about as good as I was.

It was afternoon. The band was in the assembly hall, arranged around the piano. I was sitting at the front with the other kid, our violins under our chins. That much we did know. We went through the motions, pretending to play, keeping an eye on the other band members. When their bows went up, our bows went up, when theirs went down, ours followed. We tried not to make too much noise, if any. For a day or two we got away with this. But you can't get away with something for ever. You'll always be caught out in the end.

One day the teacher pulled us out in front of the band. 'Play something,' she said, pointing at me.

'What?'

'Anything.'

I pulled my bow over the strings. I made a noise like two cats fighting.

The teacher couldn't work out how the other lad and I had got into the band in the first place. In fact, neither could we. Was it just because we had violins? No one had asked if we could play and we hadn't told anyone anything different. Well, why would we? If we'd said anything we wouldn't have got out of the class-room as we had and for that it was worth the risk. Yes, it was worth it, even though we looked like fools in the end.

Football was my game, and I was good at it. Number nine, up front. The only thing Dad ever told me about it was this: get the ball into the goal. Good advice. Our home ground was Paddington Rec and I couldn't wait for Saturdays.

It was a training day. The boys of the Queens Park Primary School squad were on their practice pitch on Wormwood Scrubs. The Scrubs were open and flat and, as we waited for Sir to organize us into teams, we could see all the way to an old building with high walls.

'What's that place, sir?'

'That's where they put the bad boys,' he said.

What was he on about? I wondered. Then I caught on.

Sometimes, when I was sitting at Mum's feet having my head stroked and my back rubbed, there'd be something on television about these places. I'd not paid much attention but I'd taken in enough to understand what they were and now I knew that this was one of them.

It looked horrible. But it was only for bad boys. Wasn't that what Sir had said?

So what exactly did those bad boys do to end up in that grim building? I'd no idea but it would be worse than anything I could think of, let alone do, I was sure. I would never end up in a place like that, I thought.

And the boys with me, they thought the same. Standing there, looking at Wormwood Scrubs jail, we shuddered, and we all thought, No, not me, never – I'll never go to a place like that.

'Right, lads,' shouted Sir. 'Listen up.'

The place with the high walls went right out of my mind as we started to train.

5

My father left the Gas Board in 1970, after eleven years as a fitter. At first he didn't let on to Mum, but when he did they had an awful row and Mum said something about leaving him.

Now that he was out of work, Dad was drinking every day. He went to Horton Hospital at Epsom in Surrey for treatment but discharged himself after five weeks. Later he went back but discharged himself again. Then he got work, first as a fitter at a factory in Park Royal that made double-glazed windows, then at William Press and finally on the Mozart Estate, which was being built close to our house, as a night-watchman.

Some evenings I would go with my brothers to visit him there. We would sit in his little hut and drink tea or muck about on the site. For me, the attraction was the dogs that came with the job: Brandy the Alsatian bitch, who lived at home with us, driving Mum mad and terrifying her, and Whiskey, who lived on the site.

One night, coming home with Dad, I asked if I could hold Brandy's lead. I was big enough, I believed, for the job. 'Yes,' he said. 'But you can't let go.'

I wouldn't have dreamt of letting go. That would have defeated the whole purpose, which was to be seen walking along the road with a huge Alsatian.

I took the lead and we walked on. I felt so proud, Brandy and me together, Dad behind. There was the corner. Once round it, we'd be on the last stretch to Kilravock Street and home.

We made the turn, Brandy first, me, then Dad.

Next thing, the lead snapped taut and my arm jolted.

A cat had been sitting in the middle of the pavement until we turned the corner. Now it was bolting.

I heard Brandy's claws scuffling on the pavement and Brandy barking as she took off after it. Behind, I heard Dad shout, 'Hold on! Don't let go!' He was laughing too.

Brandy ran faster and I had to speed up too. If I let go I'd never get to walk the dog home again and I couldn't have that. Oh, no, whatever happened, I was holding on.

Next thing, just like in *Tom and Jerry*, there was a tree ahead. The cat flew up it and got on to a branch. Brandy, with me behind, ran up to the tree and jumped up, putting her front paws on the trunk, barking and whining.

Dad came up and took the lead off me. With some difficulty he yanked Brandy away and we went on towards home. 'Well done,' he said, laughing.

I just walked on beside him. Praise from Dad gave me such a good feeling, one I relished. It was one of the best feelings I knew. Maybe even *the* best.

One afternoon when I came in after school, I heard voices in the front room and popped my head round the door to see who it was.

Dad was on the settee, in his usual place, and a mate from his Gas Board days was in the armchair. Each had a dictionary on his lap. I knew what they were doing. I'd seen it before. They were playing the game. One would call out a word, and then the other spelt it and gave a definition without looking in his dictionary. Then they'd both check to see if the answer was right. They were playing for pints. I loved hearing the words being called, the definitions offered, then read and the discussions that followed.

I slipped in, sat down quietly and crossed my ankles. I'd listen for as long as it lasted. I wouldn't remember the words later, I knew that, but it didn't matter. It was the words and all the talk I loved. It was from this that Dad got his nickname when we were kids. We called him 'The Dictionary'.

Some time in 1970, Westminster Council, who owned most of the Queens Park Estate, started renovating the houses on Third Avenue. They were brick-built Victorian terraced houses, larger than our current home, with a few bits of fancy plasterwork on the outside. Mum decided she liked number forty-three and when she walked past, which was many times every day, she always said, 'Oh, I wish that could be our house.'

When I heard this, I became interested. On my way to school, I would jump on to the low wall separating number forty-three from the pavement, lean against the front window, put my hands on either side of my face to keep out the light and look in. The front room was great. I began to wish, too, that number forty-three could be ours.

Mum talked to the workmen and to the official on the council who allocated housing. He knew Dad from his days as a gas fitter. He also knew that Dad was a security guard on the estate the council was building opposite 43 Third Avenue, and now, suddenly, everything fell into place. We needed a bigger house, and they needed someone to keep an eye on the building site all the time, not just at night, which Dad could do from number forty-three. The council decided to move us in. When the renovations were complete, we left Kilravock Street for Third Avenue.

The new house was not just bigger than the old one but nicer, with everything freshly painted. When you went in there was a front room to your left and behind it another that looked out over the backyard. This was the spare room, for people like Sean Smyth, my mum's brother, when he came to England. The kitchen was at the very back, with the bathroom beyond.

Upstairs there were three bedrooms. I slept with my brothers at the front, with Mum and Dad in the room over the spare, and Anne-Marie in the tiny one that overlooked the garden.

It was a nice, snug, happy home.

Although Dad was no longer a North Thames fitter he continued to do private gas jobs as he had when he worked for the Board.

One afternoon, the phone rang. Mum answered, then called Dad. He came to the phone, listened for a few moments, and hung up. He had another job to do for the landlord who used his services.

'Son,' he called, 'we're going out.'

When Dad had an unofficial gas job, I always helped.

I ran out to an old kitchen unit we kept in the garden as a sort of shed. It had a low door, which I opened. There, on the shelf inside, were Dad's overalls in a plastic bag and, underneath, his tool bag. It was an official North Thames Gas Board one, made of hessian with rope handles.

I took the overalls and the bag and carried them to the front door, then sat on the wall to wait.

A few minutes later a Jaguar pulled up, deep red, with chrome bumpers and trim, all shiny and bright.

I waved to the driver, ran in and told Dad the landlord was there. He gathered his tobacco tin, his lighter, his watch and his coat. He was in no hurry. He never was.

I was the one in a hurry. I liked cars, but the one waiting by the kerb was exceptional. Even then I knew a good car when I saw one and I couldn't wait to drive off in it. I buzzed about, went to the front door, came back, went out a second time, then came back again to check on Dad's progress.

He noticed me. He couldn't have failed to – I was so restless.

'Hold your horses,' he said. 'There's no need to rush. The landlord can wait,' he added, 'and, what's more, it'll do him good. Patience is a virtue, you know.'

Finally, he had everything he needed. He ambled out of the front door, me running behind. I picked up his overalls and tool bag from the wall and lugged them to the car. They went into the boot, too oily to go anywhere else, and Dad got into the passenger seat, with me in the back.

The doors closed. They were heavy and made a deep solid noise when they shut. The seats were leather, deep red, and the dashboard and the trimmings on the doors were wood. There was a strong smell of leather.

The landlord drove down Third Avenue towards the Harrow Road. I put my face to the window. I was hoping to see someone I knew. I would wave to them and then they would tell everyone they'd seen me in the back of this wonderful car.

We turned on to the Harrow Road. No one I knew had seen me and now I didn't think there was a chance that anyone would. We were that bit too far from where I lived. I stared at the dashboard, the indicator, the gear lever and the steering wheel. I watched the landlord as he drove. It looked easy. I could do that, I thought.

We turned off the Harrow Road and crossed the canal, passing the old gasworks. Now we were at the top of Ladbroke Grove, close to the job, I knew. All of the landlord's properties were round here. He turned into a side-street. It was wide, lined with big white houses, five or six storeys high. He parked. We'd been here before. I remembered the house.

We got out. Two girls were on the pavement turning a skipping rope and singing while a third jumped. Further away, a couple of boys were kicking a football between the parked cars.

Dad lifted his tool bag from the boot, I took his overalls and we followed the landlord up a flight of steps. There were several bells by the front door and a slip of card beside each one with a name written in Biro. The house was all bedsits.

The landlord took out a bunch of keys and opened the door. We stepped into the hall. It was long with a high ceiling and a staircase at the end. The paint was peeling from the walls. The lampshade was dusty. There was a rickety table with sooty letters piled on it, a faint smell of gas and fried onions.

We climbed the stairs, which seemed to go on for ever, arrived at a door and went into a small kitchen. There was a cooker, a gas meter and a water boiler. The landlord explained what had to be done, and listed other jobs around the building he had in mind for Dad. Then he said he would go away and let Dad get on with it.

He left. I heard a radio playing far away and the sound of cutlery rattling.

Dad took off his jacket. His watch was on his wrist. He pulled it off and handed it to me. When I went on a job with him, it was my responsibility to look after his watch. I pushed it deep into my pocket.

He put on his overalls and asked me for his big screwdriver. I opened the tool bag. The inside was black with grease, which had bonded with the hessian over the years. I found the screwdriver and handed it to Dad. He approached the boiler and set to work. The first thing was to get the casing off. I stood behind, my hand in my pocket holding his watch, feeling its weight and shape. As he worked, he explained what he was doing. If I ever wanted to be a gasman like my dad, I thought, I'd have had a good start.

Dad finished in the kitchen, gathered his stuff, carried his bag to another place and started again. I'd seen enough by now and I was restless.

'All right, you can go off but not too far,' said Dad.

I went down to the front door, opened it and stepped outside. The girls were still skipping and singing, the boys still kicking their football. I would have loved a game but I couldn't – I was working.

I slipped back into the dingy hall and started up the stairs. On the way, I met a man coming down. He looked at me in a funny way. He didn't know what I was doing there: that must be why, I thought. 'I'm with my dad,' I said. 'He's a gasman. He's doing a bit of work upstairs.'

The man nodded and went off, and I returned to the place I'd left Dad. I found him working on another boiler.

I was still restless. 'I'm going up top,' I said.

I could, he said, but I wasn't to go near the edge. He didn't want me to have an accident.

I didn't either. 'No, no,' I said. 'I won't go near the edge.'

I climbed up the stairs and got out through a door on to the flat roof at the back. From there, I could see the backs of houses like the one we were in and their gardens. They were very long and big, and you could have a great game of football in them, I thought. It felt good to be in that peaceful place, right at the top of the world.

Later, Dad came out and lit a roll-up. An aeroplane passed overhead, far away. Dad told me how high it was and the countries it might be going to, places I'd never heard of. The only foreign place I knew was Belfast. He finished his fag and went back to work. I stayed outside, looking at the sky and the clouds. Later he came to call me in. He had taken off his overalls but his hands were black. He rubbed a dirty finger along my forehead, making a nice black smear.

Back inside the house I checked that all his tools were in his bag, and closed it. After we'd washed our hands I gave him back his watch. He put it on, buttoned his cuffs and pulled on his jacket. We went downstairs and out on to the front steps.

The children who'd been there before were gone and the street was quieter. It was nearly dark. The red Jaguar returned. I put the tools and overalls into the boot. As we drove off, the landlord asked about the job.

'It was hard,' Dad said. 'Luckily I had help.' He jerked his thumb over his shoulder at me on the back seat with the grubby face of a worker. 'I don't know how I'd have managed without him,' he said.

We got home. I put Dad's things away. When I went back into our house, he and the landlord were saying goodbye. When the man had gone, Dad put his hand into his pocket and took out my wages. That evening it was a half-crown. 'Put that somewhere safe,' he said, 'somewhere you won't lose it.'

I said I would.

'Now go and wash your face,' he said. 'Your mum won't want you round the house looking like that.'

I went to Sunday school after church to prepare to make my first confession. In the class I was told many things, but these went in one ear and out the other. However, what I heard from some of the other children in the playground afterwards did stay with me.

If what you confessed was very bad, they said, the priest pulled a lever and the floor that you were kneeling on in the confession box opened up, and you fell into a black hole and then you went on falling and you didn't stop until you hit the fires of Hell.

Then came the day itself. First there was Mass and then the children making their first confession gathered near the confession box. I sat on a pew and waited along with everyone else. The green light was on over the entrance to the box. A boy shuffled in. The box squeaked and rocked like a boat at sea as he settled down inside. The red light came on. Now no one could go in.

I stared at the bulbs, which reminded me of the top of a Dalek's head. My mind was churning. What was this all about? What did I have to say and do when I got in there? And what would the priest say and do? I should have known this by now but I didn't. I really should have paid more attention in Sunday school.

I felt a tap on my shoulder. It was Mum, who was sitting behind. 'Your turn, in you go,' she whispered.

I had been so lost in my thoughts I'd not seen the boy come out or the light go green.

I went in to the dark, musty box, knelt down and miraculously something came out of my mouth – I don't remember what. The priest told me to say one Hail Mary and one Our Father.

I left the box feeling chuffed. For a first timer I'd done all right, I thought, and the priest hadn't pulled a lever and sent me down to Hell. The following Sunday I found out that one of the other boys had been given four Hail Marys and three Our Fathers. What had he been up to?

6

I had discovered television and I couldn't wait to get home after school because the programmes were so brilliant. There was *Loony Tunes* with Bugs Bunny, *Road Runner* and *Tom and Jerry*. Dad loved them too and would watch them with me. We liked

Wacky Races and *Top Cat* too. Then there was *The Land of the Giants, Lost in Space, Captain Pugwash* and, best of all, *The Magic Roundabout*.

On Saturday mornings, I'd go to the pictures with a gang of mates. One of us would pay to get in, then open the back door and let in the rest of us for nothing. We saw *The Lone Ranger*, *Flash Gordon* and *Lassie*.

On Sunday the TV programmes weren't up to much, but I liked the black-and-white films with the old stars, like Charlie Chaplin, Buster Keaton, the Marx Brothers and, the greatest of them all, Laurel and Hardy. Dad always called me when they were on.

I was in the lounge at the coffee table. I had paper, coloured pencils and the *Beano*. The comic was open at one of my favourite strips, Dennis the Menace. Slowly, carefully, as I loved to do – I'd been practising for a while and I was a dab hand at this – I drew my own version of Dennis. The image finished, I sat back and checked my drawing against the one in the *Beano*. Not bad, I thought. I'd got his solid hair spikes, his thick socks rolled to his ankles and his heavy boots just right.

Now I had to do Dennis's dog, Gnasher. He was easy in profile but I wanted him with the full width of his face and his body tapering behind. This was trickier than side on.

I started with the pencil. I had to rub lines out and redo them several times but when I'd finished, yes, I was pleased again. It wasn't bad at all. I'd really got Gnasher's face, his huge mouth, his teeth, big and white. Now all that remained was to colour my drawing. This wasn't hard. Everything was either red or black, with Dennis's hands, face and knees left white.

With my red pencil I began on the red stripes of Dennis's jersey. Dad came into the room and sat down on the sofa behind me. I didn't look round, absorbed in what I was doing, watching the point of my red pencil moving backwards and forwards, and trying to keep the pressure even.

I heard Dad open his tobacco tin, roll a fag, close the tin and spark up his lighter. I smelt the puff of smoke he blew out.

'You keep your drawings in a folder, don't you?' said Dad.

'Yes,' I said.

I kept them in a paper folder at the bottom of my bookcase with my pens and drawing-paper.

'I shouldn't do that any more,' he said. 'I should get them up on the walls of your bedroom where you can see them and everyone else can too. They're good.'

I stopped colouring. 'Do you mean it?'

'Yes,' he said. 'I wouldn't have said so if I didn't. Just check with Mum first, and if she says it's okay, I should put them up without delay.'

I finished my colouring, then ran into the kitchen where Mum was making our tea. 'Can I stick my pictures up in my bedroom?' I said. 'Dad said to ask you.'

'You mean your cartoons? Yes, of course,' said Mum.

Using what, though? I wondered. Then I remembered. 'Can I use the black tape in Dad's tool bag?'

'Ask your dad.'

I went back to the lounge. 'Dad, can I use the black tape that's in your tool bag to stick my drawings up?'

'You're welcome to it,' said Dad.

I got the tape and my folder, then ran up to my bedroom. I chose the ones I liked best and stuck them up. I called Mum and Dad up to see when I'd finished. I was a clever boy, they said, and they liked my drawings. I should keep up the drawing because I was good at it.

It was evening, dark. I was in the front room.

'Son?'

'Yeah?'

'Would you like to go for a walk?'

This was unexpected. I would never normally be out at that time of night. 'Yes,' I said, not asking where we were going or why. Anything that involved being with him was fine with me.

'Get your coat. I'll just fetch something. Meet you in the hall.'

Dad went into the garden and came back with Anne-Marie's

old pram, one of those big Silver Cross ones, heavy with big wheels.

'Where are you going at this time of night?' asked Mum, from upstairs. 'And what are you doing with the good pram?'

'I'm just going up the road,' said Dad. 'Son, open the door. We won't be long.'

I did as he said and he pushed the pram out quickly.

'And where's *he* going?' said Mum, meaning me.

'He's keeping me company,' said Dad. 'Back soon.'

We went up Third Avenue, sticking to our side of the street, then crossed and entered the Mozart Estate, where I'd never been since it was finished even though it was only across the road from where I lived. People had been in there a while now. The flats were mostly full and the estate was brightly lit. Dad, of course, wasn't working there any more though he was still working for the same security firm who'd employed him as the night-watchman in other places around London.

'That looks nice,' said Dad.

What was he saying? What was nice? I could only see pavement, a low wall with a block behind it, some blank windows, others with lights on, one or two with television screens glowing.

'The grass,' he said.

I hadn't noticed but there was grass behind a little wall. Dad took a long look up and down the street, satisfied himself that it was empty, clambered over, knelt down, and rolled up a piece of grassy ground as if it was a carpet. Then he popped it length-wise into the pram.

'Come on,' said Dad. I stepped over the wall. He had another look up and down the street. 'Keep your head down. You get the little pieces, and I'll get the big ones.'

We filled the pram with turf, wheeled it home and got it in through the front door. Mum was still upstairs. Dad pushed the pram straight down the hall, through the kitchen and into the garden.

'Turn on the lights, son,' he said, meaning the bathroom and toilet ones. I did so he could see what he was doing outside. He unloaded the pram. We went back to the estate, filled it a second time, got it home, then went back again. 'That should do it,' said Dad.

As we came out on to Third Avenue, Dad said, 'Oh.'

A police car was coming up the road.

'There, there,' said Dad, addressing the rolls of grass in the pram. 'There, there. No need for crying.' He bounced his baby and cooed like a mother.

The police car slowed right down. I saw the faces of the policemen behind the windscreen, staring straight at us, and I heard Dad saying, 'There, there,' and the pram creaking as he bounced it up and down. The patrol car passed but Dad kept going until it had vanished. Then we rushed home. Mum was in bed, which suited us. We pushed the pram through the house and into the garden.

'Let's get it laid now, shall we?' said Dad.

I was up for it.

'Go and find Mum's scissors.'

I fetched them from the kitchen and Dad set to work. Laying the turf seemed straightforward. He rolled out the pieces, like bits of cloth, and trimmed them to size. My job was to find him odd bits and patch them into corners or the spaces where two pieces didn't quite meet. Then I did a lot of jumping around to smooth out the lumps under the new grass.

The job done, we admired our work by the light from the bathroom and the toilet. It did look nice.

'Well done, son,' said Dad, rubbing my head.

We headed for the door.

'Listen, son,' said Dad, 'if your mum asks where did it come from you say, "One of Dad's mates."'

I went to bed, chuffed. We'd grassed the garden, so we had. When I woke up, though, I'd forgotten about it. I was halfway through breakfast when I remembered. 'Oh, Mum,' I said, leaping up, 'come and have a look.'

Mum was drinking a cup of tea at the table. She gave no sign she'd heard me; in fact, it looked to me as if she didn't want to hear.

'Mum, quick!' I opened the back door. The smell of grass wafted in. 'Come on.' Mum got up and headed towards me. I shot off as she got nearer and ran out to the middle of our new lawn. 'Look! Look at this!'

'Jesus Christ, Mother of God, where did this come from?' The last time Mum was in the garden, it was a mud patch.

'One of Dad's mates,' I said, as instructed.

'All his mates work for the Gas Board.'

Yes, they did.

'Look, you can roll it up.' I dropped down and lifted an end to show her.

'Well, you and your dad can roll it up and take it away.'

'Don't you like it? I think it looks nice,' I said.

'Tell me,' said Mum, sounding tired, 'who is going to cut it and water it? It won't be me. I've enough to do already in this home.'

It looked all right for a bit, but then it died. On the Mozart Estate, the new grass laid by the council maintenance men thrived. Perhaps we should have got them to do our garden, I thought.

7

It was winter, late 1971 or early 1972. The alarm clock went off and I opened my eyes. The curtains were drawn but the yellow light from the streetlamps came in around the edges.

Vincent got up and dressed. He left the room. A few minutes later I heard the front door bang as he left the house. He was off to Lacey's, the newsagent, on Kilburn Lane. He'd been a paperboy but recently he'd been promoted. Now he marked up each paper with the customer's name and address for the other boys to deliver. He had to be there first with the shopkeeper.

I went back to sleep.

Later, Mum came in. 'Come on, Patrick and John,' she said. 'Get up now.'

John was a Lacey's paperboy and this morning I would become one too.

I got dressed and went downstairs. I was excited: I was going out to my first paying job. I found Mum in the kitchen. 'You're a big boy now,' she said.

John and I left the house together and headed up Third Avenue. The streetlights were still on and their yellow beams spilled over the pavement, the trees and the few cars parked along the kerb. It was early, so no one but us was around.

'All you got to do,' said John, 'is deliver each newspaper to the address written in the top right-hand corner. So, if you see twelve and, say, "Nutbourne" written in the corner, you take that paper to twelve Nutbourne Street and put it through the letterbox. Do you see?'

'Yes,' I said. I did.

'Now, it isn't an easy job delivering papers. It takes time and you don't want to be rushed,' he said. 'You know what I mean?'

'Yes, I do,' I said. Vincent had said the same the night before.

We turned on to Kilburn Lane and approached Lacey's. There were two large glass windows each covered with a grille, and an open door in the middle. As we got closer, two or three boys came out, bags bulging with newspapers slung over their shoulders. They looked as if they were sleepwalking as they headed off to do their rounds.

The shop inside smelt of confectionery. Vincent was behind the counter, papers in neat rows in front of him, marking them up. He looked up from what he was doing, gave me a smile, then went back to the job.

John got his bag and was gone. The shopkeeper was serving a customer. I was staring at the chocolate bars arranged on a slanted section of the counter. Each had its own compartment. Like most kids, I liked my sweets. I liked Mars Bars best and, now and then, Turkish Delight.

'Oi,' Vincent called. 'That's yours.'

He pointed at a bag on the floor, white canvas with *Evening Standard* written on the side. Suddenly I felt anxious. Though I'd been told what to do I hadn't really understood, and my reading wasn't very good. I didn't know if I could do this.

'Are you all right?' Vincent must have seen my worried expression.

'Yes,' I said. I picked up the bag. It was very heavy. I got the strap across my shoulder and felt myself tilt sideways as the weight of it pulled me down. I went out through the door.

Outside, a couple of cars were crawling along. I set off down Kilburn Lane. As I went, I pulled the bag round so it was in front of me like a bus conductor's ticket machine. I began to count my papers. 'One, two, three, four . . .'

Something was wedged between two. What could it be? A Mars Bar! Good old Vincent, I thought. That's why he was so keen for me to pick up my bag and get off on my round.

I tore off the wrapper and bit into it. Because it was so cold, the chocolate and toffee were hard. It made the walk along Kilburn Lane rather pleasant.

I reached Third Avenue. I knew I had to make my deliveries all round the Avenues, so I turned in there. On either side I saw terraced houses with small front gardens, just like the one we lived in. I was back in my world.

I looked at the newspaper at the front of my bag. A word was written in the corner. I was cold and the bag was heavy. I wanted to get this done and go home. The trouble was, I couldn't puzzle out the word. I looked up. The first street on my right was Nutbourne. Wasn't that what Vincent had scribbled on the first newspaper? I decided it must be. What was the number? I looked back at the paper again: '5'. I went to number five and shoved it through the letterbox. Where next? '7'. Easy, next door. I pushed it through, and heard it land on the floor inside. Number eight was next. Over the road and through the slot.

I finished Nutbourne. I looked at the scribble in the corner of the newspaper now at the front of my bundle. Marne? Yeah, thought so. The next street was Marne. Lovely. What number? Three. Then it was four, five, six, and seven . . .

I went on, not stopping, and suddenly my bag was empty.

Vincent and John had said doing a paper round was hard work and took time. What were they talking about? This was easy.

I started back for Lacey's. I felt good, and when I got to school I'd tell the other kids I was working, earning money. They'd be impressed.

At the end of Third Avenue, I turned on to Kilburn Lane. The streetlights were off now. People were on their way to work or waiting for the bus, and there were more cars and vans. The streetlights must have only just gone off because the vehicles still had their headlamps on.

I got to Lacey's and stepped in. Vincent was where I'd left him but without any papers. He was almost ready to leave. 'That was quick,' he said. 'You're the first back.'

I felt pleased with myself.

The shopkeeper was also behind the counter. Unlike Vincent, he didn't seem pleased to see me, more like surprised and doubtful. I thought he was going to say something, but before he could, the phone in the storeroom began to ring. He went to answer it. 'Good morning, Lacey's,' he said. There was a long pause while he listened and then he said, 'I'm very sorry. It's the new boy's first day.'

He came out of the storeroom. The customer on the phone lived in Nutbourne Street but the newspaper I'd delivered was for a house in Oliphant Street. Had I delivered all the papers to the wrong houses? That was what he thought I'd gone and done, though he hoped I could tell him different.

But I couldn't. Vincent's writing was never any good and nor was my reading.

The phone rang again. The shopkeeper disappeared into the storeroom and picked it up. 'Lacey's, good morning.' He knew what was coming. It was in his voice.

I did too. I dropped the canvas bag and walked out. I never went back.

Dad was on the settee. He'd done the crossword and now he was reading the paper. The TV was on. Mum, as always, was in the kitchen, cooking (as often as not it was apple pie, which had a lovely smell) or doing the laundry. I was sitting on the floor at Dad's feet, using the coffee table to work on. I had drawing-paper and coloured pencils to hand, my folder, where I kept everything that wasn't stuck on my bedroom walls, at my side. I had no comic, no *Dandy*, no *Beano*. I wasn't copying today. I was doing something different. This picture was made up of lines and shapes, some of which I was colouring in.

I sensed Dad looking over my shoulder. 'Son, show me that,' he said.

I got up from the floor and handed it to him, then sat beside him on the settee. He looked at the drawing the way I'd handed it to him, squinting as if he was finding it hard to see, his head bobbing this way and that.

Then, still with his eyes half closed, still moving his head from side to side, he turned my drawing through ninety degrees.

'You had it the right way up the first time,' I said. 'You've got it on its side now.'

'No,' he said, 'there are many ways to look at this.' He went on turning the drawing until he had it back to the way it was when he'd started. 'Look, do you see that?' he said.

I looked at the bit he was pointing at and couldn't see anything except shapes, which weren't shapes of anything and which I'd coloured in. 'What?' I asked.

'There,' he said. 'That's a face. There's the eyes, the nose and the mouth.'

He moved the paper just enough, and there it was – a face. I had drawn a face and didn't even know it.

He turned the paper and showed me one shape, another and then a third. Yes, you had to look hard, they didn't stand out a mile, but they were there and he had found them. My drawing was full of different shapes and what had started out as a plain piece of paper had life. I had given it that life.

'Did you know there's a word for this kind of drawing?'

'No,' I said.

'I know it already,' he said, 'but let's look it up so you can see it in black and white on the page.'

Dad picked up his dictionary, which was never far from his side, flicked through the pages, then pointed to a word. 'There we are,' he said. 'There's the word for your drawing.'

I stared at the word. It was true: there was a name for my drawing and it was in his dictionary.

'"Abstract",' he read. '"Not relating to concrete objects but expressing something that can only be appreciated intellectually."'

'Abstract,' I said.

'Did you understand what I read out?'

'No,' I said. But that didn't matter. If it was in his dictionary, that was good enough for me. 'Can I borrow your dictionary?' I said.

'Sure,' he said. I carried it to the table, sat down, and carefully copied, in my best writing, 'Abstract' at the bottom of my drawing, then added my signature and the date. It was my first proper drawing, I thought. I was now an artist.

Mum came in.

I showed her my abstract. She didn't have her glasses on so she couldn't see what I was showing her properly (and even with them on, her eyes being so bad, she wouldn't have seen much more), but she peered at it anyhow and moved her head about like Dad had. She said she preferred my cartoons but she agreed that the colours in this one were very good.

I was still at Queens Park Primary School, in my last year. It was a Saturday morning. John was in the house with two mates and a couple of girls. Their plan was to get Red Rover tickets, which would let them travel on any bus they wanted, and spend the day trundling around London. It sounded marvellous and I wanted to go, but John wasn't keen. They were his mates, weren't they, not mine? I pleaded. No, he said. Hadn't I heard? I wasn't coming. They weren't my friends.

I wasn't going to be put off. I went to Mum and told her the old sad story of how my brother didn't love me. Mum went to John. He had to take me, she said, and that was that.

A few minutes later I was walking down Third Avenue with John and his mates. I was pleased to be going out for the day with these bigger boys and girls, and I was already looking forward to Monday morning, back at school, telling my friends what I'd been up to and the great day I'd had with John and his mates zooming around London.

We bought Red Rover tickets, caught the number eighteen from Harrow Road to Edgware Road, then a bus to Marble Arch, and a third up Oxford Street.

We got out at Selfridges. I was surprised. I'd thought the plan was to stay on the buses. I hadn't expected us to get off and go somewhere. I said nothing, of course. I was as happy as Larry to be out and about, and not with Mum or Dad. I was going to like whatever we did.

John's mates were talking. It was something important: I could tell from the tone of their voices. I tuned in. That was when I discovered why we'd got off the bus outside Selfridges. We were going shoplifting.

I knew what it was, of course, though I'd never done it. They all had – at least, it was my impression that they had. They seemed very sure of themselves as they made their plan and synchronized their watches. Now there was only one detail that had to be sorted. Did I want to come with them?

'You don't have to do this,' said John. 'You can wait outside until we come back.'

It sounded too good to miss, and I wasn't going to be the odd one out on the bus home later. Oh, no, I was in. Definitely.

We filed through the doors and headed for the toy department. There, everyone fanned out. I held back and watched how they looked around, picked up whatever caught their eye, and slipped it into a pocket or under their jumper, all without a sales assistant seeing.

That looks easy, I thought. I looked about for something to take and decided on a yo-yo. I sidled up to the shelf where the yo-yos lay, glanced around and saw that no one was watching. I took one and put it deep in my pocket.

From the toys we moved to another department, and from there to a different floor, stealing what we wanted as we went. Eventually, our coats and trousers bulging, we moved to the ground floor and headed for the door. Unfortunately, two store detectives blocked our way and we couldn't get out.

They took us to an office in the basement, where a third detective sat behind a desk. The room was full of TV monitors, each of which showed a different black-and-white image of part of the store. We saw customers browsing along shelves and racks as they looked for what they wanted. So, they'd seen us nicking and now we were for it.

Suddenly I felt sick. It wasn't what was about to happen to us that worried me but what Dad would say when we got home. That I could predict. He'd go mental.

'Empty your pockets,' said the man behind the desk. The five older ones started, and as he watched them pile what they'd taken in front of him, he shook his head.

'And you,' he said, pointing at me. 'Empty yours too. Let's see what you have.'

I pulled everything out. It wasn't as much as the others had, and I didn't want any of it any more. I just wanted to go home.

I won't do it again, I thought. I wanted to say, 'I've learnt my lesson, and I'll never do it again, promise. Please, just let me go home,' but as none of the others had spoken, I thought it was best that I didn't either. Instead I copied what they were doing: I bowed my head and did my best to look guilty and ashamed. It worked. The man behind the desk spoke to us sternly, then told us never to come back to Selfridges. We have your photos, he said. When he'd finished, the other two took us back upstairs, told us to piss off and kicked us out into the street.

It was early summer 1972. I was in my last term at primary school. In the autumn, I'd start secondary.

It was Prize Day. As I filed into the main hall with the rest of the children, I saw the table at the top with cups and medals laid out, the teachers sitting behind it in a row.

Anything on that table would do me, I thought. Just something I could bring home and show Mum and Dad. I was sitting next to my best mates, Barry and Paul. One whispered, 'What do you think you'll get?'

The headmaster called out the name of the first boy or girl to get a prize. The winner went up. Everyone in the hall clapped and cheered. Then the next went up and the third, and all the time this was going on I was waiting for my name, convinced I'd hear it.

Then the headmaster announced he was about to give out the prizes for football. There weren't many games in which I didn't score a goal or two. I sat up. The first name was given, not mine, another boy's. He won all the prizes as it turned out, every single one. I'd thought he was good but not that good.

I walked back from school with tears streaming down my face. When I got home, the door was locked and I hadn't a key.

I sat on the doorstep, crying and feeling sorry for myself. A woman walked past, a friend of my mother's. 'Isn't your mum in?' she asked.

I shook my head.

'Are you all right?' She gave me her handkerchief. It was small, lacy, and smelt of makeup. 'You can keep it,' she said. 'I'll come back and see your mother later.'

Her son was the boy who had won all the prizes for football.

My life wasn't all bad, though. In the last year I was at Queens Park I had started playing for Westminster Borough football team. Soon after that miserable Prize Day, the borough presented me with a badge they called 'Colours of Westminster'. Two boys and two girls from every school in the borough got it for being good at sport. The other boy from Queens Park Primary School to get the badge was the other kid who couldn't play the violin. He was a brilliant swimmer.

At the end of July 1972, Queens Park Primary School broke up for the holidays and I left the building for the last time.

A few days later, the whole family were at Euston station. Under the sooty canopy, I could smell scorched diesel and stewed tea. Mum and Dad found the Heysham train. We children and Mum got on. Dad followed, with the big suitcases. Someone opened a sliding door to reveal an empty compartment. We piled in, and Dad put the cases on to the overhead racks. We bounced up and down on the dusty seats. He left the train. A few moments later, he was outside on the platform, looking in at us.

The guard's whistle went. The train shuddered and moved off slowly. We gathered by a door with the window pulled down, Mum standing behind us with Anne-Marie in her arms, and waved to Dad, shouting, "Bye, Dad, 'bye.'

As the train moved, so did Dad. As the train got faster, so did Dad. Then the train began to go faster still and Dad slipped behind. Then the train went faster again and Dad gave up trying to keep up with us and stopped altogether. We went on, and, as we did, I looked back, and I saw my dad getting smaller and smaller.

'Why isn't he coming, Mum?' I said.

'Someone has to look after the house,' she said, 'and, anyway, he has to go to work.'

We moved back to our compartment. I sat down on the dusty seat and looked out of the window. The train had come out from under the canopy and into the open now. I stared out at offices and factories, houses and blocks of flats. It was dusk and some of the windows in the buildings were squares of yellow and white because the electric lights behind were on, while other windows were squares of black. With my mind's eye I saw Dad on the empty platform. I felt sad to think of him going home to an empty house.

Then I remembered that this was the start of our journey to Belfast. I had made it many times before. I knew how it went and I knew what was waiting at the other end. The picture in my head of Dad vanished. Now I could think only of what lay ahead. I felt a surge of excitement. I think it was the same for my brothers, because suddenly we all got up.

We had the compartment to ourselves and began to jump on the seats and dangle from the luggage racks, pretending to be monkeys. Mum let us burn off our excitement, then told us to settle down. If the train man found us jumping on the seats or swinging from the racks he'd put us off at the next station and then we'd have to walk to Heysham.

We knew all about the train man. Sometimes, on earlier journeys, there hadn't been enough money to buy John and me a ticket. When the train man came round, we'd hide under the coats and lie there without moving until he had punched Mum's and Vincent's tickets and left. Anne-Marie, as an infant, was free. Today there were tickets for everyone. Still, no one wanted to get on his bad side. You didn't mess with the train man. He was a serious figure and I respected him.

The train rushed on and it grew dark outside. We had books to read and paper to draw on. We came out of the city and into the country. The fields were dark, and so were the trees and hedgerows. The animals grazing – cows, sheep and horses – were dark shapes.

Mum opened a biscuit tin of sandwiches she'd made. She had crisps, cakes, sweets and drinks in her bag. We feasted until our bellies were full, then went quiet and floppy. I looked out of the window again, but there was nothing to see now. It was as if someone had put up a blackboard while we'd been eating.

We lay down to sleep on the seats with their itchy, rough covers. John dropped off first – he could sleep anywhere – then Anne-Marie and Vincent. But I couldn't stop thinking about the journey ahead, getting off the train and boarding the ferry.

I asked Mum, as I had several times, 'Are we nearly there?'

'Go to sleep,' she said.

The next thing I knew, Mum was shaking me and telling me we'd arrived. I sat up. Vincent's face was pale and he was rubbing his eyes. He looked only half alive. Through the window I saw the dim yellow streetlights of Heysham, and the funfair with a few lights still on.

Mum woke Anne-Marie next. At that point she didn't bother with John: he would have gone straight back to sleep.

'Put on your hats and coats,' she said, 'or you'll get cold on the way to the ferry.'

Once we'd got our coats buttoned, we got the cases down from the racks. Mum gave Vincent and me something to carry. We weren't to lose it, she said.

The train was slowing now. Outside the window, on the dark platform, one of the old-fashioned British Rail signs swept past. It said 'Heysham'. The wheels screeched. Mum woke John, lifted him to his feet, helped him into his coat and gave him a case to carry. He sat down. He couldn't go back to sleep, she said. He had to help. She pulled him to his feet again. He rubbed his eyes. The train stopped and we were thrown forward. There was the sound of many doors banging open and passengers getting out.

One after another we humped what we'd been told to carry along the corridor, out of the door and on to the platform. Mum had the biggest suitcase. It was cold off the train, as Mum had said it would be, but that was good. The night air woke us up and we felt a bit perkier. We could still smell burnt diesel but now it was mixed with a salty, brackish-harbour-and-rotten-fish smell. There was no doubting that we were by the sea. In the distance the horn of a ferry hooted, low and deep.

We hauled our bags down the platform, through the station and on to the quay. Here was the ferry that would take us to Belfast, all lit up and with smoke coming out of its funnel.

We went towards it and soon found the gangplank, a steep wooden ramp. We climbed it in single file. It was tied, but I could feel it moving beneath me. I didn't like that. At the top I stepped off it and on to the ferry, which was solid underfoot.

Next, I went through a door with a lip at the bottom so I had to lift my bag high to get it through. The others followed. Now we needed to find somewhere we could sit together and sleep during the night as the ferry sailed to Belfast. We followed Mum upstairs, along corridors and through great lounges filled with seats that passengers had bagged with coats and newspapers. Eventually she found somewhere near the front. We dropped our cases and flopped down.

The propellers churned and the ferry shook. It was like a vast animal lumbering to life. We got up again and went out on deck.

There were men on the quay and others on the ship, shouting to one another. The ropes that moored it were loosed. The engine revved. The ferry edged out. There was clanking and gurgling. The men on the quays and the buildings behind them got smaller, while the stretch of black water between the ship and the quay-side got bigger. Then we could see the whole dock and Heysham stretching behind. Then the town got smaller and we were headed towards the open sea.

We went inside. As the ship moved on, we grew restless again. We said we'd go and explore.

'All right,' said Mum, 'but be careful. Stay away from the side and don't climb on any railings.'

'Don't worry,' we said, and hurried away.

I went out on deck and ran right round the ship. I loved the sound of the sea hitting the front and the sides. When I got cold I went in to explore the inside. There were a few bars with men drinking in them but mostly all there was to see was passengers stretched out, eyes closed, trying to sleep. One circuit was enough.

When we got back to Mum, she opened the tin of sandwiches again. The ones that remained were a bit bent now but still good. Soon John fell asleep. Vincent read. Mum began to nod off. Anne-Marie was asleep with her head on Mum's lap.

The ferry began to pitch and Mum's head – she was now asleep – rolled from side to side. Now and then, Mum would half-open her eyes, but she was too tired to ask why I was laughing at her. Soon the waves got bigger and the ferry reared up when it hit one, then smacked down once the wave had passed.

I began to feel tired, even though the ferry was being thrown about. People around me were folding coats to make pillows, putting them under their heads and closing their eyes. The lights were dimmed and everyone around me fell asleep.

When I opened my eyes it was morning and the ferry was moving steadily.

People stirred. They went to the toilet and combed their hair. I could smell makeup, perfume and tea. I went out on deck. The air was fresh and clean. There was a brown and green line of land in the distance: Ireland. Our journey was coming to an end and I couldn't wait to get off.

The ferry pulled up at the quayside in Belfast and on the Tannoy a voice said the passengers should disembark. We gathered our suitcases and went down the swaying gangplank. Among the crowd in the arrivals shed we saw Hugh McCaffery, Mum's brother-in-law, married to her sister, Mary. He had a red face and a big smile.

He also had a car. We squeezed in and he drove out of the docks and towards the city centre. It was early so only a few people were on their way to work, waiting at bus stops or crossing the road. None of this was very interesting. But in Belfast one thing was very interesting and I was impatient to see it. Come on, I thought. But I didn't see it. Then we left the centre and drove into West Belfast and now, at last, I saw.

A line of British Army soldiers was moving down a street, guns out, the last man walking backwards, guarding the others from attack. Lovely.

Then I saw something even better: a Saracen armoured car. It was big and green and looked so heavy when it roared along in the opposite direction to us.

We stopped at traffic lights, the windows wound down. I heard a helicopter hovering above. I'd only ever seen one on TV so I looked towards the sky, but I missed it.

Then the lights changed and Uncle Hugh drove on. I forgot my disappointment because there were patrols and Saracens galore now. There was normal life too, of course, people waiting for the bus, walking to work, carrying shopping, but with the army mixed in. It was this jumble of everyday life and war that I found so exciting.

I didn't know the ins and outs of the 'Troubles', of course. I didn't know that in 1969 the army had been sent into Derry because the Royal Ulster Constabulary had lost control. I didn't know that later the army had been sent into the rest of Northern Ireland and that, although at first they were welcomed, it wasn't long before they became the enemy to Catholics, Nationalists and Republicans. I didn't know that the people of certain districts, like West Belfast, and the British Army now fought battles in the streets. I didn't know that the Provisional IRA, who saw themselves as the defenders of the Catholic population, were at war with the British Army and were attempting to drive the soldiers out of Northern Ireland by shooting at and bombing them. I didn't know that the IRA wanted to take Northern Ireland out of the United Kingdom and make it part of the Republic, the other country on the island of Ireland. I didn't know any of this because we didn't talk about it at number forty-three Third Avenue. I had no idea, as Uncle Hugh drove us to his house that morning, what Belfast and Northern Ireland were going through or why. I was eleven. I was off school and I was on holiday. I was going to see my uncles, aunts and cousins. That was all I cared about.

At some point we left the streets where there were soldiers and entered a district that felt different. It was leafier, greener, and suburban. I recognized where we were. We were getting close to Uncle Hugh's. And, sure enough, there was his house, we were pulling up outside and Mary, my mother's sister, was rushing out and up to the car. She hugged everyone and brought us inside.

We had breakfast in the kitchen. Then I went into the garden and played with my brothers, my cousins Kevin and Colin, Aunt Mary's sons, and Sean, son of my mum's brother, my uncle Sean, and the dog, Jet. The holiday had started.

The cousins were taking me out. Before we left one of the grown-ups gave us the lecture we heard every time we went out anywhere. We were to stay together. We were to look after each other. We were to come home together.

We listened, promised we'd do as we'd been told, and walked into the city centre where we wandered about, played snooker in a club, then went to a public baths for a swim. We bumped into some of my cousins' friends in the hall and at the pool. They found my accent funny, but I told them I was just like them. I'd been born in Belfast.

It was another day. We had the lecture again and wandered into a busier part of West Belfast, where my cousins met some more friends. A patrol of Saracens appeared. Suddenly, everyone in our group but me had something in his hand, a bit of kerbstone, a brick or a bottle, and this stuff was flying through the air, whacking the Saracens, making a dull clang and falling to the ground. Then the Saracens passed on and there was just the road with debris everywhere.

'How come you don't throw anything?' This was one of my cousins' friends. 'Is it because you're a Brit?'

I didn't understand the background to what they'd done but I understood this: I hadn't done as he had and he didn't like it. I'd have to change that if I wanted to keep in. At the same time, though, I didn't want to do what everyone else had done. The Saracens were full of soldiers. I didn't want to throw anything at the soldiers. I liked the soldiers. I wanted to be a soldier one day, like my dad had been.

Another convoy appeared in the distance. Everyone picked up something. This time I did too. The convoy drew closer and the chucking started. Bang, bang, bang. Everything bounced off the Saracen's steel sides. I threw too, using my left arm so that my stone fell in the road, well short. I'm right-handed, but no one knew that. And no one could say, after the convoy passed, that I hadn't joined in. I was one of them now.

It was evening, just my cousins and me. We were walking home. Our route took us past a housing estate. It looked like any other to me. It wasn't, but how was I to know the meaning of the Union flags fluttering from the lamp-posts and the kerbstones painted red, white and blue? There was nothing like that at home, round the Avenues.

Suddenly a gang of kids rushed out of the estate. Some were our age, some older. There were lots more of them than there were of us, maybe six or eight.

'Run!' my cousins shouted. They sprinted off. I followed and caught up. We ran on together. My cousins were frightened, I could tell. I heard running feet behind as the gang got closer and closer. I heard them shouting too. One phrase stood out: 'You Catholic bastards.'

The running didn't stop. The gang behind wouldn't give up. The road we were on turned into a hill. I was short of breath – I'd been running fast for a while. But I was frightened like my cousins were. Very frightened.

Kevin was slowing and dropped back. I didn't stop but pushed on with Sean. We went on a bit but then we realized there was a different sound behind us now. Sean and I stopped and turned. The gang was in a circle around Kevin, kicking and pummelling him.

We had a problem. What had the grown-ups said? That we were to stay together and look after each other. We were not to get into trouble. We were to come home together. Sean and I should do something, but what? We couldn't go down and ask them, please, to leave Kevin alone. Nor could we take them on or drive them away. There were too many of them. So we did nothing, which left me feeling helpless – a horrible feeling.

The circle parted. Kevin was on his feet. The gang manhandled him towards us. Someone kicked him from behind to send him on his way.

Kevin ran up the hill towards Sean and me. The gang stayed below, watching, waiting, but they made no move to follow. Kevin reached us, breathless, his face wet with spit and swollen from their blows.

'We don't want him,' one of the gang shouted up. 'That's why we let him go. He's not our size. We want you, yeah, you and him, because you're bigger.' They meant Sean and me. 'You're good at running, but come down here and we'll see how fucking good at fighting you are. Come on, come down. Let's see if you've got any balls.'

Sean shook his head. 'Piss off, you wankers,' he shouted. Kevin and I started shouting too. We gave our pursuers all the fucks we had and a lot more besides. My cousins, I noticed, also used a word I'd never heard before: 'Protestant'. 'You Protestant this, you Protestant that,' they shouted. I assumed it was just another bad word, that calling someone a 'Protestant' was like calling them a 'shit' or a 'bastard'.

The gang below had some new words too: 'Fenian' and 'Taig'. I guessed they went into the bag with 'prick', 'arsehole' and the rest.

After a bit, we got hoarse with all the shouting and they must have too. Eventually they started walking back towards their estate, with its flags on lamp-posts and painted kerbstones. That was our signal and we set off towards my uncle and aunt's.

As we went along, did we talk about what happened? I don't remember. And if we did, would I have understood that they'd come after us because, as Catholics, they assumed we were Republicans and supporters of the IRA? I doubt it. All being Catholic meant to me was that I had to go to church every Sunday and sometimes Sunday school afterwards. I knew Dad was a Catholic but he never went. I knew nothing about Catholicism and Irish history. Why would I? I didn't live in Belfast. I just came for a fortnight in the summer.

8

The holidays ended, and we went home to London. I was eleven now and in September I would start secondary school. Quintin Kynaston was a modern comprehensive in St John's Wood. Vincent had been there but he'd left now. 'And thank fuck for that,' he'd said, meaning he wouldn't have to be there when I started. But John, who was only two years older than me, was still there, so I wouldn't be alone.

When Vincent had started at Quintin Kynaston, it was a hard school to get into. By the time it was my turn, anyone with half a brain and a school blazer could walk in.

A week or two before the beginning of term, Mum took me to get my uniform. In the shop I was kitted up, then brought to the big mirror. In it I saw Mum, all smiley and happy, then myself in my blazer, trousers, shirt and tie. All I needed now, I thought, was a bowler hat and an umbrella and I'd look like a City gent. I hated what I was seeing, especially the tie. I got a headache trying to knot it and I hated the tightness around my neck, as if I was being strangled. But there was nothing for it. The school had a uniform and you wore it.

The first day of term came. I put on my uniform and Mum gave me a new black briefcase to carry books and schoolwork. I set off for Quintin Kynaston.

First day at big school you're always a bit nervous. But once I was inside the building I ran into a few boys from the Avenues, which helped things along. There were some preliminaries in a hall and then we went, my class and I, to our classroom. 'Stand at the top with your backs to the blackboard,' said the teacher.

We lined up. In front of us the desks stood in columns of two.

'Right, boys,' said the teacher. 'Find somewhere to sit and someone to sit with. Remember where you are because that's where you'll sit from now on. Do you understand?'

'Yes, sir.'

'Off you go, then.'

There was the sound of rushing feet, shortly followed by chairs dragging on the floor, desk flaps opening and banging shut, with much talking and laughing throughout.

'Enough, settle down,' said the teacher.

The room went quiet.

'Hello,' said the teacher. 'Did you hear me?'

The question was addressed to me and another boy. We'd been standing at one end of the line with our backs to the blackboard, as he'd said. But when everyone dashed forward to find a desk, we'd stayed put, talking to each other.

'Go and sit over there,' said the teacher. He pointed at the pair of desks in the row that ran beside the windows.

He was TK – Tony Kinsella – and he lived in Kilburn. We got on well and we spent the period, as we would spend so many over the coming year, planning a bank robbery. I did the drawing and TK supplied the time, date and so on.

At break I found Smokers' Corner. There was John, as I'd expected, with his mates. 'This is my little brother,' he announced. That helped things along a bit more.

I went home feeling pleased with my progress, my briefcase as empty as it had been when I'd set out.

On the days that followed I carried my empty briefcase in and out, and made more new friends. One day I decided I'd had enough of the briefcase. I left it in a classroom. I never saw it again and Mum never asked about it.

Now that I was going to 'big school', I began to knock about the local streets a bit more. Most of the boys I hung around with went to QK. We formed a loose gang.

We didn't get up to much, not at the start. We'd go to the adventure playground, or kick a ball about on the Tarmac pitch. We'd ride our bikes or go to the Harrow Road Baths to swim. We were all eleven or twelve, still kids. We hadn't it in us yet to be really bad. And I wasn't allowed to rampage around at all hours. I had to be home at a set time.

It was a Sunday, early. I was up and about to go off on my bike with my mates.

'Back by five,' said Mum.

'Did you hear that?' said Dad, as he always did.

'Yeah,' I said, and left.

I spent the day tearing around the streets and then down on the canal towpath.

I got back well after tea. I was hungry and went into the kitchen. Mum was there. 'You're late,' she said.

'I didn't notice the time. Is there anything to eat?'

'We're going to church, you know that, and now we're going to be late.'

'Sorry, I didn't mean to be late.'

'Where have you been all day?'

'Well,' I said, and the words flew out before I could stop them, 'around the streets and then on the towpath.'

'By the canal?'

'Yeah.'

'But you're not allowed down there. You've been told that. Kids have fallen in. They've been pushed in the canal, and they've had their bikes taken off them. It's dangerous down there.'

'Yeah, yeah,' I said. 'Where's my dinner?'

The toilet was just off the kitchen. The door opened suddenly, and there was Dad. He flew across the kitchen, grabbed me by the neck, pushed me against the wall and began to slap me.

Mum jumped in and grabbed his arms. 'He's only a kid and you'll hurt him if you go on like that.'

Dad stopped. 'No more bike-riding on the towpath. Have you got that? Disobey once more and no more bike. Got it?'

'Yes, Dad.'

A couple of days later I was out on my bike with my friends.

'Fancy coming down the canal?' someone said.

I thought about it for a second. 'Nah, I don't think so.'

'Why not? It's great down there.'

'Nah, don't fancy it.'

That was the towpath and me finished for the time being.

The security firm who had employed Dad on the Mozart Estate now sent him to work in an office block. His hours were from six at night to eight the next morning. One Friday he asked Vincent, John and me if we'd like to go with him. Vincent and I said yes and John said no, though I can't remember why.

Dad put on his uniform – black trousers, a light-blue shirt, a dark tie and a black jacket with silver buttons. There was also a cap. He didn't like wearing it so he would carry it to work in a bag. But he had to have it: it was one of the stupid rules employers specialize in. On his cap and jacket, there was a badge: 'Security,' it said.

We left the house. The streetlights were on and it was cold because it was winter. We walked to Queens Park station and caught the tube. We got out at Morden, at the end of the Northern Line, and came out of the station on to a wide street with office buildings on either side. Dad led the way to the block where he worked, tall, grey, with a lot of big glass windows and all its lights on because the working day had only just ended.

We went through the plate-glass doors at the front and into the lobby, which was full of light and the sound of a floor-polisher. A cleaner was buffing the floor. This was much better than the building site. It was nice and warm.

There was another security guard in the same uniform as Dad behind a desk. He and Dad talked. Dad signed a book. The other guard handed him the keys, said goodbye and left. The cleaner who'd been operating the floor-polisher and a few others who'd been upstairs were not long in following him. Soon we had the building to ourselves. Dad locked the front doors.

'I'm going on my round,' he said. 'You coming?'

I certainly was. Vincent too.

Dad took his cap and put it on my head. It smelt of him, a mix of Old Spice and Brylcreem, and dropped over my ears because it was too big. I was pleased to have it, though. 'You can always wear my cap when you come on the rounds with me,' he said.

We left the lobby, got into the lift and pressed the button for the top floor. As it went one way, my stomach went the other. At the top, we stepped into a corridor with doors leading off it. At each door Dad stopped to check it was shut. Most were locked. Then we came to one that was open. We went into a big office with windows at the end. We crossed the room to look at London spread out below us. I'd never been so high in my life. I could see only the yellow streetlights and the headlamps of the tiny cars. 'We'll come back in the morning,' said Dad, 'and you'll see more then.'

He flicked the lights out and locked the door. He checked the other rooms and locked them too. On my own, I'd have found it creepy, the empty rooms, the humming neon lights and no one around, but with Dad and Vincent there, I didn't.

Finally, Dad went to a box on the wall, put a key into a little hole and turned it.

'Why are you doing that?' I asked.

'To show I've done my round.'

I didn't understand.

'When I put the key in there and turn it,' he said, 'the box records the date and the time. There's one on every floor and when I finish a round I do this to show I've done it. It keeps them right, and it keeps me right.'

We went to the next floor, then the floor below and all the others, and on each one he checked the rooms, then put his key into the box on the wall and turned it.

Eventually we were back in the lobby. In the street, on the other side of the big windows, I could see lights glowing in the darkness. Dad found some drawing-paper and a pencil and put them on the desk. He glanced at his watch. 'I'm going to pop down to the pub,' he said. 'It isn't far, only a minute or two from here.'

I wondered where this was leading.

'While I'm away,' he said, 'I want you to hold the fort.'

Vincent, I noticed, had pulled on his coat and was making for the big doors.

'Will you do that?' Dad said. 'Will you hold the fort? We won't be long.'

I realized my brother, who was fourteen but looked older, was going with him, and I was being left alone. I felt excited but uncertain. On the one hand Dad trusted me, which was good. On the other, they'd known all evening they were going to the pub but they were only telling me now. I didn't like that.

'You can draw while we're out,' said Dad.

He crossed the lobby, his footsteps echoing, to Vincent. 'We won't be long,' he said.

The door closed with a squeak and Dad locked it.

He waved, and I watched them through the glass until they'd vanished. I sat down behind the counter at the back of the lobby. There were big black phones and copies of the *Daily Mirror* and the *Evening Standard* that the day security guard had left. There was the book Dad had signed, and the paper he'd left for me to draw on. And there was a bank of CCTV monitors. On each monitor, there was a different fuzzy black-and-white picture.

There was the lobby on one monitor but the counter was so

big I couldn't see myself. I stuck my arm up and waved. I saw that on the screen all right. On another monitor, there was a picture of the hallway where the lifts were and on a third, the plate-glass front doors.

The minutes passed and my excitement drained away. I didn't like being there on my own. I went to the big front windows and looked out into the street. Dad had said they wouldn't be long. But how long was that?

I went back behind the counter and sat down, anxious. What if someone passed by and saw me behind the counter? I was a child, obviously not the night-watchman, so Dad would be in trouble.

I decided to get down on the floor behind the counter. That way, I'd be invisible. I opened the old *Mirror* the day guard had left, laid it on the floor and sat on it. At least I wouldn't get a cold arse.

From the floor, I stared up at the monitor that showed the front doors. This was the one to watch because this would show Dad and Vincent coming back. Suddenly, with the corner of my eye, I thought I saw something moving on the monitor that showed the lobby. I stared at the screen carefully but I saw nothing, just the familiar space with the sofas and the plate-glass front doors, in fuzzy black and white. But there had been something there, hadn't there? I had seen something, hadn't I? And now, whatever it was, it was with me, inside the building, wasn't it?

I wanted to run – out of the door and down the street and all the way to the pub where they were, which couldn't be far away. Of course I couldn't because the door was locked. I wanted a pee too but I was too frightened to get up and go to the toilet.

After some time, I saw something on the monitor that showed the entrance, two blurs, far away but approaching. I'd have recognized them anywhere. Soon they came into the light at the front of the building – Dad in his uniform and, just behind him, Vincent in his leather jacket, swinging his arms in a way I'd never seen him do before.

I didn't want them to find me hiding behind the counter so I jumped up, put the *Mirror* back where I'd found it and sat on the chair. Dad unlocked the front doors, which squeaked as they swung back. As he and Vincent walked towards me, my brother was smiling. I realized he was pissed – which accounted for the funny way he'd been swinging his arms. Dad looked much the same as he had when he left but that wasn't a surprise. He drank every day. He had to have a lot to make him different.

They came up to the counter. They smelt of beer and tobacco.

'You all right, son?' This was Dad.

'Yeah,' I said. 'Fine.'

'We got you crisps and a bottle of Coke,' said Dad. He put them on the counter. There was a straw floating in the neck of the bottle. I rushed off to the toilet, then came back, drank the Coke and wolfed the crisps.

'I've got to do my rounds again,' said Dad. 'Do you want to come?'

Of course I did. I wasn't going to let him out of my sight now.

We took the lift to the top, put the key into the box, and repeated this on every floor. By the time we got back downstairs, Vincent was asleep, stretched out on a sofa at the side of the lobby. I lay down on another . . .

When someone shook my shoulder I thought I was at home, in bed, but when I opened my eyes and saw Dad I remembered where I was. Vincent was sitting up with a mug of tea, which he was sipping.

'Here, there's tea for you too,' said Dad, and he put a mug into my hand.

I drank it, then Dad and I went to do his last round. At the top of the building, he took me into the office we were in the night before. We went over to the big window and looked out. It was neither day nor night. The streetlights were on but there was light in the sky and I could see the shape of the street below, the outline of the buildings that stood along it. We opened up the other offices, turned the key in the box, then went on down all the floors. By the time we arrived back at the lobby, the day security guard had turned up. Dad signed the book and handed over the keys.

After the warm building, it seemed especially cold in the street, but I soon warmed up. I started thinking about the breakfast I'd have when we got home. I'd have a bowl of Sugar Puffs, then egg, bacon, sausage and beans, the works.

There weren't many people around because it was Saturday. Dad bought tobacco and a newspaper, and we went into the station, down to a platform and stepped on to a train. It was empty, like the streets outside.

Vincent's face was white, from the beer the night before. He was reading Dad's paper because he didn't want to talk to us. Dad rolled a cigarette, lit it – you could smoke on the Underground in those days – and blew a smoke-ring. It was heavy and blue and hung in the air for a long time before it dissolved and rose as smoke towards the handles above. Magic.

We came to Queens Park, got out and began to walk home.

'Listen, son,' said Dad. 'You won't say anything to Mum about Vincent and me going to the pub, will you?'

Of course I wouldn't. If she knew, Mum would kill him.

We got home. Vincent went to bed, Dad and I sat down at the kitchen table and Mum got out the frying pan. Dad told her we'd had a nice quiet night and I'd been good. Home, sweet home.

When I'd been at Queens Park Primary School, I'd joined the Cub Scouts. The uniform was a green cap, green jumper with matching long socks, and grey shorts. My brothers had moved up to the 8th Paddington Scouts Group and eventually the time came for me to follow them.

We met in a school off Kilburn Lane and I had a lovely new uniform: a green beret, mushroom-coloured long trousers, a green shirt, and a scarf that was fastened with something called a woggle.

Scouting was a challenge. For a start there was map reading, but as I found it hard to read a book, this was lost on me. Then there was knotting. I couldn't do my own shoelaces, so I'd no chance there either. But it was all good fun.

The annual highlight was a fortnight's camping in the New Forest. Vincent and John had done this trip and had told me how good it was. I had been down with Mum to wave them off in the past, but now I was a Scout like them, I'd be going with them.

The morning we were due to leave, the boys and their parents met outside the church hall where the local youth club was. A Blake's removal van pulled up. While our parents watched, we loaded our tents, cooking things and rucksacks, which we piled on top of each other to make a wall that ran right across the back. Mum gave Vincent, John and me a packed lunch each in a plastic bag. There were hugs and kisses, then we piled into the back of the van with the tents and the luggage and away we went, shouting and waving.

After we'd sung a few Scout songs, everyone settled down. Vincent was talking to his mates, John was having a sleep and I was watching the world fly past as we drove out of London.

Halfway into the journey, the van pulled over. We got out to stretch our legs and eat our lunch. Someone had a ball, and a little game started. How green the world was out of London, and how peaceful, I thought.

After an hour we got on the road again and kept going until we got to our campsite. We all helped with unloading the van and pitching the tents we'd be sleeping in. Then we put up some bigger ones, those we would use for group activities.

That evening, we were told what we'd be doing over the fortnight to come and there was more singing, around the campfire now, before bed. It had been a long day so I was straight into my sleeping-bag and had soon conked out.

The next morning the scoutmaster got us up early. It was cold but after I'd got some cold water on to my face and had my breakfast, I was ready to go, and I didn't stop.

After we'd been there a week, a coach came with our parents. Mum had brought Anne-Marie, and gave us some goodies. We gave her our dirty clothes. There was a cricket match, the fathers versus the Scouts, and Mum sat with the other women to watch.

One night, halfway through the second week, another lad and I decided we wanted some treats. We waited until everyone was asleep, then made our way to the tent with the food in it, including Jaffa Cakes. The trouble with Jaffa Cakes is that once you start you can't stop. We gorged ourselves. By the time we crept back to our tents we felt sick.

The next day I expected someone to say something about the missing Jaffa Cakes. But no one did.

In the evening, when we were sitting round the fire, the scoutmaster stood up. Someone had gone into the food tent, he said, and scoffed a load of Jaffa Cakes. Would those who had done this please come forward? It was a mad idea, of course, to ask the culprit to own up. I didn't move a muscle. I didn't look at the mate I'd been with, either. That would have been a giveaway. I kept very still and made sure I had my innocent face on.

There was a long silence. A few boys shifted in their seats. No one was going to put his hand up. Even the scoutmaster realized that. We moved on to a song.

At the end of the fortnight we returned to London and for the next few weeks I went to the weekly Scout meetings in a school off Kilburn Lane.

One evening we were playing Bulldog in the gym. You had to get from one end of the hall to the other without getting caught by the Bulldog. I was a lightly built, nimble child, but another kid, bigger and older, came at me from the side. He pushed me so hard that I tumbled and slid away. When I got up, he was laughing. Big mistake. I punched his nose hard.

There was blood. There was shouting. The scoutmaster came over. There was a bit of talk, by him and me, followed by a quick decision. I'd overreacted. I'd hurt a fellow Scout. There was no room in the 8th Paddington Scouts Group for that sort of behaviour. I was asked to leave. My Scouting days were over.

It wasn't only the Scouts I fell out with around this time. When I'd started at Quintin Kynaston I'd probably have been better off going to work but, of course, that would have been illegal.

In the first days, big school was an adventure, a novelty. I liked expanding my circle of friends, finding my way around a new bit of the world. And I think I did try at the start, not very hard but a bit. I'm sure the teachers tried too, but it wasn't fun sitting in a classroom, and I just couldn't get my head round any of it. For a start there was far too much going on at QK. Go to this room on that floor, then from this floor to that room, lots of people coming and going, like ants, all day. On top of that, everywhere you went someone was trying to fill your head with shit. For instance: they told me that I couldn't write or talk English. So what fucking language had I been speaking all my life?

I wasn't bad at art – the head of art said I had it in me to get to art school – but my actual art teacher and I, we didn't see eye to eye, so as often as not, I'd get kicked out of the art class too. That was the way it went in all the other subjects. I'd argue, act up, and get thrown out. It even happened in PE. So the football I'd loved never took off either.

I wasn't alone. They were other kids like me – many from around the Avenues – who became my mates. It was bound to happen, wasn't it? Like attracts like. We all hated school and we all wanted to leave and get on with our lives and we all hated our teachers because they stopped us doing that. And because we all thought the same, we couldn't imagine there was any other way of looking at the world but our way.

Word had gone round: after lunch, the lads from our school were going to march down Carlton Vale to fight St George's. I'd heard about these regular pitched battles from John before I even started at Quintin Kynaston, and I was excited that at last I was going to see what I'd heard him talk so much about.

After lunch, everyone flooded out and marched down the hill. There was a patrol car with coppers inside and the teachers told us to go back. We ignored them. At St George's there was another patrol car and more teachers. 'Go back,' they said. The bigger lads ran for the wall surrounding St George's and climbed over. Some were dragged back, but others made it. I asked a big kid at the top to help me up. He extended an arm and hauled me on. He jumped down and ran forward. I stayed put. If I got down I'd be unable to get out. I sat and watched the scrap instead. St George's was a mixed school and one or two of our boys, I noticed, were chatting up the girls rather than fighting. Eventually teachers appeared to break it up. This hadn't been anything like the pitched battles John had reported. I jumped down and started up the hill for Quintin Kynaston.

I asked Mum if I could join the Army Cadets. I wanted to go into the British Army when I left school and this seemed a good step. Mum was all for it. The trouble was that the Cadets met a long way from Queens Park and I wouldn't get home from the meetings until very late. So that was the end of that idea.

I was disappointed but then I discovered that a branch of the Sea Cadets met in a church in First Avenue near Tesco on the Harrow Road.

I then found out that Cadets were banded by age. I should have been in the band for ten- to twelve-year-olds but it was full so I'd have to go into the next band up if I was going to get in. I asked Mum to tell them I was thirteen. She didn't want to but she did and I was in.

Six weeks of basic training followed, with a lot more knot-tying than I cared for. Then I was measured and given my uniform. I had just started to get interested in the opposite sex and my current interest was Julie. Once I got the uniform home, I started wearing it round to her house, where I'd strut about like a sailor home on leave. My God, I thought I looked the bollocks.

I was taken one weekend, by minibus, with the other Cadets to the river Thames, and there was our training ship. She was grey, with one funnel, sooty around the top, smoke pouring out of it. We carried our rucksacks on board and were ordered to stow our things below deck.

The engine came alive and the boat throbbed. We slipped our moorings, and sailed down the Thames towards the sea.

We were put to work, scrubbing the decks and polishing anything above water. I hated that so I hid in the engine room. The old boy there didn't mind me hanging around. He tried to explain how the engine worked but I couldn't hear what he was saying above the noise it made.

We passed out of the Thames estuary and into open sea. The waves were huge now and the boat was rocked this way and that. They were cooking in the galley – you could smell it – and several Cadets were sick. I'm proud to say that I wasn't. Maybe all those years going to Belfast by boat had given me sea legs.

Before dark, we pulled into a Navy shipyard. A couple of warships with big guns were moored there. That night I was woken and taken up on deck where I was given a pair of black binoculars and told to keep watch. Watch what? We weren't at war – or had it started when I was in my berth?

The binoculars were huge. I could hardly hold them up to look through them and I was still half asleep. It was dark and cold, the wind was blowing and I couldn't hide from it.

I was given a cup of tea. I put the binoculars down, nearly dropping them overboard, and drank it. I was told again to watch for anything that wasn't right. My eye fell on the dock. If anything was going to happen, that's where it would be, surely, I thought.

So I kept my eye on the dock, and that's all they got, one eye. It took all my might to keep that one open. Keeping watch was like watching paint dry. Time passed. It got darker and colder, and the wind picked up even more. Then I saw something. I didn't know what it was so I gave the warning. Half the ship's company turned out. All the officers and petty officers took turns with the binoculars. There was only the one pair on board, it seemed, the big black pair I had. They all wanted to know what I had seen. I didn't know what it was so I said it was a dark figure, a man running.

Someone got on the radio to the dockside. Within minutes Military Police, with lights and dogs, were crawling all over the quays, looking for this man I'd seen. They never found him. Everyone went back to bed, and when my watch finished, I followed.

In the morning, a captain from one of the ships in the dock was to come on board ours. I was given the job of piping him on by blowing into a whistle of a kind I'd never seen before. The captain arrived and I piped. I sounded, I thought, like Roger

Whittaker in 'Durham Town'. The captain smiled. When he left I had to pipe him off. I think I was given the honour as a reward for my vigilance the previous night.

Later that day we sailed for home. Somewhere along the Thames we had to stop. Some Sea Cadets from another part of London whose ship had broken down needed a lift.

Once on board they came below decks. One started taking the piss out of someone from the Avenues. A fight kicked off and we slaughtered them.

Shortly after I left the Sea Cadets. It wasn't for me. The Royal Marines – that was where I knew I belonged.

9

In the autumn of 1973 Dad got another job, as an assistant care-taker at Willesden College of Technology this time. In the evenings, Vincent, John and I would sometimes take the bus over there. By the time we arrived, the place was empty and we would have it to ourselves.

There was a full-size snooker table and the four of us would have a game – or try to. Vincent and Dad weren't bad. Then Dad would set off on his round and I would go with him. He would check each classroom, make sure no one was inside, then lock the door. He always ended at the stationery store, a long room with no windows. He would walk up and down the shelves selecting coloured chalks, pencils and blank paper for me to draw with. Then we would collect my brothers and catch the bus home.

One evening when I came in from school Mum called me into the kitchen. She told me she knew a lady who knew a woman who owned a shop on Chamberlayne Road, in Kensal Green, that sold men's clothes. There was a job waiting for me. I was now twelve, so I was up and able for it.

The next day after school I went there. It was a small shop and looked as if it had been there for years. Inside it was the same. With its wooden counter, glass cabinets and drawers with brass handles, it reminded me of something from an old black-and-white film. I thought, I'm the youngest thing ever to have walked in here, and I didn't like that.

The owner was behind the counter, a Rothmans smoking in the ashtray beside her. She was small, round and old. I said hello. A man was sitting very still on a chair beside her. He looked old, too, and unwell.

'Are you the son of the Irish lady?' she said.

'Yes.'

'And you've come about the job?' she said.

'Yes.' I wondered who the old man behind the counter was but I didn't ask and she didn't say.

'Well, it's a nice job,' she said, 'and the hours are good. You do two hours after school Monday to Friday and all day Saturday. You clean the shop, run errands, make the tea and serve any customers who come in for small items, belts, socks, ties or hankies, that sort of thing. Anyone wants anything bigger, I'll take care of him. You just come and get me. I'm never far away. If I'm not in the shop, you'll always find me in the back room.' She pointed to its door. 'Do you know how to knot a tie?'

'No,' I said. When I had to wear one for school Mum or someone else always did it for me.

'You have to wear a tie, you know, for this job.'

'Oh.'

'Never mind. I'll teach you. Let's start now. No time like the present, is there?'

She draped a tie round my neck and showed me. Then she told me to do it. I made a mess of it. 'You just keep doing it,' she said. 'You'll get it right in the end. Practice makes perfect.'

Then she remembered the most important detail, at least to me, which she'd forgotten until now. 'The pay's a pound a week,' she said.

I was twelve and a half. I would have liked more but it was

better than nothing. I had a post-office book and I was good at saving. I would pay in all the money I got and build up my balance, then buy some Christmas presents, or some toy soldiers, of which I had a great number at home.

'All right,' I said, and I was taken on. Every day after school that week I worked in the shop and the following Saturday morning I was there again.

The morning passed and lunchtime came. The owner helped the mysterious old man to stand up. He did this with difficulty. Then they walked the length of the shop together and disappeared into the little room at the back. She closed the door after them. Her husband, her brother, her father, I still didn't know who he was.

For the next hour, I had the shop to myself. Then the door opened. They made their way back and the old man sat down in his seat behind the counter.

It was afternoon. She lit a Rothmans, took a drag and then, as a customer came in, set it down in the ashtray. I looked at it, at her, then at the fag again.

When I was eleven I had taken one of my dad's half-smoked roll-ups from the ashtray at home and smoked it in the garden. I hadn't liked it and vowed I'd never have another. It was a resolution that didn't last. Nearly all my mates at school smoked. I'd started taking the odd drag off them, then the odd fag and it wasn't long before I was buying my own. I got them, as we all did, from sweet shops, most of which sold cigarettes singly at a penny each. Sometimes I spent my bus fare on fags and walked. My mates did the same so we did a lot of walking. If the weather was nice, so was the walk. If it was raining, we'd jump on the bus and stay there until we were kicked off. Then we would hop on another bus until we were nearly home. I got plenty of exercise and excitement, plus I got to smoke.

By this stage I was on two or three or, at most, five a day, but watching the smoke from the woman's Rothmans and smelling it, I wanted one now. In fact, I was desperate.

I looked at the owner again. Her back was towards me. I could get away with this, I thought. The old man was drowsing in his chair. Yes, definitely, I could do it but I had to be quick.

I took the burning fag from the ashtray. 'Just popping to the toilet,' I said, and went down the shop, out of the far door and into the yard at the back. I went into the toilet, took a few puffs, and flushed the butt.

When I went back into the shop, another Rothmans was burning in the ashtray on the counter.

From now on, I decided, I'd be going to the toilet a lot.

After about a month I asked if I could have a pay rise.

'What's a little boy like you going to do with more money?' asked the owner.

I didn't have an answer.

'Well, you're getting quite enough for what you do,' she said. 'I'm not going to give you any more and that's that.'

I decided I'd have to help myself.

The end of my two hours was nearly up and she was in the back room with the old fellow. Perfect.

I opened the till quietly. The tray inside was full of money. I took one of the new fifty-pence pieces that had replaced the old red ten-shilling notes. My plan was to take the same each weekday and each Saturday afternoon. That plus my pay would give me four pounds altogether each week. Stealing, of course, was completely against the way I had been brought up. Mum and Dad would have been disgusted if they'd known what I was doing. But I felt I had no choice. A pound a week just wasn't enough.

The owner's Rothmans were on the shelf under the till. I opened the packet. Inside I saw a neat row of fags with their filters, pale brown with tiny white spots. I took one, then put back the packet where I'd found it. As well as the extra money, I'd have one of her fags every day too. And so I did and so I did . . .

It was another Saturday, just after five, when I left the shop, my wage plus fifty pence in one pocket, and one of the owner's Rothmans hidden in my hand. I had to smoke it before I got home but I didn't have a light. The first person I asked didn't either. Neither did the second, nor the third. Along the way I was also told to fuck off and that I was too young to smoke, but eventually I got it lit.

I had a couple of puffs and then a hand landed down on my right shoulder – a heavy hand with a familiar watch on the wrist. A familiar voice spoke: 'All right, son?' it said. 'Just finished work?'

I was pissing sweat. I shoved my left hand with the cigarette into my coat pocket and said, 'Hello, Dad. Yes, just finished.'

We started the walk. I could feel the heat from the cigarette I was holding but I didn't dare pull it out. First I was not allowed to smoke and, second, how was I to explain where the cigarette had come from? There was nothing for it but to keep walking, with the cigarette hidden, my hand getting hotter, and hope my best jacket didn't catch fire.

Dad took the longest way home and he kept his hand on my shoulder until we got there. Then he said, 'Tell your mum I'm going for a beer, and try not to burn a hole in your coat.'

He walked away, laughing. I pulled my hand out in a puff of smoke. My ashy fingers were puffy and cooked. The cigarette was just a butt and a red tip.

I went on working in the shop after school and on Saturdays, helping myself to fifty-pence pieces and cigarettes. After three or four months, I decided I'd had enough. The work was dull and I was now a big football fan and I wanted to watch Queens Park Rangers' home games on Saturdays. I loved walking up the Harrow Road wearing my blue-and-white scarf and matching bobble hat, getting the train at Westbourne Park, riding the three stops to Shepherds Bush, buying a bag of chips and a drink, arriving at the ground with no ticket and getting over the wall, helped by some bigger lads, or crawling under the turnstiles, hidden by the legs and feet of the people going through.

One evening I said to Mum I wasn't going back to the shop. She told me to keep my job. But I'd made my mind up. I wasn't going back, and I never did.

There was a Tesco on the Harrow Road. Mum shopped there and knew the manager. She had a knack of making friends wherever she went. His name was Seamus. His parents came from somewhere in the south of Ireland and he'd grown up in London. Vincent and John were working in the shop and one afternoon when I got home from school Mum told me that I had a job there too. My hours were Friday evenings and Saturday mornings, which left me free in the afternoons to watch QPR.

It was a small Tesco, with only two aisles, but it was the biggest shop at the time on the Harrow Road, and many people used it.

At the back I found Seamus's office. It was a tiny room with a big desk. He gave me a coat to wear and told me what to do. I had to check the shelves and see what was running short, write it down on a bit of paper, go upstairs, get what was needed from the storerooms and carry it down. I had to put the new stock in place and price the items with a little machine that shot out stickers.

I set to work. At some point, when I was upstairs, I found a box of Mars Bars. I took one out and ate it. Then I had a drink on the house. Of course, Mum would have done her nut, Dad too, if they'd found out I'd done this. But stealing, I now believed, was only wrong when or if you got caught. That was how I saw it. So long as I wasn't caught, everything would be fine.

At the end of the evening, another boy and I were given a bucket of soapy water and a mop to wash the floor. The water was hot at first and when I ran the mop up and down, steam rose. By the time I finished, the water was black and cold. I poured it into the sink in the washroom. It was full of grit tramped in from the pavements – I'd never noticed the streets were so filthy.

The next day, Saturday, I was back in Tesco. I spent the day stacking shelves and helping myself to the odd treat. There was so much stock upstairs that whatever I took would make no difference to Tesco.

I was thirteen now and hung around the corner of Farrant Street with a gang of others: the brothers Paddy-Joe, Frank and Charlie

I, John and Dave I, Mark C, John B – they're all dead now – plus Garry and Steve M, Larry W, Terry M, Mick L, Frank M, John-John, Robert (Trebor), Winston, Ricky Mac, Delroy, Roy C, Phillip R (Tilley), Eddie O, John and Carl G, Lee and Mark N, Jimmy Derick, Brian B and Tony W.

We passed the time with games. There was 'Penny off the Kerb' – sometimes 'Penny-up' – though I never saw anyone playing with a penny, always 2p and above. The aim was to get your coin as close to the edge of the pavement as possible: the nearest was the winner. There were other coin games too, like 'Up the Wall' and 'Heads or Tails'. I was never very good at any of them so I didn't play much. If the police caught you playing they could nick you, but more often they would nick your money and send you home with a kick or a slap.

We smoked and broke the windows of old houses, taking care to avoid the ones where the squatters lived. They'd had us in to tea once and explained that they didn't like it.

One evening, we decided to have fun ringing people's doorbells and running off. We loved doing that and we did it to everyone, English, Irish, whatever, as long as they'd a front door. We even did it to our own homes. That evening we went to the house of a Pakistani family we'd done earlier. Normally, between knocking and the door opening, you had a chance to run but no sooner had we knocked this time than the door opened and men came flying out, some with sticks, others with knives. I began to run. I was nippy and they weren't going to get me. I also had the wind up. God, I said, inside my head, as I was running, I won't ever do that again, I promise.

I made it to Third Avenue, and stopped, puffing and a bit shaky. I'd lost them. There were no feet pounding behind me, no voices calling.

I got my breath back, then pulled a piece of chalk out of my pocket. It was big and fat, one of a box of ten Dad had brought home from Willesden College for me. I carried it round so I could do something else I loved doing.

I turned now and wrote 'Paddy' on the wall. I never wrote

Patrick – I hated my name. If anyone called me Paddy in front of Mum, though, she would always say, 'His name isn't Paddy, it's Patrick.' That was what she always called me and that was what I heard now, coming down the street.

She was calling me to come indoors. She didn't like me staying out late – she didn't like any of us staying out late.

10

It was the autumn of 1974. Murphy's were doing the pavements in Ilbert Street, just round the corner from my house. The team was small, just three. Two were young, with long hair, and one had a beard. The third was the gaffer and drove the lorry so he was older. You could tell he'd worked hard all his life. The young lads wore jeans and jumpers, but the old boy always wore a suit. When I'd worked in the clothing shop, men like him would come in on Fridays, looking for a cheap suit to wear over the weekend, to church, down the pub and then to work until the next Friday, when they'd buy another.

About halfway up Ilbert Street, the workmen had a shed made of corrugated iron. They'd go in there to shelter from the rain, or to have tea on their breaks. That was when we'd get them. We'd throw stones, and when they hit the corrugated iron what a noise they made! The two younger ones would fly out and run after us. They wore wellington boots so we felt quite safe. We could always get away when they came after us.

One day I got the chance to make my mark in a new way. I came across a square of fresh concrete in Ilbert Street that the Murphy's men had left to dry when they'd gone home. I found a stick and wrote my name in it: Paddy. Once the concrete set, I'd be there for ever.

It was evening, a day or two later. The sky was blue and the sun was out. The gang was hanging around the corner of Farrant Street as usual. Some were playing 'Penny off the Kerb', others were smoking and talking, and we were all spitting too. We did a lot of spitting in those days. I think we thought it made us look hard.

Out of nowhere, the workman with the beard appeared. 'Hello, Paddy,' he said, not at me, to all of us, but I, silly bollocks, said, 'Hello,' back. Well, now he knew who'd written his name in the new cement, didn't he?

He got me by the neck and pulled me up the street in the direction of the hut. My mates followed, shouting. They told him to let me go, and called him a Paddy-wanker, which didn't help but that's what friends do in your hour of need. I tried to get away, kicking at his legs, but he had a firm grip and wouldn't let go.

'Where do you live?' he said.

Well, why not lie? I thought.

'Miles and miles away, mate,' I said. 'I got to take two buses and a train to get here.'

'You're having me on,' he said.

'No, I'm not.'

'You tell me where you live right now,' he said, 'or I'm going to drag you over to the phone box and then I'm going to ring the police.'

Now I'm in for it, I thought.

At that moment, the truck drove up with the old boy who wore the suit at the wheel. He got out and asked what was going on. The workman with the beard told him. The old boy clipped me on the ear and pushed me on my way . . .

Later that autumn, a bit after four o'clock one wet weekday, I was with some mates in the street. We were talking about the Murphy's hut. The workmen used it in the day but after they'd gone home it was empty until they came back the next morning. It was empty now.

'It's going to waste,' said someone.

'We could break in,' said someone else. 'No one around, no one to stop us, easy.'

'Brilliant place to get out of the rain,' said a third.

'Brilliant place to smoke,' said a fourth.

'And with the Murphy's men not back till tomorrow there'll be no chance of getting caught. We'll be long gone.'

None of us could believe we hadn't thought of it before. It was a cracker. We waited until we thought enough time had passed since the workmen had clocked off, then sauntered across to Ilbert Street and walked up to the hut. There was a padlock, as we'd expected, on the door. I found an iron bar and hit it twice, without success. Others had a go, hitting it with all sorts. Finally it was off.

We pulled open the door and piled in. There was only the light coming in through the door so it was dark. The place was damp and smelt of earth, pavement, men's sweat and tobacco. But we weren't fussy. It was ours now.

The workmen's clothes were hanging up – jeans and donkey jackets. We rifled through them. I found an old knife and put it straight into my pocket, finders keepers and all that. One of the other lads put on a pair of wellingtons and started talking like an Irishman, making everyone laugh.

There was a big old Primus stove, a big black kettle filled with water, a bit of milk in a bottle, some sugar and tea bags, all the ingredients for a brew. Someone got the Primus going, and as we waited for the water to boil, we sat about, talking and smoking.

The kettle boiled and someone made the tea. It was handed round in big old chipped mugs. We left the Primus going so we could see what we were doing and to keep warm. Through the half-open door we could see grey lines of falling rain and the pavement dark with wet. Someone said we couldn't be in a better place than where we were and we all agreed. We closed the door, not completely but so there was just a slit with light at the side and no wind or rain blowing in.

Snug, we sat about with our mugs, huffing and sipping. Then the lad by the door said, 'The lorry's coming!'

We jeered. As far as we knew, in all the weeks they'd been at work, the Murphy's men had never come back after they'd knocked off. When they finished, that was it. This was a wind-up. Had to be.

'No,' said the lad, still squinting through the slit at the side of the door. 'They're coming, I tell you.'

'Yeah, yeah, nice try,' one of us said. Then we heard it: the low rumble of a diesel engine and it was right outside the hut. The lorry had pulled up outside.

We crowded up to the door and looked out through the gap. There it was, just a few yards away. If we ran out now they'd see us. Maybe the best course, someone whispered, was to stay put. Maybe they wouldn't notice that the door was ajar and the padlock gone. (In fact, it was in the bucket we'd been using as a toilet.) Maybe they'd just pick up what they'd come back to collect, sling it into the back of the lorry and drive away. Maybe.

The driver's door opened and there was the old fellow. He jumped down on to the road. He was looking at the door of the hut and we knew he had seen that the padlock wasn't there.

'Come out, you bastards!' he shouted.

Clearly the other two in the cab heard this. Their gaffer was on to something and they wouldn't let him face it alone. They opened their door and jumped down.

It was every boy for himself. We shoved open the door and ran. The Murphy's men tried to grab us as we pushed past them but we were frightened so we were quick. The only one they caught was the lad in the wellingtons.

When we were far enough away we stopped. We saw them give our mate a dig in the ear and a kick up the backside. They made him take off the boots and then they let him go. He ran down the road. Once he'd joined us, we started shouting. We called them wankers and shitfaces, and told them to fuck off back to Ireland.

I started for home. I still had the knife in my pocket. I got it out. It was only a little one and it was covered with dirt. When I got home I gave it, and myself, a good clean. The knife came up lovely, just like new. The tip was broken but, other than that, it was all right. I knew I had to hide it from Mum and Dad. They'd have asked a lot of awkward questions about where I'd got it and they wouldn't have let me keep it. I'd have to keep it with me all the time, I realized, if I didn't want to lose it.

The next day, with the knife in my pocket, I set off for school at the usual time. I knew the Murphy's men wouldn't be long finding the padlock in the bucket we'd pissed in, if they hadn't already. I knew they'd recognize me, too, and if they got hold of me it would be very unpleasant. I'd have to give Ilbert Street a wide berth for a while.

A week or so later I was out one night. I had on my parka, the one I wore to school. It was dark blue with a horrible orange lining, and had a hood with a fake-fur trim. I would have it zipped up as much as possible because of the lining. I was on my way home. In front of me I could see the old red telephone box a few yards from our house.

There were cars parked along the kerb and in one there were some men but I had eyes only for the phone box.

As it was dark the inside light was on, weak and yellow. Someone, a girl, was on the phone. When I got closer, I recognized my brother John's girlfriend, Maxine.

I pulled open the heavy door. 'Hello, Maxine,' I said.

She turned.

'What you doing?' I asked.

'Phoning John,' she said.

I told her not to bother. 'Come with me. I'm going home now.'

Maxine put the phone down. 'I don't know if I'd be welcome.'

Why wouldn't she? She and John were going out, weren't they?

'We've had a row,' she said. 'When I called at your house earlier he wouldn't come to the door.'

Ah, I knew about this sort of thing. I'd seen it with Mum and Dad. This was what happened with couples. One minute they'd be lovey-dovey, the next they wouldn't be talking.

Maxine dialled our house again. As she waited for someone to answer, I held open the door with my shoulder, picking away at the cashbox with my knife. I knew there was no chance I'd open it, yet I hoped I might.

Next thing, a man jumped out of the car by the kerb. 'What are you doing, son?' The accent was Scottish. He had red hair and looked hard.

'Nothing,' I said, and slipped the knife into my pocket.

He got me by the arm. 'Put the phone down,' he said to Maxine. 'Step out of the box.'

He wasn't in uniform but I knew he was a policeman. He pulled me into the street. Maxine followed.

'What were you doing?' he said to her.

'Phoning someone,' said Maxine.

'It didn't look like that to me,' he said. 'Now, go home.'

Maxine walked away towards the Harrow Road.

'Have you got anything on you that you shouldn't have?' he said to me.

'No.'

'Oh, really? We'll see about that.'

The man patted the sides of my parka, then put his hands into the pockets. He pulled out a ten-pack of No. 6, a box of matches and the knife.

I thought he'd be satisfied with that but his hand came up and he swiped the side of my head. I heard ringing in my ear. 'You're a liar,' he said.

I said nothing. I thought that was for the best: by keeping my mouth shut, I wouldn't make him angrier.

'How old are you?'

'Thirteen.'

'You're too young to be smoking, and what's with the knife?'

'What do you mean?' I said.

'Where did you get it?' He held the knife so he could see it better by the light that came out of the phone box.

'I found it up the road.'

'Oh, yeah?' he said. 'You found it, right? When?'

'Just now.'

'And what were you doing with it when I found you in the box?'

'Nothing.'

'Don't lie to me,' he said. 'You were trying to open the cashbox, weren't you? That's what you were doing with the knife, wasn't it? You had it stuck in and you were trying to get the front off.'

'No, I wasn't. I was waiting with Maxine while she phoned. She's my brother's girlfriend.'

'Well, you're nicked.'

He led me to his car. There were two men in the front. They weren't in uniform either, but I guessed they were policemen, too, like him. He yanked open the back door, shoved me in, got in after me and closed the door. I'd never been nicked before, except in Selfridges, so I'd no idea what would happen.

'Where do you live?' asked the Scot.

The driver turned the engine over and put the car in gear. He was smoking a fag. The windows were closed so the interior was full of smoke but not so full I couldn't see my house. The car headlamps came on and the handbrake came off.

'Number forty-three, just there,' I replied. I thought it was a great stroke of luck he'd asked the question at that moment. Now I'd shown them where I lived, I thought, the driver would stop the car and the Scot would get me out and walk me to my front door. But I was wrong. The driver didn't stop.

'That's my house there,' I said. 'You're just passing it.'

'Shut up,' said the Scot.

Dad had always said to us, 'Fear me, not the police, when they bring you home.' By this he meant that if the police caught us for something, whatever they did wouldn't be a patch on what he would do when he got his hands on us. Until that moment I'd always believed it, but now I wondered if these men wouldn't turn out to be far worse than my dad. I wanted to shout, 'Mum, help me.' I was very frightened.

The driver pushed on. We looped round and drove to the Harrow Road. The further we went from my house the worse I felt.

The policemen began to speak quietly. I heard what they said, but I couldn't understand it. They were careful to make certain I couldn't follow, not quite talking in code but almost. That added to my anxiety. They must be talking about me, I thought.

The policemen talked for a long time, maybe twenty minutes, maybe longer. Then the Scot turned to me. 'What's your name, son?'

'Paddy Maguire.'

'Is it Paddy or Patrick?'

'Patrick, but I don't like it. All my mates call me Paddy.'

'So you're Irish?'

'No, but Mum and Dad are.'

'Who lives at home?'

'Mum, Dad, my two brothers and my little sister.'

'Anyone else?'

'Yeah, my uncle Sean.'

'Why is he living with you?'

'He's working over here.'

'Are Mum and Dad working?'

'Dad's not but Mum is.'

'What part of Ireland do Mum and Dad come from?'

'Belfast.'

'What work is Mum doing?'

'Cleaning. I help her sometimes.'

'Where's her work?'

'Up the Harrow Road.'

'What about your brothers and sister?'

'What about them?'

'Were they born in Belfast like your mum and dad?'

'No, only me.'

'Why was that?'

'Mum was on holiday at the time.'

'In Belfast?'

'Yes.'

'Do you ever go back to Belfast?'

'Yes, we do but not Dad.'

'Why is that?'

'I don't know.'

'What about this knife? Where did you get it?'

'I found it in the street.'

'You're lying. It's too clean.'

'I gave it a wash.'

'When was that?'

'The other day.'

'But you told me you'd just found it.'

'No.'

'Yes, you did. You said you'd just found it in the street when you were walking down to the phone box.'

I said nothing. It was true. I had told him I'd just found it. He'd caught me out.

'Why did you lie to me?'

Again, I said nothing. What could I say?

'If you don't tell the truth, I'm going to lock you in a cell until you do,' he said. 'Understand?'

I'd never been in a police station before. But some of my mates had. They'd told the rest of us all about it and it wasn't nice. They were locked up for hours, no food, no water, plus they'd had a beating. The police at Harrow Road were well known for that.

When you've got a policeman talking at you and making threats, you start to think, What can I tell him? What does he want to know? I thought about the hut. Had the workmen told the police we'd smashed the padlock off, helped ourselves to tea and pissed in a bucket? It was possible. I decided I'd better mention the Murphy's hut. I was about to open my mouth when the Scot said, 'Where is it you said you live?'

'Forty-three Third Avenue.'

To my surprise, the driver turned into Third Avenue, drove to forty-three, and stopped outside.

'What are Mum and Dad going to say about all this?' the Scot asked.

The police had picked me up and it was at least half an hour past the time I was supposed to be indoors. 'They'll go mad,' I said.

'Move it,' said the Scot. He got out and so did the one in the front passenger seat. I got out, too, and then, with a policeman on either side of me, I walked up to our front door. One of them knocked.

John answered. 'Mum, he's here,' he called.

I went into the front room, with the Scottish policeman behind me. The second hung back, staying in the doorway.

Mum was on the phone. She put down the receiver as I came in. Uncle Sean, her brother, was watching TV. He gave me a smile. He'd been living with us in London for the best part of a year. He slept in the little spare room behind the living room that looked into the yard.

The Scot introduced himself and the other man as policemen. He confirmed who my mum was. Then he said, 'We found this in your son's pocket.' He held the knife out so Mum could see. 'He was in the phone box, the one outside here. He was using the knife to try to open the cashbox.'

I looked at her. Mum, my face said, the policeman's lying. I didn't do it. I'm innocent.

'He shouldn't be carrying a knife like this,' said the Scot.

Mum agreed with him. No, I shouldn't. 'But I didn't know he had it,' she said.

The other policeman, who hadn't spoken, was still standing half in, half out of the room. I could feel him behind me. I glanced back to see what he was up to and saw he was looking around, taking everything in.

'Are you the father?'

The question was addressed to Uncle Sean.

'No,' he said.

The Scot asked Mum where Dad was.

'He's at the police station,' she said.

After I hadn't come home when I was supposed to, he had gone there to ask about me.

That's all I need, I thought, Dad going down there. He'll find out I've been picked up and when he gets back he'll kill me. That's if Mum hasn't already.

'I'm going to keep the knife,' said the policeman to Mum. He slipped it into the pocket of his overcoat. He went to go, then stopped. 'I nearly forgot. These belong to your son as well.'

He handed my pack of No. 6 and my box of matches to Mum. Then he and the other policeman left. I heard them shut the front door behind them and walk across the pavement towards the car.

Mum had been worried sick, Dad too. Maxine hadn't gone home, she explained, as she'd been told to do by the Scottish policeman. She'd gone on up the road a bit, then stopped where she couldn't be seen and watched. She'd seen me bundled into the car and driven off, then gone straight to my parents and told them what she thought she'd seen, which was me being put in a car and driven away by strange men. Maxine didn't know they were policemen. They weren't in uniform and their car wasn't marked. It had looked to Mum and Dad as if I'd been abducted. That was why Dad had gone to the police station. To report me missing.

Mum told me to go to bed. I didn't argue, just went straight up. My room was at the front. I shared it with John. If I'd wanted I could have stuck my head out of the window and seen the phone box where the evening's trouble had started. I didn't, of course. I just got into bed. It was nice under the covers. I heard Dad coming in later. I didn't go down and he didn't come up.

I saw him the next day at breakfast. He said I shouldn't have had the knife or the cigarettes. But he was more upset with the policemen for not bringing me straight home. He couldn't understand why they'd taken me away in their car and driven me around for so long.

December 3, 1974, was a Tuesday. The day started quietly. Downstairs, Uncle Sean was asleep in the little back room and Dad was in the front room. He and Mum weren't getting on. He'd given up his job as assistant caretaker at Willesden College about a month before. He was drinking and arguing with Mum a lot, which was why he was sleeping in the front room. Upstairs Vincent, who was working as a gas fitter's mate and going to night school to get his qualification as a fitter, was asleep in the little room that had been Anne-Marie's. My sister was asleep in my parents' bedroom, as was Mum, because there was space now that Dad was downstairs. John and I were in the front room we shared.

Uncle Sean got up first and left for work. He was a tractor driver for Fitzpatrick's, a subsidiary of Tarmac Ltd and the site was at Wembley Stadium. I didn't hear him go.

Mum and Vincent were up next (my brother was second out after Sean) and then it was my turn. Mum woke me gently. She didn't trust me to see myself to school. She thought I'd bunk off unless she put me on the bus so she took me to work with her, then saw me on to the bus. In three months I would be fourteen.

I said I'd get up and she went out.

I didn't want to get up, of course. Why shouldn't I lie on? The school would still be there tomorrow.

Mum came back. 'If you don't get up now,' she said, 'I'll be late for work and you'll be late for school.'

'All right, I'll get up,' I said, and she went away.

Without her there, well, it was easy to doze on. Then I heard her at the bottom of the stairs. If I didn't shift now I'd be in trouble. I pushed off the covers and fell out of bed. 'I'm up,' I called.

I wanted something to read at breakfast. I looked around my room and found an annual, the *Beano*.

I carried it down to the kitchen and sat at the table. A cup of coffee and a slice of toast appeared in front of me. I opened the book and picked up the toast. I began the first story and took a bite. Mum told me to put the book down and hurry up. Otherwise we'd both be late.

'I don't mind if we are,' I said.

'But I do,' she said. 'I mind very much. If I don't turn up when I'm meant to, I could lose my job. They don't pay me to be late, you know.'

'All right,' I said. I could be awkward but not that morning. I polished off the coffee and toast. Then I had a wash, got dressed and off we went.

We walked up Third Avenue, turned on to the Harrow Road and arrived at Morris Apple, the accountants. We went inside and Mum began hoovering and dusting. I went round with a black bag and emptied the little bins that sat beside each desk. Next I gathered up the mugs and put them into the sink for Mum to wash. Finally, I got a bucket of hot soapy water and mopped the stairs. I was happy to help (and I helped Mum after school with her evening cleaning jobs as well), and I knew Mum put money for all the work I did into my post-office savings account.

We finished. Mum locked up and we went to the baker's as we always did, and she bought me a cake. I ate it in the street as we walked to the bus stop outside the cinema. I liked to look at the posters that were sometimes stuck up outside.

At the stop Mum gave me my day's money. I got free dinners, because of my parents' income and the number of children they had at school, so it was just the bus fares and she gave me the exact amount. If I'd extra she knew I'd spend it on fags.

It was early and still dark but there were people around. Mum said, 'Hello,' to one, 'Good morning,' to another and 'How are you today?' to a third. She knew everybody because she had cleaned or was cleaning every shop and business on the Harrow Road.

After a bit, my bus pulled up. Mum kissed the top of my head, told me to be good and reminded me of the importance of school.

'Yeah, yeah,' I said. I hated school. Henry VIII and his six wives. What good was that to me? None. The problem was, no matter how hard I tried to listen, my concentraton was gone after five minutes, which led to my getting bored and irritated, which led to my being rowdy and troublesome, which led to my getting a reputation, which led to rows with teachers and endless trouble with the staff. The only part about school I liked was meeting my mates and home time. Of course, I wasn't going to tell Mum this.

''Bye-bye, Mum.'

I jumped on and ran upstairs. Some of my mates were already up there, keeping a seat for me. The deck was about half full with people going to work, none of them looking very happy (and it didn't help having us lot fucking about at the back), some staring out of the windows and probably wishing they were back in bed – it was cold and dark outside – others reading newspapers. There were women too putting on makeup, and the air was thick with cigarette smoke.

Someone gave me a No. 6, already lit, and I slid up to the window and wiped away the condensation.

Mum was on the pavement looking up. She waved. I nodded. The bell tinged and the bus moved off. Mum was on her way home now. Dad would have got Vincent off to work, John off to school and given Anne-Marie her breakfast, and now Mum would take her to school. I was dying for my first puff. In case Mum looked back, I ducked below the window.

As the bus rumbled on we talked about last night's TV, pop music, which of us was going to the youth club that night and football. I was a QPR fan but most of my mates supported Arsenal or Chelsea so I got a lot of stick.

With two stops to go we went down the stairs to the open platform at the back. The bus speeded up. We were coming to the hill that had our school at the top and the driver liked to get a run at it. We mucked about, swinging round the pole, shouting to each other, keeping an eye open for the old man on the bicycle we passed each morning. Sure enough, there he was, pedalling hard, wearing his old white crash helmet with flaps that covered his ears and a strap that fastened under his chin.

'Whey, Chopper, Chopper,' we shouted, and as the bus passed we leaned out and tapped his helmet.

'You bastards,' he shouted.

The bus went on and he dismounted and began to run after us, pushing his bike as he ran. But we knew we were safe. When we got off at our stop, we'd run across the road and disappear into the housing estate with the school on the other side. And he'd run after us shouting, 'Chopper, I'll give you Chopper, you fucking bastards.' We would be laughing as we ran, looking back to see where he was. Eventually, he would stop running and so would we, and then we'd give it to him one more time, 'Chopper, Chopper.'

But one morning there had been no sign of him. We didn't think much about him as we got off the bus and slowly made our way towards school. Had he died or been run over by a bus, maybe? Then, out of the blue, we heard, 'Fucking Chopper, I'll give you fucking Chopper,' and right there in front of us, absolutely mental, in his helmet, there he was. Oh fuck, I thought.

We scattered and ran, like headless chickens, this way and that way but not the right way, Chopper behind, trying to grab anyone he could. He didn't get anyone and as I ran towards school I heard him laughing, and shouting, 'Chopper, Chopper.' That day for once I was in school on time.

This Tuesday though, which was what usually happened, I wasn't. When I sailed into school the bell was ringing. I was late for class. I should have run but I didn't. I'd only just got there but already I wanted to go. School was a chore. I was way behind with everything, so all my classes, with the possible exception of art, were a nightmare. Plus, some of the teachers didn't like me because of how I acted up, and they picked on me, which got on my nerves, which made me more irritated, which made me act up even more. And on it went. The end of the day when I could go home could never come quick enough for me.

After lunch I went to the changing rooms. The other boys in there were changing into shorts and singlets but I sat on the bench. The PE teacher came in.

'Where's your kit?'

'Forgot it, sir,' I said.

'Right, go to the secretary and get a note,' he said. 'I'm sending you home. If you can't be bothered to bring in your kit, I can't see why we should be bothered to keep you in school.'

I went to the secretary's office. She wrote a note for my mum. I was being sent home because I'd forgotten my kit. She gave me the note sealed in an envelope. 'Thank you,' I said.

I walked down the corridor, out of the building and into the yard with the note in my hand. Did Mum need to see this? All right, forgetting my kit was no big deal but nothing was going right at school and I didn't want her knowing about any of it, this included. So I did what I always did when I got a note: I went to the first bin and chucked it in. Then I walked out through the school gate. I felt quite chuffed. I was on my way home early.

I set off down Carlton Hill and thought about Christmas. On Sunday, the one just gone, Dad had got out the lights and tested them. It had been great to see them lit up. Now it only remained for the tree (we'd got it in Whiteley's some years earlier) and the decorations to go up. That wouldn't happen until twelve days before Christmas, 13 December. On that day I'd come in and the tree would be decorated, like magic, and the house alive with colour. It would stay that way until the twelfth day after Christmas when it would all come down. That was how it was every year. Mum insisted on it. She said if you did it any other way it was bad luck. If I'd had my way, of course, the decorations would have stayed up all year round.

My favourite bit was the crib. Dad had made it out of boxes and inside it went small figures of the baby Jesus, Mary and Joseph, the Three Wise Men and other bits and pieces. There was a hole at the back through which Dad always poked one of the tree lights. When the lights were on the crib was always lit up.

I ambled into Maida Vale, then on towards home. I bought a fag in a sweet shop and smoked it. I reached home. I had a key – Mum didn't like us roaming the streets – and let myself in. My brother John, Maxine and John's mate Hugh McHugh, known as Ginger, were in the front room. I went to the kitchen. 'Hello, Mum.'

'Hello,' she said. 'What are you doing home so early?'

'The coach didn't show up,' I said, 'so there was no PE.'

'What sort of a school is it if they send boys home if the coach doesn't show up?'

'A good one,' I said.

'Well,' she said, 'seeing as you're home, you can make yourself useful. You can collect Anne-Marie from school and she'll have her friend Marie Baker with her.'

There were a few minutes before I had to set off. I went up to the room I shared with John and changed out of my uniform into my home clothes, then set some books in a circle on the floor and put my soldiers on them. The carpet beyond was the sea and here I put my warships and aircraft – Airfix models I had made and painted.

I didn't know much about war. I'd got my ideas from films and the pictures on the front and back of the boxes that my soldiers came in. Then I used my head. I had one or two books on the army and they were useful too. One was an A–Z of guns and tanks, quite interesting to look through, and the other was about the uniforms and flags of soldiers around the world. There was a picture of a Royal Marine and for a while now I'd known that was what I'd be when I was sixteen. Then after a few years, I'd leave and become a long-distance lorry driver.

I never gave any thought to what it was like to be a soldier, go to war and kill. I just wanted to be a soldier. I remember, though, that I asked Dad once if I'd be sent to Belfast when I joined up, and he said no: I wouldn't serve in Northern Ireland because I had family there. I heard what he said but actually I didn't give a shit. I would have gone anywhere the army sent me and I didn't care what was going on over there, or anywhere else for that matter. That was me.

It was only a short walk to Anne-Marie's school so I took my time, thinking about the war that had been going on in my bedroom with the soldiers. I couldn't wait to get back to the battlefield. Then I realized I'd been dawdling and picked up speed. Left, right, left, right. I reached the gate of what had been my old school in no time.

There were lots of mums there, talking to each other, waiting for their little ones. Several called to me: 'How's your mum? Is she all right?'

'She's fine,' I said.

I went to the playground. As I looked about for Anne-Marie and her friend, it seemed smaller than I remembered it, but it was so bright and cheerful. No uniform was worn, so the children were like coloured crayons as they ran through the gate and jumped into their mothers' arms, some with things they had made, all with happy faces.

The headmaster was in the playground. 'Still daydreaming, Patrick?' he said.

'Ye— No, no, sir,' I said. 'I was looking for my sister.' I hadn't realized it but she was standing next to me, trying to show me what she had done with a corn-flakes box and some paint. Her friend, Marie Baker, was with her.

'How are you getting on at your new school? Are you working hard?' He had a very deep voice.

'I'm doing fine, top of the class. I love it,' I said.

He's reading my mind, I thought. He knows I'm lying.

'Say hello to your mother and Vincent and John,' said the head-master. 'Vincent was a good boy.'

He gave me one more look, then walked away. I had to get off in case he called me back and read my mind some more.

I took Anne-Marie's hand, tucked the corn-flakes box under my arm, told Marie Baker to hurry along, then sped out of the gate and up Third Avenue. As we went I was aware that Anne-Marie was trying to tell me something but I wasn't stopping until I was safely indoors.

We arrived at number forty-three. Mum opened the door, as she usually did when her daughter came home. She gave Anne-Marie a kiss and a hug and asked how her day had been, then said hello to Marie Baker. Then Mum frowned and said, 'You're all covered in paint. What are you like?'

Anne-Marie was staring at me too. 'I've been trying to tell you all the way home, only you wouldn't listen,' she said.

'What?'

'The box was wet.'

I was cross. It wasn't the paint though. It was because I wasn't wearing my school uniform. If I had been, Mum would have had to wash it, which would have meant that the next day it would have been wet and I wouldn't have had to go to school. Should have kept it on. Big mistake not to.

I changed out of the clothes with the paint on them and ran a couple of errands for Mum. I got milk from the corner shop near the phone box and took a box of Christmas presents, ordered from a catalogue, that had come in the post to one of Mum's friends across the road.

Back in the house, I found Dad in the front room with another man. They'd been drinking together in the Grey Horse, a pub off Kilburn Lane. The visitor was old, a bit stooped and he suffered from TB, though I wouldn't have known it then. He was my uncle, Giuseppe Conlon.

Giuseppe wasn't Italian – he had been named after his godfather, who was. He was Irish, born and raised in Belfast. During the Second World War he had been conscripted into the British Army but deserted. He was married to Sarah, my dad's sister. I had met him before, in Belfast, but knew his son Gerard better. From time to time Gerry had come to London to work, and stayed sometimes with Uncle Hugh Maguire, Dad's brother, and his wife, Kathleen, or Kitty, in their flat in Westbourne Terrace Road, near Paddington station. On one visit Gerry had stolen a Giro from Uncle Hugh for cash to bet on a dog and had been told to leave Uncle Hugh's flat. Since then Uncle Hugh had forgiven him and Gerry had been back to stay with him.

He'd also stayed at our house in Third Avenue, until Mum and Dad thought he had taken money from the box in the front room I used as a piggybank. They'd asked him to leave but hadn't forgiven him. Dad had told Uncle Hugh that if Gerry came near our house he'd kill him because of the bad things he'd done to us. But the London-Irish world was small, and even if someone stayed away from your door there was always the possibility you'd run into them somewhere else, and that was what happened.

In the early autumn of 1974, Uncle Hugh bought tickets for an Irish dance and invited Mum. She normally never went to these sorts of things, in fact she didn't go anywhere really, but the group performing were the Wolfe Tones, an Irish traditional group popular on the London-Irish circuit, and Hugh said that a night out would do her good.

The dance was in the Carousel Ballroom, one night early in October. When she got there, Mum saw Gerry Conlon. It was an Irish event so that wasn't surprising. He was with friends, including Paul Hill, from the Quex Road hostel in Kilburn where he was living. Mum had seen (but not properly met) Paul Hill once before at the Conservative Working Men's Club in Maida Vale and now they spoke briefly. She'd worked with his mother in Belfast: that was the connection. But she didn't talk to Gerry that night in the Carousel Ballroom and indeed she told Uncle Hugh to keep him away from her because she was still angry with him. And since that night she hadn't laid eyes on Gerry either. Giuseppe, Gerry's father, on the other hand, was a different story: there'd been no falling out between him and us and he was as welcome as he'd ever been at Mum and Dad's house. But why was he here now? That's what I wanted to know. What had made this sick man come all the way from Belfast to forty-three Third Avenue on Tuesday 3 September 1974?

I found out soon enough. I was sitting at the bottom of the stairs with John, waiting for Mum to call us into the kitchen for tea. I asked John about our visitor. 'There's some sort of trouble with the police,' said John. 'Gerry's been arrested, something to do with bombs.'

I had seen something on TV about IRA bombs exploding in pubs in a town called Guildford, but it meant nothing to me. I couldn't imagine what Gerry might have to do with it either. Perhaps John was pulling my leg.

'I'm going to the youth club,' I said. 'Are you?' We had youth club Tuesdays and Thursdays.

'Course.'

'We'll have to get some money off Mum.' You couldn't go without a bit of silver in your pocket.

'Don't worry, we will,' said John.

From the kitchen, Mum shouted, 'Have you washed your hands and face, Patrick?' Before you ate in our house you were always supposed to do this. I hadn't but I shouted, 'Yes,' anyway.

There was stew for tea and I ate it quickly. I liked Mum's stew. At some point Uncle Sean came back from work. Mum fed him too. Then Pat O'Neil arrived. He lived in Stockwell, south London. He had his three daughters with him – Jacqueline, Sharon and Jean, aged eight, six and four. His wife, Helen, was in hospital having a baby and Mum had said she'd take his girls for the night. Suddenly our house was very full and very noisy. I got some money from Mum, pulled on my boots and coat, then left with John.

The youth club was on the same side of the street as our house. It was in an old church hall and it was closed when we arrived but I liked to get there early. I enjoyed what happened outside as much as what went on inside later.

Some of our mates joined us. Then Mum passed, with Anne-Marie and Jacqueline, on their way to Jason's, the chip shop. When they came back it had started to rain. Mum told us we were mad, hanging about getting wet. I said I'd just seen Mr O'Leary drive past to park his car and he'd be along in a minute to open up. Mr O'Leary helped out at the club.

Soon he'd arrived and we ran in through the double doors to the hall. There was a stage at one end and windows down the sides. It was cold, but after ten minutes of us running about, it warmed up and the windows were steamy.

Once, Mrs Crotford, who ran the youth club, had given a party for all the children who attended. First, she made us all sit down – a job on its own – then gave us sausages, beans and mash. Candles were lit, the lights went off and food flew everywhere. It was one of the best nights ever at the club.

Now Mrs Crotford came in and the activities got under way. I played table tennis and listened to records – Sweet, Marc Bolan and Alvin Stardust. Bottles of orange were handed out from the kitchen at the back through a hatch.

That evening I had a good time. I always did. I remember thinking, Pity I have to go to school tomorrow. Then I reminded myself that in three days it would be the weekend, and after a couple more weeks, we'd break up for the Christmas holidays. I loved Christmas more than any other time of the year.

The club shut, and the children swarmed out through the swing doors into Third Avenue. We milled around on the pavement, a vast mob, and then my mates and I went to the corner of Farrant Street. At some point I'd noticed that John wasn't around, which was strange because usually he stayed on. He must have gone home already.

Now Vincent walked up.

'Where've you been?' I shouted.

'College.' Of course he had – every Tuesday evening he went as part of his training to be a gas fitter. I'd a head like a sieve for that sort of thing.

He told me I was out too late and Mum would come for me any minute now.

I didn't know how late it was – I had no watch and, of course, couldn't read the time. But I knew Mum didn't like me running about the streets late at night. I got maybe half an hour after youth club before she brought me indoors.

Time passed and I thought she would be coming any minute now, but she didn't. It got later, and still she didn't appear. I began to think something funny must be going on. It was not only that she hadn't come: vehicles had appeared in Caird Street, directly opposite where we were standing. One was a police van and the rest were cars. They were parked but their engines were running and the headlights were on. They were all police, obviously, and they were about to swoop, weren't they? Yes – but on what or whom?

We swapped ideas. When we were out on the streets we got up to quite a bit of mischief and we knew the police at the Harrow Road station were fed up with us. They'd said as much to several of my mates. They'd told them they'd get us. So, when you put it all together, there was only one answer. They were about to swoop on us.

Suddenly the cars and the police van took off. They came up Caird Street, straight at us. They really *were* after us. We bolted up Farrant Street. When we were halfway up, one of the lads shouted, 'They've gone! They're not coming for us.' I stopped, and looked back. He was right. They'd turned into Third Avenue.

We went back to the corner. A bit of time passed and now another police car came up Caird Street, and the strange evening took an even stranger turn. Dad and my brother John were sitting in the back, staring straight ahead.

After John had slipped out of the youth club he'd headed home. When he got there, he found that Dad, Giuseppe, Uncle Sean and Pat O'Neil had gone to the Royal Lancer for a drink. The O'Neil girls were in their nightdresses, playing on the carpet in the front room with Anne-Marie. Mum was in the kitchen. She had things to do. There were clothes to wash and she had to sort the laundry into piles by colour.

What she didn't know yet was that she was wanted in connection with the Guildford pub bombs, the ones John and I had talked about at the bottom of the stairs before tea. They had exploded on 5 October 1974, in two public houses in Guildford, Surrey: the Horse and Groom and the Seven Stars. Five people were killed at the Horse and Groom: Caroline Slater and Ann Hamilton, both in the WRAC, Paul Craig, a civilian, William Forsyth and John Hunter, both of the Scots Guards. No one was killed at the Seven Stars. The IRA had claimed responsibility, saying that, as intended, they had killed soldiers drinking while off-duty. They had carried out six further bombing attacks in England during October and November 1974. Late in November, in connection with those bombings, the police arrested, among others, Paul Hill and Gerard Conlon.

In the opinion of the police, they were murdering Irish bastards, and once they were in custody they were treated as the police believed murdering Irish bastards deserved to be treated: they beat them, they deprived them of sleep and food, and they threatened to hurt or kill their families or loved ones. The only way Hill and Conlon could see of making the police stop doing this was to tell them what they realized the police wanted to hear. They agreed that they were part of the IRA unit that had been planting bombs throughout the autumn, and they said the IRA's bombmaker was Mum.

It isn't clear which man gave her name first. Hill, who was arrested first, says in his book, *Stolen Years*, that it was Conlon. In his book, *Proved Innocent*, Conlon says it was Hill. What is clear, though, from both men's accounts, is that they believed the idea that Mum was an IRA bombmaker was so preposterous that it wouldn't stand up in court. Big mistake.

The police took the opposite view. They believed Conlon and Hill were hard-nut IRA men but they'd managed to make them confess, and now they had two witness statements that named Mum: never mind that they'd been extracted with violence and threats, they had a result, and that was all the police cared about.

They decided to move against Mum and the day they chose was Tuesday, 3 December 1974.

*   *   *

The team collected in Caird Street at about nine o'clock. I saw them when I was standing with my mates in Farrant Street. Then they set off and we ran because we thought they were coming for us. But, of course, they weren't.

While I was running up Farrant Street, they were turning down Third Avenue. They stopped outside number forty-three, piled out of their cars and rang the front doorbell. Anne-Marie answered the door. The instant she turned the knob, Detective Chief Inspector David Munday stormed in, followed by the others, all in plain clothes except for the dog-handlers, who were in uniform.

Mum saw Munday (though only as a shape) through the little window in the kitchen door that gave on to the hall. She thought it was Dad or one of the others back from the pub. Then the door opened and he came in. 'What is it?' she asked.

'Do you know who we are?' said Munday.

'You're the police.' The uniforms behind him had told her that much.

'We're the bomb squad,' Munday said.

He told her to put the children somewhere. She led them into Uncle Sean's room and lit the gas fire so they'd be warm.

Once she'd done this, Munday told her he wanted to search the house.

'Certainly. All you'll find is a rubber bullet. I'll get it for you,' she said. On our last visit to Belfast, one of the family had given her one that they'd found in the street – a holiday souvenir.

Munday wasn't interested and told her to sit down in the living room. 'Do you know why we're here?' he said.

'Is it because of Gerard Conlon?'

'What makes you think that?'

'Because Gerry's father arrived here today, didn't he? He's come to get a solicitor for his son because he's been picked up for the Guildford bombings.'

'Yes, we know that.'

Munday asked where Dad was. Mum said he was over in the pub, the Royal Lancer on the corner of Lancefield and Mozart Streets. It was agreed that John would go over with some policemen and help them to identify Dad and the others. John went off, and Mum explained that Dad was with Giuseppe Conlon, Pat O'Neil and Sean Smyth, her brother. She said that Sean had been in England for some months because Loyalists had murdered the uncles for whom he'd been working in Belfast.

Outside, John made his way to the Royal Lancer. He went into the pub, which was crowded. Dad turned and saw him with the policemen behind. They asked Dad, Giuseppe, Pat and Sean to leave the pub. Puzzled, the men came out. Giuseppe, Pat and Sean were put into police cars and driven away. Dad and John were put into a car together. The plan was to drop John at home and take Dad to the Harrow Road police station.

A few minutes later, when I saw that car, I couldn't understand why Dad and John were in it. Sometimes, when I don't understand something, my mind freezes. That happened now. It stopped. Then, as if from a distance, I heard someone talking to me. It was the mate beside me.

'The police are outside your house, Paddy,' he said. 'They're everywhere.'

I looked down the street. Outside my house, there were men in uniform, several police cars and a crowd, attracted by the commotion.

I ran home. The front door was shut, and I'd forgotten to take my key with me to the youth club. I knocked. A policewoman opened the door. 'Yeah?'

'I live here.'

She pulled me into the hall and called, 'I've got another one.'

Briefly I wondered if it was a party.

The policewoman pushed me down the hall to the kitchen. The door to the front room was open and I saw Mum sitting down, with Munday towering over her. 'Mum? Are you all right?'

She looked up and I saw she was crying.

It wasn't a party.

'What are you doing with my mum?'

The policewoman pulled me out and opened the kitchen door. 'In there. Sit down and shut up,' she said.

In the kitchen, the laundry was still in piles – whites and colours – and the twin-tub machine was pulled out from the wall with black tubes running to the sink. There was a sheet of newspaper on the floor under the machine in case it leaked. The stewpot was on the cooker. The room smelt of meat and potatoes. John was sitting at the table. I hadn't seen the police drop him off, so this was a surprise.

John looked at me. I looked at him. I sat down.

The police were all over the house. I could hear them pulling open drawers and throwing things on to the floor. Vincent was with them. They wanted to go into the attic and he was showing them the hatch. He'd always wanted to be a policeman and later he would say this was the closest he ever got to being one.

There was another policewoman in the kitchen. She was making tea and toast, breaking biscuits out of packets and putting them on plates. Once she'd everything ready, she called. Policemen came for their tea, toast and biscuits, then carried them away. She offered John and me nothing.

I stood up, intending to walk to the sink for a drink of water.

'Sit down, you little bastard.'

I did sit, but then I gave her my worst. I called her a fat pig and a cunt and I told her to fuck off. They weren't new words. I'd used them when I was with my mates in Farrant Street, but I'd never used them indoors. I wouldn't have dared. None of us would. Mum and Dad didn't allow those words. John wasn't slow to join in. We swore at them partly because we were cocky, partly because we were angry and mostly because we were frightened.

A police officer came in. Now I'd been in the kitchen for a few minutes and taken everything in, I couldn't contain myself any more. 'What the fuck's going on? What are you doing with Mum?'

'She's in the front room, helping the other officers,' said the policewoman.

'What are you doing here anyway? Why are you searching our house?'

'We're looking for bombs.'

'Well, you're not going to find any here,' I said.

Then John chipped in: 'Have you got a search warrant?'

'One of the other officers has it,' said the male officer.

'Are you English or Irish?' asked the policewoman. The police had come expecting Northern Irish accents but we talked like Londoners.

I remembered my conversation with John on the stairs, his mention of Gerry Conlon's arrest having something to do with bombs. Suddenly I understood. 'Oh, that's it,' I said. Right, well, I'd tell them. They had Mum in the front room and they'd been taking the piss out of John and me. 'You think we're bombers. Well, I'd like to blow up the Harrow Road police station and Scotland Yard.'

'You're a nice boy, aren't you?' said the policewoman.

'I've got some money upstairs,' said John.

He had been saving his money – we all had – for Christmas. Mine would have been in my piggybank only Mum had emptied it earlier in the day to pay it into my post-office savings account the following morning. She did things like that for me or sometimes we'd do them together.

'I hope my money's there when you lot go,' said John, 'because if it's not, there'll be some fucking trouble.'

I said, 'It wouldn't surprise me if they planted something in the house.'

A bit later I said, 'I want the toilet.'

'Where is it?'

'Down there, at the back of the kitchen.'

'All right.'

I got up and went past the laundry. I opened the bathroom door and went in. The light was already on. I made to close the door.

'Leave it open,' the policewoman shouted.

She could see me from the kitchen.

I walked to the WC. It was in the corner directly down from the door. There was a window beside it, which was open. There were officers with their dogs in the garden. It was bad enough that the policewoman was watching from the kitchen without this lot looking in too. I went to close the window. There was a policeman right outside.

'Just piss and leave it,' he said. He had a gun in his hand.

When I came out of the toilet Mum was in the kitchen with Munday. She was still crying and he was explaining she would have to go to Paddington Green police station with Vincent, John and me.

'Don't touch them! They're English,' she cried.

Munday wondered who could look after the O'Neil girls and Anne-Marie. Mum thought of Mrs Roach who lived across the road. It was to her that I'd brought the box of Christmas presents ordered from a catalogue earlier. They were old friends, Mum and Mrs Roach, and she was a kind woman. Munday sent someone over for her.

Mum went upstairs, a policewoman with her. She put Anne-Marie and the O'Neil girls to bed. Vincent, John and I were brought into the hall to wait. Mum came down the stairs. She wore her good coat, leather with a fur trim, and she had her handbag with her purse inside, stuffed with the money from my piggybank. It made her handbag heavy – I could tell from the way she was carrying it.

Someone opened the front door and we were herded on to the pavement. There was still a crowd outside and across the road, among them some of my mates who shouted out, 'What's going on?'

Mum was put in a police car and driven away. Vincent, John and I got put into the back of a van. There were wooden benches on either side and it smelt of diesel. I took one side; John and Vincent were opposite. The big doors at the back were slammed shut.

The driver put the van into gear and moved off. The seat was slippery and I held a strut so I wouldn't slide about.

John had something in his pocket and he got it out carefully, so the driver and the policeman in the front wouldn't see. It was a ten-pence piece with a hole through the Queen's head.

'Oh, no,' said Vincent, when he saw it. 'What do you think the police are going to say when they see that? It'll give them ideas –

they'll think you're IRA. Best thing you can do is show it to them and get it over with.'

That was Vincent. He always thought the straight way was best and there was no point in trying to be clever.

John wasn't fussed, at least at the start. As for me, it was just a ten-pence piece with a hole in the middle and a waste of good money. You could get a lot with that in a sweet shop.

Vincent and John didn't stop talking about that coin throughout the journey. In the end, John decided to lose it. He put it on the floor under the bench.

The van stopped. The doors at the back were yanked open. We were at Paddington Green police station on the Harrow Road. I could hear the traffic on the Marylebone flyover.

I had a strange, light feeling in my head. I must have been thinking about Mum and Dad. Where were they? When would I see them? I was fearful as well. I didn't know what was coming. I had fuck-all to hide. I knew that. We'd done no wrong. But would I get a beating anyhow? This was the police. You had to be prepared for that. Well, if I did, I'd give them nothing. I'd my brothers with me. I could hold out. Frightened but cocky, that was me.

We were taken into the station and put in a holding cell. There were benches in it, like in the police van, and nothing else. It was grey, lifeless.

John and I turned to Vincent. He was the eldest. He must be able to tell us what was going on and what would happen. Of course, he didn't have a clue, so John and I started pissing about and laughing. Vincent didn't approve of our carry-on. We'd been arrested. But we didn't care and went on regardless.

I don't know how long we were in that cell. It's hard to judge time when you're locked up.

Then I heard the key turn in the lock. The door opened and a policeman said, 'Vincent Maguire?'

'Yeah.'

He was taken away.

The door was locked. A bit later, it was opened again and John was taken away. The door closed again. Now I was alone. In the past, when I was naughty, I might have been sent to my bedroom, but when that happened, Mum and Dad were always downstairs. I could call them if I had to. Here, they weren't nearby and I really was alone. Suddenly I wasn't so cocky any more. I wanted to cry. Then the cell door opened.

'Patrick Maguire?'

'Yeah.'

I date the end of my childhood from that moment.

11

I was brought along corridors and into an interview room. There was a table, two chairs and a window. I sat on one side of the table. Detective Sergeant Hunt sat opposite. He had on a jacket but under it I could see a holster with a revolver butt sticking out of it. There was another detective with him and a uniformed constable at the door.

'Are you a Catholic family?' asked Detective Sergeant Hunt.

'Yes.'

'What do you think about these people planting bombs?'

'I don't know.'

'When these bombings occur, what happens in your house? Do you all talk about it?'

'No.'

'Have you any idea why we came to your house?'

'Because we're Irish, I suppose.'

'But there are hundreds of Irish round where you live.'

'I don't know why you came.'

'Do your parents talk about bombing?'

'Mum and Dad think it's bad, all those people being killed for nothing.'

'Do you know what explosives look like?'

'Yes, I've seen them on the telly.' I was thinking of cartoon bombs, big black round things with a fuse coming out of the top.

'There was a roll of black tape in the lounge. Who does it belong to?'

Was that the roll that had come from Dad's tool bag? Or had I nicked another from school or Willesden College of Technology? I couldn't remember.

'It's mine,' I said. 'A boy at school gave it to me a couple of years ago. I use it for sticking things up on my wall.'

'Do your mum and dad ever ask you to take parcels to anybody?'

This question unnerved me. Earlier, I'd taken that parcel to Mrs Roach for Mum. 'No,' I said.

'Where did your brother get the coin with the hole in it?'

'I don't know,' I said. This was true. 'I've never seen it before.' This wasn't true but he didn't know that.

'Do you know what the Tricolour is?'

'No, I don't.'

'You don't know what the Tricolour is?'

'No, I don't.'

'I'm sure you do.'

'I don't know what the Tricolour is.'

'It's the Irish flag.'

'I didn't know that's what it's called. I only know the colours. It's green, white and gold.'

'So you do know the Irish flag?'

'I know it by its colours but I don't know its name . . . whatever it is.'

'The Tricolour. And you really don't know that's what it's called?'

'No,' I said. This was the truth.

'I find that very strange. You're in an Irish family and you don't know it's called the Tricolour?'

'But I don't.'

'Do you have one at home?'

'What?'

'The Irish flag, the Tricolour?'

'Yeah.'

'Where?'

'In my bedroom.'

'You've got a Tricolour in your bedroom?'

'I've got two flags in my bedroom. I've got the Irish one and I've got the Union Jack. They're up on the wall over my bed.'

They weren't big. They were the little ones you wave, not that I did a lot of waving with them and I'd only put them up because they looked good. If I'd had other flags they would have gone up too.

'Let's go back to the roll of tape. Why do you have it?'

'To stick things up on my bedroom wall.'

'Like the Tricolour?'

'The flags are heavy. They're held up with drawing pins. I stick things on my wall with it,' I said again. This was true. I'd stuck up some posters and my drawings. 'Sometimes when parcels come I open them by mistake, then reseal them using the tape.'

This was a lie. When parcels came, I didn't open them by mistake. I opened them deliberately. With Christmas just round the corner, I wanted to see if there was anything in them for me. Then I'd reseal them with the black tape so Mum wouldn't be cross with me. I couldn't see how I'd explain this, though, and I was beginning to think he wouldn't believe me anyhow.

'Do many parcels come to your house?'

'Quite a lot from John Moore's.'

That was the mail-order company Mum used. The things I'd dropped over to Mrs Roach had come from it.

'What's in them?'

'Toys and things.'

'Who's Gerry Conlon?'

'He's my dad's nephew.'

'Your father's sister's son?'

'Yeah.'

'Do you know him well?'

'Not really.'

'Do you know him by sight?'

'Yeah.'

'So you know him well enough?'

'No, I just know what he looks like.'

'How come you know what he looks like?'

'He came to stay.'

'When was this?'

'I don't know. A while back.'

'A year ago?'

'Maybe. I don't know.'

'How long for?'

'I don't remember. A few days, I think. Then he left and I haven't seen him since.'

'Who's Giuseppe Conlon?'

'He's Gerry Conlon's dad.'

'Has he been staying in your house?'

'He was going to.'

'When did he come?'

'He came today. He was there when I got home from school.'

'Why did he come?'

'To see his son.'

'Why?'

'He's in trouble, isn't he?'

'You tell me.'

'He was arrested, wasn't he?'

'Do you know him well?'

'Who?'

'Giuseppe Conlon.'

'No.'

'You've met him before, though?'

'Yes.'

'Have you met him in Belfast?'

'Yes.'

'When?'

'When we were on holiday.'

'Whose are the rebel records?'

I asked what he meant by 'rebel', not knowing the word. He explained. He meant the songs from the days of the old IRA, the 1916 Easter Rising, the War of Independence, and the Irish Civil War, events that were in the far past.

'They're Mum's,' I said.

'Has she had them long?'

'Yes, she has.'

'Does your dad play them?'

'No.'

'What about your mum?'

'Hardly ever, really.'

'Really?'

'Yeah.'

'So they hardly see the light of day, you're saying.'

'Yeah.'

'What are the clear plastic gloves for?'

'They're Mum's. She's got bad hands.'

'Have you ever used them?'

'Once, to make a water bomb.'

I'd filled one with water, tied the end and thrown it outside in Third Avenue. When it had hit the road it had made a wonderful splat and the water had spread everywhere.

'Whose are the black woollen gloves with the fingertips cut off?'

I used to watch *Steptoe and Son* on telly and Albert Steptoe wore mittens with no fingers. I wanted some and one evening Dad said I could cut the ends off my gloves. Then Mum came in. 'What are you doing to them good gloves?' she asked. Then she turned to Dad. 'And you just sitting there watching him!'

'He's all right. Leave him alone.'

Mum picked up the bits and put them into a drawer in the kitchen. I thought she was going to get Dad to sew them back on again, but she didn't.

'They're mine,' I said.

'What did you cut the fingertips off for?'

'My dad said I could.'

'We found a rubber bullet,' he said. 'What was that doing in the house?'

It was the one Mum had offered to fetch.

'It was a souvenir from Belfast.'

Uncle Sean and Aunt Teresa still lived in Abyssinia Street. One day their son Michael had been playing outside the house when a commotion started. Aunt Teresa pulled him in and as she did a rubber bullet landed near her door. It would have hit him if he had still been playing. Aunt Teresa picked up the bullet, yelled at the soldiers, 'That's one you won't fire again,' and slammed the door.

In the summer of 1974 my mum had visited her sister-in-law and Teresa told her about Michael's narrow escape. She said the Americans would pay a fiver for the rubber bullet she had. She showed it to Mum, who thought it was very heavy. Teresa said she should take it as a souvenir. Mum refused but Teresa dropped it into her shopping bag and she left without knowing she had it.

When she got back to 43 Third Avenue, she showed it to Dad. He told her to hide it – he didn't want his children seeing something like that. She put it into the drawer of the chest in the back room downstairs, and there it stayed until the police came on 3 December 1974. It had no significance. I wanted to get this across to him so I told him about some other things. 'We've also got leather wallets made in Long Kesh prison at home,' I said. One was mine and it was in the pocket of my jeans. Many people had them. It didn't mean we supported the IRA. We had them because Long Kesh was famous. A wallet that had been made there was a talking point, and gave you a bit of an edge, like a personalized numberplate might.

Detective Sergeant Hunt stood up. I thought he must have run out of questions. I was wrong. He'd just got his answer. He'd got a result.

'Stand up,' he said.

I stood up.

The constable opened the door.

'Go on,' said Hunt.

I went out into the corridor. He followed. I began to walk. Where were we going? Suddenly another man was with us. His clothes were dirty and he stank.

We got to a door. It was opened. I went in. Hunt and the other man followed. This room smelt like the chemistry lab at school, but it was an interview room like the one I'd just left. There was a table and some chairs. The stranger sat down.

'Are you a tramp?' I asked. He looked like one.

'I'm a policeman,' he said.

I told him he didn't look like one.

'That's the idea,' he said, sounding pleased with himself. Detective Sergeant Kenneth Day worked under cover.

'Sit down,' said Hunt.

I sat down.

'Hold out your hands,' said Detective Sergeant Day. He wiped each hand in turn with dry cotton wool, which he then put in a plastic bag. Then he wiped each hand again with wet cotton wool. The ether – I found out later that that was what it was – felt very cold and made my skin tighten.

'Give me your right hand,' he said.

He took the thumb firmly and put the point of a cocktail stick under the nail, which was very short – I'd bitten it as I had all my nails. As soon as the point was underneath, it was digging into the top of the soft red part below. Now he ran the point up and down as if trying to dig out whatever might be under there. It hurt. I wouldn't shout, though. That would only show me up in front of him. But I wriggled and tried to jerk my hand back. It was automatic. When you're hurt, you flinch. He gripped my thumb even tighter.

When he finished it, he got a new cocktail stick and was about to start on the next finger.

'What are you looking for?' I asked.

'I'm seeing if you've been playing with bombs.'

'You'll not find anything in there,' I said, 'only gunpowder from Bonfire Night.'

Guy Fawkes night had been about a month earlier, but not knowing better, I thought something from the fireworks I'd handled that night might have stuck to me.

'We'll see,' he said, though I could tell he didn't believe me.

He scraped every nail on both hands, then bagged the sticks. He also sealed up a piece of cotton wool he hadn't touched me with.

Next I was photographed, front and side. Finally, my finger-prints were taken. Afterwards I was given a cloth to wipe off the ink, but the blue-black shadow on the tips of my fingers wouldn't come off no matter how hard I rubbed.

I was brought to a hallway. Vincent and John were already there. Their fingertips were stained like mine.

Mum appeared. She told us they were finished with us and we would be going home soon.

Just then Munday walked in with a bundle. 'Who owns these wigs?'

There were two. They were Mum's, but only my sister and her friends wore them: they used them for dressing up. Mum had bought one a month before. She had been in Brixton market with Helen O'Neil, looking to buy a doll's pram for Anne-Marie's birthday. Helen had spotted the wig and persuaded her to buy it. When Dad got home later she'd had it on. He got a shock – which was the idea. Afterwards she never wore it again.

The other wig was blonde. Mum had been given it a year before but had never worn it. This was the one the police were interested in. They were looking for a blonde-haired woman in connection with the Guildford bombings.

Next, Munday asked about the plastic gloves. He hadn't them with him but he'd seen them in the house.

Mum said they were hers.

Munday wanted to know why she had them.

I knew. It had started after Granny Smyth died in 1967. When she'd got back to London from the funeral, a rash had appeared on Mum's hands and forearms. Dermatitis was diagnosed. Her arms were bandaged and she was kept in hospital for a week. When she was discharged, she was given a supply of disposable plastic gloves and told to wear them for all household chores.

Over the years, the dermatitis came and went but never cleared up completely and that was why she always had disposable plastic gloves in the house. There had been twelve pairs in the kitchen drawer when the police came.

But Mum didn't go into this. She just told Munday she had

dermatitis. She wore the gloves if there was redness or soreness; and for other things, she said.

What other things, Munday wanted to know.

'I use them when I clean my brass ornaments.' She had a lot of these. 'I use them when I'm doing the garden.' This surprised me because she had so much to do she was hardly ever in the garden. 'And sometimes I even wear them for dusting,' she said.

'When did you last use your plastic gloves?' he asked.

'Earlier this evening,' she said, 'when I cleared out one of the kitchen drawers.' Among the things she had removed from it, she explained, was a pair of woollen gloves with the fingertips cut off. They were mine. She kept throwing them away but every time she did I'd find them in the bin and get them out again and put them back in the drawer.

'What did you do with everything this evening when you finished?' Munday asked.

'You'll find the woollen gloves in one of the dustbins some-where, and the plastic gloves I wore this evening at the top of the dustbin that's full up.'

Because of the questions I'd been asked earlier, I knew they'd already been through the dustbins but I didn't say so, and neither did Munday.

A policeman came over and said he would take us home. Mum stood up. 'Not you,' he said to her.

I said I wouldn't leave without her and so there should be no misunderstanding I sat down again.

The officer told me not to make trouble.

Mum told us to go home. She said Anne-Marie needed us. We should tell her that she and Dad would be home soon.

The three of us were put into the back of a van and driven off. It was about 3 a.m., very cold, and through the windows I saw shops with Christmas lights. I had never been out so late before. In different circumstances I would have enjoyed it.

The driver stopped outside number forty-three. As I got out with my brothers I wondered what we'd find indoors.

* * *

Two policemen and a policewoman were waiting for us. They said Mrs Roach had taken Anne-Marie and the O'Neil girls to her house. Ours wasn't too tidy. Vincent asked if we could put it back to the way Mum liked it. He thought she'd be home in the morning, and she wouldn't be pleased to see it all messy. The police said no and told us to go to bed. Instead we went to the kitchen and Vincent made a pot of tea.

When I'd had mine, I went up to the room I shared with John. It was a mess. We were never the tidiest, John and I, but I couldn't tell if the police or we had left everything lying about.

My headboard had stickers all over it, from the Westminster Schools' Sports Association and QPR. I also had Aries, the astrological sign, and a US Army sergeant's stripes with the CND logo in the middle. The bed was unmade but I got under the covers and went to sleep.

In the morning, I lay in bed waiting for Mum to call me, as she did every day. Then I remembered she wasn't there, and why. I went down to the kitchen. Vincent and John were drinking tea with the two policemen.

I made myself a cup of Nescafé, then sat at the table with my brothers. None of us spoke. We just looked at each other and our expressions all said the same thing. Had it really happened? Could we be sitting in our house with two policemen on a Wednesday morning while Mum and Dad were at the police station?

The policewoman came in. She told me I was to go to south London with Anne-Marie and stay with Aunt Teasy and Uncle Bill. Mum and Dad had stayed with them on their first night in London after they were married. Since then there hadn't been much contact. I didn't know Aunt Teasy or her family very well.

'I want to stay with my brothers,' I said.

The policewoman said no. Someone had to look after Anne-Marie and Mum had decided it should be me.

My sister and I were put into a police car and driven to Harrow Road police station. There, we were taken into a big room and left on our own. Later a policewoman brought us drinks and biscuits. Later still, again in a police car, we set off for Aunt Teasy's. She lived in De Laune Street, just round the corner from Kennington Underground station. When we arrived no one was in so we sat in the police car and waited. Then one of Aunt Teasy's sons appeared.

The police left and he brought us inside. He was about twenty, a Londoner, and talked like me. I told him as much as I could. I think it came to him as a bit of a shock. He gave us each a glass of milk and made us what he called an omelette.

Later, everyone got home from work or wherever they had been. Aunt Teasy was motherly, small and round. She wore her hair in a bun and spoke with a Belfast accent. She'd worked all her life as a silver-service waitress, doing banquets for judges and doctors. Everyone in the street thought highly of her. Bill Kearney, her husband, was slim, had grey hair and spoke so quietly you hardly noticed his Belfast accent. His uncle Peadar Kearney had written the lyrics for 'The Soldier's Song' (1907), which became the Irish National Anthem after independence. He was thoughtful and helpful, and smoked all the time, which was fine by me. He always wore a suit, and when he went out, a cream-coloured raincoat and a trilby. Besides my aunt and uncle, six children, a lodger and several cats and dogs lived at the house, so that evening it was pretty full.

Teasy made us some dinner. She wanted to know what had happened. I told her what I could but as I didn't really understand what had happened myself, I didn't explain things very well. I think she rang Vincent to find out more.

It was Saturday morning, three days later. I was in a bedroom at Aunt Teasy's, asleep in a double bed, Anne-Marie beside me. Someone was shaking me – 'Get up, son.'

I opened my eyes. 'Who are you?' I asked.

Anne-Marie sat up.

'I'm a policeman,' he said. 'You've got to come with me.'

'Where?'

'To the police station. Come on, get up.'

'Why? What for?'

'I don't know,' he said. 'I was just told to come and get you. Come on, hurry up.'

Anne-Marie started crying and I got dressed. The three of us went down to the kitchen. Three more policemen in plain clothes were waiting there. Aunt Teasy wanted to make me some breakfast but one of the policemen told her I'd get something at the police station. Anne-Marie was still crying. I told her I'd be back soon.

We left Aunt Teasy's. The four police officers set off at a furious pace. I had to be on my toes to keep up. The car was in another street.

I got into the back between two officers and the others went in the front. I asked where we were going.

'Carter Street police station.'

'What you done?' one asked.

'I've done nothing,' I said.

I sat quite still for the rest of the journey. It was best to keep quiet, I had decided.

We got to the Carter Street station and I was brought in. A few policemen were standing around and stared at me as I passed, but no one said a word. I noticed that police station smell, a mix of fear and loneliness.

I was put into a cell and the door was locked. I sat on the bed. Some time later I heard feet scuffling on the floor outside, and metal banging on metal. Next, an eye was at the spyhole. Then the door opened. 'Are you Patrick Maguire?'

The speaker was a giant with a red face. He wasn't in uniform and he was sweating.

'Yes, that's me.'

He told me to stand up. I could tell he was very angry so I got up straight away.

'Do you remember the testing done on you at Paddington Green?'

Oh, no, back to that again. How could I forget? It wasn't every day I got cocktail sticks dug under my nails.

'Do you know why that test was done?' the Giant asked.

I was shitting myself now. 'To see if I'd been playing with bombs,' I said, though I thought this was stupid.

'Well,' said the Giant, 'the test proved positive in your case. They found nitroglycerine under your fingernails.'

I'd never heard the word before and didn't know what it meant. 'That's stupid,' I said, 'I've got no nails. Look.' I showed him my hands.

'It's not stupid. You've been touching bombs.' He said this as if there was no argument about it.

'Well, that's daft,' I said. 'I never touched any nitro— whatever it is. They must have made a mistake. The police aren't always right.'

I wasn't trying to argue. This was just a simple statement of fact. They weren't always right. Everyone knew that.

'It wasn't the police who did the test,' said the Giant. 'It was a civilian scientist and he said you had touched nitroglycerine.'

The Giant had a pair of handcuffs. He put one band on my wrist and closed it – the click was like the tick of a clock or Dad's watch when he wound it, only louder – and the other round his own and he closed that too. Now we were attached.

I'd only ever seen handcuffs on television or in the newspapers. Handcuffs meant real trouble. Handcuffs were for criminals. This wasn't, I thought, like the time the detective had caught me in the phone booth with Maxine. This wasn't even like the night the police had come to the house and taken us all away. We had reached a new level.

The Giant led me through the station to the car park and over to a white Ford Escort. A policewoman in ordinary clothes was sitting at the wheel, and from the look on her face I knew she'd been waiting for us. She seemed quite old.

The car had only two doors. The Giant opened the one on the passenger side and dropped the front seat forward. I got into the back and he followed. The front passenger seat was left folded forward and he was able to put his feet on the dashboard.

We set off, and the Giant began to talk. 'We're going to Guildford,' he told me.

'Where's that?'

'It's where your fucking bombs went off,' he said.

That wasn't an answer. Where was Guildford? That's what I wanted to know. But I wouldn't ask him anything else because obviously he wasn't in the mood to answer.

'Right,' said the Giant. I knew he'd a list of questions for which he wanted answers. I also knew I wasn't going to enjoy this.

'Where did you get the bombs?' said the Giant.

'What bombs?' The car drove on. Nobody spoke. 'You've made a mistake,' I said.

'Your mum and dad had bombs in the house,' he said. 'Where did they get the fucking bombs?'

'You've got the wrong people. We don't do that sort of thing.' Northern Ireland wasn't mentioned much in the house, and if it ever was, my parents were very clear: bombing and shooting were wrong. We weren't a family who'd anything to do with violence.

'Don't fucking lie,' said the Giant. The way he said this was frightening. It was as if he knew otherwise.

'Where do you think the traces of nitroglycerine from under your nails came from?' said the Giant.

Bombs, according to the test. I understood that but we had never had any in the house. 'There were no bombs in our house,' I said. 'They've made a mistake.' I thought if I said it enough, I'd be believed.

'They don't make mistakes,' said the Giant. 'They've been doing this job for thirty years.'

There it was again. He was certain. There was nothing else for it but to press on and tell him they were wrong.

'They've made a mistake this time,' I said.

He wasn't impressed. 'Did your mum show you how to make bombs?' he said.

'I told you, you've got the wrong people.'

'By the time we get to Guildford,' said the Giant, 'you'd better have told me something. I'm not fucking around, all right?'

'I can't tell you anything,' I said, 'because there's nothing to tell you.' Then I added in my sincerest voice, 'If there was, I would, believe me.'

We passed a place full of trees, all without any leaves. The Giant saw them and so did I. 'You know what I'd like to do to you, you little bastard?'

I didn't but I guessed it wouldn't be nice.

'Take you in there,' he said, pointing at the trees, 'and blow your fucking brains out. That's what you IRA bastards do in Belfast, isn't it?'

How was I to know? 'I don't know what they do,' I said, 'and I don't know anything about Belfast.' I didn't live there, did I?

'By the time you get out of prison you'll be an old man, and you'll not see your mum and dad again,' he said.

I didn't reply to that because I was still thinking about getting my brains blown out. I didn't remember any woods in Northern Ireland, just roads and houses.

'There are six lads,' said the Giant, 'with big boots on, waiting for you at the nick, and they're going to kick the shit out of you and your brothers.'

I'd not thought Vincent and John might be there, but even knowing that they would was of no comfort. I saw the driver watching me in the mirror. She'd been watching me since Carter Street. Did she see how frightened I was? She must, I thought.

We drove on, the driver's eyes going to the mirror every few seconds to check on me. After a while, the Giant said we'd got to Guildford. I was tired, hungry and squashed from sitting with him. I wished he'd put me in the boot. Anything would have been better than this.

The Giant said we were nearly at the police station. He said that when we got there he was going to put his coat over my head.

I'd seen people with coats over them, looking like ghosts.

'It's all right,' I said. 'I don't need your coat.'

'You don't?' said the giant. 'You're fucking having it.'

'What do I need it for?'

'So no one can see your fucking face.'

'Who?'

'The reporters,' he said. 'Now shut up.'

The car stopped. The Giant put his coat over my head. It was a mackintosh and smelt of rubber. I went to throw it off but he stopped me.

The door opened, and he yanked me out. I felt concrete or pavement under my feet. I tried to throw off the coat but he stopped me again. Then he tugged me and I went forward.

12

The mackintosh came off and I was in a big room with a counter. A lot of policemen were hanging about, all watching me. I had the feeling they'd been waiting to see me and their attitude wasn't friendly. A sergeant came up. He was scratching his head.

'Who's this?' he said to the Giant.

'One of the bombers.'

'He's only a boy,' said the sergeant. 'Get them cuffs off him.'

Suddenly, I felt I was in safe hands. The cuffs came off. I was booked in.

'Had anything to eat, son?' asked the sergeant when that was done.

'No, nothing. I was told I'd get breakfast at the last place, but they forgot.'

'All right, I'll get you something.'

He told me to follow him. We went along passageways and came eventually to a cell. The door was open and there was a chair outside in the corridor. I knew the cell was for me but I didn't want to go in. I asked the sergeant if I could sit on the chair outside.

'All right,' he said, 'but don't go away.'

Where could I go? I didn't know where I was. I told him I'd stay on the chair. I sat down and the sergeant went away. I felt better in the corridor than I would have if I'd been in the cell. I started to think maybe Guildford wasn't so bad. I hadn't had the shit kicked out of me. My brothers were somewhere. And the sergeant was all right.

A new policeman appeared with a plate of chips, baked beans and a sausage. I took the plate on my lap and ate a mouthful. It was cold but I wasn't going to ask for it to be heated. I didn't want to push my luck. I did ask for some coffee, though. He went away and came back with a cup that had a small hole in it. Tea was dribbling out.

I finished my food and emptied the cup. The policeman who'd brought it came back and told me my brother would be coming.

'Which one?'

'How do I know?' he said. 'Anyway, when he comes in, don't say anything to him, all right?'

'All right.'

A few minutes later, there was Vincent. As soon as I saw him, I was off the chair and straight over to him. 'All right, kid?' he said.

'Where's John?'

'At home, and he's all right.'

I asked what was going on. He told me not to worry, and that everything would be fine.

'What about Mum and Dad?'

He didn't know about them.

Before I could say any more, the policeman who had brought the food came up. 'Since you're so talkative, you can stay in there now,' he said. 'On your own.'

He pushed me into the cell I'd been sitting outside.

'But he's my brother.' I said. I didn't see why I shouldn't talk to Vincent even if this policeman said not to. We'd the right to talk, didn't we, whatever he said? And it wasn't as if it was a crime talking to my brother, was it?

'I told you not to say anything to him,' said the policeman.

He slammed the door and turned the key and then I heard another slam, which I knew was Vincent being put into a different cell.

How's our John got away with all this? I thought, funny though it was to be having that thought just then. We're here, I thought, and he's not. Well, he'd always been a bit slippery. But at least

Vincent was in the building, even if he was in one cell and I was in another, and I felt better knowing that.

I looked at the bed. The base was made of wood. It stuck out of the wall and was only a couple of feet above the ground. The mattress was blue. I lay down, hoping for sleep, even though this wasn't very likely seeing as I was terrified with not knowing what was going to happen. The mattress smelt of sweat and piss and God alone knows what else.

After a few minutes, I heard the cover on the slit in the door being lifted and I knew someone was looking in at me. The cover went down and I'd another try at sleep but after a few minutes, the flap banged and I knew someone was looking in again. After this had happened a couple more times, I gave up trying to sleep and just lay there with my eyes open, alert and tense and waiting for the worst to begin.

Time passed slowly and even school was starting to look good. Then the door flew open and banged against the wall. There he was again – the Giant.

'Get your shoes off.'

'Why?'

'Just get them off.'

I was wearing my favourite socks and they were full of holes. Mum had put them in the dustbin many times but I'd always fetched them out. Those socks had come to Teasy's and I'd put them on that morning. They were multi-coloured. I didn't want the Giant to see the holes in them and my big toes sticking out.

I bent over, pulled one lace undone as slowly as I could.

The Giant told me to hurry. They were coming off, whether I liked it or not. That was it, and no arguments. He told me to put them outside the cell on the floor. I carried them out. He took my wrist – he'd a firm grip – and pulled me down the corridor in my socks. I wasn't running but I was on my toes trying to keep up. We passed many cells, all with pairs of shoes outside the door, some with cigarettes and matches too.

The Giant stopped. 'That's your dad's tobacco there,' he said.

Yes, it was Dad's leather tobacco pouch, the one we gave him for Father's Day, the one I used to fill with Old Holborn. I asked the Giant what it was doing there but he ignored me.

At the end of the corridor, we went through a door. On the other side there were stairs and we climbed them. At the top, we went through another door and down another corridor. At last we came to a door that the Giant opened.

We went into a large room, the sort used for briefing policemen. There were tables and chairs stacked against the walls. In the middle there was a table with one chair on one side and two on the other. The policewoman who had driven me to Guildford was sitting in one.

The Giant pointed to the single chair and told me to sit. He sat beside the woman. They stared at me. At least my feet were under the table and they couldn't see my socks.

'Right,' said the Giant. 'Where did you get the bombs?'

'What bombs?'

'You know the bombs I'm talking about. Where did they come from?'

'I've told you. You've got the wrong people. We had no bombs.'

'Don't fucking lie. Tell me, where did you get the bombs?'

'There ain't no bombs.'

He got up and walked out of the room.

'Look,' said the policewoman. 'Tell me where your mum got the bombs,' she said. 'That's all we want to know.'

'There ain't no bombs,' I said. 'We're not that kind of family.'

'When he comes back he'll be really mad,' she said, meaning the Giant, 'so you'd better tell him something, anything.'

'What can I tell him? I don't know anything. You've made a mistake.'

The door opened and the Giant walked back in. This time he didn't sit down. He leant on the table with one hand and put the other on his hip. 'The bombs, where did they come from?'

'I've told you, there ain't no bombs!'

He took his hand off his hip and punched the side of my face, nearly knocking me off my chair. I grasped the table. I knew there was more to come and I didn't want to be sent flying.

'How come there were traces of nitroglycerine under your nails?' he said.

The bone under my cheek hurt and there was a whooshing noise in my ear. 'I don't know what you're talking about.'

He began to walk from one side of me to the other. He asked me the same questions over and over again. Then he changed tack. 'You saw your mum in the kitchen making bombs, didn't you?' he said.

'No, you've got it all wrong.'

He hit the other side of my face. I managed not to fall off the chair but I started to cry. I wanted this to stop. At the same time I knew there was nothing I could do or say to stop it.

'Stop crying,' he said, 'and tell me where the bombs are.'

'I can't tell you. There are no bombs.' He hit the top of my back, just below my neck.

I went on crying.

'Your mum's a murderer and she's getting it too,' he said.

'No, she's not.'

He hit me again. 'Your bloody bombs,' he said. 'I've been picking up all the mess they made, so don't tell me there ain't no fucking bombs.' He hit me again. He told me that everyone in our house on the night the police came had had traces of nitroglycerine under their fingernails and that we were all guilty and we were all going to get it.

I asked if that included Anne-Marie. He gave me a nasty look and walked out of the room again.

I went on crying, the tears running down my face, and I told the policewoman it was impossible we had bombs in the house. Then I asked what the bombs were supposed to look like. She told me I was the one who should know since the bombs had been in our house.

I told her she was wrong and began to cry again. She took her hankie from her pocket and gave it to me. I tried to dry my eyes but I couldn't stop crying so I gave up.

'Look,' said the policewoman. She spoke in a reasonable voice. It said, Listen, I'm about to give you some good advice. Pay attention.

'Stop crying,' she said, 'and tell him what you know, anything. He'll leave you alone then.'

The Giant came back into the room. 'You know someone called Armstrong?' he said.

'He plays for Arsenal.'

I wasn't trying to be funny but for the first time since the questions started here was one I could answer. Armstrong was a winger and had played with the team for years.

'What's his first name?'

'George,' I said, which again was true.

'Nah, it's Paddy Armstrong,' he said. He hit my head again. 'Carole Richardson, Paul Hill, Gerard Conlon – those names mean anything to you?'

'I know Gerry Conlon,' I said. I told the Giant he'd stayed with us once and nicked some money. The other two, I'd never heard of.

The Giant didn't believe me. He said all those people had been in our house and, worse, my mum had shown them how to make bombs.

'No,' I said. We hadn't seen Gerry Conlon since he was asked to leave and the others I didn't know.

This annoyed the Giant. He pointed at the window in the far corner. He said he was going to throw me out. I should have been frightened but instead I saw an opportunity. This could be my escape. When I hit the ground, I thought, I'd get up and run away. But where? I didn't know where I was and it was raining and dark. This wasn't going to work, I realized. The window wasn't a way of escape.

'Your dad's a drunk,' said the Giant. 'You know that?' He said this in a nasty voice.

I knew he wanted to upset me. But he couldn't because I knew this already. 'Yeah,' I said. 'I know my dad likes a drink.'

The Giant didn't like this so he hit me. 'What about the nitroglycerine under your nails?' he said. 'How do you explain that?'

Suddenly I had an inspiration. 'I could have got the traces in the Murphy's hut,' I said, and I told him what and where it was. 'Me and my mates went in there to make some tea.'

It wasn't so far-fetched. The hut was a strange place I didn't normally go. Perhaps I'd touched something inside it, which was why the test had turned out as it had.

'When was that?' the Giant asked.

'About a month ago,' I said.

'Stuff as dangerous as that wouldn't be left in an unlocked hut.'

He was right there. But the hut had been locked and we had broken the padlock to get in, then run away when the workmen returned. However, I was in enough trouble as it was so I decided not to tell him about this in case it made an already bad situation worse.

'Where else do you think you could have touched nitroglycerine?' he asked.

'At school?' I said.

'I'm sure they wouldn't let young boys play with nitroglycerine.' Then he added, 'You must have touched something in your house.'

Well, obviously. If I hadn't touched it anywhere else, it had to have been in the house. Except I hadn't. 'Well, I haven't,' I said.

He hit me again.

'I'm not going to talk to you any more,' I said.

'Why not?'

'Because every time I do you hit me.'

'You're a liar,' he said. 'You know that?'

'I'm not a liar,' I said.

'Yes, you are.'

'I'm not a liar and I was brought up to tell the truth.'

'Oh, yeah?' He hit me again and left the room.

Now I heard Vincent. The Giant had told me he was next door but I'd have known without being told. I could hear his head being banged against the wall. That was what it sounded like anyway. And I could hear him crying out, but I couldn't make sense of what he was shouting.

I started to cry again. (Vincent told me later he could hear me shouting and crying through the wall, just as I'd heard him.)

Now, next door, Vincent went quiet. The Giant returned and

this time he had another man with him. They stood by the door, smiling.

'I tell you what,' said the other man to the Giant, 'you and me will swap over. Then you can get something out of Vincent and I can get something out of this one. How about that?'

I looked at the new man. I knew the Giant wasn't worth asking but maybe this new man would help before he got stuck into me. 'Can I see my mum and dad?' I asked.

'No,' he said, then added, 'You know they got a pasting?'

The two men laughed and the new man left the room.

'I've got some news for you,' said the Giant. 'It's about Gerry Conlon. He's said your mum showed him how to make bombs in your kitchen, and there were people there and you were one of them.'

I shook my head. This was all nonsense.

'What's this stick of white stuff?' he said.

When he was helping the police with their search, Vincent had found it under Uncle Sean's bed. Here was another question I could answer. 'That's chalk,' I said, 'and I got it from school.' In fact it had probably come from Willesden College of Technology but I wasn't going to tell him that.

'Stand up,' said the Giant.

I stood. I felt shaky but I didn't fall.

'Your mum's trained you all well for this,' he said.

He grabbed my wrist and dragged me from the room. Then he led me back the way we'd come to the cell from which he'd fetched me earlier. There were my shoes standing outside where I'd left them. He pushed me in.

'Can I have some water?' I asked. I was thirsty. The Giant said nothing, just closed the cell door and locked it.

While I'd been away, the cell had got very hot. There was a window but it didn't open. I discovered the coolest spot was by the door so I went and stood there.

I could hear everything in the corridor. Whenever anyone walked by I'd shout, 'Can I have a cup of water?' and they'd shout back, 'In a minute.' But that was all I got. The water never came and I realized that a policeman's minute and the minute I knew were two different things.

Besides the thirst, I was finding it hard to breathe. I had to have water. I had to cool down. Finally, I went to the corner where there was a toilet but no handbasin. I pushed the flush on the wall. As the water surged from the rim, I cupped my hands and caught some. I drank it. Then I pushed the flush again, and with the water I got I splashed my face.

Through the window I saw it was getting dark. Was I going to be here for the night? Had I been forgotten? Was there more of what I'd already had to come?

There was a bell on the wall near the door so I pushed it. A policeman came and looked at me through the slit. 'What?' he said.

'Where's my mum and dad? Can I see them?'

'No, you can't. Now leave the bell alone and shut up.'

'There's no air in here,' I said, 'and I've got asthma. Can I sit outside?'

'Where do you think you are? This is a police station. No, you can't.'

He went off. I sat on the bed. The internal cell light was on. I heard footsteps, the flap clanging and realized someone was looking in at me. Whoever he was, he said nothing. 'Yeah, I'm still here,' I said. They came to look at me several more times.

It was night outside now. I felt very tired but when I lay down I couldn't sleep. I put the mattress on the floor; it looked better there. I lay down again and closed my eyes. I waited for sleep but instead I began to cry.

I got up and walked around the cell. I kept hearing footsteps and the rattle of keys outside. Whenever I did, I would think someone was coming for me but no one did. No one unlocked the door and told me to come out.

At some point that night, exhausted, I fell asleep.

The next morning the cell door opened, waking me. A voice told me I was going outside for exercise. I had a sore neck and a sore head.

I was given my shoes to put on, then handcuffed to a very tall policeman in uniform. He took me out into a yard. It had four high walls, or perhaps they only appeared so big because I was small.

It was fresh and cold. I put my free hand into my coat pocket. The other was still cuffed to the policeman. I asked if he could take the cuffs off so I could put it in my pocket too, but he said no.

We walked round the edge of the yard, like in a prison film.

'What have you been up to?' he asked.

'I haven't been up to anything,' I said. 'They think we've been making bombs in our house, but they've made a mistake.'

'You'll be all right, then. Where are you from?'

'London, the Harrow Road.'

'I know it well,' he said. 'I was there for years. Bit rough round there, isn't it?'

'The police are,' I said. He didn't say anything but he didn't seem to mind.

'Have you got a fag?' I said.

'Not for you I haven't. You're too young to smoke,' he said. We walked on.

'You go down the canal much?' he asked. 'Do any fishing?'

'I go down there with my mates on our bikes, but that's about all. We don't fish.'

We walked on and he made small talk with me about school, football, things like that. After a bit, since we were getting on so well, I thought he might help with some of my questions. 'Has my brother been out here yet?' I asked.

'Your brother?' he said. 'Is he here as well?'

'Yes, and my mum and dad, I think.'

'I don't know,' he said. 'Sorry, I can't help you. No one's told me anything about your family.'

We stayed out for about half an hour. Then I was taken back to my cell. I had been told at some point that I was going home with Vincent but now my shoes were taken again. Why did they do this if I was going home? It was all very puzzling.

The door closed. An hour or so passed. Then it was opened again and I got my shoes back. A policeman told me I was going to have a wash and led me to a washroom. Here I found Vincent at a sink, washing his face.

'You're not allowed to talk,' the policeman said.

We looked at each other. We didn't need to speak. Our faces said it all.

13

Someone told us we were being let out on bail. I didn't understand what that was. All that mattered was getting out.

Two policemen drove us back to London. Very little was said on the journey, except that Vincent told me he was going to show the policemen a stick of the chalk they'd got so excited about when he got home. That was the point at which I realized I wasn't going with him.

'I want to go home too,' I said.

'No,' said one of the policemen. 'You're going to your aunt's, and that's that.'

We arrived at Aunt Teasy's. I said goodbye to Vincent and he said he'd see me soon, and told me not to worry. I got out and the police car drove off.

In her kitchen, I told Aunt Teasy and her family what had happened to me at Guildford, but they didn't believe me. They didn't believe it could have happened the way I told it.

She made me a meal, but I couldn't eat it. I went to bed, but I couldn't sleep. My mind was not my own any more. I couldn't make it think about what I wanted to think about. Instead it threw up question after question to which I didn't have a single answer.

Mum's first letter arrived, addressed to Aunt Teasy and us.

I have not stopped thinking of you and it breaks my heart to know you are also suffering this pain and we all know that I am the innocent person and have been [wrongfully] accused of this terrible crime. My loving boys I want you to be brave as I am trying to do, for please God soon I will be able to prove my innocence. Promise me to go to Church and Holy Com, every Sunday. Pray hard to God to listen to children's prayers. Patrick my Son, be brave be good and love Anne-Marie as I did. Say your prayers with her and for your Mum and Dad . . . Please God Dad will be with you, love him be good to him for I know he loves you and me more than anybody or anything in the world. Aunt Teasy Anne-Marie wanted a cot for her dolls for Christmas. Vincent will get it for her . . . Tell my family . . . to keep praying hard, that God will help me prove I am innocent . . . If you get to see Paddy give him my love and tell him to pray for me. I hope he gets home for Christmas . . .

Dad didn't get bail like she hoped. Neither did she.

I had breakfast in Aunt Teasy's kitchen, then left the house and walked to Kennington station. I crossed London, changing twice, and got to Westbourne Park tube station. From there it was a short walk to Tesco on the Harrow Road.

The shop had steel swing doors at the front. I went in. After the cold in the street it was hot in there. Music was playing. I walked down the aisles to the office. Seamus, the manager, was at his desk.

He spotted me, got up and came out into the shop. He was very quick. 'Yes. What can I do for you?' He said it as if I was a shoplifter and he was on to me.

'When can I come back to work?' I asked.

'You can't work here now,' he said.

'Why?'

'People won't come into the shop if they know you're here. Not with the police and all that.'

'But I haven't done anything wrong. What are you talking about?'

'Look,' he said sharply, 'you can't have your job back and that's that.' He went back into his office and sat down behind his desk.

'You big-chinned, spotty-faced bastard,' I shouted. Then I turned and ran out.

Vincent and I had an appointment with our legal people in Middle Temple. We went there with Aunt Teasy's husband, Uncle Bill, and, not knowing our way around, we got lost and arrived late.

The meeting, like the others that followed, was in a lifeless office, heavy curtains over the windows keeping the light out, the lower half of the walls covered with dark wood panels, the top with shelves crowded with books, big heavy ones with gold writing on them.

We told the team our stories and answered their questions. I didn't follow what was happening. All I could think was, This is one big huge mistake. Why does nobody see that?

After the meeting, Jenny Sterring, our solicitor, took me aside. 'I'm going to Guildford to see your mum,' she said. 'Would you like to come?'

I knew the police still had Mum and that if I went I might run into the Giant again. But it was a risk I was prepared to take. I'd do anything, absolutely anything to see her. 'Yes,' I said. 'I want to come.'

I got into Jenny's car and off we went. When we arrived, the police station wasn't the one in Guildford. It was in Godalming. That was a relief. No possibility of seeing the Giant here.

We went in and were searched. Then we were taken into a room full of policemen and some policewomen. A door to the side of the room opened, and a woman was standing there between two officers who, I later discovered, were Detective Inspector Powell and Detective Sergeant Robinson. The woman was squinting, as if she'd lost her glasses, her clothes were in a state and her hair was messy and grey. She stretched her arms towards me. 'Son, are you all right?'

If I hadn't recognized her voice I wouldn't have known her. It was Mum. She said everything would be all right and that we hadn't done what they said we'd done and I started to cry. Everyone in the room laughed and I hurled myself at Powell. I kicked his leg and threw a punch that didn't connect. I was dragged off him by some of the other policemen. I could hear Jenny telling me to calm down while I was taken into the corridor. From there I could hear Mum crying inside. Eventually we were let back in.

Mum told Jenny that while we were out of the room Powell had been talking to her and what he'd said wasn't very nice.

'What did he say?' asked Jenny.

'He said he's going to get me for murder,' said Mum, 'and if he doesn't get me for murder, he's going to get me for the gloves because the tests showed I'd worn them to handle explosives, and either way I'm going down for a very long time.'

Jenny asked Powell if this was true. He smirked. Mum and Jenny went on talking, with the two detectives listening and sometimes smiling.

We'd had our time. We had to go. The policemen were laughing again. I went for the nearest uniform but I didn't get far. I was dragged outside and told not to come back.

I was in Jenny's car and we were on our way to London. 'What's going on?' I asked. I'd realized that Mum had been knocked around.

'What do you mean?'

'Mum's had the shit kicked out of her, day and night, which I know isn't right. She's a woman. What's going on?'

'I don't know,' said Jenny.

As we drove her eyes kept going to the rear-view mirror. She thought an unmarked police car was following us. She pulled over and let the vehicles behind go past.

Back on the road, her eyes kept going to the mirror. She still thought we were being tailed.

She stopped again to let the traffic by and later still she stopped a third time.

It was very late by the time we got to Aunt Teasy's.

Mum had been sent to HMP Brixton so Aunt Teasy took Anne-Marie and me to see her there. When we got out of the station, we were at the bottom of Brixton Hill. As we climbed it I had strange feelings. Obviously I was looking forward to seeing Mum, but I didn't want to leave her later, and I already knew that was how this visit would end.

When you visit someone in prison, it is generally thought that you must be no good yourself, and prison officers go out of their way to let you know they think so. We got to the main gate, which was closed. There was no shelter and it was raining, but we had to stand and wait. That was what all the other visitors were doing.

Eventually the gate opened and Aunt Teasy handed the screw our VOs – visiting orders. Then we gave our names and that of the person we were visiting – 'My mum, Mrs Maguire,' I shouted, at the top of my voice.

The screw looked at me as if I was a piece of dog shit.

We filed in and handed over everything we had brought for Mum – clothes and food. Then we sat in a large room with everyone else who was visiting. We were there ages. I went to the toilet for a fag. Anne-Marie couldn't keep still for more than a minute or two. Every time she'd go off I had to bring her back to her seat.

I could do without all this, I thought. I wished I was at home, or out with my mates playing football. I wished we were all at home. I wished this wasn't happening.

Eventually the screws moved us all across the yard to the visiting rooms. Then they took Aunt Teasy, Anne-Marie and me upstairs. We were searched again, even Anne-Marie, then put in a room full of screws. We had to wait there, but we knew that Mum was on her way because all the screws were acting as if something was happening.

Then Mum was at the door. The screws searched her, then let her in. She gave Anne-Marie and me a big hug and lots of kisses. She asked us if we were being good with Aunt Teasy, doing what we were told and helping around the house. I had not yet gone back to school so Mum was worried about that. I promised I'd go back in the New Year.

Then she said we were not to worry and that everything would be all right in the end. She said she was innocent, that she hadn't done anything wrong and that she shouldn't be there. She said this over and over again. As she did, Anne-Marie jumped all over her and held on to her. Every now and again she asked, 'When are you coming home? I miss you,' and all the normal things that a little girl would say to her mum.

I could see Mum was doing her best to hold back her tears as she went on talking, but I was too young to understand what was really going on or what she was going through.

Nor had I Mum's certainty that all would be well in the end. All I had was rage. I hated the police, the courts, the screws, Gerry Conlon, Paul Hill and everyone I believed had done us down, and if anyone had mentioned forgiveness to me then I'd have said no, never, not as long as I drew breath would I ever forgive.

After fifteen minutes the screws called time. I knew we had to go and that Mum was staying, but Anne-Marie couldn't understand why she couldn't come with us. Mum told her Brixton was a hospital and she'd come home when she was better.

As the screws led Mum away, she began to cry.

'What's wrong with Mum? I want to stay with Mum,' said Anne-Marie. She cried most of the way home.

I waited until we got to Aunt Teasy's house, then went off and had a cry on my own.

14

It was Sunday. Christmas at Aunt Teasy's had been and gone. I went up to Third Avenue to see Vincent and John. They were living at number forty-three, trying to keep the house together. I saw some of my mates too.

Around half past three it was getting dark. Aunt Teasy had told me not to be back late. As I left our house to walk to Westbourne Park Underground station, I knew what I was going to do.

From Third I cut across to First Avenue and headed towards

the Harrow Road. As I went I picked up two half-bricks and I had them with me when I got to Tesco. The shop was closed. The lights were off inside, but I could make out the aisles and the tills with grey covers over them.

I had a good look up and down the Harrow Road. There were only a few people about, no one very close. I could do this, I thought, and get away with it.

I threw the first brick. It went though the glass door. I threw the second and broke another plate of glass. The door was in a right old mess, glass everywhere.

As I legged it up the road, with the alarm ringing in my ears, I thought, Seamus won't need his keys to open up in the morning, the bastard.

That evening, I told Aunt Teasy, 'I don't have a job at Tesco any more.'

'Not to worry,' she said. 'I know the manager in the Tesco at Elephant and Castle.' It was down the road from her house. 'I'll have a word with him,' she said. 'He's ever so friendly and I'm sure I can get you in there.'

I was doubtful but, sure enough, a few days later, Aunt Teasy told me I'd a job there, Saturdays only.

The next Saturday I got up early, had breakfast, and took the bus to Elephant and Castle. This Tesco was a lot bigger than the one on the Harrow Road. There were a lot more people working there and some were girls.

I walked around the shop like a little boy who had lost his mum. I was trying to find the manager. He found me and took me to his office. 'How old are you?'

'Thirteen.'

'Why did you leave your other job at Tesco?'

'Because I'm living with my aunt now.'

'Why are you living with your aunt?'

'My mum isn't well.'

'If I phone up your other job, will the manager tell me good things about you?'

I didn't think about it. 'Yes,' I said.

'Right, you can start today. Let's see how you get on. Here, put this on.' He gave me a tie.

It was brown and long and I was small. It was about the same length as me. Dad had tried to teach me how to knot one and so had the owner of the men's outfitters where I'd worked. Both had failed. Mum did my tie when I had to wear one to school.

The manager took it back. He put it round my neck and told me to watch what he was doing. I nearly went cross-eyed. He was too fast for me. 'Next time you come here to work,' he said, 'you are to wear black trousers, black shoes and a white shirt. Do you understand?'

I understood, but I didn't have them.

He left the office and I followed. He gave me a quick tour of the shop floor. As we went along he told me what to do and what not to do. We finished off in the storeroom. It was about three times the size of the one in the Harrow Road Tesco. The manager introduced me to the storeman and left.

He was older than me – and could he talk? He wouldn't stop. He told me how many birds he'd pulled, how many pints he could put away. It all went in one ear and out the other. I took home two pounds at the end of the day. I had decided I needed every penny I could get.

I had promised Mum when I saw her in Brixton that I would go back, but since then school had been far from my mind. Now that it was January I had to think about it and I didn't like the idea. I'd always hated questions and I knew I'd be plagued with them when I went back. There would be questions about what had happened, and what was going to happen. The trouble was, I knew neither what had happened nor what was going to happen, so how would I answer?

I explained to Aunt Teasy and Uncle Bill. I said I wasn't up to it, and that I didn't want to go back. They said I had to go back, that people would talk if I didn't.

I wasn't convinced so Aunt Teasy suggested finding me a new school, one closer by. She had already done this for Anne-Marie.

I said I'd still get asked loads of questions *and* I'd be the new boy. At least at my old school I could tell them to fuck off. So that was that settled: I'd go back to my old school.

School was only a bus ride away from Third Avenue, or I could walk. But from where I was living now, in Kennington, south London, St John's Wood was miles away.

The weekend before term began, Uncle Bill got out the London Underground map and we worked out the best route from Kennington to St John's Wood. On the Monday morning he got me up early, and after breakfast, we left the house together. Why was he coming to the station? I knew the way there.

We got to Kennington Underground. I was expecting he would say goodbye there but he didn't. 'I'm coming with you,' he said.

'To school?'

'Yes,' he said.

'The last time anyone took me to school,' I said, 'I was about eight. I can manage, you know. I've been on the tube before.'

'I know,' said Bill, 'but I'm coming anyway. It's a complicated route and I want to be sure you don't get lost.'

No, it wasn't complicated, there was just one change, and there was no chance I'd get lost. The truth, as I knew, was that he thought if he didn't take me I'd bunk off.

We got tickets and found the platform.

'Now,' he said, 'so you can do this journey on your own, I want you to make a mental note where we change this morning.'

'Of course I will,' I said.

The train came. We got on. The carriage was packed. We changed at Waterloo on to a Bakerloo Line train for St John's Wood that was also packed. For the rest of the journey I was dodging elbows, big feet, bigger newspapers and an army of black briefcases. I might have left Aunt Teasy's half asleep but I was wide awake when we reached St John's Wood.

I got off. So did Uncle Bill. We went up to the barrier where the ticket man stood. Was he going to walk me all the way to the school gate? What would my friends say if they saw us?

I shouldn't have worried.

'This is as far as I'm coming,' he said, 'but I'll meet you after school. I'll be waiting outside the gates. I want to be certain you get home.'

We said goodbye and I went out into the street. I saw my school on the far side of Wellington Road. I got a fag out and lit it. Why didn't I bunk off, I thought, and just be at the school gate in time to meet Uncle Bill later? I could do it easy. But where would I go? It started to rain.

It wouldn't be worth it, I thought, skiving off. I'd just get wet, and that was no way to spend the next six or so hours.

I crossed the road. The gate was on the other side of the school from where I was and I couldn't be bothered to walk round so I hopped over the low wall and headed across the asphalt. There was no one around. School had started while I'd been smoking, not that I cared.

I got up to the main building. A window opened and a teacher stuck his head out. 'You're late,' he shouted.

'Bollocks,' I said, and went on my way.

I didn't care if he reported me. I didn't care if I got detention. I'd never liked school. Now I liked it even less. I didn't want to be here. What good was school to me? Was it going to get Mum and Dad out of jail? Was it going to get the family living back together again? No, of course it wasn't and no amount of detention, or anything else they threw at me, was going to make me change my mind – it was pointless and a waste of my time that had no relevance to my life or to what really mattered to me.

I got into the building, no one around, of course, because everyone was in class, and began to climb the stairs to where my form's classroom was. Suddenly I realized there was one thing I did like about school: my mates. I was looking forward to seeing them. I hadn't expected that.

I got to my classroom door and walked straight in.

'Knock before you come in,' said the teacher, sharply. 'What do you want?'

I saw it wasn't my class. 'I thought this was Two D,' I said.

'Well, it's not,' said the teacher. 'Are you a new boy?'

'No, I've been off.' I walked out and went to the toilets at the end of the corridor, sat down on one and lit another fag. My class had moved, but could I be bothered to find it? The thought of bunking off crossed my mind again.

I finished my fag. I still didn't know what I was going to do – walk out or find my class. I went to the stairs and began to go down. I was probably going to walk out. However, as luck would have it, I met the headmaster coming up the other way. He was doing the rounds, making sure everyone was where they should be.

'Patrick, where are you going?' he said. 'Why are you not in your class?'

'I don't know where it is,' I said. 'I've been away.'

'Yes – and how are you?' he said, and he looked at me in a funny way.

'All right.'

'And what about your mum?' he said. 'Is she all right?'

It was nice of him to ask. 'Yeah,' I said, 'I think she is.' I wasn't going to tell him anything about what had happened to her in Guildford or visiting her at Brixton prison. If I did there'd be no end to his questions.

'Your form is on the fourth floor now,' he said, and told me the number of the room where I'd find everyone.

He went on his way and I set off for my new classroom. I got to the door and had a look through the window. I didn't recognize the teacher but I knew the boys at the desks. It was Two D all right.

I opened the door and went in.

'Yes, and who are you?' said the new teacher.

'Patrick Maguire.'

'You're late.'

'I was talking to the headmaster.'

'Well, go and sit down at the back there.'

I walked between the rows, saying, 'Hello,' to one or two of my mates as I passed, got to an empty desk and sat down. I felt like I'd been away from school for years rather than weeks.

For the rest of that period I gazed out of the window, dreaming the time away.

Break came and everyone streamed out.

'All right?'

It was TK, the boy I'd hit it off with on my first day, the boy I'd sat beside in the first year planning bank robberies.

'What happened to you?' said TK. 'Where've you been?'

'Got nicked.'

I told him what I understood, which wasn't a lot.

One afternoon, not long after I'd gone back, a mate and I decided to bunk off. We didn't get far, just to the other side of the main road, when two policemen stopped us. What with there being only two of us, we couldn't have been on an official school outing, and they wanted to know where we were going.

We gave them some story but they didn't believe us.

'Right,' said one, 'you're going back to school and we're coming with you.'

So off we set, them and us, and as we marched along my mate and I looked at each other. That was enough. Together, we flew over the low school wall, across the asphalt and vanished into the main building. I learnt a lesson that day. There was no point bunking off like that. I'd only get caught.

From now on the trick with bunking off was to stay inside the building. So from now on, whenever I skipped a class, that's what I did. I hid in the toilets. I hid in the bicycle sheds. I hid anywhere and everywhere. I even found a broom cupboard from where I could climb up into the roof. That was a brilliant place: up there, I could smoke and chat away with someone for hours. One day, when I was up there, whoever I was with said he'd better go – and vanished. It took me a moment to realize he'd fallen through the roof and landed in the hallway below. It wasn't a long way down, so he was all right. I followed him through the hole he'd made and we ran off laughing.

*　　*　　*

Mum to Hugh and Mary McCaffery (brother-in-law and sister) in Belfast, 10 February 1975:

> Inside me something keeps telling me not to worry for when you're innocent and tell the truth, how can these people punish you, but the hardest cross is being away from my kids and them to suffer for nothing, and them, God help them, to know their Mum and Dad are as innocent as themselves.

Living over in Kennington had its drawbacks. I didn't know anyone there, apart from Aunt Teasy and Uncle Bill, so I didn't get out much. Vincent and John were at 43 Third Avenue, and my mates were around there too. I really wanted to go home, but that wasn't going to happen – well, not for a while. I didn't like having to get up so early for school either. By the time I got there, I felt as if I'd done two lessons already, one being PE, what with dodging elbows and big feet on the Underground.

Coming home at half past three wasn't so good either because I was in my Quintin Kynaston uniform. I was stopped endlessly by boys from other schools and asked what school I went to. I ran when I could but sometimes I was cornered. Then I'd always make sure of getting one of them who I'd poke, punch and bite even as the others were steaming into me. If I could get one howling, it would drive the others off.

I found different routes home, but there were always other kids somewhere along the way. I also tried leaving school early, which worked but didn't go down well with the teachers. Or instead of going to Kennington, I'd pop around to see Vincent and John at home, getting back to Aunt Teasy and Uncle Bill's late. They didn't like that. So I never did find a satisfactory solution to the problem.

15

It was 24 February 1975. Uncle Bill brought me to Waterloo where we met Vincent and the three of us caught a train to Guildford. My brother and I had to appear before the juvenile court. When we got there, we saw a crowd waiting outside another court, the one in the Guildhall. They were waiting for Mum, Dad and the others, and they weren't there to wish them luck. Vincent said that if the people in the crowd knew we were connected to Mum and Dad, they'd kill us.

A policeman told us to come with him. He walked towards the crowd, us following. What Vincent had said was going through my head. I could see people staring at us as we got nearer. Then a line of police vehicles passed, lights flashing, and the crowd turned to watch them instead. It was the convoy with Mum and the others, and later she told us she had seen us, through the blacked-out windows, walking along the road.

The police convoy stopped outside the court and the crowd was made to stand back as Mum, Dad and the others were got out, with blankets over their heads, and brought in, everyone shouting abuse at them. Our policeman followed them, and we followed him, and as we slipped in I could feel the crowd's eyes on us. I hoped they didn't know who we were.

We were taken through the court and across a yard to a holding cell where we saw Mum, Dad and the others. It was then, maybe, or it mght have been earlier in the day that Mum was told the murder charge against her would be dropped and that she was to be charged instead with possession of nitroglycerine. One of the rubber gloves she had used for housework had some on it, or so the tests said. She was also told that Vincent and I, on the strength of the tests done three months earlier, would be charged with the same offence.

As I only found out much later, this test, which had been used on us all and was the reason why most of us were charged, was known as the Thin Layer Chromatography or TLC test. For this test the substances to be tested (the swabs from our hands and the scrapings from under our fingernails) had been taken away to a laboratory and dissolved in a solution, and then a drop of that solution put on a special plate and allowed to dry. A spot of nitroglycerine was then put alongside the dry spot and the plate was then stood upright in a dish of solvent, sample end downwards. The solvent was drawn up the plate like water up a sheet of blotting paper. As it rose, it carried the spots with it and how the spots travelled and where the spots finished was measured on a scale. If two spots behaved identically, then that proved they were the same – that was the theory at any rate – which in everyone's tests but John's was what happened. However, the fact the spots ended in the same place didn't prove any such thing and that was because this wasn't a positive test designed to determine whether two substances were the same but a negative test designed to work out if substances that were thought to be similar were in fact different. So if spots ended in the same place it didn't mean they were the same. In order to prove that, another confirmatory test was required, but this was never done, with the result that we were now being charged with a crime of which we were innocent. One final point: it never occurred to anyone in authority to ask what John was doing while we were supposed to be making bombs. Of course it didn't make sense that one brother hadn't made bombs while the others had. But had they asked this question their case would have unravelled, which presumably was why they never asked the question.

When it was time to go to court, we were taken back the way we'd come, across the yard. There were police dogs everywhere and men on the roofs with rifles pointed at us. It was like a scene from a war film. Mum held my hand.

Once we got to the courtroom, we sat together on long hard benches. People were coming and going, whispering and looking important. Behind us the court was packed and everyone was staring at us. It was only bearable because Mum and Dad were there.

Then the magistrate appeared. Mum applied for bail but was refused. She and all the other adults were remanded back to jail.

I said goodbye to her and Dad and left with Uncle Bill and Vincent
for the station.

We got on to the train and sat down. It slid off along its tracks
with a lot of clacking and banging. I looked out of the window,
at the backs of houses and then at fields. I didn't understand the
ins and outs of what was going on but I knew what it was: a load
of bollocks.

Mum to Hugh and Mary McCaffery (brother-in-law and sister)
in Belfast, 20 March 1975:

> Well, what do you think of them not giving bail? They are
> trying to break me one way or another. It's heartbreaking
> being here four months doing nothing. Even the boys are
> taking it hard, but they don't show it. At court on Thursday
> they were laughing and joking, but I could see our Sean's
> face when they said [to him] no bail . . .
>   The two kids are still on bail, God help them, Hugh, they
> never done any wrong, never had any trouble from them
> and the law plants this on us all. I feel sorry for Vincent just
> started his apprentice[ship], and it all could be wasted
> because of lies. Hugh, I also say the Rosary every morning
> and night. Sometimes I think my mind is going to go, when
> I look at Anne-Marie. I ask myself, is there a God to let this
> happen to innocent people? . . . Anne-Marie said, 'Mum, I
> won't make my first [Holy] Communion until you come
> home in May.' That was one day I was always looking
> forward to, her being the only girl. Hugh, they have got to
> believe us, we are innocent people, and not mixed with
> those people who do these bombings. I know Mary, and the
> kids and yourself are praying hard and you are doing your
> best for us.

It was May, a school day. The sun was shining and the sky was
blue. It was after dinner and I was back in class. The door opened

and the headmaster came in. There was a small stir of excitement. Someone in trouble, were they? Was one of us due to get a bollocking?

The headmaster and the teacher talked in low voices. It was impossible to hear what they said. We were all curious as well as anxious. Trouble with authority was unpleasant, but so long as it wasn't you it was exciting too.

The adults broke off. Well, I thought, now we'd find out what this was about. I hoped it wasn't my name that was called.

'Maguire.'

Oh no. 'Yes,' I said.

'You're to come with me,' said the headmaster.

I got up. What had I done now? He was standing by the classroom door, holding it open. As I passed him, I tried to see from his face if he was cross, but it was blank and I couldn't tell.

In the corridor there was another surprise: my brother John was standing there. We looked at each other. What was going on?

The door closed and the headmaster was beside us.

'What's this about?' asked John.

'You'll see,' said the headmaster. I still couldn't tell from his face if there was trouble or not.

He set off down the corridor at a good pace. We followed.

'What have you been up to?' whispered John.

What indeed? 'Nothing,' I said. I thought that was the safest answer. 'Nothing. I haven't done nothing.'

John shrugged. He didn't know whether to believe me or not.

We followed the headmaster down the stairs, across the front hall and out of the door into the playground. He was still ahead, striding towards the gate where a man was standing. With the sun behind him, his face was in shadow and I could see only his outline.

Perhaps, I thought, I'm in really serious trouble. Perhaps I should run. It might be a policeman. It might be the Giant. It might be anyone.

But it was my dad's brother, Uncle Hugh, who lived in Paddington, not far from us in the Avenues. He wagged a finger at John and me as if we were in trouble. Then he and the headmaster began to talk. We stood and waited. I couldn't hear what was said. Then Uncle Hugh pointed at a car just beyond the school gates, parked by the kerb. 'In you get, lads,' he said.

'What's this about?' asked John. 'Are we in trouble or something?'

He said nothing, just went to the back door. He opened it and up jumped Mum, who had been lying across the back seat, hidden from view.

I fell into her arms, then John pulled me off and took his turn. Then we got into the back, Mum in the middle. She had got bail that day, and couldn't wait for me to get back to Aunt Teasy's and John to get home to 43 Third Avenue so she'd persuaded Uncle Hugh to drive her over to fetch us.

Vincent was at work so he didn't know anything about this until he walked into the kitchen that night. His face was a picture.

I was happy to have Mum back but I couldn't stop thinking about Dad in prison. He'd be over the moon that Mum had got bail, but it would have been so nice if he had been there too.

My other worry was Mum. Was this for keeps? 'Mum,' I said, 'are you going back to prison?'

'No, I'm home now,' she said, 'and I'm home for good. I'm not going back to prison.'

Her sister, Mary, had come to stay and they made us boys our favourite dinner, shepherd's pie. The next day Mum went to Kennington and brought Anne-Marie home.

After we were nicked, I went almost overnight from being an ordinary lad, though no angel, to one who didn't give a shit about anything. At Aunt Teasy's Uncle Bill kept me in check but once I returned home that stopped. Dad wasn't around because he was in prison and Mum was up to her eyes. There were the police, of course, but after what they'd done to me, how much influence could they have? Zero. From now on I did what I wanted.

There was work being done to the exterior of Queens Park Primary School. In the evening, when there was no one around, some of us would climb up the scaffolding, bringing the end of the scaffolding rope up with us, while others stayed below. When we got to the top, we'd feed it through the pulley hanging over the side of the scaffolding. Then one of us would hold the rope at the top and another kid would hold the rope at the bottom (or so you hoped) and then the lad at the top would jump off and the kid holding on to the rope below would come up as the lad from the top went down, just like that. Yes, you hit the scaffolding now and then but it was great fun.

The council was renovating Farrant and Ilbert Streets, which backed on to each other and made a great square where you could mess about all day and night.

It was evening. I was in Farrant Street. At the far end there were houses with families who were waiting to be moved on, but I was at the empty end. One mate's family had moved recently and in front of us was their old house. He got a stone, flung it. The glass broke. He threw another, smashed another pane. He threw a third and then we were all at it.

It was another day in Farrant Street. We smashed a ground-floor window and swarmed into the house, a bunch of us. Inside, we moved from room to room, wrecking them. We went upstairs and did the same in the bedrooms. Then we got into the small dark attic. Someone kicked a hole in the slates and we climbed out. With the sky above me, I felt as if I was on top of a mountain. Someone pulled one of the roof slates free and lobbed it. It hit the ground and shattered. Next thing we were all at it. We never thought we could hit someone. We were having too much fun.

Another roof, another afternoon. One of us was on the ridge keeping a look-out for a police patrol car or van and the rest were at the chimney. It was brick and old.

We put our shoulders to it and pushed. For a moment nothing happened. Then there was a tremor and whatever was holding it in place was tearing and ripping. Suddenly the whole thing was tilting sideways and then it was gone.

Bang! It hit the roof, dust billowed, and then it started to slide, faster and faster, with the screech of brick rubbing on slate. It dropped over the eave. There was silence and then – crash! Dust swirled, and we had a great feeling in our stomachs.

'They're here!' someone shouted.

At the end of the road, a police van was crawling along.

We piled back through the hole in the roof we'd come out through, surged down the stairs and ran out into the front garden.

Not far away, the police van was coming up the road slowly, Mr Plod behind the wheel. When he saw us in the garden his face got hard and determined. He braked, opened his door and jumped out, followed by a dog-handler with an Alsatian.

We picked up some small stones. A hail of missiles flew and pitter-pattered on the roof of the police van.

We turned and ran through the house to the garden behind, then into the one that backed on to it, then into the house belonging to it and then out into the next street. The Alsatian was barking but we'd got away.

Another roof, another day. Instead of slate-lobbing or chimney-tipping, something riskier. I'd been dared and, well, I wasn't chicken so I was going to do it.

I was on my bottom. I slid slowly down the incline. Now and again a slate, dislodged by my weight, dropped over the gutter and smashed on the ground. That was what would happen to me if I wasn't careful. That was why I went so slowly, why my heart thumped.

I got to the bottom. The gutter was at my feet. Now, easy does it. I turned slowly on to my hands and knees. I got one foot then the other on to the roof and edged back the way I'd come. Up, up, I went, until at last I was back with my mates, sitting on the ridge. For that moment I was a hero. I'd been dared to go down and come back and I'd done it.

I looked along the roofs of the houses beside me and saw a couple of bigger lads on one. They were pulling away the lead flashing from the chimneys and hurling it into the garden below where a mate was gathering it up. What was that about? I didn't ask because one of my mates was doing the dare, slithering down. I was having far too much fun to worry about what those bigger lads were up to. That was what the times on the roofs were about. Fun. And because it was such fun we never thought of what might happen if we took a tumble.

No, we thought, the worst that could happen was a cut on the head or the hand, or a splinter, and of course you got filthy black crawling round the condemned houses. By the end of the day you looked like a miner fresh from the pit, or so we liked to think. It was pure fun, the best going – and, as we saw it, constructive in its own way. All the houses in Farrant and Ilbert Streets were coming down, weren't they? All we were doing was helping things on a bit. Even when I lit fires, and I did that many times in houses and skips, I was helping things on a bit. And I always called the fire brigade, didn't I? I was never an irresponsible fire-starter.

It was after school and we were in the ticket hall at South Hampstead overground rail station, the lads from the Avenues and one or two others who lived close by. We heard a train pulling up to a platform. This was our cue if we wanted to be certain that no kid from another school had a chance to escape us. We'd done it before and got it down to a T.

We jumped the barrier, sprinted down the stairs banging into people just off the train as they came up. When we got to the platform the train was creeping off. We ran beside it, opened the doors and jumped aboard as it accelerated away. Perfect. Our enemy was trapped until we got to the next station.

We fanned through the train shouting, 'Here we are! Come on, then.' As soon as they saw us, kids from other schools were up and the fighting started. There was some punching but it was mostly wrestling.

I spotted a kid from another school sitting by the window, clearly wanting nothing to do with what was happening. I'd change that, I thought.

I went up to him. He looked me in the eyes, like a puppy, and raised his right arm. It was encased in a plaster cast covered with graffiti.

Without a word, I walked away. I didn't get far. He hit me on the side of the head with the cast, then hit me again. I punched his nose, and knocked him into the seat he'd been sitting in.

I heard the train slowing and through the window I saw the platform at the next station. We opened the doors and jumped out. A few minutes later, we caught a train back to South Hampstead, leapt over the barrier and caught the thirty-one bus home.

I was in school with my mate Francis – Frank to his friends. He worked in an off-licence in Lancefield Street, opposite the Royal Lancer, where Dad and the others were arrested.

'Listen,' said Frank.

'What?'

'I need someone to give me a hand at work,' he said.

'Right.'

'So I've put your name forward.'

God bless you, Frank, I thought. Dad away, Mum struggling, there wasn't much money at home. A job would change all that. I couldn't wait to start.

With Frank, I went straight from school to the off-licence. The couple who ran the business interviewed me. Tom and Bridget were Irish: they lived in the flat above the shop and they had a new baby, who kept Bridget busy. They knew Mum. They had seen her sometimes on her way to work. Well, everyone knew Mum, didn't they?

They knew Dad too. Many a time, before he was arrested, he'd been in to buy his Old Holborn before he went into the Royal Lancer.

I got the job.

I couldn't wait to tell Mum. I ran home. 'Mum! Mum! Mum!' I shouted, as I dashed through the hall.

Mum was in the kitchen making dinner. She saw the smile on my face as I burst in. 'Well?'

'I got a job! I got a job!' I said.

'What job?' she said. 'Where?'

'The off-licence, the one opposite the Lancer. I have to start straight away, soon as I've had my tea. Tom's expecting me.'

I bolted my food and set off. I cut through the Mozart Estate and came out on the far side by the Royal Lancer. I hadn't thought about Dad when I'd passed it on my way to the interview because when I did, like when I was trying to go to sleep, as sometimes happened, I always ended up crying. But with the excitement of having got the job I couldn't stop myself thinking about him now. I imagined putting my head through the door of the pub, calling him out and telling him my news. 'Dad, I got a job.'

'Where?'

'In the offy.'

'Across the road?'

'Yeah.'

'Well done, son.'

Then I imagined him looking at the watch that would be mine one day, and saying, 'You don't want to be late, son. You want to get a move on.' Then he was waving to me as I crossed the road and I was waving back, and then he was disappearing through the doors of the pub, which were swinging shut after him . . .

I opened the door of the off-licence and went in. Frank was behind the counter with Tom. It was a dark wooden one, shaped like an L with a flap that lifted to let you go behind. Tom said he'd pop upstairs to check on Bridget and the baby. 'Yeah, sure,' I said. He was going upstairs for a drink. I knew the signs.

He hurried off.

'Come on.' Frank took me down the corridor at the back. A small storeroom was filled with spirits and wine, another with crisps, nuts, cigarettes and tobacco. 'You'll never have to buy another packet of fags,' he said.

Not with a room full of them, I thought, and pocketed the first of what I knew would be many packets.

We continued the tour. The third room was the coldest and biggest. This was where the deliveries were made, and where the beer and lager were stored.

'What about Bridget?' I asked. 'Is she ever down?'

'We don't see much of her,' said Frank. 'It's mostly Tom we have to deal with.'

We went back into the shop. I took fifty pence from the till. A few customers came in. We served them. One or two of our mates appeared. We didn't charge them.

A bit later Tom came down. He smelt of drink. We'd have to charge everyone from now on, but no matter, we'd had a good evening.

Then the time to shut came, the 'closed' sign went up and I set off home.

A few days later Mum was on the doorstep at number forty-three, bags of shopping at her feet. I opened the door when I heard her outside, just in time to see a police car stop at the kerb. The window on the driver's side was wound down and the policeman behind the wheel leant out. It was Flash Harry – Mum's name for him. He was a right bastard. All the lads on the street knew him, and some had been at the end of his boot.

'If we can't get you,' he said, 'we'll get your son.' Then he said something about Mum being an IRA bomber, had a good laugh about it and drove off.

A few days later I turned fourteen.

It was the day Mum had said I'd go with her to see Dad. We got into the jail and then into the visiting room. There were bars on the windows and the paint was grey. I knew the man sitting across from us was my dad and yet I didn't think of him as my dad any more. I never came home now to find him in the lounge playing his dictionary game with a mate, or snoozing on the sofa after the pub. He was out of my orbit.

'Here, son,' said Dad, 'why don't you hold my watch.' He undid the strap and passed it across.

'Take that watch back now,' shouted a screw. 'Prisoners are forbidden to hand personal items to visitors.'

I couldn't work it out. I'd always been allowed to hold it in the past. Why not now?

It was yet one more thing that made no sense.

16

The adventure playground in Ilbert Street had been pulled down and replaced with a new one in Caird Street. I helped to build it, with the rest of the area's lads, and then I helped to brighten it up with some paint. I loved to muck around there but I also loved the old site in Ilbert Street. It was now just waste ground and became a new meeting point for my mates and me.

We got stuff out of the condemned houses in Ilbert Street – floorboards, doors, sheets of corrugated iron – and built makeshift camps. Then we had battles, one camp versus another, throwing stones, half-bricks, anything we could get our hands on, at each other. Someone always got hit on the head but it was fun.

Then the builders moved on to the site. They put up sheds to store everything they'd need for the renovations they'd be doing to the houses still standing in Ilbert and Farrant Streets.

One evening, after they had gone home, we broke into the site. All their machines were parked in a corner. They were like Tonka toys, the same colour but a lot bigger. Among them was a dumper truck with the starting handle stuck in the engine at the back. Two of us turned it, giving it everything we had, and the engine roared into life, with a puff of black smoke. Next the engine was ticking, like a fast heartbeat, and the truck was rocking from side to side. Someone climbed up, put it in gear, took off the handbrake and off they went.

Everyone had a turn driving it around the building site, with kids sitting in the front part that tips up, laughing and telling the driver to go faster. A corrugated-iron fence surrounded the site, so no one could see us – but they could fucking hear us. The poor old dumper truck had never worked so hard in all its mechanical life. At the end of the evening we hid the starting handle so we could always be sure of getting the truck started.

We went back often. Inevitably someone called the police. As the patrol car approached we saw the blue light over the corrugated fence. We jumped off the truck and ran into the gardens at the back of Farrant Street. Here we hid until the police had gone and it was safe to come out.

Over the following weeks and months we'd always see the blue light before the police arrived and hide, and then we'd go back next day after the workmen had gone home. It was just so brilliant, breaking in, starting the dumper and driving it around, though we were fed up with the police stopping our fun. I'm sure they were getting fed up too.

One evening, on the site, someone had a new idea. Why not rig it up so it would drive itself without anyone at the wheel? The police would be welcome to come then. Not a bad idea, we thought, and set to work.

We got the old dumper truck started, turned the steering wheel as far to the left as it would go and wedged a piece of wood under it to hold it there. Next we wedged the accelerator with another bit of wood so the engine was roaring. Then the handbrake came off and down we jumped. Off went the dumper truck, round and round, looking like it was going faster and faster each time it made a circle. We stood well back to watch. We weren't worried that it might run us over. We knew it wouldn't be long before the police turned up and we wanted to be sure we could get away.

Sure enough, a few minutes later, the blue light of the car sent to investigate was flashing over the top of the fence. We disappeared like rats into the gardens of the surrounding houses to watch what happened next.

The police came on to the site. It was dark and they thought someone was driving the dumper. They shouted and waved their arms. We laughed our heads off.

Then they twigged. There wasn't anyone driving. They needed to get up on the truck to stop it, or it would keep going all night.

The first man got alongside and tried to jump up. But the truck was like a raging bull, kicking up mud and bucking. He couldn't make it so another tried. He failed too. In the end there was only one thing they could do: wait for it to run out of fuel. Eventually that was what happened: as the tank began to empty the truck slowed and a policeman scrambled up to stop it.

I'd seen it all now. As I ran home I couldn't stop laughing, and I didn't stop until I fell asleep.

I was in the off-licence. It was Thursday. The bin men came on Friday. Frank and I flattened the boxes as we were meant to, then took the rubbish and a box of spirits to the place where the rubbish was collected, around the corner in Bravington Road. We piled the rubbish up and hid the spirits beneath it.

'All right, Tom?' said Frank, when we went back in. 'We put the rubbish out.'

'You're good lads,' he said.

'We hope so,' said Frank.

'Yes,' I agreed.

And it was true. When Tom was around, we did work. We kept the storerooms tidy, we mopped the floors, and we stocked the shelves. It was fun. In fact, Frank and I were almost running the place.

Later that night we went to Bravington Road, picked up the box of spirits and carried it to a house in the Avenues where we knew there was going to be a blues party. We rang the bell. A man answered the door. We showed him the box. 'You interested?'

He paid on the spot. We went away and split the money.

We pulled this stunt on many a Thursday and many a Sunday night – the bin men came on Monday too. We could have got a lot more money but we were happy with what we made and it wasn't as if it was hard work.

One afternoon in the early spring of 1975 I was on my way home from school when a car pulled up and out jumped Flash Harry. Before I could make a run for it, he grabbed my arm, opened the back door, flung me across the back seat and got in beside me. I was for it, I knew, unless I could get away. The best chance was the door opposite the one I'd been thrown in through. If I could get it open, maybe I could escape.

I slid down the seat, reaching for the handle. But I never got to it because he yanked me back and hit me on the head two or three times. Then he slammed his door and the driver moved off sharply.

He punched and slapped me round the head some more, shouting at me between blows. I didn't take it all in but I heard enough to get the gist. I was an IRA bastard and if we fucking Maguires thought we were above the law, well, we'd better think again because we were going to get taught a fucking lesson, a fucking lesson we would never fucking forget.

'Take your hands off me,' I shouted. 'Leave me alone.'

I was wriggling and ducking, sticking my elbows out, covering my head with my arms, throwing my fists in his direction, but it was an uneven contest. He was big and strong while I was slender, petite as Mum sometimes said, lightly built and not very tall.

After a while, I realized the car had stopped and the door on my side had swung open. Flash Harry shoved me sideways. I tumbled out and landed in the road.

The door slammed. I heard the tyres squeal. When I got up the car was some way down the road. It was a relief to see the back of it.

My face and shoulders hurt and my knuckles felt as if I'd punched a wall. I hobbled on to the pavement and looked around. I was in a residential street in Maida Vale. The houses were big and white. I pointed myself towards home and I trudged off with my head down. My face was swollen, and wet with tears.

When I got home Mum asked what happened. At first I said I'd had a fight with someone. Then she got the truth. She contacted the A.10, the internal Metropolitan Police complaints unit, but, as had happened before and would happen again, she got nowhere.

After this, Flash Harry and other policemen would sometimes meet me on my way home from school and give me a going-over. If I was lucky it was just verbal abuse. They always said more or less the same thing: Mum was an IRA cunt, we Maguires were all IRA bastards, and why didn't I fuck off back to Belfast where I came from? They also liked to remind me that sooner or later they'd get me, and when they did they'd teach me a lesson I'd never fucking forget, and that I'd be going to prison for a very long time too.

Usually, though, they'd yank me into their car or the back of their van. I only got away if they stopped me near Paddington recreation ground. If I could get in through the gates I was safe because they couldn't drive after me. But then they got wise. If I got into Paddington rec, they would drive to the far side and catch me coming out. So that escape route was closed.

Once they had me in the car or the van, the pasting would start. I would always try to put up a fight, which didn't help. But fuck it, I thought, I was going to get the shit kicked out of me anyway so I might as well.

When they'd had enough and were too tired to thump me any more, they'd push me out into a street somewhere. I got dumped all over west London: Edgware Road, Bayswater Road, Queensway, Kilburn High Road. I knew those streets: I'd been to them shopping with Mum. They were quite a way from home and so then I'd have to walk back to Third Avenue, like a wounded soldier.

It was all a long way from *Dixon of Dock Green* and the old style of policeman who sent you home with a clip around the ear.

Mum had never been one for going out and leaving us alone, especially after she got bail and we were waiting for the trial. However, when some friends invited her to bingo, she thought she might go as she hadn't been out for a while. We thought she should too, and it was decided that she'd go.

The evening came. Mum gave us our tea. Then she got ready, put some money on the kitchen table in case we wanted chips later, and left.

After an hour or two, everyone decided they wanted chips. How I was volunteered for the chip run, I don't know but I was. I decided I'd cycle, except my bike had a flat tyre so I borrowed Anne-Marie's, pale pink, with a little white basket on the front that would be handy for the chips.

I started pedalling down Third Avenue towards the Harrow Road. The chip shop was at the bottom on the other side from number forty-three. It was getting dark, and rather than hang around in the street my mates were at their homes. This was a relief. I didn't want them to see me.

Then, suddenly, a police siren was blaring behind me and a blue light was flashing. A car drew up alongside and Flash Harry was at the wheel. He looked like a madman. He was waving frantically and shouting through the open passenger window. I didn't hear what he said but I got the message. He wanted me to stop and it wasn't to say, 'Hello.'

I mounted the pavement and flew on. The police car kept going beside me but now that there were parked cars between us, I felt better, safer. In fact, I was doing all right, I thought, and Evel Knievel would have been proud of me. If I'd had my own bike, a Chopper, I'd have got away – but, like the great man himself, I took a tumble. A car door opened in front of me. I managed to scoot round it but lost control. I went over the handlebars and landed near someone's front garden. The wind was knocked out of me and I was stunned.

I tried to stand up, thinking perhaps I might run, while Flash Harry had braked, jumped out and run over to me. A couple of punches followed on the nose and the mouth. My lip split. There was blood on my tongue. Now I made an effort to get up and run but he held my arm and gave me another couple of punches, this time to the side of my head. My left ear took the brunt. It was so painful, I thought it had fallen off.

I wasn't on for any more of this. I somehow got to my feet, turned away, and at the same time lowered my head to avoid the next thump. He called me a 'little shit' and kicked me from behind. 'Whose bike is this?' he said.

'My sister's,' I said.

'No, it ain't.' He hit me again.

'It *is* my sister's.'

'No, it ain't.' He thumped me yet again.

'I swear.'

After a while, he let me go. He was exhausted and he knew I wouldn't change my answer. He carried the bike to his car and tried to put it into the back. It wouldn't go so he threw it on to the pavement and gave it a kick. Then he made his way round to the driver's side, got in and drove away.

I bought the chips, then set off for home, dragging the bicycle behind. When I got back, having no key, I knocked.

John answered. 'You didn't forget the salt and vinegar, did you?'

I was at the off-licence. I'd been there ten or fifteen minutes on my own with Tom. 'Where's Frank?' I asked.

'I sacked him,' said Tom.

'Why?'

'For always being late.'

It was true. Frank was usually late but I wasn't having that. 'If he can't work here, I won't,' I said.

Tom didn't put up much of a fight. 'Go round to his house and get him,' he said.

I went to Frank's and knocked. He came out. 'I got you your job back,' I said.

'Really?'

'Yeah.'

He seemed pleased. 'I've just got to get myself ready,' he said, 'and we can walk back together. Will you hang on?'

I waited a long time. Now we were both late, but at least we were back in business.

17

It was summer, and I hung around the streets with my mates on the long evenings and at weekends.

Halfway up Bravington Road there was a chocolate factory – that was what we called it, anyway. It was a big building full of food. You name it, they had it. One Saturday, all the kids in our gang got in and had the biggest food fight ever. Then everyone filled boxes with stuff, either to bring home or to sell. John and I were the only ones who didn't. If we'd taken anything home Mum would have done her nut. We weren't stupid though. We packed a box and gave it to a mate and told him to bring it round later, saying it was a gift. We didn't know whether Mum would believe this but she did.

The following day, Sunday, Anne-Marie was making her first Holy Communion. John and I got into our Sunday best. There was still plenty of time before we were due at church. 'We're just popping out,' said John. 'Won't be long.'

We half expected Mum to say no, you can't, not on your sister's big day, but to our surprise she said, 'Okay.' Then she told us what time we had to be back, and to keep clean.

In the street outside we found some mates. We ran to Bravington Road and broke into the factory. We hadn't been in long when someone shouted, 'Police!'

They swarmed in, and we scattered. John, a mate and I were on the first floor and heard the police running up the stairs. We headed for the roof but were grabbed before we got there, punched and slapped, dragged outside and taken to the Harrow Road nick. There, we were booked and thrown into a cell together.

Our nice clean white shirts were filthy.

'We have to get to our sister's Holy Communion,' shouted John, 'so you'd better fucking let us out.'

The cell door opened. John was punched and slapped, then thrown back in.

Eventually, Uncle Hugh came. John told him the officers had hit him, so he had a word with a policeman: if they dropped the three charges against us, he'd say no more about the hitting. The police agreed, and we left the station. We'd missed Anne-Marie's Holy Communion. On the way home, Uncle Hugh gave each of us, John, our mate and me, a good slap.

It was a Saturday not long after this. Mum set off with Anne-Marie to see Dad in prison (Anne-Marie in her Holy Communion dress so Dad could see how she looked) and Vincent went off somewhere too. This left just John and me at home on our own. I had some money and I decided to go to the shop on the corner of Ilbert Street for sweets. I sauntered along the pavement and found a group of mates playing 'Penny off the Kerb'. As I passed them, the questions started.

'You and John coming out?'

'Don't know.'

'Ah, come on.'

'Maybe later.'

Mum had asked me not to go out that afternoon – with the beatings I was getting she didn't like me being out when she wasn't around – and I was trying to be good.

I went on to the shop. Inside, it smelt of boiled sweets, sugar and chocolate. I chose some chews and other things. The shopkeeper put them into a white paper bag. I paid. He nodded.

I came out of the shop, fished a sweet from the bag and put it into my mouth. Then I saw a police van parked by my mates.

An officer was sitting at the wheel and two others were on the pavement. From the way my mates were standing, I could tell that they were being told off for smoking in the street, hanging around and getting up to no good.

I didn't want to get involved. I put my head down and walked past without making eye contact.

I was further down the pavement when I heard a bang, which made me turn.

The police van had just moved off when one of my mates had thrown something and hit the back.

Well, that was that. The van stopped, the doors opened and policemen piled out. Strangely, it wasn't towards my mates they now ran but to me.

'Maguire!' one shouted. 'Come here, you little fucker.'

Bollocks, I thought, and ran, shouting ahead to John to open the door. When I got there I pounded on it, yelling his name.

John was quick to open it and saw the police coming down the street behind me. I dashed in and he went to close the door but he wasn't quick enough. The police got to it first. We both pushed it frantically – my sweets were now all over the carpet, popping under my feet, and the door was nearly coming off its hinges. That was all we needed, I thought, Mum coming home to find sweets ground into the hall carpet and no front door.

I needn't have worried because that wasn't going to happen. They were men and we were boys, and we were never going to keep them out.

They forced the door back, knocked John to the floor, and two grabbed me, an arm each. They pulled me into the street and ran me towards the police van. There was a lamp-post in the way, which they clearly wanted me to collide with. I swung my legs up and got my feet on to the post, but they pulled me round it to the back of the van. They got the doors open and threw me in. Then they climbed in after me and closed the door. Now I was in a dark metal box with two policemen. I was quite small and young and they were quite big and grown-up. They started hitting and kicking me. I tried to get into the corner where at least I could keep half my body out of the way, but no sooner had I got there than they flung me against the wall on the other side, not hard for them as I was light as well as small. I slid down on to the bench. At least there was something to hold on to. While one tried to prise my fingers free, the other slapped and punched me. There was just pain and noise but it was far away now and I was somewhere they couldn't get at me.

Next thing, the van was stopping. Without my noticing it had been moving. The doors opened and we were in the yard at the back of the Harrow Road police station.

I was dragged inside and booked, probably for resisting arrest. Then I was taken to a cell and slapped around some more. Finally, the cell door slammed and I was alone.

It was several hours before the door opened again. I was brought back to the front desk, where Mum was waiting. She saw the conditioon I was in and tears welled in her eyes.

When we out outside the streetlights were on.

'They made me wait a very long time,' said Mum, 'until they brought you up.'

* * *

Before our troubles Mum had always worked and Dad, who was at home then, would keep an eye on the kids while she was out. Now, with Dad in prison, she couldn't do this. She had to fit the work in around us, with the result that she did less work, which, in turn, meant less money. Things were tight at forty-three.

One night I was at the off-licence and Tom was upstairs with his wife. There was a five-pound note in one of the trays. I'd taken coins before but never a note. I lifted it out and slipped it into my pocket.

When I got home, I shouted, 'Hello, Mum.'

She shouted something back from the kitchen. She sounded busy. Good. I didn't want to be disturbed in case she thought I was nicking from her. I found her handbag, opened her purse, slipped the note inside, then put it and the handbag back where I'd found them. She'd never know, I thought, and she didn't, not that time, not all the other times.

On another evening when I came in from work I found her sitting in the front room watching the TV. This was the perfect moment to ambush her. 'These are for Dad,' I said.

If you're going to steal, make it worthwhile – it's still nicking however little you take. I dropped five or six pouches of Old Holborn, some cigarette papers and matches on to her lap. She'd a visit in a day or two and she always brought Dad something to smoke.

'Where did you get them?' she said, looking at me hard.

'From the off-licence,' I said.

'Did you steal them?'

'Yes. I took them,' I said. 'Took' sounded better than 'stole', I thought. 'There's a storeroom full of tobacco and that.' A few pouches wouldn't be missed was what I meant.

I could tell from her expression that she wasn't happy. 'You can bring them back tomorrow,' she said. 'You know it's wrong.'

'I can't bring them back.'

'Why not?'

'Because,' I said, and went up the stairs.

The next day nothing was said and after that I often brought things from the off-licence before her visits to Dad.

* * *

I started nicking from shops, anything I could get into my pockets or a bag. Then it was motorbikes, easy to take and start up: often a screwdriver was all you needed. I loved them. My mates and I would take them down to the canal and race them up and down the towpath, going as fast as we dared.

Next it was cars. I used to go out with a mate, Luggy – he's dead now. He'd a bag of car keys. We would walk the streets together, trying this car, then that, until we got lucky, and we always did. It was a lot easier back then. Cars didn't have complicated security systems, and people seemed to leave them unlocked more often. Then all we had to do was start her up, and one of Luggy's many keys usually did the trick.

When we began, Luggy did the driving because he knew how to do it and I'd sit in the front passenger seat and watch him. As he drove, he'd tell me what he was doing. Then he'd find somewhere quiet and I'd have a go.

Then came a night when, using either a screwdriver or a borrowed key, I nicked a Mini somewhere in the Avenues with a different mate, and this time, as there was no Luggy, I did all the driving. We went round the Avenues. I was hoping I'd pass some of my mates. I wanted them to see me driving. I was exhilarated. I was in charge, powering along, going where I wanted.

The only trouble was, I was fourteen and every officer at the Harrow Road police station knew me by sight. A fair number of them thought I was a mass murderer and I needed manners put on me. Under these circumstances, my first night of driving could only end badly.

The end came as we were turning a corner in the Avenues. We passed a police car. The driver and the officer in the front passenger seat saw me. I realized they had and, worse, I saw the delight on their faces.

I put my foot down and screeched off. Behind me I heard the siren and then, a few seconds later, a whirling blue light was in my rear-view mirror.

I sped down one of the Avenues' narrow streets, cars parked on either side. I knew there was no way they could overtake, which was good. On the other hand, there was no way I could escape. But there we were. I was in front; they were behind. I wasn't going to stop. But they weren't alone. They had back-up. My pursuers must have radioed for help because suddenly a police van was blocking my way to the Harrow Road.

But we weren't caught yet. My mate and I could still run. I stood on the brake, and as soon as the car had slowed to a reasonable speed, we bailed out. Unfortunately I forgot to apply the handbrake, so the Mini sailed on, slowly, sedately. And here's where it got interesting, though I only heard this later.

The driver of the police van saw the Mini coming. It was going slowly and he had time to act. He got out of the way. Now the road wasn't blocked: it was open, empty, and it led in a straight line to the Harrow Road. The stolen Mini cruised out on to the Harrow Road, narrowly missing a number eighteen bus, and came to a halt on the far side when the front wheels hit the pavement. It was a happy outcome: if it hadn't stopped it would have parked itself in a shop window.

But back to me: when we bailed out, my mate and I went different ways. He disappeared into the night but I ran back up the street I'd driven down. It wasn't long before I met, coming the other way, the policemen from the car that had been chasing us.

'Maguire!' one shouted.

They hadn't got me yet and I wasn't giving up that easily.

I ran back down the street. Maybe I could dodge the two from the van coming up towards me. If I could get past them and on to the Harrow Road . . .

Out of the corner of my eye I saw a front door open and a man come out to look at what was going on. I hardly paid him any attention, which was a mistake. As I passed, he grabbed me. I kicked at his legs so he wrapped his arms round me and lifted me into the air. He didn't let go until the police came up. And they were delighted. They had me.

Meanwhile, the lad who had been with me had reached the Harrow Road. He found John and some others by the chip shop. He told them what had happened and they ran back to see if they could help. By the time they got to the scene, I was already cuffed and in the back of the police car, with a policeman laying into me.

We got to the station and I was dragged inside. I felt sick, and I wanted my mum to come down and take me home where I would be safe and nothing could happen. At the same time, I felt hard, defiant. I'd fucking show them. I wouldn't cry. They could do their worst. Bring it on.

In the room with the counter the cuffs came off. But there was no booking. The officer from the police car dragged me to a cell. The door was open. He threw me in and said something. I didn't hear it but I turned. Then he delivered a blow straight to my nose with as much force as he could.

I hit the concrete floor. Blood was pouring out of my nose into my mouth. My head was throbbing from all the punches I'd taken in the car. Perhaps now he'd be happy, I thought. I wasn't going to get up in a hurry. I hoped he'd leave me alone.

He had other ideas. He came into the cell. He started to kick me, and when he couldn't get a good kick in, he stamped on my chest. My face and my head were on fire. I rolled myself into a ball and put my arms over my head and face. I was desperate for him to stop and leave me alone to cry.

But he didn't. He went on kicking and stamping, kicking and stamping, kicking and stamping. All I could do was wait for it to stop. But it went on and on and on . . .

Then I heard the cell door bang. He was gone and, like a football in the corner of the school playground, I didn't move. I wanted to be absolutely sure he had gone and that he wasn't coming back. Eventually I lifted my head. The door was closed. He really had gone.

It was a relief to know that but then the pain set in all over my body. From the tips of my toes to my skull I ached like I'd never ached before.

Then the cogs started to turn. He'd be back, wouldn't he? Of course he would. Maybe with a friend or two. They'd open the door and pile into me. I strained my ears.

Every time I heard a footstep, a key turning, prisoners calling or any kind of noise outside, I thought, Hopefully, someone's coming to my cell. They're going to let me out. I'm going home.

Finally, the cell door opened, and to my surprise, Luggy was with the policeman who'd given me the beating. The officer pointed at me and told Luggy I'd grassed. He said I'd told the police that we'd stolen the Mini together, and that while Luggy had got away I'd got caught. Later, I discovered that a mate of ours had told them this (to put the police off) but all I could do now was deny it and hope Luggy believed me.

'Bollocks,' I said. 'I've not seen him all night.'

Luggy gave me a wink (he knew it was bollocks) and asked if I was all right. Before I could answer the cell door was banged shut.

Later, someone from CID interviewed me. I said only that Luggy hadn't been with me in the car. I said it was someone else but as I'd never met him before, I couldn't say who he was. That was nonsense but the officers didn't seem to give a shit. They had me, and that was enough for them.

Later still, I was brought out to the front of the station. Mum was waiting. When she saw me, I could tell from her expression I looked bad. She turned to the nearest policemen. 'Who has done this to my son?' she asked.

She got a snigger or two but she didn't get an answer.

They let us go. As soon as we were out in the street Mum said she wanted my lumps and bumps looked at. We went to St Mary's, just up the road. There, X-rays were taken. I'd a broken nose, a cut lip and a size-ten boot print on my chest. 'What happened?' asked the doctor.

'He was in the Harrow Road police station,' said Mum.

'Ah,' said the doctor. 'I've seen a lot of patients with the same injuries as your son after a visit there, and I'm so sick of it that I'll come to court with my X-rays and my notes on his injuries and I'll speak on his behalf.'

When the time came for this trial the doctor couldn't be found, or his notes, or the X-rays. We went to the court anyway but as the bombings case was about to start at the Old Bailey we were told that it had been adjourned. If I got off, we understood, a new date would be set for the car-theft case to be heard.

One Sunday afternoon a mate and I went up to Beethoven Street, which runs from Third Avenue to Kilburn Lane, and broke into a factory. We'd hoped it'd be full of good stuff to nick but it wasn't, just table lamps packed in cardboard boxes. We searched the main office, and one or two other rooms, but there wasn't anything for us there either.

Then, in a loading bay, we came across a van with its keys.

'Tell you what we'll do,' my mate said. 'We'll fill the back with lamps and drive it out.'

'Great idea,' I said. At least we'd get something out of it.

We filled the back of the van with boxes. That was easy. All that remained was to start it and drive off.

We turned the key in the ignition. Not a glimmer of life. We tried again and again. Nothing. The van was dead. It wasn't going anywhere.

Now that Plan A had failed we moved to Plan B. We set the van and the factory on fire, and then, a lamp under my arm, we left. It had taken quite a long time to break in but we were out much quicker.

When we got into Beethoven Street the fire was really going. Windows had shattered with the heat and thick black smoke was pouring out.

We started to run and two fire engines appeared, followed by a police car, all heading for the factory. Oh, no. With my reputation the police would scoop me up instantly.

We stopped running, dropped our heads and walked on while the sirens and blue lights roared towards us, then turned into a little alley that ran down to the Mozart Estate. Now we were out of view, we could run, and we sprinted as fast as our legs would carry us. We wanted to get as far away from those policemen and the fire as we could.

When we stopped, well away from the factory and Beethoven Street, we sat down, got out our fags and lit up. We could see black smoke from the factory rising above the rooftops, and we could hear another fire engine racing in the distance.

Time passed. There was still plenty of smoke but there were no more sirens. It was safe to go home, or so we thought. We decided we'd go to my house, 43 Third Avenue.

We had an uneventful walk until we came round the last corner. There was a police car right outside the front door and Mum was talking to an officer. A lot of my mates were there too, sitting on the wall just below the front-room windows. And in the sky you could see black smoke from the burning factory.

Did I turn? Did I run? But if the police saw me running, they would come after me, and then they'd kick the shit out of me until I told them what they wanted to know.

There was only one thing to do. With the lamp tucked under my arm, my mate and I walked towards the little crowd outside my house, and when we got there, we sat down between some mates on the wall and I dropped the box behind us.

From there I could hear Mum and the policeman and it wasn't long before I'd everything worked out. It wasn't me the police were looking for but another kid. He was a mate and he was standing on the front doorstep beside Mum with a strange look on his face: worried and defiant at the same time. His name was Terry and he's now my sister's partner. The police thought he'd done the factory fire and they wanted to nick him.

'He hasn't done it,' Mum said. 'He couldn't have, for the simple reason that he's been outside my house since before the fire started. I saw him with my own eyes. It wasn't him. Couldn't be. I'm sure of it.'

The policeman went back to his car. In the back there were two boys who had apparently seen two other boys running out of the factory shortly after it was set on fire.

'You see him?' said the policeman to the two witnesses, and pointed at the lad beside Mum. 'Is he one of the boys you saw running away?'

The witnesses stared at him from the back of the police car.

What would I do if they said he was the one they saw running

176

off? He'd be charged for the fire I'd started. I couldn't have that. If they did, I'd have to put my hand up and say it was me, not him. Now it only remained to be seen whether I'd have to.

I sat very still, my head cocked, listening carefully. Come on, I thought, say your piece, you two.

Finally, one shook his head. 'No,' he said, 'he wasn't one of them.'

'No, it wasn't him, definitely,' the other said.

The policeman pointed at the rest of us, sitting on the wall under the window. 'What about this lot?' he asked. 'Did you see any of them running out of the factory?'

They stared.

'No,' said one.

'No,' said the other. 'It wasn't any of them.'

The policeman got into his car and drove off. He'd drive around and hope his witnesses spotted the culprits out of the back window.

The crowd cleared. I went indoors and gave Mum her new lamp.

18

While I was on bail I went to Middle Temple several times to see our legal people. I found those visits baffling and didn't understand what was being said. Mostly I thought about the fag I'd have when I got out. Fortunately, Vincent was always there to do the talking and listening.

What I got from the meetings was this: we were all going to court and when we got there someone with a fucking brain was going to explain that they had the wrong people, and then the court would let us go home.

As for prison, I never thought about it, ever, all the time I was on bail – at least, not as somewhere we'd be going. Why would I? We hadn't done what they said. Prison was just the place I'd seen Mum and was still seeing Dad. And I was sick of visiting Dad in prison but after the trial I'd never have to go inside another, would I? That was what I thought, when I thought, before the trial, about prison . . .

It was Monday, 26 January 1976, two months from my fifteenth birthday. It was lunchtime. I was in the Quintin Kynaston dinner hall with friends. They knew the score so it was possible that the talk was about the trial, which was due to start the next day, Tuesday, 27 January. On the other hand, it is possible it wasn't mentioned. What I can remember, though, is this. I had a bowl in front of me. There was custard, thick and yellow, and under it was the pudding. I didn't know what it was because I hadn't paid any attention when it was being dished out.

I dug my spoon in and out came fleshy red rhubarb. I put the spoon down. 'I hate rhubarb,' I said. Someone else could have it.

Before I could give it away, the younger brother of a mate grabbed my bowl. 'If you don't want it, I'll have it,' he said. But he hadn't asked. He hadn't said 'please'.

'No, you can't,' I said. 'Let go.'

'No,' he said.

'Let go.'

He wouldn't. I pulled. He tugged. I won. You cocky little sod, I thought, I'll show you not to take without asking. I put the bowl upside-down on his head. Custard dripped over his ears and face. He pushed the bowl off. It fell on to the table.

'You didn't even want your rhubarb. What you do that for?' he said.

'Headmaster's office now, both of you,' someone shouted.

We trailed through the corridors, got to the headmaster's door and went into his office.

'Right,' said the headmaster, pointing at the other lad. 'Go to the toilets and get cleaned up. Come back when you're done, quick as you can now.'

The lad went off.

'What was all that about in the dinner hall?' asked the head.

'I don't know,' I said innocently. 'I thought you wanted to see me about the trial.'

'Oh, yes,' he said, as if he hadn't forgotten when I knew he had. 'I want to wish you all the best,' he said, 'and I hope to see you back here soon.'

'Thank you, sir.'

He wrote something on a bit of paper, then handed it to me. 'You can have the rest of the day off,' he said. 'Go on.'

I put his note carefully in my pocket. This one wouldn't be going in the bin like so many others, oh, no.

'On your way out,' he said, 'tell the other boy to come in, please.'

He was in the corridor outside, his hair dripping. 'He'll see you now,' I said, as I walked past.

'Wanker,' he said. I didn't care. This wanker was going home and he wasn't.

I made my way out of school. I felt good but then I heard the headmaster's words in my head: 'I hope to see you back here soon.' The very fact that he'd said it made me think, for the first time ever, that perhaps the opposite was equally possible and he wouldn't see me again.

Horrible thought. I hurried up the road and saw my bus, the thirty-one, pulling up at the bus stop. I jumped on to the platform at the back as it was pulling away.

'Hold on tight,' shouted the conductor.

I ran up the stairs. There was only a handful of passengers on the top deck. I got the best seat, right at the front. The conductor came. I paid for my ticket and he went downstairs again. I was safe now.

I got my fags out and lit one. The bus was quiet, not like in the morning or late afternoon when it was full of noisy kids. I saw the road stretching ahead, the roofs of the cars in front, the pavements filled with people. This was lovely. Next thing though, as the bus trundled on, I heard the headmaster again: I hope to see you back here soon. I hope to see you back here soon.

If he hoped he'd see me it meant he wasn't sure he would. Why else would he have said it? Maybe I wasn't coming back. Or, at least, there was a possibility I wasn't. I might be found guilty. I might go to jail.

This hadn't occurred to me before, nor had Mum and Dad said anything about it. True, after the raid, my mates talked about it for a bit: but then time passed and they didn't mention it any more. As for me, I'd given it no thought. Before the raid I was just a boy: while after, almost overnight, I became a little fucker who didn't give his future any thought at all.

It was my last evening at the off-licence. I wouldn't be working while the trial was on. I knew I'd get back too late from court to go to work.

'Well, goodbye,' said Tom.

'Goodbye,' I said.

'Your job will be waiting when it's over,' he said. 'Don't forget now, will you?'

I thanked him, walked home and went straight up to my bedroom. John was lying on his bed, listening to music.

'Good night at work?' he asked.

'Yeah, not bad,' I said, and threw two packets of B&H at him.

On 27 January 1976, Mum got me up early. After a cup of coffee, I popped out to the shop. I bought a packet of ten No. 6 and ten tubes of Polos.

Back home again, I nipped up to my bedroom, inserted a fag into the middle of each packet of Polos, and then sealed the end so it didn't look as if I'd tampered with it.

With my pockets full of Polos we set off, Mum, Vincent and I. The police had said they'd come round and take us to court but we didn't want that. We took the tube into central London and walked to the Old Bailey. As we went in we were searched. The man found the Polos but not the fags. He said something about my sweet tooth and waved us on. I was delighted. Not only was I guaranteed a smoke in the bogs that day but now I had a system for getting fags in that'd work every day.

We were brought down to the holding area under the court.

Here, Dad, Sean, Pat and Giuseppe joined us. When it was time, we formed a line: Mum, Vincent, me, Dad, Giuseppe, Sean and Pat, then climbed the stairs to Court Two. For the rest of the day, the first of the trial, the so-called Maguire Seven sat in the dock.

At the end of the afternoon, we returned to the holding area. The men were taken back to prison, and Mum, Vincent and I were brought through the court and back to the front of the Old Bailey. We caught the tube home and had I been paying attention I might have noticed our case was in one or two evening papers that people around us were reading. Except for when the judge's sister died ('That's all we need,' Dad had said) and the court didn't sit for three or four days, this was the pattern I followed for the next six and a half weeks. At first it was good to be off school but I soon got bored: it was the same every day and I didn't know what was going on. Plus I missed my mates.

On Monday, 1 March, Mr Justice Donaldson started his summing up. It took him all day. Dad and the men were taken back to jail, while Mum, Vincent and I went home in the evening as usual.

On Tuesday, 2 March, the judge finished his summing up. After nearly seven weeks it was now time for the jury to make up their minds.

It was now afternoon, and I assumed that while the jury did what they did, Mum, Vincent and I would go home, as we did every evening. But the judge decided we too should be held in custody, with our four co-defendants, until the jury had reached a verdict. This took me by surprise. I didn't like the sound of it and a great wave of fear went through me as I imagined what might lie ahead.

The seven of us were taken from the dock and brought down below. Mum had her worried face on. It wasn't because of what might happen to her, she explained, but what might happen to Vincent and me. She hated the thought of us in custody. Dad told her that everything would be all right and she wasn't to be anxious.

The screws came to take him and the other three men away. They said goodbye and left.

Next an officer came for Mum. 'Be good, boys,' she said. 'Do as you're told and everything will be all right.'

'Don't worry, Mum,' Vincent said.

She gave us each a kiss, and then she was gone.

Vincent and I were put into a cell. What exactly was happening? Where was I going? I asked Vincent but he'd no idea. The door was unlocked and the officer in the doorway ordered Vincent out. He rubbed my head and told me he'd see me in the morning. He said I wasn't to worry.

The door closed, the key turned. I listened to Vincent and the screw walking away. Once they'd gone, there was silence. I was alone, in bits. Mum wouldn't be too pleased, I thought, when she found Vincent and I weren't together. Memories of the cell in Guildford flooded back. I felt anxious and hot, and soon sweat was running down my back.

I paced up and down the cell, biting the ends of my fingers and my nails, spitting out the bits. I hated being locked up, and I hated the uncertainty. I kept thinking, Where are they going to send me?

Then I thought, Maybe they're not sending me anywhere. Maybe I'm going to be here all night. That was a horrible idea. Now I wished someone, anyone, would come and tell me.

At last I heard footsteps, voices and the jingle of keys in the corridor. I put my ear to the door.

I was right. I had heard something and the noise was heading my way.

I didn't want to be discovered listening at the door so I sat on the bench. My heart was beating like a drum as the door opened. 'On your feet, lad,' said the screw. 'You're going with this man.'

I hadn't seen the other bloke because he'd been standing behind and to the side, but then the screw moved and I did. He wasn't in a uniform, just jeans and an old coat. He came into the cell pulling something out of his pocket that turned out to be hand-cuffs. Without saying a word, he cuffed us together, my left wrist to his right wrist.

The three of us went up the stairs and back into Court Two. It was empty now, apart from the cleaning woman mopping the floor. She gave me a half smile.

We went out the big doors and into the corridor outside. As we walked on we passed other courts and lots of people, all looking at me handcuffed to this bloke with an officer for an escort.

We reached the front and headed for the main doors, which I'd come through that morning with Mum and Vincent. It had never have occurred to me that I'd be leaving like this.

The screw left us and we went into the street, me and the bloke I was cuffed to. It was dark and raining lightly, not that I minded. I'd always liked the rain, ever since I was a kid and Anne-Marie and I would sometimes sit on the front porch wrapped in a blanket, watching the rain falling and people walking past.

The bloke led me to a red mini bus with its lights on and its engine running. I got into the front and he got in after me. I was now wedged between him and the driver.

There were kids in the back, all boys about my age, laughing, joking, scooting up and down the seats and having a wonderful time.

The driver shouted at them to pipe down. Then he put the minibus into gear and drove off. It wasn't long before the kids were playing about as before. That was when I realized they weren't cuffed.

'Can I have the cuff off?' I asked. 'It's hurting my wrist.'

'Oh, no, you're one of the bad boys.'

If only I was a bit skinnier, I thought, I wouldn't have had to ask. I could have just slipped it off.

The minibus moved on. The windscreen wiper flipped backwards and forwards. The demister was on, blowing hot air. The kids in the back were laughing as if they had been out somewhere good for the day. My escort and the driver were talking. They never stopped except when the driver told the kids in the back to pipe down. I watched the red tail-lights of the cars and buses in front, the people on the pavements with their umbrellas up, hurrying home, the shutters coming down on some shops for the night. I thought about Mum and Vincent – I knew where Dad was – and wondered how they were. And what about John and Anne-Marie? What were they doing? And where was I going?

Suddenly I saw we were on the Edgware Road, going north. Then the driver went up on to the Paddington flyover and from there on to the Westway. Next thing, we were over the Harrow Road. We weren't far from the house in Third Avenue. My stomach churned. Were we going to Shepherds Bush? If we were, I thought, then we must be going to Stamford House. Some of my mates had been in there, or their elder brothers had. It was a jail for boys aged twelve to seventeen, run by the local authority not the prison service.

The driver turned on to the spur that ran beside Notting Dale and came out at Shepherds Bush roundabout, then headed for Shepherds Bush Green. I'd guessed right. We were going to Stamford House on the Goldhawk Road, near the QPR ground. Could I remember anything my mates had said about it? No.

We arrived. The driver went through a gate, then headed for a building that made me think of an old people's home. He stopped and opened the door at the back. The kids piled out, ran to the building and disappeared inside.

The driver slammed the back door. Now it was my turn. The escort pulled me out and the driver got my other arm. He must be after overtime, I thought. I was handcuffed to a big bloke. Where did the driver think I was going?

Inside, the driver left us. My escort led me down a corridor to a white door with the word 'Doctor' painted on it in black. He knocked.

'Come in.'

I found myself in a room with an old woman behind a desk in a white doctor's coat. She stopped what she was doing. 'What have we here, then?'

'This is Patrick Maguire,' said my escort. 'He's come up from the Old Bailey.'

'And what have you been up to?' she asked me.

I said nothing.

She got a piece of paper from a drawer, asked me questions about myself and wrote down my answers. The questions finished, she passed me a small vase.

'Go into the toilet,' she said, 'and wee into that. It's over there.' She pointed at a door.

The handcuffs came off. I hurried off to the toilet.

'Come on, hurry up.' It was the escort.

I filled the vase to the top, then went back to the doctor's room and put it on her desk without spilling a drop. She was at the filing cabinet and had her back to me so she didn't see how careful I'd been.

The cuffs went on again. The escort was smiling. I was smiling. What a good boy I was, I thought. Not a drop spilt.

The doctor turned. 'You silly boy,' she shouted.

She was supposed to be pleased, not grumpy.

'I didn't mean fill it up. Go and empty it.'

Attached to my escort, I carried the vase back to the toilet and poured everything away.

We went back to the doctor's room. I put the empty vase on her desk.

'I didn't mean all of it!' she yelled.

The escort was shaking as if he wanted to laugh but couldn't let himself.

'Oh, take him away,' she said.

As soon as we got into the corridor and the doctor's door was closed, my escort started laughing. He went on as we crossed a yard and he rang a bell.

Two men opened the door. We walked in and one of this duo locked up behind me.

The cuffs came off. I was in a hall full of kids, including some from the minibus. They were running about, playing ping-pong and watching TV. It was like the youth club on a Tuesday or a Thursday night, same noise, same atmosphere, same smell.

The escort went off and the duo led me to a door and towards some stairs. I could have done with something to eat and drink but didn't know if I should ask. I couldn't see food but I could smell it – like in the dinner hall at school.

We climbed the stairs. The screaming and shouting of the kids in the hall fell away and instead there were just footsteps, theirs and mine. We came out into a corridor and walked past doors, one after another. Where were they taking me? I thought of Guildford again and felt hot.

At last we stopped outside a door. One of the duo took a bunch of keys from his pocket and opened it. I walked in before he got a chance to tell me. The door closed. The lock turned.

The room was dark. The only light was coming in through a window from outside. I went to look out. I saw the red minibus and the yard I'd walked across after I'd seen the doctor.

There was a bed under the window. I lay down and stared out at the night sky, the cloud a sort of pinky purple from all the streetlights below.

I wondered why I was there. I'd done nothing wrong. I thought about Mum and Dad and wished I was at home with them. If I went home, I decided, I'd never be late for school again. Never. I'd be up early and down the road in plenty of time for the bus. I'd be a brand-new child.

Then I thought about my mates. Did they know where I was? Well, of course not. But I'd tell them about it when I saw them next. They'd be so impressed.

Now came the questions. Did anyone know I was here? How long would I stay? A week? For ever?

Then I thought I could hear crying, very close, in the room with me. My heart raced. I'd thought I was by myself and the men who had locked me in hadn't said anything.

I sat up. There was a bed on the other side of the room.

'Who's there?' I called, because I couldn't see anybody.

'Leave me alone,' came a voice from under the covers.

'What's the matter?' I said. I used my nice voice.

'Leave me alone.'

I wish I could, I thought, but I'm locked in with you.

A head came out from under the bedclothes. It was a lad. I couldn't see him very well, just his outline. His face was in shadow.

'I've been in here for a week,' he said, 'and I've got another week to do. I fucking hate it here!'

I haven't been here two hours, I thought, and I fucking hate it too.

'What did you do?'

'Nicked a car.'

'And you got two weeks?'

'A week for nicking the car, the other week for running away from court.'

'So what's this place like, then?' I said.

'Stamford House?' he said. 'I don't know. I only get out for meals and a walk in the yard you can see from the window. I have no idea what it's like.'

That was my questions over. Now it was his turn.

'What you here for?' he said. 'What you do?'

'Something to do with nitro something or other,' I said. I still hadn't got the hang of the word. 'It's an explosive and I'm charged with handling it, but I never did.'

I remembered then. In my pocket I'd two packets of Polos, each with a No. 6 rammed down the middle, left over from the ten I took to court every day. 'Do you want a fag?' I said.

'Oh, yeah.'

I pulled them out, handed one to him, then broke the filter off mine.

'Why'd you do that?' he asked.

'The mint taste from the Polos gets in the filter,' I said. 'It makes it taste like a Consulate and I hate them.'

'Oh, right,' he said, and broke the filter off his.

I struck a match and got us lit. We sat in the dark, our cigarette ends glowing, and smoked. We talked about football, mates, where we lived, all sorts, and at some point I noticed he wasn't crying any more.

Later, I got under my covers in my clothes, and closed my eyes. I hope I'm not kept here for two weeks like this lad, I thought. At some point I fell asleep.

In the morning we were unlocked by two men and taken to a bathroom. We washed our faces. The men brought us downstairs to the dining room. It was full of noisy kids. We went to the servery and got our breakfast: two slices of bread, a pat of butter, a boiled egg and a cup of tea. The men led us to a table away from everyone else. We sat down and they stood behind us. I hadn't an egg cup. I turned to the man behind me. 'Could I have an egg cup?'

'Just fucking eat it,' he said.

I looked at the egg on my plate. I wanted to eat it but without an egg cup I didn't know how I'd manage.

Then I heard tapping on the table. The lad I'd spent the night with was breaking the shell of his egg, then peeling it off. 'Here,' he said.

He put the egg on my plate and took mine, which he peeled for himself. I squashed his egg inside the bread slices and wolfed it down, then drank the tea.

In a couple of minutes breakfast was done. We were handcuffed separately and brought out into the yard for our exercise. It was cold out there and it was raining too. We walked in a circle for a quarter of an hour. Then the two men brought us back inside, removed the cuffs and put us back in the room where we'd spent the night. We were dying for a fag. We ate my Polos instead.

An hour or so later, the door was opened. It was the man who'd brought me from court. He had the cuffs. I knew the routine. One went on me, the other on him. I said goodbye to the lad, and my escort led me out.

The red minibus was in the yard with the same driver and the same kids. We went through the gate and headed for the Old Bailey, following the route we'd come the night before. Every now and again the driver shouted at the kids in the back to pipe down.

They all knew where we were going and one said to me, 'Mate, what you done?'

I went to turn so I could answer, but my escort shouted at everyone in the back, 'Keep it down.'

That was the end of the conversation.

At the Old Bailey I went in through the front, still cuffed to my escort. A screw led us down to the holding area. The cuffs came off and I sat on a bench near the stairs to our dock, with two or three screws standing around. Vincent joined me first, and not long afterwards, Mum, Dad and the others came.

'Where did they take you last night?' said Mum. 'Was it all right? And did you get a wash this morning?'

She knew Vincent would have had one, but that if I could get away with it, I wouldn't. 'Yes, I had a wash,' I said.

'What about breakfast?' she wondered.

By now Dad and the other men were listening. I described the egg-cup incident and everyone laughed. Then the grown-ups were talking among themselves. I asked Pat O'Neil for a smoke. He gave me a pinch of tobacco and a couple of Rizla papers.

I bunked off to the toilet, rolled a fag and lit up. One puff, and I felt light-headed, woozy. Lovely.

The jury spent the day trying to decide but didn't manage it. That evening I went back to Stamford House and spent a second night in the same room with the same lad. I'd got some tobacco and papers off Pat, and once we'd been locked in, we smoked ourselves silly.

The next morning, Thursday, 4 March, I was driven back to the Old Bailey, same van, same driver, same everything, and brought downstairs to wait. Mum, Dad and the others came. There was a lot of talking. Surely the jury must have made up their minds by now.

Midday came. A screw we knew as Jock hurried up and said the jury was coming back in with their verdict.

We got in line, one behind the other as we had been doing for weeks: Mum, Vincent, me, Dad, Giuseppe, Sean and Pat.

'This is it,' said Dad, as we started up the stairs, 'the big hurdle. Get over this one and we're home.'

I presumed he meant horse racing, which surprised me. He'd never bet on a horse in his life.

'Good luck,' shouted Jock, the screw.

We came out into the dock. The court was full. The judge came. The foreman stood.

Mum was pronounced guilty.

'I'm innocent, you bastards, no, no, no,' she shouted.

Some screws picked her up and carried her, shoulder high, out of the dock and down to the holding area.

The word 'guilty' was said several more times. The jury was done.

The judge, Mr Justice Donaldson, said, 'The fact that these offences were committed for terrorist purposes gives the unique character to this case that must and will be reflected in the severity of the sentencing, which it is the duty of the courts to pass.'

He sentenced Mum and Dad to fourteen years' imprisonment, Giuseppe Conlon, Sean Smyth and Pat O'Neil to twelve years' imprisonment and my brother to five years' imprisonment.

The screws brought us back down the stairs to the holding area. Mum was in a cell somewhere and Dad went to see her. Sean and Giuseppe were whisked away. The Maguire Seven were down to three, me, Vincent and Pat O'Neil. We sat in a hallway on a bench. Pat made a roll-up and handed it to me. 'You're going home, son,' he said.

I didn't understand. I thought they'd found all of us guilty.

'No,' said Pat. 'They haven't reached a verdict on you. They're still deliberating. In a bit you'll have to go back up and hear what they've decided. But I wouldn't worry. You're going home.'

I felt a great rush of anger. 'If the jury finds me innocent,' I said, 'I'm throwing the chair I've been sitting on at the judge. I've come this far. I'm not going home alone.'

Pat gave me a little smile.

A screw came. I was to follow him, he said, back to the dock. I got up and at that moment Dad came back.

'Is Mum all right?' I asked.

'Yes,' he said. 'Now, don't do anything silly up there, son, and you'll be all right.'

The screw took me up the stairs and into the dock. I stood in the same spot I always stood and looked straight at the judge, the target. I knew everyone in the court was staring at me, but no one had the slightest idea what was going on in my mind. I had my plan, and when I was ready, I'd strike.

'Have you reached a verdict?' the judge asked.

Go on, tell me I'm going home, I thought. Go on.

The chair was just behind me. I could feel it against the back of my legs. In my mind I ran through the motions, turning and picking it up, turning back, then firing it through the air, straight at his head.

'Yes,' said the foreman. I was guilty by a majority of eleven to one. I got four years' imprisonment.

No need to throw the chair, I thought. Well, I could still have a go, I thought, but I was grabbed by my upper arm and pulled away before I got the chance.

When I got downstairs, the holding area was empty. Where had everyone gone? Then a screw opened a cell and I saw Vincent inside. It was a relief to see a friendly face.

I went in and the door shut.

'I was found guilty,' I said.

'I know,' he said.

'How do you know?' I said. 'I only just told you.'

'You wouldn't be in the cell with me if they hadn't found you guilty,' he said. 'Would you?'

We talked for a bit until I heard voices in the corridor. I didn't know who it was. The door opened and in walked Dad with two prison officers, one on either side.

We got up and I met Dad halfway across the cell.

I had tears welling in my eyes, which I didn't want Dad to see, so I lowered my face. Dad put his hand under my chin and lifted my head until our eyes met. 'Don't cry,' he said. 'You've got to be strong.'

I said nothing.

'Sons, I'm sorry, I have to apologize,' he said. 'I've always told you that British justice was the finest in the world and that you should trust and respect it. I was wrong.'

'That's all right, Dad. It's not your fault,' said Vincent.

I was looking at my feet again.

'Head up, son,' he said to me. 'Now, here, if you're old enough to go to prison, then you're old enough to smoke.'

He gave me his tobacco pouch. Then he took off his watch and put it in my other hand.

He gave us both a hug, then the officers led him away. The cell door banged.

I looked at the watch in my hand. 'What happens now?'

'We're going to prison,' said my brother.

'Will we go together?'

'I don't know.'

'What do I say when I get there? I haven't done anything. What do I say?'

'Say you've been found guilty of unlawful possession of nitro-glycerine.'

'Nitro – I can't even say the fucking word.'

'Nitroglycerine,' he said, slowly and carefully, so I could take the whole word in.

'But I haven't done anything.'

'Then tell them that. Tell them you're innocent.'

The door opened again. The officer shouted, 'Vincent Maguire.' Was I going too? Apparently not. The officer hadn't called my name.

Vincent rubbed my head and told me I'd be all right, then gave me a half-smile as he headed out.

I sat down, but then I was on my feet again, pacing up and down the hot, brightly lit cell with nowhere to hide. The number '4' and the word 'years' filled my head.

'Four years,' I said, to hear what it sounded like.

Maybe if it didn't sound right, it couldn't be.

'Four years,' I said again.

I'd never seen my life in years. Minutes, an hour, a day, a week at the most, yes, that's what I could hold in my head. A month, no, and a year, that was out of the question. I didn't do years. I lived in the moment, just enjoying one thing after the next as a year rolled on, the first highlight being my birthday, followed by going to Belfast for our holidays, followed by Christmas. Then it started all over again. I didn't tick days off on the calendar either. I'd never had one. And why should I? I had all the time in the world, as far as I knew. Well, not any more. I'd four fucking years to do. Just as well I wasn't any good at maths, I thought, or I'd be working out how many days there were in four years.

Then my mind changed tack. Where was I going? Maybe back to Stamford House. I'd only stayed there a couple of nights, but I already hated it. To go there for four years was too horrible to think about.

Then I remembered what Vincent had said: 'We're going to prison.' Stamford House didn't qualify. Not like this place. Wasn't this cell a prison? Perhaps they were going to keep me here. No, that didn't make sense. They wouldn't have taken Vincent away if this was it. Why didn't I go with him? Where's he gone? Am I going to see him again? And what's happened to Mum? The last time I saw her, she was being carried down the stairs. Will I ever see her again? And what about Dad? What's going on? Why is this happening to us? We should all be at home now, a family once more. I'm not ready for this – I'm not ready. Please, I just want to go home.

The door was unlocked again and I was ordered out. The screw led me along a corridor to another door. He unlocked it. 'Go on,' he said. 'In you go.'

I stepped forward. The door closed. Pouch in one hand, watch in the other, I looked around, not making eye contact with any of the men in there. I didn't want trouble.

This cell was three or four times bigger than the one I'd left, with fifteen or even twenty men in it. Most were sitting on a wooden bench that ran round the wall, staring at the floor. A few were pacing about. No one was talking. The air was thick with cigarette smoke. They're all grown men, I thought. This doesn't make sense. I can't be going to the same place as them. I'm a boy.

Time passed. I didn't move from where I was standing. After a while the door opened again. Immediately, as if they'd been suddenly woken, some men started to talk, others to stretch, while others gathered up books and court papers. I stuffed the tobacco pouch into one pocket and the watch into the deepest part of the other. I didn't want to lose it.

Names were called two at a time and prisoners were going out in pairs. I hoped that somehow I would be going home. Then I heard, 'Maguire,' and another name. He looked like he knew what was going on and I followed him through the door.

'Right,' said the screw, when we got out into the corridor. 'In there.'

I went through a door and found myself in a reception room with a lot of screws hanging around, drinking tea and smoking, as well as a large desk covered with papers and files. Three screws stood behind it, processing prisoners.

I got into the queue, and when my turn came, they asked my name, date of birth and what court I'd been in. They asked the lad whose name had been called with mine the same questions. Then we were handcuffed together and told to wait on one of the benches in the corner. We went and sat down and I recognized, among the others waiting, several faces I'd seen in the big cell.

The bloke I was cuffed to got out his cigarettes and lit one. I won't ask for one, I thought, but I couldn't stop myself staring.

'Do you want one?' he asked.

'Oh, yeah, thanks.'

I took one and he gave me his fag to light mine. When mine caught I handed his back to him.

'How old are you?'

'Fourteen,' I said.

'Well, don't let the screws see you smoking,' he said. 'They'll take it off you.'

I turned sideways and kept my head down.

When everyone was handcuffed we were led outside. It was cold and raining. We were put on to a coach, two by two, like the animals going into Noah's Ark. Then the big gates at the side of the Old Bailey, which Mum, Vincent and I had walked past twice every day during the trial, were opened. In the road outside, a policeman stopped the traffic going both ways, and the coach nosed out. I looked through the window, which had rain on it, and saw people on the pavement and in the cars that had to stop. They were gazing up at us. With a burst of speed the coach pulled away and they vanished.

'How long did you get?' asked the lad I was cuffed to.

'Four years.'

'What did you do to get that?'

'Didn't do anything. We're innocent.'

'Who's we?'

I outlined the story, as much as I was able, and added Mum and Dad had got fourteen each, the most out of the seven of us.

'Fourteen fucking years,' he said. He sounded appalled.

'They did.'

'You don't sound fucking Irish.'

'I'm not. I'm from the Harrow Road, Paddington.'

Now it was my turn with the questions. 'Where are we going?'

'To the Scrubs.'

'What's it like?'

'It's a shit-hole, but we're not getting off there. We're going to Ashford.'

'What's that like?'

'Another shit-hole.'

We got into Wormwood Scrubs. I didn't recognize the building I'd seen when I was training on the common and our teacher had told us what prison was. I wasn't seeing it from the same direction. That was why. Also it was dark.

Some prisoners got off. The coach doors closed and we drove away. We were going to Ashford now. Out on the street the traffic was heavy and we went slowly.

The bloke I was cuffed to and I had another cigarette. We were getting on. He was eighteen and had been in prison several times already. I told him I'd never been away before.

'Oh, don't worry,' he said. 'Just keep yourself to yourself and don't mind when the screws mouth off at you. It makes them feel good, the wankers, but they don't know any better. Do as I say and you'll be all right.'

19

I saw Ashford from miles off. It looked like a cross between a lightbulb and a UFO that had landed in the middle of nowhere. When we got nearer I saw that the walls and fences were topped with barbed wire, and the buildings had rows of windows with white-painted bars.

The coach slowed as it approached and the driver beeped. The gates opened, like a giant's jaws, and the coach went through. We headed towards a building with its door open, and two screws standing outside.

The coach stopped.

'All out.'

We trooped off in pairs and went through the door. Inside, the cuffs were taken off. There was a lot of noise. People talking, people shouting, doors banging, gates locking, and keys jangling. I'd never heard so many keys.

Everyone sat down to wait. Obviously they'd been through it before so they were at ease. I sat down too. I didn't feel at ease. My mind was far away, at 43 Third Avenue, with Mum, Dad and everyone else. I wished the rest of me was there too.

Next thing I heard, 'Maguire.'

That's me, I thought. I got up, trying to see where the voice had come from.

Suddenly a screw was in front of me. 'Are you Maguire?'

'Yeah.'

'Then get your arse down there when your fucking name's called.' He pointed to a room along a corridor.

I went off, hands in pockets, as if I was going to see the head-master at school. When I got inside the room, three or four screws were waiting. One was sitting behind a desk. 'Get your fucking hands out of your pockets and stand up straight,' he said. He got a Biro and a form. 'Full name?'

'Patrick Maguire.'

'I said full name.'

'Patrick Joseph Paul Maguire.'

'Could your mum not make up her mind what to call you, then?'

'I'm named after the saints.'

'Well, you're not a fucking saint, are you? Haven't you just come from the Old Bailey?'

'Yeah.'

'And you got four years?'

'Yeah.'

'That'll teach you to fuck about with bombs.'

'I'm innocent. I shouldn't be here.'

'Well, you're here now and let me tell you, there are no innocent people in prison, all right?'

'Well, I am.'

'I'll tell you what you are. You're a fucking number. You are 333892. Got it?'

'No. Could you write it down for me?'

'You're not in fucking school now, 333892. Now get out.'

Outside, a screw told me to sit at the door of another room. I did as I'd been told. Right, I thought, I mightn't be able to remember the telephone number at home but I must get this off by heart . . . 33 . . . Was there a third 3? Yes. 333 . . . and then what was it? 9 . . . Was it 9? Oh, sod this . . .

The door opened and I saw a screw in a long white coat. 'Come in,' he said. He sat down at a desk. 'Name and number?'

'My name is Patrick Joseph Paul Maguire,' I said, 'and I've forgotten my number.'

'I'll write it down on a bit of paper for you.' As he handed it to me he told me I didn't have to give my full name every time I was asked. The number would be fine.

'I'm the prison doctor,' he said. 'Is everything all right?'

'I shouldn't be here,' I said. 'I'm innocent.'

He gave me a strange look, then started a list of questions I knew he'd asked before.

'Do you take drugs?'

'No.'

'Are you a homosexual?'

'No.'

'Have you any sexually transmitted diseases?'

'No.'

I told him I had asthma, which had troubled me since child-hood, and I needed lots of fresh air.

He gave me another strange look and then he stood up. 'Drop your trousers.'

He cupped my balls. 'Cough.'

I coughed.

'Pull your trousers up.'

I left with the piece of paper with my number. At least I'd got that. I folded it in half and stored it carefully in my back pocket.

Outside, another screw directed me to a dining room where the lads who'd been on the coach were eating. I sat down and an inmate put a meal in front of me. It was a slice of cold pork, very grey, mashed potato, also grey, and cabbage with green water coming out of it, plus a bread roll and a cup of tea. It was inedible except for the bread roll and the tea.

'Don't you want yours?' asked the lad who'd been cuffed to me, pointing at my plate.

I shook my head. I'd never seen food like it. He took my plate and gave me his roll in return.

The meal over, I was taken to another room. There was a screw with a box, light brown, cardboard. 'Everything out of your pockets,' he said.

I pulled out the tobacco pouch and the watch. That was all I had, other than the paper in my back pocket and that didn't count, I thought.

'In the box,' he said. 'It will go into prisoners' property, and when you leave its contents will be returned to you. Understand?'

'But can't I keep them?'

'For a start,' he said, 'you're too young to smoke so, no, you can't keep the pouch.'

It was logged and went into the box.

'What about the watch? Can't I keep it? It's my dad's.'

'You don't need to know the time,' he said, 'because you're not fucking going anywhere for the next four years, are you? So, no, you can't keep it.'

The watch followed the pouch.

'Right, everything off, and into the box.'

'Everything?'

'You heard. Now hurry up.'

All my clothes went into the box and I was naked. My face reddened. I had never been naked like this, not even at school. I put my hands in front to cover myself.

I could hear water running and see clouds of steam.

'Shower,' said the screw. He pointed.

I'd never had a shower before either. At home we had baths. I'd always put up a fight when Mum said, 'Bath-time.' How I wished I was at home now. I'd have a bath every day if Mum told me, even twice a day, if she said so. Anything had to be better than this.

I got under the water, which was too hot, and the soap was like jelly. I came out and dried myself with a coarse, frayed towel.

I was issued now with my prison uniform: grey trousers, a horrible blue and white shirt, a grey jumper and a pair of slip-on black shoes. I rolled the trouser legs up four or five turns though there was nothing I could do about the waist, which was for someone with the build of Desperate Dan rather than a fourteen-year-old boy. The shirt would have fitted two of me; and the shoes would have looked better on a clown. The only good thing was the jumper. It was big, too, but it hid the shirt.

After I got my day clothes, I got the rest of my issue: socks and underwear, PE kit (singlet, shorts, different socks, plimsolls) and a pair of good trousers for visits, plus my bedding (sheets, blankets, pillow), everything bundled up in a roll, and finally my piss pot. Now that I had everything, I expected to be moved on but no one said anything. So I stood there with my hands in my pockets, waiting for something to happen.

A screw came over to me. 'Get your hands out of your pockets,' he said.

'My trousers'll fall down if I do,' I said.

'Oh, yeah?'

I took my hands out and down they went. He went off laughing and came back with another uniform that fitted better. Then the lad from the coach gave me some cigarettes and matches. 'Whatever you do,' he said, 'don't let the screws see you smoking. You're too young and they'll take everything off you.'

'Don't worry,' I said. 'I know how to be careful.'

'I'll see you later,' he said. I never saw him again.

More time passed and still nothing. Then another screw came over.

'Name and number?' he said.

'Maguire,' I said. I reached into my pocket for the bit of paper with my number on it, but it wasn't there. It was still in my own trousers and they were in the box. 'I don't know my number,' I said.

'Not to worry. You'll learn it soon enough,' said the screw. Then he said we were going to H Wing. My cell was waiting.

I got my bundle and the piss pot and followed him outside to a yard lit with floodlights. It was cold, raining and very quiet, but I had the feeling I was being watched. We were making for a building that seemed to go right up to the sky. I saw the same little windows with the white-painted bars that I'd spotted from the coach. We went in and up some stairs. The bundle was heavy and I had to stop to swap it with the piss pot. The screw waited but said nothing. At the top there were doors, grilles and then a corridor. There was no one around except a screw who came out of an office. As he spoke to the escort, I put my bundle down and looked around at H Wing. Though Ashford was a remand centre it also housed convicted prisoners serving short terms, while this wing was for sentenced prisoners waiting to be shipped on.

How the fuck did I get here? I wondered.

The escort went off and the other screw took me to my cell, unlocked the door, turned the light on inside and told me to go in. He pointed to the bed and told me to get some sleep. I went in, the door closed and the light went out.

After a moment or two my eyes adjusted. I could see the bed by the light from the floodlights coming through the barred windows. I lit one of the fags I'd been given, lay down and looked at the white-painted bars and the wire cage on the outside. My mind was full of jumbled thoughts, all racing around.

'Paddy Maguire.' Someone was calling my name in a broad Belfast accent. 'Come to your window.'

I jumped off the bed and up on to the table that was under the window. 'Hello, who's that?' I shouted back, in my best Belfast accent.

'Never mind. Are you all right?'

'I'm – I'm all right.'

'Them bastards, putting you all away for nothing. Have you got fags?'

'I'm sorted.'

'Be careful, if they see you with fags they'll take them off you. Okay?'

'Okay.'

'God bless.'

'God bless.'

I got off the table and smoked a second cigarette, sitting on the bed this time. I felt a bit better now I'd spoken to someone, even if I didn't know who it was. At least he was on my side. Then I stretched out, pulled the covers over and fell asleep.

I opened my eyes. It was Friday morning, 5 March 1976. Sunshine streamed past the bars and filled the cell with light. I lay, warm and snug, under the covers and wondered when Mum would be up to wake me. There was a bang on my door.

'Everyone up,' shouted the screw outside my cell.

Another bang, this time from the next cell. He was giving it everything he had with his truncheon.

'Hands off your cocks, pull up your socks and make your beds.'

He walked off. Then, from the far end of the wing, I heard a door being unlocked and the same screw shouting, 'Slop out.'

He came back, opening every door and shouting, 'Slop out.'

I had no idea what he was talking about so I stayed put.

Then the door opened wide and in walked a prisoner. 'All right, Paddy?' It was the Belfast accent I'd heard the night before.

'Yeah, I'm all right,' I said, in my London voice.

He looked puzzled. 'I thought you were from Belfast.'

'No, mate, I'm from London, Paddington.' I explained that I'd spoken in a Belfast accent the night before because I didn't want him to think he'd got the wrong person. I also told him that I didn't know anything about Belfast and had only been there on holidays.

He didn't mind. He gave me some fags and a box of matches, as well as toothpaste and a bar of soap. 'Have you slopped out yet?' he said.

'I don't know what you're on about,' I said.

'Get your piss pot and follow me,' he said.

We ended up in the toilet – the recess, they called it – where several lads were rinsing their pots. I didn't need to do mine because I hadn't used it, but I washed it anyway. I took some hot water in a bowl to my cell for a wash, and then I had to slop that out. Then the lad from Belfast took me to a room at the top of the wing and I had something to eat. No one talked to me and there was an atmosphere, sort of unfriendly.

After breakfast we were locked up again. A bit of time passed and then my door opened. A screw came in. 'You're for the hospital,' he said.

'But I don't need to go to hospital,' I said. 'I'm all right. There's nothing wrong with me.'

'Just do as you're told,' he said. 'Get your things together.'

He slammed the door and locked it.

I made up my bundle, stashed my fags in the middle, then sat on the bed to wait. Hospital had to be better than this. It would be outside, in the world. In which case, I realized, it would be much better than this. Suddenly I was looking forward to hospital.

Two screws came. I followed them out of H Wing, feeling quite perky. We walked across the prison grounds and arrived at a building well away from the main block. A door opened and I stepped into a place filled with men in white coats and a medical smell. Now I discovered prisons – or this one, anyway – had their own hospitals. I didn't feel quite so perky any more.

In reception I was strip-searched, and then my bundle was searched. The screw found the cigarettes and matches. 'You're too young to smoke,' he said, 'so I'm going to be keeping these.'

He brought me to my new cell.

It was white, with a big window, very low, unlike in the previous cell where the window had been small and high. It had bars, of course, but it also had a toilet and washbasin, and there was a bell to press (I was told not to press it) if there was an emergency. But it was still a fucking cell and I was in it.

'Right,' said the screw. 'In the day you've got to leave your bed made up our way, understand? The blankets and sheets have to be folded to the same size, like this, and then you pile them up at the head of the bed, one blanket on the bottom, the two sheets on top, then the other blanket, and finally the pillow.'

I folded the bedding like he said and piled it up.

'If it isn't done like that, you'll have to do it again until it is. Got that?'

I said I had.

'Your clothes and your other bits and pieces, you've got to fold them too,' he said. 'Like this.'

He folded one or two of my things to show me how it was done. I had to do the rest.

'One more point. Daytime, you don't lie down on the bed. Sit on it, yes, but no lying. Prison rules. Break the rule, and you'll be charged. That means you'll go to the punishment unit, which is a lot harder than it is here and you don't want to go there. So, my advice, do exactly what I've told you, exactly, keep your nose clean and you'll be fine. Got it?'

He went off and I tried to remember what he'd said about how everything had to be. I could hear moaning and crying in the cells around me, and I could hear an officer shouting, 'Fucking shut up.' What would happen if I pressed the bell? 'Fucking shut up.' That's what would happen.

The door opened. It was a screw and an orderly with the dinner trolley. The orderly handed me something to eat, which included margarine and bread. 'I don't have anything to eat with,' I said.

'Give him a spoon,' said the screw.

The orderly gave me a plastic spoon.

'How do I spread the marge?' I said. 'Isn't there a knife?'

'No,' said the orderly. 'No knives. Use the handle of the spoon.'

Meal finished, the plate and spoon were taken. I was locked up again. A bit later the door opened. 'Yard,' said the screw.

I went out. There were some prisoners already by their cell doors, waiting for the rest to be unlocked. None was bandaged or had anything wrong with him that I could see. Then I twigged. It wasn't the kind of hospital I'd thought it was. It was the other kind, for the mental cases, the nutters, the insane.

A couple of prisoners were talking.

'No talking,' said the screw. They stopped straight away. Amazing. Frightening.

Everyone was out by now. We were marched – about fifteen of us – to a small yard. The prisoners began to walk around the edge and I followed. Round and round we went. One or two whispered to each other and the screws didn't mind. I realized that as long as you didn't shout or raise your voice you could talk. I didn't, though, and no one spoke to me either.

After half an hour we were marched back. Everyone else was locked up but I was taken to the recess. 'You've got to clean your cell,' said the screw who had brought me there. He gave me a bar of brown soap, a dirty cloth, a scrubbing brush and a tin bucket. 'Fill it with hot water,' he said.

I did so, then carried everything I'd been given to my cell, the screw following. He unlocked the door. I went in. 'You scrub every inch of this floor,' he said, 'and you'll be all right. But you don't do it right, I'll make you do it again and again and again. Understand?'

I got down on my knees and scrubbed and wiped anywhere that was floor. When I'd finished, I emptied the slops in recess, rinsed the cloth, put everything away. Back in my cell, my floor was still wet and the air was damp.

Later I got tea. Later still it got dark. A screw told me to make my bed. I put the covers on and got under them. The main light was turned off outside but there was a red one in the cell that stayed on, watching me. I could hear whimpering in the cells around me.

'What have I done?' I said. 'I shouldn't be here.'

I called, 'Mum! Dad!' over and over, then begged them to come and help me. Then I shouted, 'Where the fuck are you now, God? I went to church every Sunday. All right, I didn't want to go, but I went, didn't I? Why didn't you do anything? Why didn't you stop this?'

I started to cry after that and didn't stop until I was asleep.

I woke to the sound of the screw banging on the door. What day was it? Was it Saturday? Maybe it was Sunday. I didn't know. I'd lost track of time. I got dressed, folded my bedding, got inspected, got told to do it again, did it again, got breakfast, got locked up, got unlocked, got marched to the yard, walked round in silence, got returned to the recess, got the brown soap and the dirty cloth, the brush and the bucket, got back to my cell, scrubbed anywhere that was floor, got inspected, did it again, got back to the recess, put the bucket and the rest away, got locked up again, got dinner, got unlocked, got marched to the yard, walked in silence, got returned to the recess, got the brown soap and the dirty cloth, the brush and the bucket, got back to my cell, scrubbed anywhere that was floor, got inspected, did it again, got back to the recess, put the bucket and the rest away, got locked up again, got tea, got told to make up my bed, made up my bed, got under the covers, lay in the dark with the red light staring at me and started crying.

That was my routine, day after night after day.

'Visit,' said the screw at the door of my cell.

I put on my good trousers and was taken to the hospital visiting room. It was small, only big enough for one visit at a time, with a table in the middle and chairs on either side. My Aunt Mary and my brother John were sitting, my sister Anne-Marie standing between them. My brother John didn't say much. Here he was, visiting his younger brother in prison; what was there to say – not a lot. Aunt Mary and Anne-Marie on the other hand weren't silent. They were crying. There were also four screws on duty, two on their side of the table and two on mine.

'Sit down and keep your hands off the table,' said one.

'And no touching,' said the other.

I lifted up a trouser leg and showed everyone the clown shoe I had on. Aunt Mary and Anne-Marie went on crying but John laughed.

I sat.

'I got some pencils and paper for you,' said Mary. She pushed them across the table towards me. 'You can draw in your cell,' she said. 'It'll help get the time in.'

'Take that back,' said one of the pair watching. 'No gifts.'

In one move, Mary took back the pencils and paper, and pushed over a brown-paper bag of fruit.

'Take that back,' shouted the same screw. 'No gifts allowed.'

'What harm can it do?' said Mary. 'The lad's in hospital and surely if he's in hospital he must be allowed fruit.'

'Only remands are allowed food brought in,' said the screw, 'and he's sentenced so he's not allowed it. However, seeing as he's new, I'll make an exception. He can have the fruit, but that's all.'

The brown bag was slid towards me. I reached forward and took it. My hands were red and the skin over the knuckles was cracked open.

'What happened to your hands?' Mary asked.

'Scrubbing my cell floor,' I said.

'Scrubbing?' she said, but her face said she didn't believe me.

'On my hands and knees,' I said. 'Every day. You have to. It's the rules.'

Anne-Marie slid something towards me. It was a key ring. She'd given it to me a long time ago but taken it back after I'd pulled the head off one of her dolls.

'Take that back,' shouted the screw. 'Didn't you hear me? Fruit only. Nothing else to be given to the prisoner.'

Anne-Marie started to wail.

'Right, that's it,' said the screw, 'time's up, visit over.'

I said goodbye and marched back to my cell with my

brown-paper bag. Once I was locked in, out came the fruit. It was gorgeous to see the colours and to smell it. Then I remembered the big bowl Mum always had in the front room of forty-three, full of apples, oranges and bananas.

I sat on the bed and as I ate I cried.

'Why is this happening?' I shouted. 'We haven't done anything wrong. God, where are you? Help me. I know I didn't pray in church, I didn't know how to. But I was there, wasn't I? Where are you when I need you?'

Another day.

'Hello? All right?'

The voice came from the other side of my cell door. I went over. 'Yeah. Who's that?'

He explained. He was Vincent. I took it as a good omen that he had the same name as my brother. He was the cleaning orderly on the hospital wing.

There was scuffling on the ground. Cigarettes and matches were sliding under my door and into my cell. Magic. He hadn't even asked if I smoked, just shoved them through.

'You can't give me all these,' I said. 'You won't have enough for yourself.'

'I don't smoke,' he said. 'You're welcome to them.'

This was even more confusing. 'If you don't smoke, how did you get them?' I asked.

'I nicked them from the screws,' he said. 'I'm in and out their office every day, making tea, cleaning up, and every time I'm in, as a point of principle, I nick as many of their fags as I can.'

That meant more cigarettes where these came from, I thought. Happy days.

'I'll see you in the yard,' he said.

'Yeah, okay,' I said. 'Thanks,' I added. 'Really. I'm dying for a smoke. You've saved my life you have.'

The door opened.

'Yard,' said the screw.

I went out and looked up the corridor. Another prisoner nodded at me. Vincent, the orderly, I thought.

In the exercise yard I made certain I was beside him in the circle of lads tramping round.

'All right?' he whispered.

'Yeah,' I said quietly.

We started to talk. I didn't ask what he'd done to get sent to prison – I don't think he knew: he was far from all there in the head. But he liked his football.

'My team's QPR,' I said. That made him laugh. Him laughing made me laugh too but quietly, of course, so the screws watching wouldn't notice.

The door opened, and a man in a suit came in. The governor on his round. 'Everything all right?' he said.

'Name and number to the governor,' I was told, by a screw standing next to him.

'Why am I here?' The words flew out.

'In case of suicidal tendencies,' he said.

He might as well have been talking French. Suicidal tendencies? Those were words, like nitroglycerine, that I'd never heard before. I shook my head. 'I don't know what you're talking about.'

'You're here because you might take your life,' he said. 'Suicide.'

The door slammed.

I was here because I might take my life?

This was amazing. I'd always thought you lived and then you died and you'd nothing to do with the dying part. It just happened when it happened because you were old or sick or you had an accident, like a car crash or something. But I was wrong. Apparently you could go from living to dying of your own accord, if you wanted. It was called suicide. It was a brand spanking new and absolutely incredible idea. Suicide. Suicide.

There was a knock on my cell door.

'Yeah?'

'It's me.' Vincent.

'I've come to tell you I'm going tomorrow,' he said.

'Really?'

'I'm going to Broadmoor,' he said.

I'd never heard of the place and I wasn't going to start asking now.

'Yeah, Broadmoor,' he said again. 'That's where I'm going.'

Cigarettes and matches floated into view as they had every day since he'd first spoken to me.

'Good luck with Broadmoor,' I said, 'and thanks for everything.'

'You're welcome.'

'Goodbye,' I said.

'Goodbye.'

There were small black ants in one of the drawers of my locker. I heard the screw outside. 'Hello.'

He stopped. 'Who's that?'

'333892.' I'd got my number on a bit of paper again.

'What is it?'

'I've got ants in my locker.'

'How many?' he asked.

I ran back and counted. 'There's five,' I shouted.

'Well, there should be six,' he said. 'They belong to the lad next door, but I won't tell him you have them. You keep them, all right?'

And off he went.

I remembered that screw had a big scar down one side of his face. I wondered if he'd got it for taking the piss once too often. I hoped so.

20

At first, I only cried in bed. Then I did a bit in the day but still mostly at night. Finally I cried most of the day and the night.

It was daytime. How long I'd been there I'd no idea. I'd lost all sense of time. Maybe a fortnight, I thought. The door opened. It was the governor on his round.

'Can I go back to H Wing? Can I go back with the other lads?' I said.

The governor looked at me. 'Yes,' he said, just like that.

The door slammed and he was gone.

It was the day after the day that the governor had said I could go back on H Wing. My door opened. Two screws. 'Maguire.'

The escort led me out of the hospital and through the main prison.

It seemed that everyone was watching me as I made my way, with my bundle and piss pot.

We reached the block and started up the stairs towards H-Wing, and as we went I noticed it wasn't so noisy. At the top, as always, the gate was locked, as the doors and gates always are in prison. 'One on,' one of the escorts shouted as he opened the gate.

I stepped forward. I was hoping to see the Belfast lad, but H-Wing was locked down. That's why it seemed so quiet coming up the stairs.

There was the usual palaver as I was handed over. Then the screw on the wing told me to start walking.

I padded along. Were we heading towards the cell where I'd spent the first night? It looked like it. The screw stopped outside a door. Yes, we were. I stepped forward – and inside, on the table, was an envelope with my name in Mum's writing.

I dumped my bundle as the door shut. I didn't have to open the envelope. The censor had done that for me. I pulled out the sheets.

At the top I saw 'Dear Son'.

After that I couldn't make out one word – my reading was never that good and nor was Mum's writing. Also, she hadn't had her glasses when she wrote this, as I found out later. Only the last few words were clear: 'Your Loving Mum, God bless.'

I began to cry. I was missing Mum and I couldn't read her letter. If I could only read the letter, I'd have a sense of her, I'd hear her voice in my head. It would be almost like having her there. But I couldn't and that made me miserable.

I heard a key going into my door. What did the screws want now?

But it wasn't a screw. It was a priest, all in black, with the little white bit under his chin, and a handful of keys on a chain, just like a screw. He came forward. 'You're upset,' he said.

'Well, yeah,' I said. I hadn't bothered to hide my face.

'What's the matter?' he said. 'You can tell me.'

'I'm innocent and I shouldn't be here,' I said.

He saw the letter in my hand. 'Who's that from?' he asked.

'My mum,' I said, 'but I can't read it.'

'Would you like me to read it to you?'

Why not? I thought. I gave it to him. He looked at it for a few moments, then started. It didn't sound like Mum. I decided he couldn't read her writing and was making it up. It didn't matter, though. I just pretended it was her anyway.

He finished.

'Thank you,' I said.

He handed the letter back. I put it into its envelope to look at another time.

'Are you all right on your own?' he said. 'You can double up with one of the other lads if you prefer.'

'No, I'm all right,' I said. 'I'm fine.'

'You don't want to share?'

'No.'

He went towards the door, as if to go out, then stopped at the last moment. 'Hope to see you in church on Sunday,' he said.

I was caught, I thought, and there was no getting out of it now. 'Yeah, I'll be there,' I said.

It was morning. A screw woke me. I got dressed and made my bed, folding the covers into squares and piling them as per the rules. Once that was done, I was marched with two or three other lads down the stairs and into the dinner hall (which was also used for visits). The rest of the prison – a mix of remand and prisoners

211

with short sentences – was already eating breakfast. We were brought through the servery and into the kitchen at the back. A screw told us what food to take and we gathered it up. We wouldn't be eating in the dinner hall. The lads on H Wing had been sentenced for serious offences; some were lifers and I was a convicted IRA terrorist. If the lifers got among the general population, they might turn them all into murderers, and if I mixed with them, I'd have them making bombs – at least, that was what the prison authorities thought. That was why, once we'd got our food, we were marched back to H Wing and into the classroom where I'd eaten on my first morning. Here, we sat down and ate our breakfast. It was the same carry-on every mealtime.

Breakfast done, everyone on H Wing put on their PE kit (black baggy shorts, light-blue vest and black slip-on plimsolls) and went down to the gym. About twenty lads from the main prison were waiting for us. They looked at us warily. We were H Wing, which meant we were hard, and we never did anything to contradict that impression.

We started, as usual, with circuit-training, hard work with the screws shouting and pushing you on. Then we'd a game of Killerball. H Wing went to one end of the gym, and the other prisoners went to the other. The medicine ball went in the middle. The object was to get the ball to the other side's end. The screw blew his whistle. It was rugby, really, without rules. There were collisions, punches and fights. Marvellous. I loved it.

After PE, the wounded were bandaged and then we went into the showers. I got my clothes off but it didn't feel natural. It never did. I went into the shower and noticed where the ones who weren't straight had gone and chose the shower furthest away from them. The water came on and I began to wash myself, but I kept my eyes open and my back to the wall. I knew if I dropped soap on the floor I wouldn't bend down to pick it up. It would stay there.

I got dressed and was marched with the others back to H Wing. I got the cleaning things out of the recess, then set about cleaning my cell. That done, I had to mop the wing, though I might as easily have been asked to clean the toilets or the office, where the screws spent most of their time doing fuck-all.

Midday came, and we were marched down to collect our next meal. Coming back up the stairs with three or four others from H Wing, I saw an old mate of my brother Vincent's coming down. His name was Brian, and he lived just up the road from us in Third Avenue; I'd knocked about with his younger brother, who had been at Queens Park Primary with me. 'All right, Patrick?' he said.

We stood and talked and he gave me some tobacco. He was a huge bloke, over six foot. I could feel the eyes of the H Wing lads looking carefully at him and me.

Back on H Wing, we went into the classroom and sat down to eat.

Then the questions started. Who was that? How tall was he? Was he as hard as he looked? I said Brian was a good mate of mine, which was a lie, but everyone was impressed with him and, by association, with me. I was the friend of big, powerful Brian and now they wanted to be the friend of the friend of big, powerful Brian. In prison, it's not what you know that matters but who you know, and for the first time since I'd arrived, I felt I had a place. I belonged. I was somebody.

I woke up. I'd been in jail eighteen days. It was Monday, 22 March, my birthday. I'd almost forgotten about it. I was fifteen. I got up and was carried along by what was happening. That way I avoided thinking about what I was missing and what I'd be doing if I was at home, the cards, the money, the toy soldiers I'd probably have been given even though Mum would have said, 'You're getting too big for toys now,' then going to Kendal's on the Harrow Road, the best clothes shop around, where Mum cleaned, and Mum buying me what I needed, and the owner writing down what I got in a book so he could dock the amount off Mum's wages. But when I was locked up at midday I couldn't stop the thoughts and I felt sorry for myself. Then I thought, Well, if I'm feeling like this, how are Mum and Dad feeling? It must be worse for them.

In the afternoon, after unlock, I went out on the wing, back to cleaning, and tried to ignore the lump I had in the middle of my chest. I thought, I'm going to cry, but I didn't.

When I got back to my cell later, I found fags and sweets on my bed – the lads on the wing had got them for me – and a letter from my brother, Vincent. I got help again with reading it because his writing was as good as Mum's. He told me he was still in Wormwood Scrubs and that he was all right. He hoped we'd be together soon, and wished me a happy birthday.

I, too, had been hoping we'd be together – not in prison, though, at home. Every day, so far, I had told myself that someone would come along and let me out. Every day. And I hadn't let go of that hope yet.

A screw came to the cell with a VO. 'Here's how this works,' he said. 'Remand prisoners can have a visit every day, but for convicted prisoners it's once a fortnight and only at weekends.

'Now, to get your visit, you have to write your visitors' names here on the VO and you post it to them. Then, on the day of the visit, they come to the prison with this. If they haven't got it they won't get in. Is that clear?'

I filled it in with Aunt Teasy and Uncle Bill's names and posted it.

The day of the visit came. A screw at my cell door, closing it, locking it. This was what they did – I knew that. They locked you in before a visit. That was the way it was done. Apparently it stopped prisoners getting agitated or over-excited.

I thought I wouldn't mind. I was locked up a lot anyway. But the time went even more slowly than usual now I was locked and I was impatient. I wanted to see Aunt Teasy and Uncle Bill. I heard footsteps in the corridor and thought, That's it. A screw come to call me. But it wasn't.

I went to my cell window. I could just about see the main gate. I would watch, I thought, and see Aunt Teasy and Uncle Bill coming in.

More time passed. Then a screw came and I was brought to the big hall used for visits.

I sat on one side of the table and Aunt Teasy and Uncle Bill sat on the other. Uncle Bill, as usual, wore his suit and raincoat. He was holding his hat.

'We've been to see your mum,' said Aunt Teasy.

'Yes,' I said.

'And she's all right,' said Uncle Bill.

'That's good.'

'She's doing fine,' said Aunt Teasy.

'Well, that's good,' I said again.

Of course, I already knew that when you visited someone in prison you just gave him the good news. I'd learnt that visiting Dad when he was on remand.

'And how are you?' said Uncle Bill. 'Are you all right?'

'Oh yes, I'm all right,' I said.

'Really?' said Aunt Teasy.

'Absolutely,' I said. 'Everything's fine. Nothing to worry about.'

That was another thing I knew about prison. I'd learnt this since I'd come in. On the inside you only gave the good news too. And I supposed they knew that, Uncle Bill and Aunt Teasy, and they knew I knew and I knew they knew, and they knew I knew they knew. And that was the way it was.

21

We got paid for the work we did, cleaning in my case, sixty-one pence per week. They didn't actually give you the money because they didn't allow cash to circulate in the prison. The money went into an account from which the prison authorities deducted the cost of anything you bought. Now it was Thursday, and I was in the canteen. I'd come to 'spend' my wage. I got in the queue. I was excited. I'd been waiting for this and I knew exactly what I was going to buy.

I got to the counter. It was like the tuck shop at Quintin Kynaston, which I'd broken into with a mate more than once, with boxes of sweets and other goodies, including fags, laid out every-where.

'Name?' This was the screw behind the counter.

'Patrick Maguire.'

'Number?'

For safety's sake I had it on the back of my hand. '333892.'

'What do you want?'

'Twenty No. 6 and—'

'No. You're too young. Pick something you can have.'

'But my dad said I could smoke!'

'I don't give a fuck what your dad said. I'm telling you you're too young.'

'But I've got no fags.'

'And you're not getting any!' With that, he gave me a white-paper bag with sixty-one pence worth of Black Jacks in it, and told me to fuck off back to my wing.

I trudged across the canteen and up the stairs to H Wing. No fags. I was desperate. Why couldn't I have them? Hadn't Dad said I could? Christ, I hated this shit-hole. I'd worked my bollocks off for sixty-one pence and what did I have to show for it? A bag of fucking Black Jacks.

I got back to my cell. There was something on my bed. Hello! It was a pile of loose cigarettes. I went back out on the wing and asked around. Someone had seen what had happened in the canteen and a few of the lads on my wing had given me these. I found out who the generous ones were and offered them Black Jacks as payment, but no one would take them.

Another visit. I was on one side of the table and Dad's brother, Uncle Hugh, with two mates, friends of the family, was on the other. They were all pissed.

'How are things?' said Uncle Hugh.

'All right,' I said.

'How's the food?'

'You wouldn't feed it to a dog,' I said.

'So, no change there, then,' said Uncle Hugh.

One of the family friends began to talk. He was too loud. The other laughed. He was too loud as well. I smelt drink on their breath and the memories started: Dad coming home in the evening, flopping on to the sofa, me getting his wristwatch, putting it on and strutting around the house.

Seeing people I knew always brought back to me what life was like before I'd been put away, what I'd had then, and that now I couldn't have any of it. I hated visits yet I went on getting the VOs, sending them out and taking visits. Anything was better than nothing.

All of H Wing was at Education, which was compulsory three times a week. We were in the room where we ate our food. Two screws sat outside and the teacher was locked in with us, a woman, quite young. The subject was English and she wore a low top, which showed off her tits. Very nice.

'Right,' said the teacher, 'I'm going to go round the class and ask you why you're here. All right?'

One after another the lads answered, taking the piss in a subtle way, while she listened carefully to everything they said.

At last my turn came. 'Well, I haven't done anything,' I said.

'Oh,' she said. 'Really?'

'I shouldn't be here,' I said.

She shifted her gaze from me to the lad sitting beside me. 'You,' she said, pointing at him. 'What did you do? Why are you here?'

Later, she tried to make us work, but none of us would have it. What could she do? Keep us in after school? One of the lads started talking about sex and asked was there a right way to do it? She seemed all right with that and the conversation rolled on. I listened to the other lads talking about the things they'd got up to on the outside, about girls and parties, girls and pubs, and all sorts of things I hadn't touched. I'd had one or two girlfriends, but I hadn't done the things these lads were talking about. At the end the English teacher tried to set some homework, but we weren't having that any more than we were having a lesson. We weren't at home now so we weren't going to do any homework.

217

Then it was art. The teacher was a young bloke, very laid back. He said he was only doing it for the money, but he was easy to talk to and didn't mind us taking the piss out of him.

He handed round coloured pencils and tried to get us to draw something.

I'd noticed he was a roll-up smoker and his jacket with his smoking things was hanging over the back of a chair. I waited until another prisoner had his attention. Then I dropped my pencil in such a way that it rolled over to his jacket. I got off my chair, took the tobacco tin out of his pocket, palmed a handful and put the tin back. Then I picked up the pencil, went back to my seat, wrapped the tobacco I'd stolen in a piece of paper and put it in my pocket. I'd get some papers off one of the older lads later and have a nice smoke when I got back to my cell.

The teacher looked at his watch. The end was coming. I'd have a couple of pencils too, I decided, and they followed the tobacco into my pocket.

That was what always happened in Education, more or less throughout my time at Ashford.

Visits again. My visitors were two mates from Quintin Kynaston comprehensive and Mr Emin, my head of year, a teacher I'd a lot of respect for. More than once he'd told me to stop messing about and get on with my art because he knew I had it in me. I'd just wanted to leave and join the army so his advice hadn't made much of an impression.

'So,' Mr Emin said, 'what about education here in HMP Ashford?'

'What about it?' I said.

'Is it any good?' he said. 'Are you learning? Are you progressing?'

'Oh, yes,' I said, 'absolutely. The education in Ashford is brilliant. I go to classes three times a week. I'm learning tons.'

'Oh, that's good,' he said. 'I'm so pleased to hear you're doing well.'

You've no idea, have you? I thought. This didn't mean I liked him any the less. Mr Emin was a good teacher, and you knew where you stood with him. I'd always liked him and it was nice to see him now. His presence reminded me, though, that I'd never go to school again. My life, or at least one part of it, was gone for ever.

Morning. A screw at my cell door. 'You're doubling up,' he said. No explanation, just the bare fact.

In the afternoon, two screws rolled in. 'Kit off,' one said.

The strip search done, they went through my things. I'd no cigarettes but I'd still a few matches left over from when I was in the hospital – you hoard anything in jail for weeks, months, years, even.

'I'm taking these,' said the screw who found them.

He probably thinks I'm too young to smoke, but I thought I'd try asking anyway. 'Can't I keep them?' I said.

'No,' he said. 'Not a good idea, believe me. You're going to be sharing a cell with a lad who's in for arson.'

'Arson?'

'Starting fires maliciously,' he said.

This would be interesting.

'Gather your stuff up,' he said. 'We're going.'

I gathered my bundle and piss pot and followed them. The new cell was two down from the one I was in. One of the screws unlocked the door.

'Go in,' said the other.

My new cellmate lay on one of the two beds, reading a book. He was a teddy boy and wore his hair in a quiff.

The door banged.

'Hi, I'm Richard.'

'All right?' I said. 'I'm Patrick.' Then I thought I might as well get it over with: 'So you're in for arson?'

'Yeah, burnt down my school – great fun.' He laughed. 'Did the screws tell you?'

'Yeah, and they took away my matches.'

He opened his locker, got out a box and threw it to me. 'Here.'

I was a bit surprised and it showed.

'Don't worry,' he said, 'I'm not going to burn down the cell.'
Then he was laughing again.

I'd a sheet of writing paper on the table and a Biro in my hand.
'Dear Mum,' I wrote and stopped. I had to write this letter. There
was no other way to talk to Mum or Dad except by letter but I
was going to find it hard now, suddenly, to talk to them like
this. I wasn't in the habit of writing letters. Also, since that day
in Queens Park School when I'd written the little piece about
playing in the park, I'd vowed I wouldn't have anything to do
with words on a page, and I'd more or less succeeded. I could
barely read. The QPR programme, my army books and the head-
line in the *Mirror* were about my limit. I could write my name.
I could copy something. The way I shaped letters was quite good.
But getting words out of my head and on to the paper? Impossible. I didn't know how to put down one word after another
until I had a sentence. Nor did I know how to put down
one paragraph after another until I had a page. I just couldn't
do it.

I chewed the end of my Biro and my nails, squirming in my
seat like a child on his first day at school.

Richard was reading a book. He read all the time. The radio
was on. 'What are you doing?' he said.

'Writing a letter.'

'Really,' he said. 'Who are you writing to?'

'To my mum,' I said. Then it all tumbled out. 'The trouble is,'
I said, 'I don't have the words to say it. I've never written a letter
to anyone before. Well, maybe a list for Father Christmas, but a
proper letter, no, I've never done that before.'

Richard nodded. 'The thing is,' he said, 'it's not a good idea to
try to write the letter straight away. You've got to break it down,
and go at it slowly. First, get a bit of scrap and write out the words
you want to use. You can copy them into the letter later when you
write it out.'

That seemed a good idea.

We started the list. He helped me with the spellings. They

included: hospital, Mary, bananas, Jenny, England, weight lifting, Richard, Ludo, radio, innocent . . .

Then I tried to write the letter.

Still nothing happened. I squirmed some more.

'All right,' said Richard. 'What do you want to say?' He'd a bit of paper resting on the back of his book and a Biro in his hand.

I told him. He wrote down what I said. When he finished he gave me the paper. 'That's what you said just now,' he said. 'Now copy it down in your best writing and you'll have your letter.'

As I copied what I'd said I changed one or two words. It was bloody hard work for someone who wasn't used to writing.

When I'd finished Richard read it over. 'It isn't bad,' he said. 'There are a few spelling mistakes, though.'

He told me what they were and I corrected them.

When that was done I looked at my first letter.

Dear Mum,

I hope you are all right, because I am. Mary came up to see me. At the time I was in hospital for Psiceatric treatment, and Mary brought me up oranges, apples, bananas and sweets.

Jenny is coming up to see me soon. She said in my letter she will go and see you and Dad and Vincent.

On Sundays I go to church and I was talking to the priest. He is from the Church of England. Every morning we do PE. We play football and weight lifting. And I am going to school. We do 2 hours every day. We do English, Maths and Art.

I am in a cell with a boy. His name is Richard. He is all right. At night we` play ludo and snakes and ladders. The food in Ashford is all right. We get a big dinner and a cup of tea. At night we get a cake and tea.

Richard has a radio. We play it at night.

221

I hope the food is good there and I hope you are eating it. Hope to see you soon, all my love, Patrick

PS: We only get one letter a week but I will soon be right [sic] again.

My head hurt and I couldn't speak. Nothing I'd ever done had tired me out like writing that letter had.

'You know what you need to do?' said Richard.

Get a new brain? Go back to school?

'If you want to learn to write, you need to read,' he said, 'and I've loads of books. You can have a go at any of them any time you want. Just help yourself, mate. And when you're reading and you come across a word you like, one you want to use in a letter, write it down on a bit of scrap so you'll have it handy for when you write that letter. And I'll help you. I'll write things out and I'll check things over and I'll correct your spellings. But you have to apply yourself. You have to make the effort.'

Well, if I could learn to tell the time in the dock, I could do this. So I started to read. It was hard, puzzling words out. I wrote down the ones I wanted to use and made sentences, then showed him what I'd done. He corrected the spellings, and I copied them out until I had down exactly what I wanted to say. It was slow hard work but within a month I could put a letter together with no help. Magic.

I sent a VO to John with his name on it, but I didn't know the names of the lads who'd be coming with him so I left them off.

Saturday came and John appeared with two mates but as their names weren't on the VO the screws wouldn't let them in. While they stayed outside, I sat with John, drinking coffee, smoking – I was careful not to let the screws see me – and slagging off the screws for being so petty. John gave me a packet of No. 6, which I slipped down the front of my Y-fronts. The screws would rub me down before I went back on H Wing but they wouldn't rub me there, so they wouldn't find them. Fuck them.

* * *

The radio was on and a rock-and-roll song came on. Richard leapt off his bed and danced, singing the words. I lay on my bed, laughing, and then I thought, Why not? I got up and danced too. For the next few minutes I wasn't in prison. I was down the youth club on a Tuesday or a Thursday night with my mates.

It was another day. The screws took Richard away. When they brought him back he was wearing shoes with crêpe soles, brothel creepers, drainpipe trousers, a drape jacket with lapels and a bootlace tie.

'Look at you,' I said.

'I'm going for my appeal.'

'Oh, right.'

He gave me a few things he didn't want, tobacco, soap, toothpaste, and packed the rest in a brown-paper bag. The screws came back.

'Goodbye,' I said. 'Thanks for all your help. You've taught me to write a letter on my own. If I hadn't been able to do that I'd have gone mad. So thank you, and good luck.'

'You too,' he said.

He picked up his sack and left. I never saw him again.

It was the weekend. I had a visit. I was in my cell, locked.

'Maguire.' A screw was outside my cell door. 'Get ready, you have a visit.'

I washed my hands and face, put on the good trousers and combed my hair. Then I sat down to wait. A visit. Yes, I hated visits. They made me sad. But that came later. Before they happened, I was always dead excited. A visit. Who was I going to see today? I wasn't certain. I'd sent out more than one VO. Well, never mind, I thought. When I got down to the hall they'd be there, whoever they were, and then I'd find out. I'd drink coffee with them, lots and lots of coffee, and I might get a smoke. It would be brilliant.

Footsteps outside.

'Maguire,' the screw shouted. He'd made a mistake. There was no visit for me. This happened more than once. They did it to wind us up.

I'd had the cell I'd shared with Richard to myself for a few days.

Screw at the door: 'Pack your bundle,' he said. 'You're moving.'

I was put in a cell with a new lad. I got on with him.

A couple of days later, screw at the door again: 'Pack your bundle, Maguire,' he said.

'Why?'

'You're moving.'

'But I've only just got here,' I said. 'Can't I stay put? I'm very happy here.'

'Cut the crap and get on with it, Maguire,' he said. 'I'll be back in a few minutes for you. Oh, I'd better warn you. The new bloke you're bunking with, he has epileptic fits all the time.' Here was another word I'd never heard before.

He shut the door.

I began to make my bundle up. 'Epileptic fits'. The words frightened the life out of me. I could feel my stomach knotting and my legs trembling. Epileptic fits. I was going to be locked up with a lunatic.

The screw came back and brought me to the new cell. I went in. The door closed. My new cellmate was by the window.

'Listen, mate,' he said. 'I have fits. Have they told you?'

'Yes, the screw said.'

He told me the drill. When he was fitting I was to turn him on his front in the recovery position and pull his tongue out of the back of his throat so he didn't choke. If he was flailing around and there was furniture, I should move it out of the way so he didn't break a limb bashing into something. Once the fit finished, I was to cover him with a blanket and leave him. After a bit he'd wake up, right as rain. That was all I had to do. Easy as pie. Nothing to worry about.

The first time, he flailed around and frothed for quite a while. I thought he'd never stop but he did. I put a cover on him and then sat on the bed, just looking and waiting for I didn't know what. Eventually, he opened his eyes. 'All right, Patrick?'

It was like nothing had happened.

Visits again. My brother John, his girlfriend Maxine and John's mate, Ginger, were on the other side of the table.

'I've something for you,' said John, quietly.

We looked around. No one was watching us. John produced three packets of No. 6 and slid them across. They went straight down the front of my Y-fronts. Sixty fags, happy days, I thought. I could smoke my head off in my cell.

Our fifteen minutes were up and the visit was over – and not just this one but all visits from John. He and Anne-Marie were going to Belfast to live with Mum's sister, Aunt Mary.

I got moved again, this time to a cell on my own.

It was another morning on H Wing. I was cleaning with another lad. He was doing life. A screw came up. 'I've a little job for the pair of you,' he said, with a smile. 'The shit parcels,' he said. 'You can clear them up.'

Most inmates wouldn't use their piss pots and have it sitting there overnight. They did it in an old newspaper, made it into a parcel, and threw it out of the window.

I never did this, but even if I'd wanted to I couldn't on H Wing because our bars, unlike everyone else's, were wrapped in wire cages.

The screw went off to get our tools – a shovel and a black plastic sack.

'You know what?' said the other lad.

'What?' I said.

'We're going to make a break for it. It's the best chance we'll get, this detail.'

Where he'd got the 'we' from I'd no idea.

'We'll hit the screw over the head with the shovel,' he said. 'Then we grab his keys and run.'

Run? Where to? I didn't know where I was. If I got outside the main gates, I'd have to ask someone the way to London.

I was all for hitting the screw but I couldn't take the rest in, so I went back to my cell and sat down. Now my mind was racing. If the lad went through with it the screws might think we'd planned it together only I'd bottled out at the last moment, and then they'd get me for failing to report him. You got charged if you knew someone was going to do a runner and you didn't report it. I'd be in almost as much trouble for that as I would have been if I'd bashed the screw.

I heard footsteps. Here we go, I thought. This is it. 'I'll escort you down to the yard,' said the screw at my door, 'and you can get going on those shit parcels.'

I had to get out of this.

'I can't go,' I said quickly. 'I twisted my knee at PE and it hurts to walk.' I grabbed my knee and winced.

The screw locked the door and vanished. Thank fuck for that, I thought.

Later, I was called to the hospital. I limped over there as best I could, saw the doctor and told him I'd twisted my knee. He gave me some aspirin and told me to go away.

I limped back the way I'd come – I had to keep up appearances. Coming up on to H Wing, I met the lad who'd wanted me to escape with him and there was the screw too.

'What happened to you?' asked the escape artist.

'Bad knee,' I said, and screwed up my face as if I was in pain. 'I had to go to the hospital and show it to the doctor. It won't be right for a week or two.'

'Oh,' he said. The madness was still in his eyes. If I'd said, 'Let's get the shovel and break out now,' he'd have said, 'Yes.' No doubt about it.

A screw was at the cell door with a lady of about fifty. She was from the Board of Visitors. They were civilians, nothing to do with the prison. They checked on you in your cell and made certain the staff weren't thumping you. I'd met a few before and I didn't like them. They always made me think of a hunter looking at the animals he'd trapped.

'Stand up,' said the screw.

I stood and she came in. The screw waited in the doorway so I couldn't slam the door and take her hostage. 'Name to the lady,' he said.

'Patrick Maguire.'

'Hello, Maguire,' she said. 'How are you? Everything all right?'

Before I could say anything the screw said, 'He's a good lad.' Then she was out of the cell and he was swinging the door shut.

'Hold on!' I shouted. 'I was a good lad before I came into this shit-hole and, what's more, I shouldn't be here. I'm innocent.'

The screw stopped the door mid-swing. The Board of Visitors lady turned. 'You can't be,' she said, 'or you wouldn't be here now. You went to court, didn't you?'

'Yeah,' I said. 'I was in court.'

'Well, then, just get on with it, and be a good boy,' she said. 'There are no innocent people in our prisons. The only people in our prisons are the people who've been found guilty by the courts.'

The only good thing you did today, I thought, was leaving your house this morning. I bet your old man was glad to see the back of you. 'Well, I'm fucking innocent,' I said.

'Right, Maguire,' said the screw, 'governor's report,' and he locked the cell door.

The next day, after breakfast in my cell, I was taken to the punishment block and locked into a cell. It was dark, damp and smelt bad.

After a while, the door was unlocked. Two screws appeared, including the one who'd escorted the lady from the Board of Visitors and put me on report. 'The governor will see you now,' he said.

They marched me down a corridor and into the governor's office.

The governor sat behind his desk. Two or three feet in front of it, there were four white tiles.

'Stand up straight on the tiles and give your name and number to the governor,' said the screw who had put me on report.

227

I stepped forward. The screws positioned themselves on either side of me, but with their backs to the governor, so I couldn't attack him, which I wouldn't.

The governor was reading – the adverse report on me, I guessed. After some time, he looked up. 'Do you have anything to say?'

'Yeah, I was telling the truth. I'm innocent.'

'We will not have the likes of you talking to a member of our Board of Visitors as you did,' he said. 'I find you guilty.'

He outlined my punishment.

I'd be locked for two weeks into my cell. My radio – I'd got one by now – would be confiscated. I wouldn't be allowed to mix with the other lads. No education, PE or visits. I'd eat all meals on my own. I'd exercise on my own. I'd get no work and that meant I'd have no pay.

The governor had finished. 'Now get him out.'

'Right, Maguire,' said the screw. 'You heard. Turn round.'

'You know, Maguire,' said the governor, suddenly, 'you were lucky you only got four years. And if hanging was still the law your mother and father would be dead by now.'

'You know nothing,' I said.

The screws marched me out.

I was taken back to my cell, the radio was removed and I was locked in.

Word wasn't long getting round the wing as to what had happened. In the evening a lad I knew stopped outside my door. 'Bad luck, mate,' he said. 'How are you doing?'

'All right,' I said.

'Look down.'

A cigarette slid into view.

I put it behind my ear.

'There'll be more where that came from,' he said.

I knew this was true. They'd see me right, the other lads on the wing.

'Have to go now,' he said. 'Don't want to be seen hanging round your door. Might get me into trouble. I'll be back later with some other lads for a natter. All right?'

He went off. I'd more callers that evening. One said that if the screws really did believe I was in the IRA, I could push my luck. Good idea, but what did I say? I hadn't a clue.

Then everyone was locked and that was that day done. One down, thirteen to go.

Next day I cleaned my cell. I went to the yard and walked in a circle on my own. I was taken back to my cell and locked up. An orderly brought something to eat. The evening came at last – though it was a bloody long time coming. More chats through the door and more cigarettes pushed under. Then everyone else was locked. Lights out. Two days down, twelve to go. Then it was down to eleven, ten, and then suddenly the sentence was done.

A screw put his head in the door. I was back on normal regime, he said. PE every morning, clean the wing every day, meals in the education room, English and art three times a week, canteen on Thursday, visits at the weekend, church on Sunday, *and* I could have my radio back. Of everything, it was the radio I'd missed most. What a joy to have it back.

In the evening we were locked in, the lights went out and the screw shouted to everyone to turn off their radios. Bollocks to you, I thought – me and everyone else. I never turned my radio off, just kept the volume down and an ear cocked in case a screw came along the wing. I put the radio to my ear and listened to a play on Radio 4. Now I could forget where I was. The performers' words made pictures in my head and for as long as they lasted I was free.

I had a visit from my solicitor, Jenny Sterring. She asked me how I was, then said, 'Look, is there anything you can tell me?'

'Like what?' I said.

'To help you with your appeal,' she said.

She said she knew I was innocent, but maybe the others were not, and that she could only help me if I told her everything.

I told her we were all innocent and she was fucking mad. Then I walked out.

22

Spring slid into summer, a scorcher. Day after day the sun shone down from a clear blue sky. Some of the lads felt we should be outside more and suggested a game of football in the yard below our cells.

'No way,' said the screws.

We decided that if they wouldn't give us what we wanted, which was hardly radical, we'd go on hunger strike.

The next mealtime came.

'Everyone downstairs! Grub up!' the screws shouted.

'I'm not going,' said one lad.

'I'm not either,' said another.

I refused, too, even though I was starving.

'Suit yourselves,' said the screws. 'You don't want to eat, that's fine by us. We don't care. It's your lookout.'

We were locked again. Time passesd. The next mealtime came. We were unlocked.

'Grub up!' the screws shouted. 'Everyone out and down to the dining room. Come on, let's be having you.'

'I'm not going,' said a prisoner.

'Nor me,' said another lad.

Again, we all refused to go down.

'Suit yourselves,' said the screws, and we were locked up again. They appeared indifferent. But they weren't. Any hunger strike was bad but a hunger strike by young offenders gave them the willies.

The next mealtime came round and we were unlocked.

'Listen carefully, lads,' a screw shouted. 'If you take your meals again, you can have your game of football.'

'Straight up?' someone shouted.

'Straight up,' said the screw. 'Take your food now, and next association you'll get your game in the yard.'

That was fine by us. We clapped and shouted and stamped our feet. We'd won.

Next association we started our game of football while several screws stood around looking pissed off. Every now and again, accidentally on purpose, we'd send the ball whizzing straight at one.

I don't remember if I was on the winning or the losing side, but that didn't matter. We'd all won and that was what we cared about.

Later, though, after lights out, my mind went walkabout. I remembered kicking a ball about the Avenues with my mates. It hadn't seemed like much at the time, but now I was in prison, I saw how great it had been. It made me realize how much I'd had when I was free, and would have had if this hadn't happened. My chest filled with pain and my throat was blocked, and I wished I could stop thinking and just lie there with nothing in my head, no memories or thoughts – dead to all intents and purposes. That's what I wished.

It was the morning after the football game. The door opened and a screw put his head in. 'Maguire?'

I opened my eyes. It was five in the morning but the cell was bright.

'Get your things together,' he said.

'Why? What's happening?' I said.

'You're moving.'

'Where?'

'Just do as I say and get your stuff together. I'll be back for you in a few minutes.' He slammed the door.

I was moving just as I was getting used to the place. And I wouldn't get to say goodbye to the lads either because I'd be gone before morning unlock.

I got up and packed.

The door opened. The screw told me to come on. Out in the corridor there were two other lads from H Wing. I knew one slightly, Fred, a lifer. They were moving too, apparently.

'Where are we going?' said Fred.

'Yeah, where *are* we going?' I said.

The screw seemed not to hear, as so often happened when you asked a question about what was about to happen to you.

'Come on, tell us! Where are we going?'

'Aylesbury,' he said finally.

It meant fuck-all to me. I'd never heard of Aylesbury. It wasn't in London, that was for sure. It was just another prison, I thought. 'Where's Aylesbury?' I said.

'Don't know,' said Fred.

The other lad didn't know either. 'Sorry, mate.'

The three of us were taken to Reception where I'd come into Ashford three months earlier. The screw behind the counter asked the same bollocks as before: 'Name? Number?'

Fred and the other lad gave their details. The screw fetched their cardboard boxes with their clothes and handed them over. 'Find a cubicle and get your kit on,' he said.

They went off. Where's my box? I wondered. Has he lost it?

A minute or two passed. There was still no sign of my box. Nor was the screw even looking for it.

'Where's my box?' I said.

'You're not getting it,' he said.

'Why not?'

'Because you're going to Aylesbury in your prison uniform.'

Fred and the other lad reappeared and handed back the boxes with their uniforms folded inside. They were handcuffed to each other but I was cuffed to a screw. Just my luck, I thought.

We were marched out. The sky was clear and blue again, the morning fresh and clean. A black van was waiting with its engine running, pointing towards the prison gates. It had bars on the windows. It was like something you'd put gold bullion in, not people, I thought. What were they so worried about?

Two screws boarded first and sat at the back. I was taken in next and sat halfway up on the left against the window with my screw. Two more screws sat down in front of me, then Fred and the other lad got in. They were put three rows ahead on the right. Finally, two more screws got on; one sat in front of the two lads and the other beside the driver.

Seven screws for three inmates?

The gates to the prison opened and the van drove out. Two police cars were waiting to escort us. One went in front, the other behind, and off we set, blue lights flashing, sirens wailing.

It was still early, about six thirty, I guessed, and there wasn't a lot to see – some people standing at a bus stop, a man opening a shop that sold newspapers. There was a red light but we went straight through it. They're in a hurry, I thought, and then I guessed this was for our benefit – well, actually, mine. I wasn't your ordinary criminal, like the lads I was with. I was a terrorist. I was dangerous. What did they think I was going to do? Pull a gun, shoot them and escape?

We hit the motorway. The police escort peeled away and on we went.

I was squashed between the side of the van and the screw. The sun was shining and it was getting hot. The screw was sweating. If they'd pulled into a town, stopped at a station and given me a ticket to Aylesbury, I'd have happily made my own way there.

Fred turned in his seat. He started to say something to me.

'No talking,' said a screw.

Fred turned away. The screws carried on gabbing.

I put my nose to the window. Trees and fields with cows and sheep flashed by. There were hills in the distance. I was surprised by the colour – had I forgotten this was what the world was like or had I never noticed? I decided I'd forgotten. In Ashford everything was grey. That was why.

We turned off the motorway. At the top of the slip-road another police escort was waiting. We drove into the centre of Aylesbury, a police car in front, another behind, lights flashing, sirens wailing, crashing every light we came to. There were people on the pavements, and as we passed, they stared at us.

I noticed some schoolkids at a bus stop, all in uniform, looking very smart. They were laughing and having fun. I felt a little tug inside. If I was at home, I thought, I'd be at my bus stop waiting for the number thirty-one to take me to school. With my mind's eye I saw it big and red, lumbering up and stopping. Then I saw myself jumping on and running up the stairs to the top deck, and there were all my mates. How you doing, mate? How are you, Patrick? All right, Pat? Here you go, try this. A hand offered me a No. 6 . . .

The van stopped in front of the heavy wooden gates of HMP Aylesbury. The driver sounded his horn. The gates opened slowly to reveal a space with old iron gates at the other end. In jail, wood and iron were always paired. Coming in, you hit the wood first, then the iron; going out, it was the other way round. Or that was how it seemed to me, anyhow.

We nosed forward and my guts churned with fear. What lay inside? At least, I thought, I'm better off than I was three months ago when I arrived at Ashford. I knew nothing then. Nothing. I knew something now. I knew, for instance, that I wasn't going to take shit from anyone. When you're a prisoner, your safety is your top priority. It comes before anything else.

I didn't enjoy thinking like this and it wasn't how I was outside. Inside I expected the worst, I expected to be attacked. Inside, I was always coiled tight and ready to fight. Outside, I was a friendly, easy-going bloke. I liked to laugh. I liked to muck about. I didn't take things too seriously. I wasn't a good boy but I wasn't a bad boy either, well, not until I went off the rails after the raid and all that followed.

But now I was not the boy I'd been. Now I was a prisoner and I thought like one.

We were through the wooden gates and stopped because the iron gates ahead were shut. A screw came out of a small office on the left and had a quick look inside the van. Then the iron gates opened, and the van moved forward, the screw walking beside us. We were heading towards a small building with big ones around it. I felt more and more frightened.

The van came to a careful stop outside the small building. The screw who had been walking alongside us opened the door to the building, then the grille behind.

Two more screws came out to meet us and we were taken inside. The grille and the door were locked behind us and at last the cuffs came off. This was Reception, part of the committal unit. I was put into a holding cell with Fred and the other lad, and we were left to stew.

At midday the door opened and food was passed in. The chef

here must have gone to the same cookery school as the one in Ashford.

Later the door opened again. I was pulled out alone and brought to the counter to be booked in.

'Name?'

'Maguire.'

'Number?'

'333892.'

'Right,' he said, looking at me. 'You don't need a uniform, do you? You're already wearing one. Good, I only have to issue a bedding roll and a piss pot to you.'

He got them out and handed them over.

'Okay,' he said. 'You'll remain in the committal unit, with the other lads from Ashford, for a fortnight, after which you'll be moved to a wing in the main prison. The fortnight here is to break you in. Got it?'

A screw brought me to my cell. There was a bed, a locker, a table and a chair, plus a big window with bars. 'Make your bed,' he said.

'Now?'

'Yes.'

'But it's the daytime. Don't I have to pile the covers up?'

'No,' said the screw. 'Just make the bed.'

That's an improvement, I thought.

I was left alone for a few hours. Then, in the afternoon, I was brought to a yard with some prisoners, including Fred and the other lad, and we walked round and round together. After exercise, we were locked up again until later when we were brought out of our cells and lined up.

'Right,' said the screw, 'you're going down to the dinner hall to get your tea, understand?'

My guts were churning again.

We marched out of Committals along a walkway, through several doors and gates, and finally into the dinner hall. There were steel trays piled up near the counter. I took one and joined the queue. Prisoners were looking at us. In jail you can tell when you're being stared at even if you can't see who's doing it. You can feel it: it's like heat. By now my heart was thumping.

If anyone starts anything, I thought, if they say one fucking wrong word, I'm going to bury my tray in their head.

Of course, nothing happened and nothing was said. I got my food, carried it back to my cell and ate on my own.

Day two in Aylesbury was like day one, except that I cleaned my cell. Otherwise I was locked in, except when I was tramping round the yard or walking to the dinner hall and back.

And day three was the same as day two.

It was day four in the afternoon and I was listening to a radio programme. I heard footsteps, which stopped outside my door. The metal flap clanged. 'You don't look like your brother,' a screw shouted.

I jumped up and went to the door. 'What the fuck do you know?'

'Watch your mouth, boy.'

'Piss off,' I said.

I heard the screw's boots squeaking on the floor as he walked away. Why'd he come to my cell door and said that? Had he seen Vincent? If he had, it must mean – No, I thought. That thought wasn't a thought to have, and I wouldn't have it.

Later, the door was unlocked. 'Tea up,' said the screw.

I went out to the wing and there he was, with a piss pot in his hand. Vincent, with the smile he always had. 'All right, kid?' he said.

'Yeah,' I said. 'When did you get here?'

'Today,' he said, 'fresh from the Scrubs, and I can't tell you how glad I am to get away from there.'

'That bad?' I said. 'What's it like?'

'Shit-hole.'

'Ashford's the same,' I said.

'Tell me about this place,' he said.

'I've only been here four days,' I said, 'so I don't know everything.' Then I explained that the only time I was off the wing was when I went to the exercise yard or to the dinner hall to get my food.

'We'll go over together, stay together. Then we'll be all right,' he said.

When I lived at home Vincent was always doing his own thing. Usually this meant playing rock music in his bedroom. It was always too loud, which drove Dad mad. They'd argue about it, Vincent would turn the volume down and Dad would stamp off. A few quieter minutes would follow but then the level would creep up again. That was my brother, up in his bedroom, listening to his records, pleasant, affable, a bit distant.

The Vincent talking now, though, was talking like an old brother, and he was on the money. Prisoners like to test a new man, to see how well he can stand up for himself, but in our case there would be an extra dimension.

We weren't ODCs – ordinary decent criminals. We were in for making the bombs used to kill people in Guildford – a heinous crime. On top of that, the IRA was still at it. When the next bomb went off, those who hated us already – and that was just about everyone else except one or two sex offenders who'd be too frightened to join in – would feel we were fair game. But if we were always together, in the dinner hall or the showers (which happened once a week in HMP Aylesbury), other prisoners might be put off starting something, and if they did start something, our chances of survival would be better if we fought as a pair.

Vincent dumped his piss pot and we went to the dinner hall together. When we got there, he nodded at one of the lads doling out the food. How he knew him he didn't say, and I never asked, but it was great that he did. My portion was that little bit larger and now I knew a friendly face in the main prison.

We carried our food back. Vincent went into his cell, two doors down from mine, and I went into mine. That was the pattern. I only saw him when we went backwards and forwards to the dinner hall, or when we were cleaning out our cells and the wing, and when we were in the showers or exercising in the yard.

Although we didn't spend a huge amount of time together, we were grateful to have each other close at hand. Word spread quickly that we were brothers. Anyone who wanted to say anything soon knew he'd have to say it to both of us. We had no trouble, but that didn't mean I let my guard down for even one fucking minute. No. I was always alert, coiled and ready.

Vincent had been on the wing a couple of days when a screw appeared one morning and said, 'Doctor for those who haven't seen him yet.'

That meant me, Vincent and eight others.

We ten new boys were brought to the hospital and put in a waiting room. A man in a white coat called one of us into his surgery and left the rest of us sitting there.

The waiting room was dark, not so dark that we couldn't see each other but too dark to sit and wait in. That was what I thought, anyway.

Where was the switch? I wanted to brighten the place up a bit. Everyone else was talking so no one noticed me looking around. Then I spotted something. That must be it. I got up and went over.

The switch was a button, which was unusual for a light, but this was a prison where nothing was the same as it was outside.

I pressed once.

Nothing.

I pressed again.

No light.

I pressed a third time.

Still no light.

'I don't think that was such a good idea,' whispered Vincent, 'what you've just done.'

'Why not?' I said.

'Because that's the alarm you've pressed,' he said quietly. 'Can't you hear it ringing in the distance?'

Now he mentioned it . . .

Probably not a good idea to stay where I was, I thought. Best to put a bit of space between it and me.

I slipped out without any of the others noticing and Vincent followed. Screws were running everywhere, pounding towards us.

They knew where the alarm had gone off and that was where they were heading.

Vincent and I took up position out of harm's way, flat against the wall. The posse flew by, a blur of blue trousers and white shirts, and burst into the waiting room. 'Right,' said a screw, 'which of you fuckers pressed the bell? Come on, who did it? Own up.'

'It wasn't me.'

'No, not me.'

'It wasn't me, sir, honest.'

'All right, all of you,' shouted the screw, 'you can stop being clever. It wasn't the Holy Ghost who pressed it. One of you little shits did. Come on, whichever one of you did it, put your fucking hand up.'

'None of us did it,' said one lad, speaking for everybody. 'We've all just been sitting here. We wouldn't touch the bell, would we?'

'Definitely not. Oh, no,' said somebody else.

'We know never to touch the bell,' said the speaker. Prisoners never touched it, full stop. It wasn't for inmates. It was for the screws. Everyone knew that.

No one had noticed we were missing. At least, not yet. But once they did notice, they'd guess one of us had done it and then we'd be in trouble. Frivolous bell-pushing was a chargeable offence. Vincent and I could get fourteen days on the boards for it.

Vincent was looking at me. He must have had the same thought, I guessed, and now he was thinking how much better off he'd be in the Scrubs, away from his little brother. Then he smiled. He must have seen the funny side. While the screws were in the waiting room, getting the runaround from the lads, the real culprits were outside, holding their breath. It was funny. Even a screw in the right mood would see that, which was what must have happened because there was no comeback.

A few days later Vincent and I were discussing pay day, our first in Aylesbury, and our first visit to the canteen.

'Aren't you looking forward to it?' asked Vincent.

'Not really,' I said. 'They wouldn't let me buy tobacco at Ashford because I was too young, and I'm sure it'll be the same here. "Can I have some tobacco, please?" "No, you're too young, fuck off."'

Vincent smiled. 'I wouldn't worry, Patrick,' he said.

He and I went to the shop together. He got me what I wanted (tobacco, Rizla papers and some matches) and I got him what he wanted (toiletries), and when we got back to Committals we swapped. That was how we did it until I was officially allowed to smoke.

Where there's a will there's always a way.

Another morning, and a screw was at my door. 'Get your stuff together,' he said.

'Why?'

'You're going to the main prison, you and the other two lads you came up from Ashford with.'

I made up my bedding bundle with my clothes and other bits stuffed into the middle, then went to Vincent's cell and told him I was off.

'I'll see you in the main prison in a few days,' he said, 'and meantime, until I get over, behave.'

F and G Wings were for first-timers who'd never been to prison before. They were big three- or four-storey buildings joined by an arm, which had a recreation room with snooker, table tennis, darts and a record player, a dinner hall (the food came from the prison kitchen), classrooms, a television room and a gym.

I was directed to G Wing, and went up to the second floor. When I came through the grille I saw a corridor stretching ahead; there was a washroom, then rows of cells, about twenty, a classroom, toilets, the recess for slopping out, and lots of windows.

The screws' office was on my immediate left, with a clear view down the wing, and beyond it there was a little spur with four more cells. I was put in the cell second from the end of the 'mini-wing'. I knew at once why I was there. It was where they put anyone they considered a security risk. There, on the spur, the screws could always see where you went and who visited you.

The screw told me to settle in and left me. He didn't lock the door.

I made my bed, put my things in the locker, rolled a fag, put the radio on and lay down. G Wing was silent. Everyone was at work. I only saw one other prisoner as I lay there. He was mopping the floor on the spur and glanced in as he passed.

A screw appeared and told me to come with him. I followed him down the wing to the office where another screw was reading some papers. He was the senior officer, or SO, the man in charge.

He looked up. 'Who do you love most?' he said. 'Your mum or your dad?'

'What?'

'Who do you love most?' he said again. 'Your mum or your dad?'

Now I knew what this was about. Sometimes, at home, Mum or Dad would ask the same question, and I would tell them I loved them both the same. But the SO was hoping I'd pick one or the other. That way he'd know whether I was a 'mummy's boy' or a 'daddy's little man'.

'What has it got to do with you?' I said.

He didn't like that, but he couldn't ask the question a third time because obviously I wasn't going to answer it as he wanted.

'When's my brother coming over? Will he be on G Wing?'

'I don't know anything about that,' he said. 'Now, you listen to me. You be a good boy, and everything will be all right. Have you got that?'

I said nothing but my heart was hammering because something was coming that I wasn't going to like. I knew it from the way he'd said that if I was a 'good boy' everything would be all right.

'You'll be having your lunch down in the dinner hall with all the other lads, won't you?' said the SO.

I nodded.

'Well,' he said, 'I have to warn you that you'll probably be booed and shouted at when you go in.'

I said nothing.

'Now, if you want,' he said, 'you can have your food brought to your cell and eat alone. Do you want to do that?'

I knew now that it wasn't just a booing problem. It was the kind of prisoner I was, a bomber, and the attitude of other prisoners to someone who'd been convicted of making bombs to kill. They knew the case, they knew the crime, and they weren't likely to be well disposed towards me. They were likely to be extremely hostile to some Paddy who'd had it in for their brave army lads. My choices were either to tough it out or, which the SO hadn't mentioned but was there, lurking behind his words, do what the sex offenders, the nonces, and other frightened, hated or vulnerable prisoners did. I could go on Rule 43 and be kept apart from the main population. Then I'd be safe from booing and everything else, but I'd be isolated and, worse, because of opting to be on Rule 43 with the kiddy fiddlers, I'd be guilty in the eyes of every other prisoner of the crime the court had said I'd committed.

But I'd not done anything, I thought. Why should I hide as if I was guilty so everyone would end up thinking I was? There was no alternative. I'd have to tough it out. 'No,' I said, 'I'll take my meals down in the dinner hall, same as everyone else.'

'Take him away,' said the SO.

I was put back in my cell and again the door wasn't locked.

I sat on my bed and waited for the ordeal to start.

The landing was quiet for a bit and then I heard prisoners coming back from work. I heard lads talking and laughing. I heard doors opening and closing. I heard officers bawling orders.

I didn't take my eyes off the door. If anyone popped their head in, I'd see them coming. The thought of being booed was going through my mind but I was up for it. I had to face them down.

The noises on the landing faded as everyone went to lunch until finally there was silence.

I heard footsteps on the landing and a screw appeared in my doorway. 'Do you want your dinner in your cell?' he asked.

'No,' I said.

'Are you sure?'

'Yes.'

'Then you should go down to the dinner hall,' he said.

I came out of the cell.

242

'Go down the stairs,' he said, 'and when you get to the ground floor you'll see the hall. You can't miss it.'

I went down slowly, thinking about what might be waiting for me when I got to the bottom, heart thumping, every muscle tight, ready to fight. I wasn't trying to be hard. I just knew this was something I had to get out of the way now, because if I didn't, and word got about that I was weak, frightened or timid, it would be worse. Once they got wind that I was weak, the ones who despised me wouldn't leave me alone. I'd be dead.

I got to the ground floor and went through the doors. The dinner hall was big and full of prisoners. They'd mostly got their food and were eating.

I started to walk forward. I could hear talking and laughing and I saw men looking at me. I walked on. They're not talking about me, I told myself. They're not laughing at me. I knew I couldn't let myself believe anyone was doing either because then I'd have to stop and ask what the matter was, what they were staring at, and then it would all kick off. That would be asking for it.

The trick was to keep moving. The trick was to act like I had nothing on my mind, and I was just a new prisoner walking into the dinner hall. At the same time, though, but without it showing, I had to be ready to take out the first nutter who stood up to have a go. And I was.

A screw came up to me. 'You see that table over there?' he said. He pointed to one with three lads already at it.

'Yes.'

'That's where you're to go every mealtime,' he said. 'Got it?'

'Yes.'

'Go and get your food, then.'

I went to the hotplate. I got a tray of food. I went to the table. I sat down.

None of the three lads spoke or looked me in the eye. They went on eating and talking as if I wasn't there, which was all right with me as I didn't have much to say anyway.

I saw the other two lads from Ashford a couple of tables down from me. I nodded to them. They were new boys like me.

I picked up my knife and fork and began to eat. Once Vincent got over, I thought, I'd have him to talk to, which would be better than this.

I spent the evening with the other two lads from Ashford. We stayed in the television room and it was a bit like being back at the youth club, only there were no girls and I wasn't going home at the end of the night.

On my second evening I decided to sit in the main room, my back against the wall, watching everyone else, just killing time, really. After a bit I saw two lads walking towards me. I wondered what to do. Did I get up and kick one in the balls? Or did I give them the benefit of the doubt?

I decided to wait.

The lads sat down, one on either side of me.

'How you doing, mate?' said one.

'All right?'

I was ready. If the talker made a move I'd pull his eyes out.

'So, you're the IRA bomber,' said the talker.

I stood up and looked down at them. 'No, I'm fucking not, so piss off.'

'All right, mate, so what you in for?'

'I said piss off.'

They got up and walked off. Had they wanted to start something or were they simply friendly? I never did find out.

Vincent arrived three days after I had. They put him on F Wing and I only saw him at mealtimes, during association or when we took visits together. It was good to have someone to talk to now and then.

I got an orderly's job, cleaning the wing, and one or two more spoke to me. After two or three weeks of cleaning I was assigned to one of the workshops. My first job was to paint little Roman soldiers. This was the sort of thing I had done at home in my bedroom, but now I was getting paid for it, sixty-one pence a week.

There were other lads sitting on the long bench painting with me, from F and G Wings and other parts of the prison. At first we got on with the work and didn't talk. Then came the thaw, and after that we talked constantly. One of the topics, naturally, was what we'd done to end up in prison.

The trial of the Maguire Seven, as they called us, at the Old Bailey had been a huge story, reported on television and written about in every newspaper. When it was happening I didn't watch the news or read the papers. By the time we got home from court, I just wanted to go out for an hour or two with my friends or, if it was very late, go to my bedroom to play with my soldiers or read comics. Also, Mum had kept me away from the news, but so cunningly that I never noticed she was doing it.

But the boys on the bench had seen the television and read the papers. They knew all about me – or thought they did. What they knew was lies of course and, as day followed day, I told them what had actually happened and that we were all innocent.

I also let them know that I could look after myself. I didn't say I'd come out of every fight a winner – that would have attracted the attention of every lunatic who wanted to make his reputation by cutting the arrogant Maguire down to size – I put it this way: I said whoever took me on would know they'd been in a fight afterwards. They might win but they'd be hurt, they could be sure of it. My words were carried out into the prison and did the trick. No one had a go.

After Ashford, Aylesbury was good. I liked mixing with other people. It was good to talk. It was good to make friends. And then, better still, it was good to stop being the new boy and become part of the furniture, just another prisoner who did his thing. Within a month, I was just another lag.

'RCs!' the screw shouted. 'Any RCs for church?'

We lined up and were taken downstairs to the ground floor and then along the G Wing landing and through the doors at the end. On the other side I found myself in the church. The walls were yellow and the woodwork was white. I sat on a pine bench. In front of me, on a raised floor, stood the altar, with barred stained-glass windows behind it. There were several vases of freshly cut flowers, put there by the nuns who cleaned the church on Saturday morning with the help of an inmate, who was also one of the two altar boys. I could smell wax polish, incense and flowers. It was good to be in a place of colour and sensation. That was why I came. After my grey cell, the work-shop and the grimy jail, those colours and smells in church were extraordinarily vivid.

The priest appeared, a great old boy, not very tall, with grey hair, a round red face, and a good laugh. The prisoners fell quiet. The only sounds now were those coming from the screws' two-way radios. 'Excuse me,' said the priest. 'Would you mind turning down your walkie-talkies or else could you leave the church? The noise will disturb the service.'

The majority adjusted the volume but one or two went out.

I liked the way the priest had spoken to them. He wouldn't tolerate them disturbing his Mass. If they wanted to stay, it would be on his terms.

It was another Sunday. I'd been coming for a while. After the service the priest called me aside. 'How'd you like to help here,' he said, 'on Saturday mornings, getting the chapel shipshape?'

'Of course,' I said. 'I'd love to.'

The following Saturday a nun was putting flowers into vases. Another was dusting. And I was polishing the floor.

'And how are you today, Patrick?' asked the nun doing the flowers.

'I'm very well,' I said.

'That's good. I'm glad to hear it.'

She went on with her flower-arranging, humming. The other went on dusting. I went on polishing. That was the end of the conversation. I didn't mind. It was better than being in my cell – just about anything was better than that – and in fact it was quite nice. I would definitely keep going with this.

I was there the next Saturday and every one thereafter. It wasn't long before I began to look forward to seeing the nuns. They lifted my spirits. And sometimes the priest popped his head in. I liked that too. He knew all about the case, although we didn't go into the ins and outs of it. I told him we were innocent and he would ask after Mum and Dad. He was a good man.

As well as cleaning on Saturday, I went to Mass every Sunday too. Well, how could I not? I was part of the church furniture. One of the alter boys was Fred from Ashford.

It was now another Sunday. I'd been in prison for several months. I was sitting in a pew and others were filing in. The priest came over to me. 'Can I have a word afterwards?' he said.

'Course,' I said. What was this about?

After the service I stayed sitting while everyone else filed out. The priest came back. 'Besides coming on Saturday mornings,' he said, 'would you like to serve on the altar at Mass on Sundays? I'm a man short, you see.'

Would I? I'd be serving with Fred. Of course I would.

It was the next Sunday. I didn't sit down to wait on a pew. I went up to the altar and lit the candles with Fred. Then the priest celebrated Mass.

Afterwards, Fred and I put out the candles and went into the side room. The leftover Communion wine had been put into three glasses, one for each of us. 'Hello, lads,' said the priest. 'Well done.' He handed us each a glass. 'Drink up,' he said.

I opened my mouth and swallowed the wine. It was warm and quite sweet. I shivered. My face went red and my head felt light. This was all right, I thought. I'd be sticking with church, helping the nuns on Saturdays, serving on Sundays, oh, yes, no doubt about it.

23

It was October 1976, Friday, very early in the morning. I was in my cell, asleep. Then something was shining on my face.

I opened my eyes. Someone had turned on my light. I heard keys. It couldn't be time to get up. I was always out of bed when the screw banged on the door to wake me. This didn't make sense.

I looked at the window bars. It was still night. Why was the screw getting me up now? He must have gone mental.

The door opened. 'Get up, Maguire,' said the figure in the doorway.

'What's going on?' I said.

'I can't say,' he said, 'but you'll find out soon enough.'

'What time is it?'

'Oh, I can tell you that,' he said. 'It's five o'clock. Now, get out of that bed and get yourself dressed.'

He closed the door before I could ask any more questions.

Did I want to get up? Why should I? I could just go back to sleep. On the other hand, what was going on?

I got dressed and had a wild thought. They'd found out we were innocent, all seven of us, and we were going to be let out. Of course the screw hadn't wanted to say anything about that. It would have been an admission of fault and it would have made me happy. And he wouldn't want to do anything as stupid as make me happy, would he? Of course not.

My heart was pounding. What about Vincent? Had the screw woken him too? Was he getting dressed and thinking the same? Were Mum and Dad in their cells getting dressed and thinking the same?

The more I followed the thought, the greater my excitement and the quicker my heartbeat.

The door opened. It was the screw who had woken me, with two more. They led me along the landing, down the stairs and out into the open. We tramped through the dark.

'Where are we off to?' I said.

'Shut it, Maguire,' one said. 'You'll find out soon enough.'

'Couldn't you give me even a hint?'

'No, Maguire, and stop the questions.'

We crossed a yard and headed for the reception building. This was where they took you before you got out. You went to Reception, got your clothes and went out of the gate.

I felt the cold air at the back of my mouth, but lower down, in my chest, I was hot.

Was I going to be let out? Was someone going to say, 'Sorry, son, made a terrible mistake. No hard feelings, are there? No, of course there aren't, good lad. Now, here's a few quid and your travel warrant. Show that at the station and they'll give you a ticket for the train. Okay, off you go, bye-bye, and don't ever think about coming back.' Was that what someone was about to say?

A door was unlocked and I was brought into Reception.

'Right, Maguire,' said a screw, pointing to a holding cell. 'In there.'

'What's happening?' I asked, as I went in. 'Can someone tell me?'

The screw closed the door and locked it.

I sat on the bench, thoughts and hopes surging. After a bit, the door opened again and in walked Vincent. 'What's going on?' I asked.

'God knows. They never tell me anything. Didn't they tell you?'

'No, they said fuck-all. Maybe we're getting out.'

Vincent smiled but didn't say anything. I could see by his expression he'd had the same idea.

The cell door opened and two screws gave us our breakfasts. I didn't bother asking what was happening – I knew there was no point. The door closed. We sat on the bench and ate quietly.

The two screws came back. 'Right,' one said, 'let's be having you.'

They brought us up to the office. There were several screws standing around and they looked at us as we came in. There was something up, no doubt about it. I could feel it in the air.

An officer was sitting behind a desk with papers in front of him. 'Right, you two,' he said. 'You're going to see your mum and dad today, and these officers are taking you.' He gestured at the seven standing around. 'They're going with you to Durham.'

That was where Mum was, which meant – since he'd said we'd be seeing Mum *and* Dad – that our father would be taken there from HMP Gartree, where he was.

'So if you want to see your mum and dad,' said the screw, 'just be good boys, all right.'

Vincent and I looked at each other. We hadn't seen Mum and

Dad since the Old Bailey seven months ago. This wasn't as good as getting out would have been but it was close. We smiled with our whole faces.

'Can we wear our own clothes,' asked Vincent, 'instead of our prison uniforms?'

'No,' said the desk screw. 'You can't.'

'Why not?'

'Security reasons,' he said.

Mum wouldn't be pleased about that, I thought. In one of her letters she'd said that when she did get to see us she hoped we'd be wearing our own clothes.

The screw with the cuffs approached. The first bracelet went on my right wrist. Then the screw bent Vincent's left arm across his chest, and closed the bracelet around his wrist.

Like this, we'd have to make the journey with our arms bent in front of us. 'This isn't right,' I said.

'This is the way we do it,' said the handcuff screw. 'Have you got a problem with that? Because if you have you can stay here.'

'Stop arsing around,' shouted another screw. 'The transport's waiting.'

Surrounded by our escort, Vincent and I set off, our arms bent in front. It felt odd moving like this and we must have looked strange too.

The blue prison van was facing the gates. The engine was running. The driver had the interior light on and was reading a paper. As one of the escorts opened the back door, he put it down and turned off the light.

Vincent and I were told where to sit. I got the window. Once we were sat, we put our hands on our knees. It was incredibly uncomfortable.

The escort got aboard. Two sat in front, two by the doors, and two sat as close to Vincent and me as possible without actually sitting on us. The seventh sat by the driver.

The gates swung open and we drove out. Two police cars were waiting outside. They sandwiched us, one going in front, other behind, sirens on, lights whirling. We got to the first red light and drove straight over. This would be like the journey from Ashford to Aylesbury, I thought. We'd be whizzed along like visiting royalty or politicians.

I looked out through the bars on the window beside me. There was condensation on the glass. I wiped it away. There wasn't much to see. It was still dark. The radio was on. The screw in the front had the driver's paper and was reading by the dashboard lights. The six around us were talking. I recognized one or two. So did Vincent. He began to talk to them. I fished my tobacco out of my pocket (hard) and rolled ten cigarettes (harder still) so I wouldn't have to go through the same bollocks every time I wanted a smoke.

'Fucking stupid, this,' I said.

I was told to stop moaning.

I got my lighter out (more contortions) and lit up. We passed a sign that told us we were in Bedfordshire. The leading police car pulled in, we passed it and the other joined it. They were Buckinghamshire police and had done their bit. They'd seen us safely off their patch and now they could go back to the station for a mug of tea and maybe a fry. Lucky bastards.

We got on to the motorway. I saw big green fields, a few with cows or sheep but mostly empty, bare hedgerows, bare trees, rivers and distant hills. It was like watching a BBC2 nature programme with the sound off.

My arse felt sore and I wished they'd let us out for a walk. No chance of that. All I could do was sit and wait until we arrived at Durham prison.

We overtook a car. There was a mum and dad in the front and a pretty girl in the back. I caught her eye, gave her a wink and blew her a kiss. The father behind the wheel scowled up at me. I wasn't to make eyes at his daughter. I gave her a final wink.

The radio was still on, Radio 1, not that anyone had started a sing-along. The six screws were still talking and now they included us.

'You know what?' said one to Vincent and me. 'We love doing escorts like this. We get overtime, and extra for the B-and-B overnight. Plus we get to go on the piss after we drop you off. Escorts are magic, so thank you, lads, sincerely, from the bottom of our hearts.'

Everyone was happy, I thought, Vincent and me because we were going to see Mum and Dad, and the screws because they were getting out of the nick and away from their wives. Who was happier, us or them? It was a close-run thing.

We'd been on the motorway for some hours when we turned off.

'Right, listen up,' said the SO.

He was the one in front by the driver. 'We're going to stop soon,' he said. He mentioned the name of a prison in the Midlands. 'We're going in there,' he said, 'to get some dinner before we go on to Durham.'

Oh, great, I thought. I could get the handcuffs off and some life back into my arse.

The van came to a stop in front of some prison gates. The driver sounded his horn twice. The gates opened. We drove forward and stopped. A screw got in, had a word with our SO, then gave Vincent and me the once-over. He directed the driver towards a building with two screws standing outside an open door.

We drove over. An SO came out. The doors of the van were opened. We were brought into the building and the cuffs were taken off. That was a relief. I could give myself a good scratch and get the circulation going.

Our Aylesbury SO and the new SO started talking.

'These two, they're SW,' said the SO from Aylesbury.

SW was Special Watch. That was how they classified us because we were too young to be classified as Category A offenders like some of the others we were in with.

'Right,' said the other SO.

'So, what's the form?' said the SO from Aylesbury.

'We've decided to park them in the punishment block.'

'No better place.'

We were brought to the block, put in the same cell and given some dinner. I was so hungry I cleared my plate quickly, then had a look at Vincent's to see if he'd anything left, but he'd cleared his too.

There was only one bed in the cell, and after eating I lay down and had a smoke.

Vincent had found a book on the table and sat on the chair, reading.

I fell asleep. When I woke up, I was confused. I knew I was in prison but which one? Then I saw Vincent and remembered. I rolled a fag and was about to light up when a screw opened the door. 'Right, better use the toilet, you two,' he said, 'because we're not stopping again until we get to Durham.'

As I pissed, I thought, Why Durham? I'd never heard of the place before they put Mum up there. If I'd a map in front of me I wouldn't have known where to find it. It was up north, but that was all I knew. Why couldn't they have put her nearer to London, where her family and friends were? Durham, I thought, they might as well have put her on the moon.

It was dark and the rain hitting the roof of the van was making a noise that went right through my head. I might have started the day in good spirits, excited at the thought of seeing Mum and Dad, but fourteen hours or so later, I was pissed off, cold, sore and stiff. All I wanted now was to get under the covers, go to sleep and lie in until late the following morning.

The van pulled up before the Durham prison gates and the driver hooted. We got through and drove to Reception, went inside and the cuffs came off. Our escort left in search of their B-and-B and beer, and the Durham screw in charge of processing started the questions – name, date of birth . . . That done, he issued us with our bedding rolls and piss pots. Then we set off for our cells, one screw behind, another in front.

We crossed a yard, went through a door, climbed several flights of stairs and turned on to a wing. It was quiet and the cell doors were locked. I guessed the prisoners were in bed. I saw a screw looking into a cell through the spyhole. He heard us, turned and stared as we walked past.

Eventually we came to a cell with the door open. Vincent was told to go in. I was walking behind him and assumed I was to follow him.

'Not you,' said a screw. 'You've a cell of your own.'

Vincent heard this and turned. 'See you,' he said. The door was slammed and locked before I could say anything back to him.

'You're in here,' said the screw, pointing to the cell next door to Vincent's.

I went in. Besides the bed, there was a table, a chair and a small locker for clothes. The window was the biggest I'd ever seen in a cell and it was open, the wind rushing in, cold and fresh. Unfortunately, all my things – my books, pens, pencils, paper, radio and so on, with which I might have furnished this spot – were in Aylesbury.

'Make your bed,' said the screw, 'and be quick about it.' He banged the door behind him.

I made the bed, then pulled the table under the window and climbed on top of it. 'Vincent,' I called, through the bars.

'What?'

'You all right?'

'Yeah. Go to sleep!'

'See you in the morning.'

'Yeah.'

'Maguire,' I heard. A screw was looking at me through the spyhole. 'Get into bed,' he said.

I got down and dragged the table back to where it had been. The light went out and I got under the covers. I rolled a fag, lit up and lay in the darkness smoking.

It was a long time, I thought, since the four of us – Mum, Dad, Vincent and me – had been under the same roof. Durham wasn't the best one to be under, but at least we'd be together as a family. I was looking forward to that.

I could feel the cold air on my face. Really I should get up and close the window, I thought, but that would mean getting out from under the covers and I was warm and cosy now.

Nah, I couldn't be bothered. I closed my eyes.

*   *   *

On Saturday I woke to banging on my cell door and a voice telling me to get up. The cell seemed even colder and fresher than it had been the night before. Maybe I should have closed the window after all. I began to dress.

I could hear doors opening and gates being unlocked, people moving about the prison. Durham was coming to life, and before long there was the most fantastic racket outside. I heard Vincent's door being opened and, guessing I'd be next, I picked up my piss pot and stood ready. My door swung open. I hurried out and into Vincent's cell. He was putting on a shoe.

'You all right?' he said. 'Now, listen. We're new boys. The moment we step out on to the landing, everyone will be looking at us and some will already know, thanks to the screws, who we are and why we're here. There might be name-calling, or worse. So, I say we go to the recess together and watch each other's backs.'

We set off along the landing, our piss pots in front of us. There were prisoners going in and out of their cells, and as we passed they stared at us, as we'd expected. Nothing else happened. No one said anything. No one jostled or pushed us. We got to the recess. We emptied our piss pots and rinsed them. We walked back to our cells. Still no shouting or aggravation. There wasn't going to be trouble.

We fetched our bowls for washing and carried them back to the recess. Vincent filled his with hot water and left. I filled mine, then came out of the recess and began to walk up the landing. We were on the third storey, and had a view into the well and the lower tiers. Suddenly, there was Dad, with his piss pot and four screws, on the ground floor. 'Dad!' I called.

He glanced up, smiled and waved. He looked better than he had when he was drinking before he came to jail. Vincent came out of his cell, soap still on his face, and waved down. Dad shouted up, 'You okay, lads?'

'Yes, we're fine,' we shouted back.

'You all right for tobacco, Patrick?'

He hadn't forgotten what he'd said: if I was old enough for jail I was old enough to smoke. 'Fine,' I said.

'I'll see you later,' he said, and walked on.

We went downstairs, got breakfast and carried it back up. I went into Vincent's cell to eat with him. I'd hardly started before a screw was at the door. 'You, young fellow,' he said, meaning me, 'go into your own cell to eat your breakfast.'

After breakfast I was locked in. Now that I'd seen Dad and knew he was just a couple of floors below, I felt good. I could wait. I could handle this.

After a bit I was unlocked and so was Vincent, and the screws brought us down to the ground floor where we found Dad waiting. This was it. Now we'd see Mum, the three of us together.

We set off. The escort was six screws, one in front, one at the back and two on either side, us in the middle, with Vincent and me on either side of Dad just hanging back a bit. Every now and then Dad would look over each shoulder in turn to make sure we were all right. I couldn't stop smiling.

We got outside. Two more screws were waiting, with dogs. We walked on, passing blocks, and at every cell window I could see prisoners looking down at us. Wherever you are in a prison, especially when you're new, you're always watched.

Suddenly Dad touched my wrist. 'Where's the watch, son?'

'They took it.'

'What?'

'The screws wouldn't let me have it. It's in my property.'

'That's not right. What happened?'

'In Reception at Ashford, I asked the screw if I could keep it. He said no, I didn't need to know the time because I wasn't . . . going anywhere for the next four years, was I?'

'Ach, no, son, you were supposed to have that,' he said, and shook his head.

We reached the women's section, which was within the prison's main walls. The building was like the others, the only difference being the high wire fence that separated it from the surrounding buildings, and the cameras on posts pointing down at the fence.

We stopped at a gate, and a screw pressed a button on the intercom unit.

256

'Who's there?' said a voice on the speaker.

'Escort with visitors for Maguire,' said the screw.

'Prisoners, look up at the camera above the gate,' said the voice.

The camera turned, moving slowly like the head of a robot, angling itself, then stopped and focused its eye on us.

I gave it a half-smile.

'Okay,' said the voice.

There was an electronic noise as the gate opened. We stepped in. The screws with the dogs stayed behind. The gate slid shut.

We walked across a yard overlooked by cell windows.

Dad turned. 'All right, lads,' he said, 'give a wave in case Mum's watching.'

We waved at the block, then went down some steps, more cameras following us, and came to a door at the bottom. Another bell was pressed.

'Prisoners, look up at the camera and show your faces,' said the intercom voice.

We looked up.

The door opened. We stepped in. Two women screws met us. The escort, which was our six and these two, started nattering. Dad made himself a roll-up. I was about to do the same when Dad gave me the one he'd made.

'Here, son, have this.'

The three of us were searched, first by hand, then with an electronic gizmo that detected weapons or explosives. Fuck knows how they imagined we'd have got either in. Then the two women brought us to another grille where we waited some more. Finally, the grille opened.

The women screws went forward, we followed, and three from the original escort brought up the rear.

'Right, Patrick, you go first,' said Dad, 'then you, Vincent, and me last.'

We formed our line and walked towards a door with glass in it through which we saw Mum talking to two women screws at a desk.

'There she is, sons,' said Dad. 'There she is.'

She turned, saw us and jumped up, smiling.

We got to the door.

'Go on in first, lads,' said Dad.

The door opened. I stepped in. Mum came forward, her arms held out and tears in her eyes. 'My sons.' She gave me a big hug and started to cry. That set me off.

The small visits room was full, what with us four and the eight officers, the two who were already in there with Mum and the six who'd brought us over, plus the screw's desk and the visitors' table.

We sat down at the table. Mum had made a pot of tea and poured it out as she did at home, giving each of us our tea exactly as we always had it. 'Why are you boys in prison uniform?' she said.

We explained we'd had to come in uniform.

'I'm not happy about that,' she said.

'Well, no,' said Vincent, 'of course you aren't, but there it is. They wouldn't let us wear our own clothes.'

'What about your cell?' she said. 'How's that?'

'Separate cells,' I said.

'I'm disappointed,' she said. 'You were meant to be doubled up. I was promised. The governor's going to pop in during this visit and when he does I'll have a word with him.'

Vincent was silent and I guess he was happy having a cell to himself because it meant he didn't have to put up with me fucking about endlessly, smoking and talking. He wasn't going to let Mum know that, though. Oh, no, he was smart. Mum wanted us together and wouldn't hear him utter a word against it.

'I want to know all about Ashford and Aylesbury,' she said.

I told her a bit, the few funny things or the good things that had happened, but the rest I left out.

Later, the talk turned to the case, the trial, to our being innocent and the fact that we shouldn't be there. I listened more than I talked and noticed that the women screws at the desk were writing down what we said.

'Do you bang your doors shut behind you after you go into your cells?' asked Dad, suddenly.

'Yes,' said Vincent.

'Yes,' I said.

Most inmates did. When they got into their cell, they kicked their door shut behind them, then the screw would come along and check it was locked. We were no different.

'Well, I don't,' said Dad, 'and not once have I ever done it, nor will I do it, ever, for as long as I'm in jail.'

'Why's that?' I said.

'I'll tell you why,' he said, 'and I want you to remember what I say, all right?'

'Sure, Dad,' I said.

'I never do it,' said Dad, 'because I don't see why I should bang myself up, not when I'm innocent. And, what's more, when the screws ask why I don't close my door like everyone else, that's what I tell them. I'm an innocent man and as such I don't see why I should lock myself up. I also like to tell the screws that when they do it, when they lock my door, they're locking up an innocent man.'

Fucking great, I thought. Only the old man could come up with something like that. What was more, I decided, I'd never slam my door again. The screws could do it and maybe, if I got the chance, I'd remind them when they did that they were locking up a boy who was innocent of the crime of which he had been convicted.

The door opened and the governor came in.

'My sons,' said Mum, 'they're not in the same cell. They're in separate cells.'

'I'll look into that straight away,' said the governor.

Time was called. The visit was over and we had to go back to our cells. But we'd another booked for the following day, another to look forward to, which meant the after-visit let-down wouldn't get a look in.

The escort took us back by the route we'd come. We got inside our block and reached Dad's cell.

'I'll see you later,' said Dad.

'All right, Dad.'

The escort brought us to a new cell, a double on the third floor. Our few things were already in there.

I got up on the top bunk. Vincent lay down on the bottom one. Within moments his slow, regular breathing told me he was asleep. Well, he wasn't going to be much good for a chat.

I rolled a fag and smoked it slowly. I thought about the visit and I thought about Mum. With my mind's eye I saw her face as I'd seen it half an hour before in the visits room. She'd looked well, I thought. And then I looked at the face more carefully. Yeah, she'd looked well but she was in pain. I saw that now. And she was holding back tears, wasn't she? She was hurting, I thought, but she'd hidden it so well I was only seeing it now. But I'd done the same, hadn't I?

I was exhausted by it all and when I'd finished my fag I fell asleep.

The screw calling, 'Dinner up,' woke me. I sat up. Vincent was waiting for me by the door.

We left the cell and walked down the wing together. We saw Dad on the ground floor going back to his cell with his food. We called and waved, and he waved back, then went inside.

We got to the dinner hall and joined the queue for the hotplate. When I got to the top of the queue I saw that the lad behind was looking at me strangely. He wasn't hostile, more puzzled and disbelieving.

'How old are you?' he said.

'Fifteen.'

'This is an adult prison. You can't be fifteen. You're having me on.'

'He's fifteen,' said Vincent. 'I know, I'm his older brother.'

I proceeded down the line and everyone gave me extra. When we got back to the cell I had so much I gave Vincent some.

After dinner, we cleaned our cell, dusted it and mopped the floor. Suddenly, we heard, 'All right, boys?'

We turned. The speaker was a mountain of a man with a frightening expression. He introduced himself as Paul Sykes. He was a professional fighter, well known outside the ring and in prison for violence. He was clever and liked his words as well, and we'd heard that he and Dad spent hours together playing Scrabble and the dictionary game that I had used to love watching Dad play when I was a child.

'We're fine,' we said.

'I've had a word with your dad, and you'll be okay,' he said, and vanished.

We went back to the mopping. I was shaky. Our visitor had had an aura. He was a man you wouldn't want to cross.

'You know what that was about?' said Vincent.

'No.'

'Isn't it obvious?' said Vincent. 'Mountain man fancies you.'

'Bollocks.'

Vincent kept this up until the cell was finished. Then we had exercise in the yard, which was full of prisoners walking round and round. We joined them. Round and fucking round we went.

We fell in with a few lads.

'All right? How you doing?' they said, the usual pleasantries.

At first we found it hard to understand each other. They had northern accents and we had London ones, but we soon adjusted.

Then the questions started.

'What did you do? What did you get?'

We told them everything.

'Fuck! How could they do that? And your mum and dad are here too? Fucking hell, that's shit, that is. And how old are you, young lad?'

'Fifteen.'

'You can't be!'

'I'm fifteen,' I said. 'I was born on the twenty-second of March 1961 and on the twenty-second of March 1976 I was fifteen.'

'That's fucking mad! You shouldn't be in here.'

'Well, I am and I can't do anything about it.'

'Here, have these.' An older man was pushing a packet of ten cigarettes into my hand.

'Ah, no, I couldn't—'

'No, go on,' he said. 'I've a son the same age as you at home, and I want you to have them. Really.'

'Oh, well then, thank you. Thank you very much.'

'Time's up,' the screws shouted.

After thirty minutes' tramping round in a circle I was freezing. I hurried inside.

Back in our cell we were banged up again. Vincent had a newspaper someone had given him. I killed time looking out through the cell window. The view was good, hills and green fields.

When we were unlocked, we slopped out for the second time that day, then set off to get our tea. I was hoping I'd see Dad again but I didn't. We carried the tea back to the cell. We were locked up. It got dark. The door was unlocked. 'Tea, milk, sugar?'

'Yes,' we both said.

The orderly poured milky tea from a kettle and handed us each a mug. 'How old are you?' he said to me.

'Fifteen.'

'Fifteen,' he said. I was getting right pissed off with this. 'I've a son the same age as you, and you shouldn't be here.' He said it nice and loud so the screw couldn't miss it. The other orderly put two slices of cake into my hand and the screw slammed the door.

Sunday started the same as Saturday: unlock, followed by slop-out, followed by a wash. As I shuttled between my cell and the recess I kept glancing down into the well. I'd seen Dad there the day before and I was expecting to see him again. Thirty-six hours in Durham and already I was in the routine. Morning slop-out was when I saw Dad.

But he wasn't below. I was a bit disappointed but I told myself we were having another visit and I'd see him then, wouldn't I?

After breakfast we were locked up for the morning. At midday we got our dinner, and then they brought us down for the walk to the women's section. On Saturday Dad had been waiting for us but this afternoon he wasn't and there were only three screws. Maybe they'd taken him over earlier.

Outside, the two screws with dogs joined the escort. We trekked to the women's section and they let us in. Once inside, I could see along the corridor into the visiting room. Only Mum was waiting.

We opened the door and went in.

'Where's Dad?' I asked.

'Ah,' said Mum. 'They sent him back to Gartree last night or early this morning.'

'We didn't say goodbye,' I said. 'Why did they do that?'

'I'll have a word with the governor when he pokes his head in. Maybe he can tell us.'

Mum had made tea again, and she'd got hold of some biscuits, cakes and sweets. As we drank our tea and stuffed ourselves, we talked about the friends we'd made, which made her happy.

The governor appeared and she had her word, as promised.

'Ah, yes,' said the governor. 'Your husband. That was a Home Office decision, out of my hands.'

He left.

'Soon be time,' called one of the screws.

'I've another surprise,' said Mum, 'just before you go. It's coming up to Christmas, the first we've ever had apart, but I've got you a few presents.'

She produced them from a bag, which until now she'd kept hidden under the table. She gave us each shampoo and soap, and I got a pouch of tobacco too.

'This is the first and last Christmas we'll spend in prison,' said Mum. 'By this time next year, Christmas 1977, we'll be home.' She described the day, Dad in the pub, her in the kitchen, and all of us lying around the lounge. 'You've always wanted a motorbike, haven't you, Patrick?' she said.

'Yes,' I said.

'Well,' she said, 'not this Christmas coming, but the one after, when we're free, you'll get that motorbike because I'm going to buy it for you.'

I felt a rush of excitement as, in my mind's eye, I saw myself on my shiny new motorcycle, flying up and down the Harrow Road.

'Time's up,' said one of the women behind the desk.

The picture vanished.
On Monday we were driven back to Aylesbury.

24

It was a Saturday afternoon, cold and windy. The F and G Wing rugby team, of which Vincent and I were members, filed out on to the pitch at the back of our buildings, along with our opponents, sixth-formers from a local school.

The referee, a screw, called us to attention. 'Right,' he said to us. 'Play hard, lads, but play clean too. If I catch any of you doing anything wrong, I'll come down on you like a ton of shit. Have you got that?'

The game began. The other team was tight and good. They played together. They knew one another. They knew their stuff. We weren't up to their standard. We only trained once a week and the only instruction we'd been given was that the ball was not to be passed forward.

Our opponents began to score. Whenever we competed it was always like that. Our opponents scored early and once they'd started they didn't stop. But we didn't care. We were just glad to get out, run about, and let off some steam, which was what we did now. We were shoving, jostling and jersey-pulling, doing everything we could to impede their victory, some of it legal, but quite a lot of it very dodgy.

The referee blew his whistle. 'Oi, Maguire,' he shouted. 'Come over here.'

I ran across.

'I saw what you just did,' he said, 'and I'm giving you a red card.'

I turned to go and the words came out: 'You're a fat wanker. You know that.'

'I'm putting you on report,' he said.

I shrugged.

On Monday I was before the governor.

'I'm giving you seven days' full lock-up in the punishment block,' he said, 'and I'm suspending you from the team for three games. Have you anything to say?'

I think he expected an apology. I said nothing. Not apologizing was all the power I had left.

'Take him away,' said the governor.

One day I found myself, with another lad from my wing, in the main office. I can't remember why I was there but I do remember I saw whiteboards on the walls with the prisoners' names in black ink. The exception was Vincent's and mine: they were written in red and stood out a mile.

'What's that about?' I said to the screw. 'Why aren't our names in black like everyone else's?'

'Security risk,' said the screw. 'If you did a runner, and a murderer, a lifer, went at the same time, and we could only go after one of you, it'd be you. That's why your name's in red, and your brother's too.'

I'd done twelve months. It was March 1977. It was the end of a day and I was lying on my bed, exhausted. What, I wondered, were they going to give us for tea tonight?

'Maguire?' A screw was standing in the doorway. 'Something for you,' he said, stepping in.

'Oh, yeah, what?' I sat up and swung my feet to the floor.

'You've got to write to the parole board,' he said, 'and ask them if they'll let you out on parole. You're to use this.' He gave me the parole form. It was covered with writing but there were lots of spaces left for me to fill in.

'Why do I have to do this?' I said.

'Why what?'

'Why do I have to fill it in?' I said. 'It's not as if they're going to let me out. Of course they aren't. So it's pointless.'

After the first year of a sentence, he explained, the form had to be filled in. No ifs, no buts, no exceptions. It was the rule.

'So what do I write?' I said.

'Just tell them you're sorry for the crime you committed, you won't take part in anything like it again and from this day on you'll lead a good life, work hard. Come on, you know the sort of thing, Maguire.'

'Hold on. What crime? I didn't do any fucking crime. I'm innocent and shouldn't be here anyway. They can stick their parole.'

'Look, I don't make the rules,' said the screw. 'My job is just to deliver the form and tell you what to do, which is what I've done. Now you have to fill it in, regardless of what you think the outcome will be. This is just the way things are. It's a prison, for fuck's sake. So will you please stop with the backchat and, just this once, do what you've been asked?'

'All right,' I said. The form had to be filled in. I'd fill it in.

That night after tea I sat down at the table in my cell and filled in the form. I gave my name, number, the address of the prison, the date of my conviction and so on. Then, in the box for the prisoner to make a statement, I wrote:

I'm an innocent man, and my Mum, Dad and brother are innocent too. If you would like to give me parole, then do, but know that as soon as I get out I will campaign to prove that we are innocent.

If you do not give it to me, I will do my four years and get out anyway.

When I'd finished I brought the form to the office and handed it to the screw who'd given it to me. Then I turned to go. 'Hang on,' he said. 'Wait until I've had a look at it first.'

He started to read. At first his face was blank but then it changed. 'You can't send this,' he said.

'I'm not the one sending it,' I said. 'You are.'

'You know what I mean. You can't write that.'

'It's the truth, so send it or put it in the bin. I don't give a toss.'

I didn't get parole.

*   *   *

266

I was in the dinner hall, at the servery, shuffling along with my stainless-steel tray, collecting my tea. That evening the food looked especially bad. When I got to the end of the line, the point at which I was supposed to walk to my table, I thought, I'm not going to eat this. I slung the tray with the meal into the slop bin.

'Oi,' shouted a screw. 'Take out that tray.'

'No.' I didn't see why I should.

'The pail's for slops, not trays, take it out, Maguire.'

'Bollocks.'

I was put on report and got seven days' cellular confinement.

In the dinner hall the rule was that if your table was served first one day, it would be last the next, by which time the food was always cold and the portions smaller.

It was tea-time. My table had been first the day before so we were last today. At the hotplate the orderlies doled food on to my plate but no carrots even though I noticed some. Mum had always made me eat two vegetables every day, so I'd happily have eaten them. 'Can I have some carrots?' I said.

'We've run out,' said a screw, even though they hadn't.

'If everyone else has carrots, I want carrots.' I said. 'Send over for more.' I fancied new hot ones, not the cold ones he had.

'In case you haven't noticed,' said the screw, laughing, 'this is a fucking jail, not a hotel. Now piss off, eat what you've got and be thankful.'

'Bollocks. I'm not leaving this dinner hall until I get some carrots.'

I went back to my place. The three lads at the next table were murmuring. 'We didn't get our carrots, either,' said one.

'You show them, mate,' said another. 'If it's carrots for one, it's carrots for all.'

As I began to eat, the dinner hall was emptying.

'What's up, mate?' asked a passing prisoner.

'I'm not budging until I get my carrots.'

'Brilliant, mate.'

Everyone supported me and several said they'd like to join my sit-in but they'd had their carrots.

Vincent strolled past wearing a smile that said, 'What the fuck are you up to now?'

The hall was empty. I'd cleared my plate and so had the three lads with me. A screw approached. 'Come on,' he said, 'you've had your fun. Upstairs.'

'Not until we've had our carrots,' I said.

After a while we were called to the hotplate and the carrots I'd spotted earlier were spooned on to our plates. I went back to my table and sat looking at mine, as did the other lads. They were overcooked, cold, and none of us felt like eating them any more. After a few minutes I want to the slop pail and threw away the carrots. I'd made my point.

I went upstairs to my landing. A couple of officers were outside my cell door. I turned in past them. The door closed sharply behind me and the key turned.

'So, Maguire, you want to play by the rules?' said one.

I noticed all my art things – coloured pencils, paper and rubbers – were gone from the locker. I pulled open a drawer. Though the regulations said prisoners were only allowed two pairs of socks and pants, I had socks and pants for every day of the week. Or I had had because now I was down to the number specified. While I'd been staging my sit-in in the dinner hall they'd reduced my property to exactly what the regulations allowed. 'You wankers,' I shouted. 'Where's my stuff?'

They laughed.

'You're just like your dad, you know,' shouted one. 'Knew him at Gartree, knew him well.'

'Why don't you piss off?'

The next morning I went before the governor. I was charged with inciting protest, refusing to obey an order and using bad language. I got two weeks' lock-up with no work, no pay, no tobacco, and all meals in the cell.

The adjudication over, I was locked in. I had hidden some tobacco and I waited until the officer had gone, then rolled myself a fag and lay down on my bed. I'd just have to start hoarding again and in a few weeks I'd be back to where I was, no trouble.

25

I was back on normal regime and sitting in my cell. A screw came to the door. 'You'll have to do this again,' he said, waving the last letter I'd written.

'Why?'

'For defacing prison property.' He pointed at the cartoon on the back page. I'd been adding cartoons to every letter I wrote for at least a year. 'Letter paper is for writing, not drawing.'

'That's bollocks,' I said. 'Who says you can't draw in a letter?'

'Home Office.'

'You tell the Home Office they can fuck right off. And I'm not coming out of this cell until I can draw on the back of my letters.'

'Suit yourself,' he said, putting my letter on top of my locker.

The next day I lay on my bed all day. In the evening a screw came to see me, not the one who'd told me I couldn't do cartoons, a different one. 'You can do your crappy cartoons, if you want,' he said.

He didn't look annoyed, as he would have looked if they'd been forced to climb down.

Home Office, my arse, I thought. It had been a wind-up.

I came out of my cell. My spur was quiet. I lifted my door card out of the frame in which it lived. It gave my name, sentence, religion, and so on. There was also a box at the bottom for 'Special Remarks'. This was where 'Vegetarian', 'Diabetic' or other important information about prisoners went. My box was empty. I wrote 'Innocent' in the space and put the card back.

The next morning the screws had taken it away and put a new one in the frame. As soon as I got the chance I took it down, scribbled 'Innocent' on it and put it back.

A few minutes later, a screw was at my door. 'You've defaced your card again.'

'No, I haven't.'

'You have.'

'How can you deface your card if you tell the truth?'

'You know the regulations,' he said. 'We've been over and over this.'

He was right. We had.

'You're not allowed to alter your door card,' he said. 'Have you got that?'

'But I'm innocent.'

'Don't touch it any more or you'll be for it. Understand? Leave it out with the door cards.'

First chance I got I wrote 'Innocent' on the new card. I was charged and brought before the governor for adjudication.

'We're at the end of our tether,' he said, 'with you and the door cards. You've been told repeatedly not to tamper with them but you won't listen. Well, you will now. This has gone to the Home Office, to the Home Secretary. If you don't back off, you'll get into a lot of trouble. Do you understand? So stop it, Maguire, now.'

'But I'm innocent,' I said.

I got seven days' cellular confinement, no work, no pay, no tobacco, all meals in the cell and so on.

A week later I came out of my cell and the first thing I did was check my door card. The box marked 'Special Remarks' was empty.

I got the card down quickly, wrote 'Innocent' on the back, and dropped it back into its frame. It was a silent protest.

The staff never knew how lucky they were with protests and me. If it hadn't been for Mum, I'd have been on the roof and all that bollocks. But I didn't want Mum any more worried than she already was, so I didn't. The only exception to this was when the Home Secretary, whoever he was, came to our nick to have a look around. Vincent and I were locked but that didn't stop me making a racket when he came onto the landing. He can't have missed it.

It was August 1977 and I was eighteen months into my sentence. It was a weekday and I was in the workshop. My job was to stick two pieces of plastic and a bit of brass together to make an on-and-off switch for the dashboard of a car. I had to make so many a day, and my numbers were written down in a book by the lad whose job it was to keep a tally.

The work was tedious and I'd still a load to make. I had to hit my quota, I thought, or I wouldn't get my quid's wages. Of course, I could always give the tally-keeper some tobacco or a Mars Bar – that always worked if I was down on my quota – but it was better if I didn't.

I glanced around. At the top of the workshop, where the offices were located, the screws had a big room, and the tally-keeper a little one. Both had large windows so we could see them at all times and, more importantly, they could see us. The tally-keeper wasn't in his office. He was next door with the screws, making tea for them, his other job, and for himself.

There was also an old boy who helped out in the shop for something to do. He was sweeping something in the corner and whistling. If we joined in he'd whistle louder and do a bit of a jig down the middle of the shop floor, with a wink and a smile.

The screw who ran the workshop was talking to someone. I liked him. We all did. He would walk about with a serious face but you could have a chat and a laugh, and as long as the work was getting done, he didn't mind.

There were also a couple of other screws in the shop, your run-of-the-mill screws, and we had no time for them. Likewise they'd no time for us. They sat on their backsides watching us. That was all they did.

Mad Stanley was about too. He was a prisoner. He wasn't from my wing, but somewhere else in the jail. We all said of him that the lights were on but no one was at home. He was Elvis-crazy, from his hair, which he wore in a quiff, to his black prison shoes. He was Scottish, his top lip stuck out, and he sang Elvis songs to himself all day long. He was singing one now.

Radio 1 was playing. It was always on in the workshop. It kept us quiet – that was the theory, anyway. I wasn't really listening but then I noticed the disc jockey was talking in a funny way. He had something urgent to say and, worse, something bad, I could tell. Elvis Presley had been found dead at his home, Graceland.

Elvis Presley dead, I thought.

'Elvis is dead,' the prisoners at the benches muttered. We all liked Elvis.

We looked at Mad Stanley.

'No! No! Not the King!' he screamed.

He stood and swept all the switches on his worktable on to the floor, then picked up his chair and hurled it at the speaker on the wall. Then he threw a second chair. The two screws ran up and grabbed him. There was a short struggle. Mad Stanley slipped from their grasp and ran, scattering switches and kicking over bins and chairs. The screws knew a maniac when they saw one. They pressed the alarm.

The chief screw and the old boy had locked themselves into the office. They didn't want to be in the way of Mad Stanley's rampage. We didn't either. Mad Stanley was at one end of the workshop, capsizing tables and throwing chairs, and we bunched together at the other as far from him as we could get. A minute or two passed, then eight screws ran in.

They laid hold of Stanley. There was a struggle but they over-powered him and carried him out. The chief screw came out of the office. 'Right, lads,' he said. 'Excitement over. Back to work.'

We took our places on our benches and went back to making switches. For the rest of the day, as I glued bits of plastic and brass together, a lot of Elvis was played on the radio.

As for Mad Stanley, he just vanished, as Dad had when they ghosted him back to Gartree. It was like that in jail.

In the workshop we were now making kids' snooker tables. I was with another bloke. Our job was to put the tabletop together from pieces that had been made in the workshop, and pack them into a box with the legs.

We'd filled a lot of boxes already that day, and the day before, and the day before that, so we were bored out of our skulls. We needed variety, we agreed. And when we were in that sort of a mood there was only one sort of fun to be had.

The bloke I was with winked at me and nodded at the office. The top screw, the two watchers and the old bloke were having tea. No one was watching. Lovely. We could have some fun now.

We got a full set of components for the tabletop – felt, cushion, nets and so on – but instead of putting them together, we threw them straight into the box with the legs. My mate wrote a note: 'Do it yourself.' We put this in on top of everything, then sealed the box.

I checked the office. No one had noticed. They were too busy slurping tea and eating biscuits. We could have another laugh.

We got another set of components but this time we assembled them. We put the finished article in a box, added three legs and closed the box.

I checked the office.

No one.

We'd do another, we decided, and if we could get away with it, another.

It was turning out to be a good day in the workshops.

In the workshop we'd switched to Wombles. These were fantasy characters that lived on Wimbledon Common, and there was a popular song about them. In Aylesbury we painted ceramic figures inspired by the costumes the singers wore. There were five or six styles.

I was in the storeroom off the workshop where the tools, paints and the other bits and pieces were kept. On the table in front of me I had dozens of painted figures. I took one, wrapped it, slotted it into its box, which involved fixing it to the bottom with wire so it didn't move in transit, then closed the box.

I took another figure, and began to attach it to a box base.

There were footsteps behind me. I turned and saw a screw. I knew him well: we'd done quite a bit of business since I'd started work as the Wombles packer. He was Wombles mad and he wasn't the only one. Lots of the screws were mad about them.

He looked at the figures on the table. 'That's one I haven't got,' he said.

I knew what he meant. 'Usual place?' I said.

He nodded.

'Usual payment?'

'Of course,' he said. 'What do you take me for?'

He went. I waited a moment, then peeped out of the storeroom door and into the workshop. The screws were miles away. I was safe.

I took a box with a figure and put it into the hiding place in the corridor that I used when I sold Wombles to officers.

Then I went back to work.

Next day I was back in the store, packing. I'd only been in about ten minutes but I wanted to get my payment.

I got off my chair and sidled out. No screws.

I went to the hiding place where I'd left the box. The figure was gone and in its place was a packet of twenty Benson & Hedges. It went straight into my pocket. Lovely. It was lovely, too, to think that I was just one thief among so many.

It was a few weeks and many packs of B&H later when the head screw sidled into the store. 'All right, Patrick?' he said.

'Yeah,' I said.

'I've news for you,' he said.

'They're letting me out?'

'Promotion, Maguire.'

I wasn't certain I liked the sound of that. Selling the figures to officers was a profitable line. Whatever he offered would have to be bloody good if it was going to replace what I had.

'Tally-man,' he said.

The tally-man determined whether each lad had his quota or not, which in turn affected his wages. With me in charge every lad would.

'Thanks,' I said.

Although the job didn't have the same opportunities as the old one, I told the lad who took over about the screws and the Wombles and I continued to get a cut of the smokes.

Vincent's working life in Aylesbury was different to mine. He didn't start by cleaning and move to painting soldiers, like me: he went straight to the Braille shop, learned to type printed English into

Braille, and passed the Standard English Braille Examination. Our Dad did it too, and was so good at it he could read Braille with his fingertips.

After Braille, Vincent started a City & Guilds (7061 and 7062) course in catering. I joined him but I only had time for 7061. If the judge had given me five years, like Vincent, I could have done both. As we used to joke, when you need more time you can't have it. Typical of British justice.

When we were studying we saw each other every day and we'd trade or sell what we cooked to other inmates on F and G Wings. At the end I passed 7061 with flying colours, which surprised me, as I'd only done it for the food, and Vincent passed both of his and was sent to work in the main prison kitchen. Now, to me that's like teaching a man to drive a car, then giving him a push bike to get around. Vincent had spent a year learning how to cook very nice food and then they had him making shit.

Me, I was put back into one of the workshops until Vincent had a word with the screw who ran the kitchen. Before you could say grub up, I was brought in, and was delighted to find I'd have Fred from Ashford for company as well as my brother.

As a rule, when a new boy came on to the kitchen floor he started with washing up and graduated to cooking. I went straight to making bread rolls, puddings and all things sweet: Vincent had put my name up for a vacancy that needed filling. With another lad, he was almost running the kitchen, which was another reason why I started so well.

In prison, as in many other areas, it's not what you know, but who you know.

A kitchen perk was that you could drink milk all day long if you wanted to, and at the end of each day you could bring a mug back to the wing. (I'd usually give mine to a mate who liked it.)

It was evening, and my mug was full of milk. I drank it and refilled it.

'Oi,' I heard.

It was a screw and not just any screw but the SO who ran the kitchen.

'You can put that milk back,' he said. 'You've had your mug's worth already and you aren't having another.'

Bollocks to that, I thought. It's only milk, and I can drink as much as I like. There'd still be milk in the morning, wouldn't there? Besides, I thought, he hadn't seen me drink one already. I was sure of it.

'This is my first fucking mug,' I said. 'I'm not putting it back.'

'No, it isn't,' he said. 'You've had one already. Put it back.'

'No. It's my first,' I said.

I lifted the mug to my mouth and emptied it.

'Right,' he said. 'You're going on report for stealing prison property and using bad language. You'll see the governor in the morning.'

The following morning I was in adjudication. I stood between two screws. The governor sat behind his desk. The kitchen screw said his piece. I said mine.

'Right, Maguire,' said the governor. 'Fourteen days' lock-up. No association, all meals in your cell and you're out of the kitchen. Take him away.'

While I languished in my cell, my brother went to see the screw who had put me on report. Vincent said he knew I'd fucked up. He couldn't deny it. I had been wrong to do what I did and to say what I'd said. I'd been punished and he wasn't going to argue with that either, he said. But, Vincent went on, could the SO do one small thing? It wasn't much but it would mean a lot to him, said Vincent, because it would affect the rest of my sentence. Once I'd finished my fourteen days, could he see that I wasn't sent to the nuthouse – the workshop with the worst reputation in the jail – where the freaks, the delinquents and the lunatics were penned together? If I ended up there, said Vincent, I'd only get into more trouble. If I went somewhere else, and it was within this screw's power to see that I did, I wouldn't get into more trouble so I wouldn't lose any more remission, which I did every time I got an unfavourable adjudication.

When Vincent had said his piece the screw said his. Not only did he not give a shit about me, he said, but he was going to make it his business to ensure that I ended up in the nuthouse.

I finished my fourteen days and presented myself for work.

'Right, Maguire,' said the screw doing the work detail, 'nuthouse for you.'

The kitchen SO had had his way.

'Welcome to the nuthouse,' said the escort, when we got to the front door.

I went in.

There he was, his hair in a quiff, his black prison shoes so shiny he could see himself in them. It was Mad Stanley.

'All right, Pat, how are you?' he said.

It was the next day, dinnertime. I went into the F and G Wing dinner hall and there, on the hotplate, doling out the food, was a familiar face. It was my brother's. But he was supposed to be in the kitchen.

I queued up and when it was my turn I asked what had happened to him.

'Long story,' he said, smiling as he always did.

'Well, tell me,' I said.

'Because the kitchen SO got you sent to the nuthouse, I handed in my notice.'

'But the kitchen's the best job in the prison. Are you mad or what?'

Vincent shrugged. 'Anyway,' he said, 'I've been reassigned to the hotplate, which isn't the worst job in the jail either.'

He ladled food on to a plate for me. 'You know the kitchen SO had you by the balls,' he said.

'No, he didn't,' I said.

'You said you hadn't drunk any milk.'

'I didn't think he'd seen me,' I said, which was true.

'That didn't matter,' said Vincent. 'You had a milky moustache. He could tell you'd had a mug no matter what you said.'

26

It was evening, a weekday. I was on association in the recreation room downstairs.

'Time,' shouted a screw.

There were the usual groans and jeers. I climbed the stairs, prisoners ahead, behind me and around me. I was with a few mates and we were talking and laughing, as was everyone else. This was when prisoners were usually at their most cheerful, the last hurrah before you were locked up.

I reached the second storey and followed the lads through the grille and on to the landing. My spur was ahead on my left, while on my right was the door to the toilets, where I needed to go. Just beyond, a screw was standing against the wall, watching us.

'Maguire,' he said.

I stopped. The other lads flooded up the wing towards their cells, leaving me behind.

'There's a bit of paper on the floor,' he said. 'Can you see it?'

There it was, a scrap torn from an envelope or a magazine, I couldn't tell.

'Pick it up,' he said.

Why me? Why not any of the other lads who were still streaming past? Why not the cleaning orderly? If he'd seen me drop it, okay, he'd have had a case. But he hadn't, because I hadn't dropped it, and now he couldn't arbitrarily select me to pick it up because he didn't like me. I wasn't having it. I wouldn't do it. 'Who do you think I am?' I said. 'I'm not your servant.'

I went into the toilet. I had a piss. I came out.

'Maguire.' The screw was standing in the same place and the bit of paper was still on the floor. 'Bend down, Maguire,' he said, 'and pick up that bit of paper like I told you.'

I wasn't going to do it. I hadn't dropped it and I wasn't going to have him single me out like that. 'Do it your fucking self,' I said, and walked on.

I turned left on to my spur and went into my cell but I didn't close the door. Since Dad had talked to me, I no longer did that. An innocent man didn't lock his own door. They had to do it.

I lay on my bed, the door half open. The screw who had told me twice to pick up the bit of paper appeared. 'Right, Maguire,' he said, 'you're on report.'

I'd disobeyed an order and I'd used offensive language. At the very least I'd get fourteen days locked in my cell, no tobacco, no work, no wage, no association, no dinner hall and no radio. Well, I'd stash some tobacco, I'd borrow a small radio with an earpiece – there were a few flying about the wing – and endure the rest. I'd done it before, and I'd do it again.

'I don't give a shit,' I said, and he banged the door.

It was early the following morning, a Friday. I was in my cell, in bed, and I wasn't asleep because something was shining on my face.

I opened my eyes.

'Get up, Maguire,' said the figure in the doorway.

I didn't need to ask: I knew from the last time that they only woke me when everyone else was asleep for one reason. It had been planned for a while, but they hadn't told Vincent or me. Well, they could hardly tell us, could they? We were highly dangerous, sophisticated and totally ruthless Irish terrorists, weren't we? If they'd told us, we'd have told the IRA. And then the IRA would have smuggled a couple of shooters into Aylesbury and on the way north we'd have shot our way free, legged it to a rendezvous where the IRA would have a helicopter waiting. We'd be taken to West Belfast or San Francisco, where we'd give a press conference, denouncing the Brits, then disappear to a safe house full of beautiful girls who would give us champagne and cater to our every whim, and there we'd stay, in the lap of luxury, until Ireland was free. As if. We were going on a visit to Mum and Dad. That was what this was about.

I got dressed and as I did the cogs in my head were turning. Maybe this wasn't a visit. Maybe when I got to Reception the screw behind the counter would tell me it had all been a terrible mistake and the world knew now that we were innocent. I was going home. He'd give me my clothes and Dad's watch, point me to a cubicle and tell me to get changed. When I came out, I'd give him back the uniform and he'd give me a travel warrant with some money. He'd say someone would run me to the station if I could just hang on a minute, and again he'd say how sorry he was about all that had happened and, finally, that he hoped there were no hard feelings.

Oh, no, mate, no hard feelings, none. You've only locked us all up for years and destroyed our family. Of course there aren't any hard feelings.

Two screws took me downstairs to the recreation room where Vincent was waiting with two more. We followed the same procedure as before and got into a van. It picked up its escort of police cars on the other side of the gate, and whizzed through Aylesbury, crashing every red light.

It was still very early. Out of the window all I saw were parked cars, closed shops and dark houses. Then we were on a slip-road to the M40, which was not the route I remembered from when we had gone to Durham the last time. 'Where are we going?' I asked. 'This isn't the way.'

'To Durham? No, it isn't,' said a screw, 'but that's because we aren't going to Durham. We're going to Wormwood Scrubs.'

We arrived at the Scrubs and were brought into Reception. The cuffs came off and the Aylesbury screws left. The Scrubs screws told us that we'd be their guests until an escort could take us to Durham. But we'd just had an escort, I thought. Why couldn't they have taken us? We were led to the third floor on the young-prisoners wing and put into a cell together.

The following morning, we were woken by the screw on the landing, shouting, 'Slop out,' as he unlocked the cells. We were new, didn't know what to expect, so we went out together and headed for the recess. There were prisoners everywhere on the landing, all young – well, older than me but not men. The looks we got weren't hostile: they were admiring. In the recess, a lad ahead of us turned. 'Is it true?' he said.

'Is what true?' I said.

'That you're brothers. One's doing four and the other five.'

'Yes,' I said.

'What for?'

'For a load of bollocks,' I said. 'What about you?'

'Just a few months,' he said. 'This is the YP wing. No one's doing more than eighteen months here.'

That was why they were impressed with us. We were in a different league from them.

After breakfast, a screw came to our cell. 'One of you can go to the gym and play football, the other cleans the cell,' he said.

Vincent was out of the door with his PE kit in a flash and I was left with the bucket and scrubbing brush. I'd never seen him move so quickly even when we played rugby.

I scrubbed the floor and cleaned the cell. When I finished I went out on to the landing, leant over the balustrade and lit up.

'You, Maguire, what do you think you're doing?'

I looked up.

It was a screw who had called over from the tier opposite.

'Having a smoke,' I said.

'Have you finished cleaning your cell?'

'Yeah.'

He raced down his side, around the end and on to my side. I didn't need to be a clairvoyant to know where he was heading. I moved back into my cell's doorway and waited.

'You,' he said, 'you call me "sir", understand?'

'Fuck that,' I said. 'I don't even call my dad "sir" so I'm not going to call you "sir". Piss off.'

'You little shit.'

There were three types of screws in my experience: good ones, bad ones and wankers. This one, I decided, was among the last. They liked to lord it over the prisoners but when push came to shove they hadn't the bottle to carry it through. 'I may be little,' I said, 'but I'm no shit, you wanker.'

He pushed me but I wouldn't give way. 'Get back into your cell,' he said.

In a fight, I stood a better chance in there than out here, so I backed in but kept my eyes on him in case he tried something.

'You know what I'd like to do to you?'

'No, but whatever it is, have a go.'

He reached for the door. 'You're a little shit,' he said, swung it shut and locked it.

'Wanker,' I shouted.

He didn't bother to reply. I was locked in and he wasn't. I hadn't given in but he'd won. They always won when they locked you in.

I rolled a fag, lay on the top bunk and smoked it slowly. What the fuck was all that about? What was his beef? He couldn't stand to see me leaning over the balustrade and smoking a fag? That was pathetic. But, then, that was jail. Everything was on that level: prisoners wanted to do one thing, often innocent, and screws made them do another.

The door was unlocked and opened. Vincent came in, his face red from exertion. The door was slammed and locked behind him.

He looked at me. I looked back.

'Well,' he said.

'Well, what?'

'"Did you win?"' he said. 'That's what you're meant to ask me, Patrick.'

Not a word, I thought, about how clean the fucking cell was. So if he wasn't going to say anything about that then I wasn't going to ask if he'd won.

It was Sunday, early morning, just after breakfast.

'Church,' said the screw in the doorway. 'Do you want to go?'

'Yeah,' I said.

Vincent was up for it too. Anything to get us out of that fucking cell.

They took us from our landing to the ground floor, then through the prison to the chapel doors. We went through them and found ourselves in a cold grey hall with rows of seats most of which, particularly the ones towards the front, had prisoners sitting on them.

The escort indicated the back right and told us to sit there. At the back on the left sat a knot of men outnumbered three to one by screws. They were high-security prisoners, I guessed, as I made my way towards the seats indicated. When I got closer, one of the high-security prisoners stood up and came towards me, several officers with him.

'We would like to apologize on behalf of the Irish Republican Army,' he said. 'We know you and your family didn't have anything to do with it. And while you're here no harm will come to you.'

He walked back to his seat and we sat down with our escort.

The service over, we were brought back to our cell and locked in.

'What was that about in the chapel?' I said. 'What did he mean?'

'He must be an IRA prisoner,' said Vincent. 'They were all IRA men probably, him and those others he was with. Look at the size of the escort.'

'Yeah, but what did he mean?' I said.

'He must know who planted the bombs they stuck on us or planted them himself. I don't know.'

Vincent was right. He had. He was one of the Balcombe Street gang, though we only discovered this later.

The Scrubs regime was as follows: unlock, slop out, breakfast, lock-up, dinner, exercise, lock-up, tea, lock-up and lights out. The only variation was that sometimes we got out to the exercise yard in the morning instead of the afternoon. I asked several times how long we'd be staying, but no one could tell me.

Another week had passed. I was on my bunk, staring out through the bars at the common that stretched northwards from the prison. I knew it well – and because it was Sunday teams of boys were chasing footballs up and down muddy pitches. I could hear the shouts of the players, and now and again the referee's whistle.

I'd practised or played on all those pitches, I thought, and then, in my mind's eye, I saw myself out there with the Queens Park team before the training session when one of the boys had said, 'What's that place, sir?'

'That's where they put the bad boys,' Sir had said.

I'd realized then that prisons weren't just for television dramas: prisons existed and I was looking at one. It hadn't looked nice. But it was only for bad boys. Wasn't that what Sir had said? I'd never end up in a place like that, I'd thought. Well, Sir had got it wrong. It was where they put anybody they fucking wanted.

What day was it? Sunday again. It was my second Sunday in the Scrubs. I shouldn't be here. I should be in Durham with Mum and Dad. This was doing my head in. When were we going? No one had told us. Was an escort really going to come and take us north? Or was this a wind-up? Were we going to be left here for another fortnight, then woken early one morning?

'Wake up, lads.'

'Are we going to Durham?'

'Sorry, lads.'

'What do you mean?'

'Couldn't get an escort. You're for Aylesbury.'

'What?'

'Come on, hurry up. You've got to be in the van in twenty minutes.'

'We don't want to go to Aylesbury.'

'We thought you liked Aylesbury.'

'We want to go to Durham. We want to see Mum and Dad.'

'Didn't you hear? No escort. Now stop pissing around. Get dressed, strip those beds and look lively . . .'

It was a terrible conversation to imagine having and in order to put it out of my mind I got stuck into the usual morning chores. I slopped out, washed, dressed, and then went to the dinner hall with Vincent. Here I picked up a stainless-steel tray and a small blue plastic cereal bowl. Now, as I knew from the previous weekend, because it was a Sunday there were corn flakes and milk for breakfast, and I loved them even if the milk was watered down.

I got to the counter and held out my bowl, waiting for the ladle heaped with dry corn flakes to come into view. I wanted to make sure I got a full helping.

'Maguire,' I heard.

It was the screw I wouldn't call 'sir' when Vincent was off playing football.

'Get a shave.'

I could have told him he could count the hairs on my upper lip and chin on the fingers of one hand. I could have said he should address his remarks to Vincent – he'd plenty of growth and needed to shave every day. But I wasn't going to argue. I just wanted my corn flakes and milk.

'I'll do it after breakfast,' I said, in my good voice, the one I used when I wanted to show I wasn't out to cause trouble and would do what I'd been asked, promise.

'You'll do it now,' said the screw.

'Look, just give me the corn flakes, will you? I said I'll do it and I will.'

'I told you to get back up to your cell and have a shave,' he said. 'Now.'

I'd been looking forward to my corn flakes and I wasn't going to give up easily. 'Listen, when I've had my breakfast I'll have a shave. Promise.'

'Now,' he said.

'I haven't got a mirror, I can't shave.' This was true. There was no mirror in either the cell or the washrooms.

'How old are you?'

'Sixteen,' I said.

'Then you know what your own fucking face looks like,' he said. 'Do as you've been told. Go and have a shave.'

Right, I thought, I wasn't going to get my corn flakes, that was for sure. But I wasn't going to let him think he could deny me like this and get away with it. No one came between me and my corn flakes.

'Wanker,' I shouted and threw the blue cereal bowl like a Frisbee. The edge caught his neck. He squealed and sank to the floor. A few prisoners jeered. Someone pressed the alarm. I heard screws running. Vincent looked at me. That's it, kid, they'll kick the shit out of us now. I put my tray down, walked out of the hall and headed up the stairs. Several screws passed me. They were going the other way, but they didn't know what had happened. They didn't know who they wanted either. I was just Maguire walking back to his landing after breakfast, minding his own business.

I got to my floor. The bell was still ringing but it was calmer up there. I turned into my cell. A few moments later the door was closed and locked. I was safe.

I lay on my bed and waited. After a while the door opened, and Vincent walked in. He gave me two bits of bread and butter with half a sausage inside.

'No corn flakes?'

'No,' he said, with a smile, 'no corn flakes.'

The next morning a screw came to the cell. This was it. Ship out. We were going to Durham.

We were taken down and put into a van. We drove north for several hours, turned into a town, drove around a bit, then came to a stop in front of the gates of a jail. I expected our driver to hoot but instead the little door in one of the gates opened and a load of screws, some with dogs, came out. They formed a half-circle around the van and the gate. The escort told us to get out and go in through the little door. Inside we were put into a cell and fed, then left for an hour or so.

Back on the road, we drove north, not stopping until we got to Durham. It was after midnight when they brought us in and put us in the same cell. Mum had had a word, I guessed, and this time they'd listened to her.

Over the following weeks we saw Mum and Dad every other day (but not at weekends), which was great except that at the end of each visit we could never be certain there'd be another because we didn't know when they were shipping us on again. (This was why we never said, 'Bye', but always, 'See you tomorrow' when time was called.) Apart from the visits, we only got out of the cell for food and our daily walk in the yard; otherwise, we were locked up. After about a month they took Dad away without warning. A day or two later, it was our turn. We were put into a coach with other inmates and off we set. We stopped at Leeds on the way, and then drove to London and Wormwood Scrubs.

We were here a fortnight and then a screw came to the cell door with the news that we were leaving. We were taken down, cuffed and put into the van. We got to Aylesbury some time later in the morning. We'd been away two months in all – one in Durham, the other in the Scrubs – and although our cells still had our stuff in them we had to be booked in properly. We were taken from the van to Reception.

'Name?' said the counter screw.

'Maguire.'

'Number?'

'333892.'

'Oh.' The counter screw looked at me. He had something to tell me – something I wasn't going to like. 'You're on governor's report,' he said.

I was puzzled, as was Vincent. This didn't make sense. How could I be on report when I'd been away eight weeks? Then it came to me. The screw who'd told me to pick up the bit of paper had put me on report.

Our escort brought us outside and we set off across the prison grounds, heading for F and G Wings.

'How come you're on report?' said Vincent.

I told him the story about the paper scrap I wouldn't pick up. He laughed. We got into our building and said goodbye. He went his way and I went mine.

I was taken up to my cell and locked in. The next morning I was brought to see the governor.

I gave my name and number, and the adjudication started. The screw who had put me on report went first.

He'd been on the wing on such-and-such a day, and at such-and-such a time in the evening, he said, when the prisoners were coming up from association, including me. 'I asked the prisoner to pick up a piece of paper from the floor. The prisoner refused and went into the toilet. When the prisoner came out I asked him a second time. Once again the prisoner refused. His language was abusive and then he threatened me. He said he could get me shot by the IRA if he wished.'

Until he said this, he'd been spot on. I'd refused to obey an order. The governor would have to find against me. So why had he said I'd threatened to have him shot? He already had me by the balls. Well, if I was going to be punished it would be for what I had done, not for something he'd made up. I'd had enough punishment because of stories made up by others to last me for the rest of my life.

'I never said anything about the IRA and getting him shot,' I said. 'And he's a lying bastard for saying so.'

'Stop it, Maguire,' said the governor in the weary voice that governors used before they gave an inmate bad news.

I was in trouble. Even if I'd the pope pleading my case, I'd made an already bad situation worse with my outburst.

'Two weeks' cellular confinement,' said the governor, 'plus no radio, no tobacco, no association, no work, no wages. Take him away.'

A screw brought me upstairs to my cell. 'Okay, Maguire,' he said. 'You heard the governor, didn't you? Two weeks no tobacco. Hand it over.'

I found my tin and made a show of reluctance in handing it over.

'I know you'll miss it,' said the screw, 'but I have to take it. Rules are rules. But you'll get it back in a fortnight. You have my word.'

I gave him a weak smile. He left the cell and locked the door. I listened to the squeak of his boots as he walked away. I waited a bit, to be sure he was gone, then stuck my hand into the back of my locker and fished around until I found one of the pouches hidden there. I brought out two ounces of Old Holborn. Happy days. I wasn't doing fourteen days' lock-up without tobacco. No way.

I rolled a fag – I still had the papers because I hadn't handed them over with my tin – and smoked it at the window. I could do two weeks of this, I thought. Easy.

Two weeks passed. My tobacco tin was returned and I went down to association.

'You're not going to believe this, Patrick,' said one of my mates.

'What?'

'That screw,' he said, 'the one who put you on report over the bit of paper?'

'Yeah, what about him?'

'While you were doing your two weeks, he upped sticks. He's gone to another jail.'

Good, I thought. I never wanted to see his ugly mug again and I didn't suppose he wanted to see mine either.

Later, back in my cell, I started thinking. Maybe he'd left because he couldn't face me, knowing he'd lied. Maybe. Or maybe he really believed I'd threatened him as he'd said I did. I never found out but it was just as well I wasn't in the IRA or had anything to do with them.

27

Early morning, light on, screw at the door. 'Get up.'

'Are we going to Durham?'

'Just get up and get dressed,' said the screw. 'When you get downstairs you'll find out soon enough.'

I dressed. The escort took me down. We picked up Vincent and went to Reception. The cuffs went on. We were taken out and put into a van.

'Are we going to Durham?' I asked.

'No,' said one of the escorts.

'Well, where, then?' I said.

'Gartree.'

That was where Dad was. They were taking us to see him. Gartree was a men's prison. That meant we wouldn't see Mum, which was bad, but we'd see Dad, which was something – and something was better than nothing.

When we arrived at Gartree we were taken to Reception. The orderly, a mate of Dad's, gave us tea and cake. Then we were brought to Visits. As it was mid-week, there were no visitors except us and we had dinner with Dad. He had a mate in the kitchen and he fixed the grub for us. I hadn't seen food like it in years: gammon steak with pineapple rings, chips, peas, onions, mushrooms, bread and butter and, to wash it all down, a jug of milk, then tea or coffee. Once we'd stuffed ourselves, it was back in the van to Aylesbury.

The last time that I could remember the three of us were together was in the office block in Morden. He looked so much better now. And how good to see him, I thought, as we drove along, and we'd got on so well too. What a day. What a visit.

One afternoon in the summer of 1978, I was in the workshop. My job now was to put ball-bearings inside a plastic housing.

'Maguire?' said a screw. 'The Principal Officer Mr Stone wants you.'

I knew Mr Stone well. Over the previous two and a half years I'd been up in front of him for lots of reasons, mostly bad, not that I minded going before him. Other officers liked to shout but Mr Stone talked to me a bit like my dad. He would tell me to stop fucking about and to make his job easy, which always made me smile. When we got back from visiting Mum and Dad, he always asked Vincent and me how it had gone. And if I bumped into him around the jail, I'd always stop and have a chat. Mr Stone was one of the few in the place I'd any respect for. When he was young he'd been a soldier – the SAS, according to the prison rumour mill and probably not true – and he'd seen a bit of life. That was why he was more flexible than the others, or so I thought.

The escort led me out of the workshop and we set off across the prison grounds. 'What's this about?' I said.

'How should I know?' said the escort. 'Why would the PO have told me? He just said to come and get you.'

We walked on. I racked my brain. What had I done wrong over the last few days? I couldn't come up with a single thing. Anyway, whatever I'd done, it didn't matter. There was nothing anyone in the jail could throw at me now. I'd seen it all.

We went into the building where Mr Stone was based, tramped

down a corridor and stopped at his door. 'Here we are,' said the escort. 'In you go and you'll find me waiting here when you get out.'

I knocked. I always observed the niceties with Mr Stone. He made me want to do things right.

'Come in.'

I opened the door and went in.

Mr Stone was sitting at his desk reading the newspaper. There was a cup of tea in front of him. He had white hair and a handlebar moustache that joined his sideburns. There were creases around his eyes. He wasn't far from retirement. 'Hello, Mac,' he said. 'Sit down. Like a cup of tea?'

'No, thanks,' I said. 'All right if I have a fag?' I waved my tin.

'Have one of mine,' he said. He passed me a packet with a lighter and I lit up.

'Well,' he said, 'there's good news and a little bit of bad news.'

'Anything to do with Mum or Dad?'

'No, everything's all right with them,' he said. 'They're fine.'

'So what is it, then?'

'Good news first,' he said. 'You're getting out.'

'And the bad news?'

'It's not for eight months.'

This was strange because my mates had got their leaving dates when there were just a few weeks to go. There was a reason for this. If the leaving date was too far away prisoners, thinking they'd never make it, got depressed or aggressive and hard to handle. But a lad with a fortnight to do was always on his best behaviour.

In which case, why was I being told I'd eight months to do? They knew that sort of timescale drove lads mad. Were they trying to drive me mental?

I was so agitated I jumped to my feet. 'You're having me on,' I said.

Mr Stone shook his head. 'I wish I was,' he said. 'I can't work it out myself. Anyway, at least you're getting out, even if it is in eight months. That's got to be good and it'll make your mum happy too.'

I felt like weeping. Eight months seemed like eternity. 'I don't fucking believe it,' I said. 'Eight months. You're having me on.'

He told me to settle down and handed me the Home Office papers. I saw my release date in bold letters, 30 March 1979.

As I stared at it I could hear Mr Stone talking. One, I had a release date; two, I was getting a year's remission. I'd been sentenced to four but I was going home after three. I had, therefore, two reasons to be cheerful. It had to be a result, he said, and would I now please stop fucking about and make his life easy?

But the remission and the fact that I had an end date meant nothing. All I knew was I had eight long horrible months stretching ahead, which was precisely why it was policy never to tell a prisoner when he was going too far in advance. 'You know what this means?' I said.

Mr Stone looked at me.

'It means another Christmas and another birthday in this shit-hole. My eighteenth bloody birthday I'll still be in jail.'

Well, the Home Office weren't going to get away with it, I thought. I wasn't going to be their plaything. They could shove their end date.

I tore the papers in half and then again into quarters. Marvellous. They had their plans – well, sod them. I wasn't having anything to do with them.

I dropped the pieces on Mr Stone's desk. 'They can stuff it. I'm not going,' I said. 'I may as well do the four years.'

'Look,' said Mr Stone, 'you've got to take it. There are no ifs or buts about this. You leave when they want, not when you decide.'

Leave when they wanted? No, fuck the Home Office. From now on it was my way. I'd do the four. That would teach them. Then I'd a better idea. 'I tell you what,' I said, 'I came in with Vincent. I'll go out with him. I'll do five.'

'Oh, shut up,' said Mr Stone. 'I haven't heard such rubbish since I don't know when. You're going in eight months, whether you like it or not, and your brother, assuming he gets his remission, and I don't see any reason why he won't, will follow you out a few months later. Do you understand? Am I making myself clear?'

He was, but what good was that to me?

'To make me wait eight months,' I said, 'when everyone I know that got out only had to wait weeks. They're taking the piss.'

'I don't disagree,' said Mr Stone.

'They're playing mind games, and I'm innocent,' I said. 'I shouldn't even be here.'

'You're leaving on Friday, the thirtieth of March,' he said, 'and if I have to kick you out myself, I will. Now sit down and have another fag, and let's talk about it.'

I sat down. He gave me a second fag and lit it.

I'd gone to see Mr Stone feeling invincible. I couldn't remember doing anything wrong, but if I had I didn't care. It had never occurred to me that my release date would be sprung on me.

That's the thing about prison: you thought you were invincible but you weren't. The system pulled stunts you couldn't have imagined. In the end, it was always going to win and you were always going to break.

Or were you? Suddenly I saw how I could screw them.

I looked at Mr Stone, with his big moustache and sideburns. 'I'll do something so they'll have to keep me in,' I said.

Then I got up, thanked him for the fags and walked out.

I found my escort lounging in the corridor. He noticed my long face but said nothing. We walked to the workshop in silence. I went back to slotting ball-bearings into plastic housings.

A mate came up. 'What was that about?' he said. 'What did the PO want?'

'I'm getting out,' I said.

'Great! When? Next week? A fortnight?'

'In eight months.'

'What? They're taking the piss.'

'No. The thirtieth of March 1979 is my release date,' I said. 'A Friday, as it happens.'

'Well, at least you're getting out,' he said. 'And it's nice to get out on a Friday, it being nearly the weekend and that.'

What the fuck's he going on about? I thought.

'It could have been a Monday,' he said, 'which wouldn't have been so clever, would it?'

My news spread through the workshop. One mate after another came over to speak to me at my bench. Everyone was appalled that the date was so far away but pleased that I had one.

'You're going, Patrick, you're getting out. That's got to be good,' they kept saying.

Workshop finished, I went back to my block. When tea was called, I went to the dinner hall. Vincent was on the hotplate but I didn't go near him. I didn't feel like talking to anyone. I got something cold to eat and sat at a table by myself.

'All right, Patrick?'

It was Vincent. He'd come out from behind the hotplate and walked over.

'I got this,' he said. 'It's from Mum.'

I took the envelope he offered but I didn't pull out the letter, eager to read it, like I usually did when one came from Mum.

'Is something the matter?' said Vincent.

Clearly, he hadn't heard the story.

'Bastards are letting me out.'

'When?'

'The thirtieth of March, next year!'

'What are you talking about? March? That's—'

'I know. Eight months away. Bastards.'

He sat down. 'In the letter Mum asks if you've got a date yet.' He said this carefully. 'So now you can tell her the good news. Well, it's not that good, but she'd be happy you're getting out.' In her letters she always said be good and just get out.

'I told them to stuff it. I said I'd wait until you get out.'

'I don't think you can do that,' said Vincent quietly. 'I'd just take it, if I were you.'

After evening association I was locked in and the lights were put out. I lay in bed looking at the shadows of the cell bars on the ceiling. I kept thinking about my talk with the PO and what I'd done. I'd threatened to fix things so they'd have to keep me. What was that about? Who'd want to stay even a second longer than they had to in this place? I must have been mad, I thought.

28

It was coming up to Christmas and I was in the recreation room on evening association with a mate. He was going in a week.

'Oh, it'll be great,' he said.

'Yeah?'

I'd heard other lads talk about going and I knew what to expect: everyone with gate fever said the same things, but he was a mate so I thought I'd better humour him.

'How's it going to be great?' I said.

'I'll walk out the gate,' he said, 'and in the car park, they'll all be there, Mum and Dad and my little sister, and there'll be hugs and kisses all round. We'll go home straight away, and in the house, everyone else will be waiting, uncles and aunts, my nan and my two big cousins, and we'll sit down to my favourite dinner, steak and kidney, and then Dad will take me down the pub and buy me a pint, and I'll see all my mates, and they'll stand me rounds, and I won't have to put my hand in my pocket once.

'Then I'll go home and fall asleep in my own warm, soft bed, and when I wake up in the morning and open my eyes, I'll be confused for a second or two. Where am I? What the fuck's going on? Then I'll remember I'm not in prison any more. I'm back at home. Then I'll think back to my cell and waking up in the bed there, and I'll snuggle down under my own covers, and I'll go back to sleep. That's how my first night and morning of freedom are going to go.'

'It sounds pretty good,' I said. I omitted to tell him that every other mate had said more or less the same.

'And then when you get out,' he said, 'we'll meet up and we'll have a drink and talk about old times, won't we?'

'Yeah, of course,' I said.

Those conversations always ended like that, though privately I doubted, as I always did, that I'd see him again. Your jail friend isn't necessarily the friend you'd choose outside.

* * *

In March Uncle Bill died. I'd never asked for home leave before –
I'd assumed I wouldn't get it – but I asked if I could go out for
the day to attend the funeral. It was only a couple of weeks from
my release date. The authorities said no.

26.3.79 [Monday]

Dear Mum,

We got your letter and also the [birthday] card, very nice.

Glad to hear everything is all right with yourself, also Dad.
Vincent and myself are still very much the same. Still
keeping fit and doing weights.

We got a visit from Hugh Maguire Saturday 24th. It was
good to see him, and he was looking all right.

Mick Egan and Shore Tully could not come up because
they were working. But they send their love.

Well, that was my last visit and I gave Hugh all my things,
letters et cetera.

He said he should be coming up to get me by car, and
when we get to his house, Kitty will have a big breakfast
waiting for me (ha).

I do remember you telling me about the £100 for Teasy,
and I will get it over to her and tell her it's from us all, for
everything her and Bill have done.

I got a card from Anne-Marie and all at '99'; also Maxine,
John and baby and Maxine's family.

And Anne-Marie sent me £2.00 so I did all right.

I'm glad you liked the cartoon and I'll miss doing them
(ha) but, like you said, I'll do one now and then.

John has still got our old gear in his house so that is all
right.

You said something about a sweater. Is that the one with
PJ on it? When I go to Teasy's I will get it.

Last Sunday a bishop from around here came to our
church, and he was all right.

He gave us 'The Optimist Creed', so I have put it in this letter for you; it is good and right.

Well, this is my last prison letter (ha). The next one will be on 'outside' paper (ha).

I sent Dad a letter last week but I will send him another one this week as well.

As I write this I have 4½ days left. So it will not be long now till we're up to see you, also Dad.

Maxine and John said they are having a party the day I get out, so I will get Hugh and Kitty to come as well, and some of our friends.

Well, I will close now, hope everything is all right, time is going fast for me, so before you know it, we'll be up to see you.

So, till we see you, all our love, your boys, Patrick Jr. and Vincent

PS Give our love to the girls.

I woke up. I opened my eyes. I was in bed in my cell. It was 29 March 1979. It was Thursday. But it wasn't any Thursday. It was *the* Thursday. It was the *last* Thursday before the Friday I was leaving. Eight months were done. This was my last day now. I'd come in at fourteen, I was going out at eighteen, I'd done four fucking birthdays, three fucking Christmases, and by the time I went I'd have done a total of three years, three weeks and six days, for something I hadn't done and hadn't known anything about.

Had I been punished? Too right I had. Part of the prison wasn't set aside for prisoners who might be innocent. I'd eaten the same shit as everybody else, lived in a fucking cell like everybody else and done the same things, day in and day out, as everybody else. The only difference between the other lads and me was that I knew I was innocent. But that hadn't made the time go any faster, or my time in jail any easier. It had made it harder. It was torture knowing I shouldn't be there. And I didn't know, as I lay there, that I was about to start another sentence when I got out because, as far as society was concerned, I was still guilty.

I wasn't like my mates. I hadn't paid my dues to society and was now going out, the slate wiped clean, to start afresh. I didn't even have the benefit of wanting to go straight like my mates. I'd come to prison confused and three years on I was no better. And I'd no idea what lay ahead except that on Friday morning I'd go to Reception, hand in my uniform, get back the lovely new clothes and shoes that had been left in, along with my dad's watch. Then I'd go out to the car park where Dad's brother, Uncle Hugh, would be waiting. That was as far as I could see into the future.

I wasn't going home to Mum and Dad. They were still in prison, Vincent too, and 43 Third Avenue was gone. John was out there, of course, but while I'd been inside he'd married Maxine and they had a young son now, Jonathan. They had a little house in Barfett Street, near First Avenue, and my little sister Anne-Marie, now twelve, was living with them. I wouldn't be going there: no room. It was Uncle Hugh's for me.

'Come on,' a screw shouted. 'Slop out. Look lively, let's be having you.'

Well, there was no point moping. I slopped out, had a wash, got my breakfast, then went to the workshop, took my place at the bench and started to stuff a cuddly toy.

I'd got to my bench and started work hundreds of times but this morning was different too. It was the last time I'd ever stand at my bench. Shouldn't I feel glad?

But I shouldn't have been here in the first place, I thought, so why should I be happy about getting out?

'All right, Pat?' said the lad on the bench beside me.

'All right,' I said.

'Good luck, and that,' he said.

The morning passed as slowly as usual.

'Time, lads,' the screw shouted.

I walked back to the wing, and got my dinner. This was the last time I'd ever collect my dinner, I thought.

I walked to the workshop for the afternoon session and went on stuffing the toy I'd left before dinner.

It was the last time I'd ever do this, I thought.

'Good luck, Pat,' someone said.

'Thanks,' I said.

'Have one for me, Patrick.'

'Yeah, sure I will, don't worry, mate.'

There was a lot of that. Just as I'd been happy for lads who'd left before me, so the lads I'd come to know were happy for me, among them some lifers who wouldn't be going through the prison gates for years. It took a lot of guts, I thought, to be as positive as they were.

'Time, lads,' shouted the screw. 'Come on, fuck off the lot of you, see you Monday. Pat, you go home now and don't ever come back, all right?'

'Yeah, don't worry, thanks, I won't,' I said.

I walked back towards the wings, lads around me, shouting and jostling.

This was the last time I'd ever walk back to F and G Wings at the end of a working day, I thought.

But I shouldn't have been there in the first place, so why should I be happy about getting out?

At that point Vincent came into my head. We'd been through this together from the start and sent to prison at the same time, so we should be leaving as one. I felt I was abandoning him. I told myself he'd be out in three months. It wasn't long. No, I thought, it wasn't.

I reached the landing and went into my cell. Everything I knew I wasn't taking was piled on my bed. I separated a half-ounce from the pile and put it aside. I'd need that, I knew, in the night to come. Everything else would have to go, especially the tobacco of which I had far too much. Over the years I'd become a bit of a baron, buying from the canteen and selling to other prisoners. I gathered everything, ambled out and for the next half an hour, like Lady Bountiful, I gave pens, pencils, paper, socks and tobacco to my mates.

I got my tea next. Then it was association in the recreation room.

'Time, lads,' called the screw. 'Upstairs, the lot of you. Come on now, come on.'

I saw Vincent heading to his wing.

'Vince, see you later,' I called.

He gave me a wave and smiled. Then he went on his way and I on mine, up my stairs. He'll be all right, I thought. I came out on my floor and walked towards my spur.

'Get him, lads!'

Out of the recess on my right hurtled five or six of my mates. I'd forgotten about last-night pranks.

The lads picked me up and hoisted me on to their shoulders.

'Come on, boys,' I shouted. 'Go easy.'

My mind raced. What was it going to be?

There were three options, I knew, from having helped to give other lads a send-off in the past.

Would it be down the toilet, a push of the flush and a wet head?

Would it be black boot polish on my face, then pants down and boot polish all over my balls and my prick?

Or would it be a good old-fashioned beating?

The lads wheeled, passed the toilet and headed for my spur.

So my head wasn't going down the toilet.

That left either a boot-polish job or a beating.

'No, lads, come on, put me down,' I said.

They squeezed through my cell door, holding me aloft, and threw me. I felt the mattress give and then the blows started, all over my body. They weren't hard but they weren't light either. I felt them. And after they'd stopped I'd still feel them. 'Come on, boys! Go easy! Don't hurt me!'

'Can't you take it, Pat?' someone shouted. 'You gave it out, you should be able to take it.'

'That's enough.'

The blows stopped. The lads moved back and I lifted my head.

There was a screw in the doorway. 'That's enough fun for one night,' he said. He sounded grim. 'Now get out and go back to your cells,' he said to the ones around me.

''Bye, lads,' I said.

I shook each of them quickly by the hand to show there were no hard feelings while the screw watched.

Everyone left and I saw he was staring at me. It was a long, hard look and I knew what he was thinking. That I was a shit and should be doing life, not walking out. I stared back at him and he turned away, angry, disgusted, banged the cell door and turned the key. He could go fuck himself, I thought. I'm getting out, matc. How long have you got to do? Don't tell me. I know. You'll still be here tomorrow night but I'll be gone, mate, I'll be fucking gone.

I sat on the bed, rolled a fag, and looked around the cell. All the things I'd got over the years to make it look a bit better had gone. I'd given them away. It looked empty. It was back to the way it was when I'd first walked in. The only thing I still had was my radio.

I had it tuned to Radio 4, as it was every night, and I was listening to a play, as I did every night. I had my eyes closed, and as I listened the words carried me away to another world . . .

'Lights out,' shouted the screw in the corridor.

I turned off the radio, lay down on the bed and looked up at the window just as I had on my first night in Ashford.

There was a knock on the door and the cell light came on. It was Mr Mac, one of the PE instructors. 'All right, Pat, take care, good luck,' he shouted through the steel.

'Thanks, Mr Mac.'

The light went out and I heard him walk away.

I rolled another fag. I knew it was the first of many. Then I lay there, smoking and thinking, mostly about the past and about Mum and Dad. I knew they were happy I was getting out but that didn't matter much to me. I kept thinking we shouldn't be in prison, that we should all be getting out.

I went on smoking and thinking for the rest of the night.

I got up in the dark, made up my bedding roll with all my prison clothes in the middle and put it by the door.

Then I sat on the bed, smoking and listening to the radio, one ear cocked, waiting for the sound of footsteps outside. Because I was going, I knew I'd be let out long before the usual unlock time.

I heard keys jangling and my door opened. I got my piss pot and went off to slop out.

This was the last time, I thought, that I'll ever go into the stinking recess, pour the night's piss away and wash the pot. That was a good reason to be cheerful, wasn't it?

But I shouldn't have been there in the first place, so why should I be happy about getting out?

I had a wash, then did my rounds again, knocking on the cell doors of the friends I'd made, calling goodbye and all the best. Some were awake, others were still sleeping, and those I left alone. I didn't want to wake them from their dreams.

I went back to my cell. My escort appeared. 'Are you ready?' he said.

'Yeah,' I said.

I picked up my bedding roll and my piss pot. We walked down the spur and set off down the stairs.

'Can you take me to F Wing so I can say goodbye to my brother?' I said.

'That's against the rules,' he said. 'I'm supposed to take you to Reception, not halfway round the bleeding jail. But seeing it's him, I'll make an exception.'

We reached the ground floor, went through the empty dinner hall to F Wing, climbed the stairs to Vincent's floor and arrived outside his cell. He was still locked in and I could hear his radio through the door. I dropped my roll and piss pot and brought my head close to the metal.

'Vincent,' I shouted, 'I'm off now. Don't forget the VO.'

'Yeah, all right,' he shouted back. 'Say hello to everyone for me, will you?'

'Do your bird.'

'Fuck off.'

'Come on,' said the escort. 'Hurry up. Don't you want to go home?'

I picked up my roll and piss pot, and followed him down to the dinner hall. There were five lads waiting for escort there; two were going out, and the other three worked in the prison kitchen, which was on the way to Reception so they were coming with us. One was Fred – I knew him well: we'd been on H Wing in Ashford and come to Aylesbury together in the van; we'd been altar boys together; then we'd worked in the kitchen until I was sacked for drinking milk.

The grille opened and we filed out. It was a cold, fresh spring morning.

'Good luck,' he said, 'and don't hurry back.'

'Don't worry, I won't.'

We reached the kitchen gate where we were to drop off Fred and the other two.

'We'll keep in touch?'

'Course,' I said.

'We'll have a drink or two when I get out.'

'Yeah.'

He was doing life so I knew it would be quite a while before I heard from him.

He smiled. I smiled.

'Goodbye, Fred.'

'Goodbye, Patrick.'

Would we meet again, I wondered, as I headed towards Reception. Why would I want to be reminded of prison by meeting an ex-inmate outside? Once I left, wouldn't I turn away from everyone connected with prison? I didn't know, but somehow I suspected I would.

We walked on. It was early and hardly anybody was about. We passed a couple of screws but they didn't pay any attention to me or the other two lads. They'd seen prisoners headed for the gate before; it was only us, on our way out, who felt the occasion was special. This was our very last walk through HMP Aylesbury's grounds. We really were on our way. This was it.

We got into Reception.

'Right, lads,' said the screw. 'Bedding rolls and piss pots on the floor, then into this cell.'

We did as we were told. It was a holding cell, quite big, with four lads already inside. Like us, they were going home.

The door slammed. We sat around a big table. We were all smoking furiously and making small talk.

'Hope it's not raining by the time they let us out,' said one.

We just looked at him. Who cared what the weather was like? It could be snowing when we got out. Would it matter? No.

The cell door opened and a screw put his head in. 'Any of you for breakfast?' he said.

There were only one or two takers but we all said we'd have tea. I wasn't eating another mouthful of their rubbish. I'd wait until I got out to have my breakfast.

A bit later the cell door opened. The screw called someone's name. The lad went off. He came back twenty minutes later in his own clothes instead of prison uniform. Processing had started. We were getting closer to the gate with every passing minute.

Screw at the door. 'Maguire?'

I got up and went out.

The screw locked the door. 'Right,' he said, 'pick up your roll and your piss pot and follow me.'

I went down some stairs with him behind me and into an office; I recognized it as the one where I'd started when I'd arrived nearly three years earlier. I dumped my bedding roll on the floor.

The screw at the desk looked up from the paperwork in front of him. 'Name? Number?'

'Patrick Maguire, 333892.'

'Bundle inspection,' he said.

I opened it on the floor. Inside were the prison-issue clothes I wasn't wearing, pants, socks, plimsolls, PE kit, and so on.

A second screw with a list checked that nothing was missing. 'It's all there,' he reported finally.

Amazing, I thought. As if I'd want to nick any of it. I pointed to the piss pot. 'Don't you want to check that?' I said.

'Oh, very funny,' said the desk screw. 'Hilarious.' He looked at his mate with the checklist. 'Give this joker his clothes and shoes.'

They were handed to me.

'Go and change,' said the desk screw, 'and bring the uniform back.'

I went to a cubicle, pulled off the uniform and got into the new stuff. It felt wonderful, after all this time, to be in good clothes that fitted.

I came out of the cubicle. How did I look? Was there a mirror? No, of course not. I should have known. I hope I look as good as I feel, I thought. I bundled up the prison uniform and carried it back.

'Right,' said the desk screw. 'Is anyone coming for you?'

I should fucking hope so, I thought. Three years in the nick and I still didn't know where Aylesbury was. It was in the country, yes, I knew that, and not too close to London, I knew that too, but that was it. I hadn't a notion how I was going to get back if Uncle Hugh didn't show.

I wasn't going to share any of this with the screw, though. What if they tried to keep me in? Worst-case scenario and no show by my uncle, I'd ask directions and walk to London. I didn't care how long it took.

'Oh, yes,' I said, 'you don't need to worry. Someone's coming to collect me.'

'And have you somewhere to go, somewhere to sleep tonight?' said the desk screw.

Fucking hell, were they worrying about me? Incredible.

'Yes,' I said, 'I have somewhere to go.'

The desk screw seemed relieved. If I hadn't, he'd have had to do something like lift the phone and call social services. He wouldn't have wanted to, of course, because in fact he didn't give a shit about me. I was just a con to him, and he was just a screw to me, and we couldn't wait to get shot of one another. And that's prison for you: you are what you are, a con or a screw, and you hold the other in contempt.

'I have to get you to sign a few bits of paper,' said the desk screw. He gave me a Biro. 'There,' he said, pointing to a dotted line at the bottom of a sheet.

'What am I signing for?' I said.

'For the money you had when you came into jail,' he said.

I signed.

The money was counted out. It was what I'd arrived with to the penny. It wasn't much. It wouldn't have even added up to a pound.

'Now, sign here,' said the desk screw. He pointed at another bit of paper.

'What's this for?' I said.

'That's for the money issued to every prisoner leaving jail,' said the desk screw.

Oh, right, I thought, the miserable bit of cash they dole out to tide prisoners over until they find their feet. I signed, with a bit of a flourish this time.

The money was counted and recounted. 'There,' said the desk screw, grumpily, as he handed it to me. From the look on his and the other's faces, you'd have thought the money had come out of their own pockets.

A third piece of paper appeared. 'Sign this.'

'Why? What's it for?'

'Don't you want your watch?' said the desk screw.

Dad's watch. That came back today too. I signed quickly, and he handed it to me.

I held it, felt its satisfying weight and rubbed the glass with my thumb. There was no ticking, but of course it had long since wound down.

It had done some bird, I thought. First, it was on remand with Dad, and then, after he had handed it over, it had spent three years in my private property.

The oddest part was now that I had it again it was if it was only yesterday I was at the Old Bailey receiving it from Dad. All the days, weeks and months between had vanished.

It had once been too big but now it was too small for my wrist so I put it into my pocket.

'Right,' said the desk screw. 'Sign here.'

'What's this now?'

'Firearms Prohibition Licence.'

'Why do I have to sign that?' I said. I'd never seen a weapon in the past and I didn't imagine I would in the future.

'Because you haven't got a choice, so do it.'

(I was sentenced under Section 53.2 of the Children and Young Persons Act, 1933, the criteria for sentencing being, 'A juvenile offender whose conviction would warrant a sentence of fourteen years or more if an adult'. Every prisoner has to sign a Firearms Prohibition Licence on leaving prison, stating they will not handle or be in possession of any firearms or ammunition for a period of years. The FPL that Section 53 prisoners like me had to sign was always a life ban.)

I signed.

'We're finished,' said the desk screw. 'You're to go back to the holding cell now.'

'How long will I have to stay there?'

'How the heck am I supposed to know?' said the desk screw. 'When everyone's processed, when the job's done, that's how long. How long will that take? I have no idea. I don't have a crystal ball.'

I was taken back and went in. Another name was called. Another lad went out. The door closed. The key turned. I sat. The small talk had stopped. We were in the same boat, desperate to go. That was all any of us could think about. Also, I was hungry now. Why hadn't I taken the breakfast? Should have, shouldn't I? Oh, well, no point crying about it now. Nothing to be done about it.

I rolled a fag and lit it. Oh, Jesus, come on. They aren't going to keep us here for much longer, are they? Come on, come on, three years, three years, this had to be over. Someone, anyone, please! Please come and let me go.

The door opened and the lad who had gone out as I came in appeared in his new clothes. Another name was called. Out he went and the door slammed.

'They're taking the piss,' I said. 'How long are they going to keep us waiting?'

'I wouldn't worry about it,' one of the others said. 'I've been in and out lots of times, and the last hour is always the worst, believe me. But it won't be long now. Any minute now someone will come along and let us out.'

The small talk started up again. One said his girlfriend was outside and he couldn't wait to see her. Another said his mum and dad would be there. I said nothing. What could I say? The ones that I wished were meeting me were still in prison. Then I thought about Vincent. It would have been so good if we were getting out together. But we weren't.

From down the corridor came the sound of keys jangling and footfalls. We went quiet. Were they coming towards us?

Yes, yes, yes.

The key slid into our cell door. The lock was turned. The door opened.

'Time to go home,' said the screw. 'Follow me.'

We hurried out and followed him down some stairs. At the bottom there was another screw by a door, which he opened as we approached.

I went through. I was outside now and I could see first the old iron gates, which were open, and beyond them, at the other end of the airlock, the heavy wooden ones. I knew them well, or thought I did. I'd seen them every time Vincent and I had gone to visit Mum and Dad. But now I was on foot they looked even bigger and heavier, more like the entrance to a fort, than they had when I'd seen them through the windows of a van.

I walked on with the other lads around me. As we got closer to the airlock, the gate screw appeared from his little office at the side. He took a bunch of keys out of his pocket – they were attached to his belt by a chain so no one could snatch them. He went to the little door set into one of the gates, put the key into the lock and turned it slowly, taking his time.

'See you all soon,' he said, as he pulled the Judas door open.

The six lads hurried out. I stood there in front of him, waited for that silly look on his face to disappear, and then stepped over the lip at the bottom.

Outside, people were milling around the six who had gone ahead, hugging and kissing. Through the crowd, I saw two policemen sitting in their car on the road beyond the car park. They worried me a bit. The court case for the Mini I had stolen hadn't been heard because I was at the Old Bailey. However, the law forgets nothing and I'd been warned, some time before, that because of this outstanding business I might cop a gate arrest. As I walked out of Aylesbury, I'd be scooped, charged and remanded back into custody: that's what I'd been told. Now, seeing the policemen, I wondered if they were there for me. That would be just my luck.

'Don't worry about them.' It was Dad's brother, Uncle Hugh. I hadn't noticed him in the crowd. He gave me a hug.

'Are you sure there isn't anything to worry about?' I said.

'The police are just here to see everybody gets away all right,' he said.

We pushed through the crowd. 'I have a car,' he said. 'It's not mine. It's an old friend's.' He gave the name. I recognized it. We got to the car and I slid into the back. Uncle Hugh got into the front. I shook the driver's hand and settled back. It was a lot more comfortable than the prison vans. This was all right, I thought.

The driver set off. We went through Aylesbury, stopping at the lights, then went down a slip-road and on to a motorway. There were lots of questions. How did I feel? How was jail? What did I want to do?

I wasn't keen to talk. I wanted to enjoy being in the car and going where I wanted, which was London. I wound down the window. It had started to rain and little drops of water splashed my face. I closed my eyes. This was marvellous.

I remembered something. I opened my eyes and closed the window. I pulled Dad's watch out of my pocket. In my mind I could hear him, 'Only twelve times now.' No need to worry, Dad. I know how to do it. I've done it before. 'One, two, three,' I counted, turning the little wheel on the side, hearing the watch come back to life, hearing its tick. 'Twelve,' I said, under my breath.

'Well done, son. You're a good lad.' He rubbed the top of my head . . .

'What time is it?' I said.

'What do you want to know that for?' said Uncle Hugh. 'I'd have thought you'd be fed up with anything to do with time after three years.'

'I want to set Dad's watch,' I said.

'Oh, right,' he said, looking over his shoulder. 'He gave you his watch, did he?'

'Yeah,' I said.

Uncle Hugh squinted at the dashboard clock. 'Is that time right?'

'More or less,' said the driver.

I turned the winder and moved the arms, setting the right time, then pushed the little knob home.

We came off the M40 at Shepherds Bush, cut through North Kensington, went up Ladbroke Grove and turned, finally, on to the Harrow Road. As we drove, I looked left and right; there was the turning to Kensal Town and the men's clothing shop where I'd worked; there were the Avenues, Sixth, Fifth, Fourth and Third, and here we turned, stopped and parked. Uncle Hugh didn't say why. I'd thought we were going straight to his flat. He must have thought I'd want to see the old place.

I got out. This was my road. This was Third Avenue. It hadn't changed. I didn't think so, anyway. It looked as it had three years earlier, I thought, but it felt different. It wasn't where I belonged any more. Our old house, number forty-three, was halfway up on the left with the phone box outside, but the Maguires weren't living there now. Another family had it. The life we had had when we lived there was over and done with, finished, and we were scattered.

The three of us went across the road and into the Pop-In café, which I knew well. It smelt of toast, cooking oil and strong brown tea. There was a radio playing and the atmosphere was warm and steamy.

We went to the counter. 'What do you want?' Uncle Hugh said.

'It'll have to be the works,' I said. 'Everything, plus tea and bread and butter.'

We sat down. When it came, I looked at it on the plate, the mushrooms, brown and black, the tomato livid red, the sausage brown on one side but lighter on the other, and the bacon rind like parcel string but curly. The smell was rich and comforting. I hadn't seen food like this, apart from on that day we'd visited Dad in Gartree, for three years.

I picked up the knife and fork and set about eating. I couldn't get enough into my mouth to start with but after a few mouthfuls I felt full. I forced down one or two more but then I had to stop. I pushed the plate aside.

'Didn't you enjoy it?' said Uncle Hugh.

'I loved it,' I said. 'I just couldn't finish. It was too much.'

'Eyes bigger than your stomach?'

'Something like that,' I said.

He paid, and we went out on to the Harrow Road.

'Hugh,' I said, 'can we walk to your flat? I want to see everything slowly, at walking pace, and enjoy it. If we're driving I'll be seeing everything too quickly, and I won't get to savour it.'

'Sure,' he said. 'Of course we can walk.'

I stepped forward, without looking, without thinking.

'Pat!' Hugh called. 'Pat!' I thought his voice sounded louder than before and I wondered why he was shouting. What was there to shout about? I was right beside him.

He yanked me back and a car whizzed past. It was close, just a few inches from me, that was all. It'd almost had me.

I hadn't been out in the street, close to cars zooming up and down, for three years. I wasn't street smart any more, not like I had been. I was going to have to relearn a lot that I'd known but had forgotten.

'Pat.' It was my uncle again. He was saying something. What was he on about this time?

I turned.

'Pat,' he said.

'Yes.'

'We have cars now.'

PART TWO

29

There was a party that night at John and Maxine's and I stayed over. After that I slept at Uncle Hugh and Aunt Kitty's on a folding Z-Bed in the front room. There was nowhere else: it was only a one-bedroom flat.

Uncle Hugh got me a job as a labourer on a building site just off Queensway, not far from Phillips, the auctioneers, where he worked. I didn't want to turn up looking out of place – I was concerned about fitting in – so I borrowed some money from him and got a donkey jacket, a pair of Dr Martens boots and some jeans. In those, I would look the part.

On Monday morning I set off early. I hadn't broken the boots in and blisters soon formed on my feet but I didn't slow my pace. I was going to be on time.

I arrived just before seven, as I was supposed to. Several men were already waiting for the foreman. They were Irish and had a look that said they'd been in the building game a long time. I, on the other hand, in my clean donkey jacket and polished black boots, looked like something that had been ordered from a builder's catalogue. I was new, all right, they could tell, and not one said a word to me. I've never worked out how people can be so cold. Over the years, if ever I came across a 'new boy', I'd go out of my way to make him welcome unless he didn't want to know. But this lot said nothing. It reminded me of prison and all the tough-guy bullshit I thought I'd left behind.

The foreman arrived. He was Irish too. 'All right, lads,' he said. 'First job of the day.'

We gathered around him.

'I want this cement moved,' he said, pointing to a lorry pulled up outside the main gate and loaded with swollen, dusty bags. 'I want them taken down to the storeroom in the basement.'

We formed a line. The first man heaved a bag on to his shoulder and set off across the muddy site. The second and third did the same. Then came my turn. I grabbed the bag and lifted. It was paper, heavy and coarse, but paper nonetheless, and I hadn't handled those bags before. As I got it up on to my shoulder, it split and cement dust started to trickle out. I didn't know what to do so I carried my leaking bag down to the basement and let it fall from my shoulder on to the pile. More dust billowed up and soon the small storeroom was full of it. I couldn't breathe or see but I could feel the dust on my face, gritty and rough, and I could taste it too, chalky and bitter.

I went back to the lorry and got a second bag. This one didn't split. I carried it across the muddy site. I got to the top of the stairs that went down to the basement and saw the foreman standing at the bottom. 'Oh, lads,' said the foreman, 'here's a fucking green one. He can't even manage a simple thing like picking up a bag of cement.'

There was a bit of jeering and laughter from the men behind him and behind me. Under the dust I felt my face going red. Everyone was looking at me, which I hated. I'd made a mistake, but surely it wasn't a big deal. It was only a bag of cement, after all. But, still, he'd had to take the piss out of me, hadn't he?

The foreman put his boot on the first step. I thought, Try this for size. I pushed the bag off my shoulder like a shot-putter pushing his shot. The bag travelled through the air, and landed on his head, knocking him to the ground. It split and the grey dust inside cascaded out almost like water.

'For fuck's sake, what are you doing?' said the foreman, trying to get to his feet.

I jumped down the stairs, and before he could get up, I landed one on his nose. Then I walked up the stairs and marched straight off the site in my coat of grey dust, and set off for home. I got some queer looks and strange calls. But I knew one person who wasn't taking the piss now, the wanker.

'I'm off out,' I said.

Uncle Hugh had a funny look on his face.

'I'll be fine.'

'Sure.'

'Just stretching my legs, that's all.'

I set off for the Harrow Road, head down, not thinking, just walking. I could hear traffic coming from behind. The cars were all travelling at about the same speed. Then I heard a diesel engine and it was slowing sharply, to walking pace if I wasn't mistaken. As soon as I'd twigged that, I knew what was about to happen because it had happened already.

'Oi, Maguire.'

On my right a police van was crawling alongside me, the front passenger-side window wound down and an officer leaning out. 'You IRA bastard, you should be in prison with the rest of them,' he said.

He pulled himself back into the cab. The driver pressed the accelerator and the van moved off.

The policeman's hand shot out of the window. He made an unmistakable sign. 'Wanker,' he shouted. 'Wanker.'

I walked on for a few minutes but my heart had gone out of it. I went back to Uncle Hugh's.

'You weren't gone long,' he said, when I came in. 'Did something happen?' He was looking at me closely. 'You met the police, didn't you?' He knew about my earlier run-ins, the ones before I went to prison, the ones since I left prison, so this was the obvious deduction to make.

I shrugged.

'You shouldn't go out,' he said. 'They're not going to leave you alone. They see you, they have to have a go. You know that.'

I shrugged again. 'I don't see why I shouldn't go out,' I said.

Neither of us spoke. There wasn't any more to say. He thought he was right. I thought I was right.

* * *

It was a few days later when Hugh said, 'I've got you a bit of work.'

'What kind?'

'Removals. It's not full time, just as and when. Twelve pounds fifty a day. That's not bad.'

'Okay.'

'It's with people your mum and dad knew.' He mentioned their names.

'Right,' I said.

It was a sunny spring morning when the removals van appeared in the street outside Uncle Hugh's flat to collect me. I was introduced to the gang: Rick and Alan, my parents' friends, and someone called Stan. He was in his mid-twenties and I soon gathered his dad and mine used to drink together.

My uncle said goodbye and we piled into the van and drove to Brixton. It was still early. We went to a café, ordered breakfast and sat down.

'So, what's the job?' I said.

'We're moving solicitors from their old offices to their new ones, which are just down the road,' said Stan. 'It's a nice handy job.'

We arrived at the premises about nine. In the early morning it had been crisp but now the sun was higher and the air had warmed. It was going to be a scorcher.

We climbed the stairs to the offices. When we got there we found they were full of heavy old furniture. With another lad, I got a table and started to carry it down. By the time we got it into the lorry, I was pissing sweat. Christ, I thought, this isn't going to be easy.

I trudged up the stairs again, face red, shirt a bit sticky under the arms, breathless. Halfway up I met Stan. 'What's your shirt size?' he said.

'My shirt size?' I said. 'What do you want that for?'

'Just,' he said. 'Now, come on, Pat, what is it?'

'Fifteen and a half.'

'Right,' he said. 'Hang on.'

He put his arm into a hole in the party wall, seemed to fish around for something, then pulled it out again. He was holding five shirts, still in their bags.

He flicked through them quickly, then handed me two, both size fifteen and a half.

I hid the shirts in the van and went back to work.

Later, the other two lads were upstairs packing files into boxes and I was at the van having a breather. Stan was there too. 'Pat,' he said, 'I think I've got some more here in your size.' He searched through a black plastic bag filled with shirts, pulled out two more and handed them to me. 'Now, whatever you do,' he said, 'don't let the others know about these. They won't be up for it and they'll go stone mad.'

He closed the bag and stowed it in the corner. I hid my shirts under some dust-sheets. Then I made a roll-up and lit it. I pulled the smoke in, and that was when I noticed a men's clothing shop next door to the solicitors'.

I finished the fag and went back in. Halfway up the stairs I saw that the hole in the plaster wall between the two buildings, which had been just big enough for Stan to put his arm through earlier, was now big enough to climb into. Everything made sense suddenly.

After that I did a few more days. I liked the work and I especially liked Stan. There was no bullshit with him. Then he disappeared and the work dried up.

30

I was out walking again. I heard brakes and looked up. A police car had stopped on the other side of the road. The driver had his window down. 'Go back to Belfast. The IRA will look after you,' he shouted.

If they wanted me, they'd have to make a U-turn across the road and traffic was pouring up and down it. I was probably safe, I decided.

'Fuck off, you wanker,' I shouted. Then I walked on smartly, looking back as I went, just in case they decided to come after me.

* * *

It was Saturday. I was in a pub with some mates, the same ones I'd hung about with when I was growing up. We were having a beer. After a bit I found myself alone with one. I shall call him Dave. I knew him of old. We'd got up to all sorts when we were kids.

'How are you doing?' he said.

'All right.'

'You working?'

This was a sore subject. I hadn't done anything since the removals had stopped. The only money I had was what Uncle Hugh gave me, and which I hated taking. Oh, yes, I wanted to work. 'No,' I said, 'I'm not.'

'You can drive, though, right?' he said.

'Yes,' I said, 'but I haven't done any for years, what with being in prison, and I haven't been behind the wheel since I got out.'

'Paddy,' he said, 'it's like riding a bike. You never forget. You might be a bit rusty but we'll sort that out.'

Some sort of offer was coming, but what? Dave worked in and around west London. I knew he wasn't going to offer me to come in with him. I was too well known in the area and the police had stopped me several times since I'd come out and warned me. They knew where I was, they were watching me, and they were dying to come down on me like a ton of bricks. So I wasn't about to come out stealing cars with him. In which case, what was he about to offer?

Was it a job driving a minicab? If it was I wasn't up for that either. Apart from the fact I didn't have a driving licence, the idea of sitting in a car talking rubbish to strangers for eight hours a day was one of the worst ways of earning a living I could imagine. No, I was going to have to tell him to fuck off, but in a nice way, of course.

'What are you saying?' I said.

'I've a mate, Bob, on the other side of the river, with a garage. He takes bent cars, either for their parts or, if the car's good enough, to sell on as ringers.' He described the money involved. It was good, a lot more than I was getting from Uncle Hugh. 'Do you want some of that?' he said.

'Yeah,' I said.

*   *   *

'Oi, you.'

I stopped.

Two policemen in uniform barred the pavement in front of me. 'Turn your pockets out.'

'Why?'

'Because you've been fucking asked. Now do it.'

'I haven't got anything in my pockets.'

'You heard. Turn them out.'

I pulled the pocket linings right out. They looked like tongues sticking out, but they were white. 'See?' I said. 'Like I told you. Nothing in them.'

'Listen, smartarse, we talk, you answer. That's the way things go. Where have you just come from?'

'My uncle Hugh's.'

'Address?'

I told them.

'Where are you going?'

'Nowhere,' I said.

'No such place on my map.'

'I'm having a walk.'

'Why didn't you say so?'

'I'm having a walk. There, I've said it. Happy now?'

'What's your name?'

'You know my name.'

'Just answer the question. What's your name? It can't be that difficult. Even an idiot usually knows their name.'

'Maguire.'

'What?'

'Maguire.'

'We're watching you, Maguire, have you got that? You put a foot wrong, and we'll come down on you like a ton of shit. Understand, sunshine?'

The only way to come out of this situation with any dignity was to say nothing. So I said nothing.

Time passed. Traffic moved. They realized I wasn't rising to the bait. They stepped round me and strolled on. I shot away in the other direction, eager to put as much space between them and me as I could.

Dave drove me to south London to meet Bob. We got on and it was agreed that I'd work for him, but not in my own area where the police knew me and would be on to me. I'd be outside west London.

This was how the job worked. When Bob had an order I'd go and meet him in a café near his garage or he'd send a letter to my uncle's address. Either way I'd be told what make of car was wanted, where I'd find it and the best time to take it. All I had to do then was take the big bunch of keys I'd acquired, nick the car and bring it down to Bob. I did this a couple of times for a couple of weeks and I got paid after each job, meeting Bob at the café to collect my money.

I was still getting money from Uncle Hugh. I couldn't stop him thrusting it into my hand. I couldn't say, 'It's all right, I've money coming in now, I'm sorted.' He'd only have wanted to know how and from where, and I couldn't be telling him that. So I just took it and put it back in his wallet when he wasn't looking.

The police car pulled up beside me in the street and two policemen jumped out.

'Right, Maguire, come on, in the car, and don't make a fuss if you know what's good for you . . .'

I was driven to Harrow Road police station and brought inside. There were no formalities. There never were. I was led straight past the desk and into the holding area, shown a cell and told to get the fuck in there. I went in – I was hardly going to argue – and the door was locked.

I sat on the bed, head cocked, and listened to the noises outside. There were only two things that could happen. Someone would come and have a go, telling me to fuck off back to Belfast or that all the Maguires were bastards who deserved to be strung up. Or someone would let me out. The trick was to work out which. Hurrying footsteps usually meant trouble. Ambling footsteps usually meant I was about to be let out. And I liked to know what to expect, which was why I was listening. Also, as I knew from past experience, if they were going to give me a bad time and shout at me, it usually happened sooner rather than later.

But nothing happened. Time passed. They were leaving me to stew, I decided, and once they'd had their fun – today it was keeping me locked up for a while rather than shouting abuse – they'd open the door and throw me into the street.

I heard approaching footsteps, the key going into the lock. I stood up. I didn't like to be caught sitting down.

The door swung open. It was a policeman, a sergeant. He stepped into the cell. I expected him to shout abuse. But he didn't speak. He just stood there, staring and staring and staring at me.

'Cunt,' he said suddenly, and his fist caught the side of my jaw.

I threw two punches straight back, one right down the middle, straight to his face, the other to the side of his head.

'Cunt,' he said again. His fist flew forward and caught my nose. Christ, it hurt.

I threw one back.

'Cunt,' he said again, and threw another.

The blows went backwards and forwards. Bash, bash, bash.

I began to feel weak. My head throbbed. How long would this go on?

Then I heard the cell door bang like the bell at the end of a boxing match and the sergeant's footsteps as he walked away.

A draw, I thought. I felt marvellous suddenly. That was a bloody good result.

I was in the café with Bob.

'Instead of coming to see me here in the day,' he said, 'why don't we make a night of it next time I have to pay you?' He'd an evening job, he explained, in an adult bookshop in Soho. 'Come in and we'll go for a drink,' he said. 'I'll show you the sights.'

We agreed a time and I went in. The Soho streets were dark and, along with adult bookshops, full of knocking shops, brothels and strip clubs. I'd never been there before but why would I? I'd been a kid. Now that I was a big lad, though, it was different. I could see there were good reasons to be there.

I found Bob. I got paid. We had a drink. We went to a club. There were a few tables and a stage on which one girl after another danced around as they took their clothes off. I'd seen porn magazines on the wing in Aylesbury but this was something else. It was fantastic.

After that first night, I met Bob regularly at his bookshop, even when he hadn't any money for me. He was well known in the pubs and clubs of Soho, not as a face, nothing like that, but he knew what was what and who was who, and he was a perfect guide to this new world.

Our routine was always the same: we'd have a bite to eat, down a few beers, then chase some speed – which was strange as I was quite speedy enough. Then we'd hit the strip clubs. Beer, speed and naked girls. What more could I want?

Well, there was one thing and that was why I was there. It involved naked girls but it wasn't watching them. It was what you did with them that I was after, but I didn't know how to ask – 'Bob, I'm a virgin and I need a shag. Do you think you could point me at the girl who could best help me out, mate?' No way.

Then, one evening, Bob said, 'One of the girls likes you.'

Back then, if a girl had had a sign on her forehead saying, 'I want you!' I still wouldn't have got the message.

'Well, I like them,' I said.

'No, she *likes* you,' said Bob, with a smile.

Oh.

He told me her name was Sam.

Cut to a bar after closing time, a lock-in and a late drink for a few punters and some strippers. Sam was there and she told me what she had in mind. I was full of beer and speed. 'I'm nineteen and a virgin,' I said. I didn't know how she'd take that.

I needn't have worried. She said nothing, only smiled, showing very white teeth.

I went to Bob. 'I'm off now,' I said.

He palmed me a little bag of speed. 'I told you, Paddy boy,' he said, with a laugh and a squeeze on the back of my neck. 'I told you.'

Outside, we flagged down a black cab. I had nowhere to take Sam. She gave her address, which was fine by me, and we hopped in.

We got to her flat. I got undressed and straight into her bed. She stood at the end and began her act. I'd seen this already and didn't need to watch it again. I wanted something else. I jumped out of the bed and pulled her under the covers . . .

After that I was mad for Sam, so much so that I let Bob down once or twice but then, given the choice of nicking a car or staying in bed – well, it was a no-brainer.

Eventually things fizzled out. A relationship based on sex sounds lovely but it can't work in the end because you haven't got anything to talk about.

It was a day in October 1979, late in the morning. I was in Marylebone station with Uncle Hugh. The place smelt of stewed tea and burnt diesel. I stopped a guard and asked about the train from Aylesbury.

He told me the platform and we walked to the gate. On the other side a couple of trolleys were piled with old-fashioned mail sacks, like the swag bags of cartoon burglars, and the platform stretched away, the rails running beside it over greasy wooden sleepers and grimy stones.

I looked into the distance to where the overhead canopy ended and the rails ran out into the pale grey light and tangled with lines from other platforms. I waited. At first there was nothing, and then there was a dot beyond the end of the canopy where the lines blurred. It got closer and I saw that, yes, it was on the track that came to the platform where I was standing. I felt a surge of excitement. In a minute or two the train would be in. Come on, I thought, come on.

The dot was growing bigger and suddenly it had a shape. It was a diesel engine, pulling several carriages. It came under the canopy. I heard the squeal of metal grinding on metal. The driver had his brakes on. He was slowing down as he came towards the buffers. The train juddered to a halt. I heard doors smacking against carriage sides and saw passengers jumping down. He wouldn't be one of the eager ones. I knew that.

The first passengers who'd got off flowed around me and I gazed along the platform. Where was he? I hadn't expected him to be first but I didn't think he'd be bloody last either.

And then I saw him moving slowly down the platform towards me. Vincent.

I waved. He waved back. It was good to see him.

We went back to Uncle Hugh's and we shared the front room for a while. I still had the Z-Bed and he slept on the settee.

After three or four weeks, a family friend offered Vincent his house in the Avenues, which was empty except for a mate of his, someone called Stan. As soon as Vincent moved in I discovered it was the Stan I already knew: we'd worked together doing removals. A month later I followed Vincent. We stayed in that house until Vincent and I got a two-bedroom council flat on the twentieth floor of a tower block on the Harrow Road.

We had little money and couldn't furnish the place, but that didn't matter. Uncle Hugh with his auctioneer contacts got us some beds, chairs and a TV, all second-hand but we were glad of it.

One Saturday morning he rang. He'd a roll of carpet, he said, that would do the front room. Two friends of his brought it over in their van and we got it up to the flat. After they'd left, brother John, who'd come to lay it – he was working as a carpet-fitter at the time – and I rolled it out. It would fit perfectly; he wouldn't have to make a single cut. We put it in place.

'You know what you have here?' said John.

'A carpet.'

'Yeah, a thousand quids' worth, if not more,' John said.

It was a big Persian rug, the sort you'd find in a large posh house, very colourful, well made, too good for the top floor of a tower block. Perhaps we could sell it, buy enough carpet to do the entire flat and still have change.

Monday morning, very early, the phone rang. It was in the front room and as Vincent's bedroom was closer I decided he should answer. I heard him get out of bed, then a few mumbled words. Suddenly he was in my bedroom. 'Quick! Get up!'

'What time is it?'

'Half five. Hugh wants the carpet back.'

I'd known it was too good to be true. 'Now? Can't it wait till later on?'

'No. It's got to be at Phillips before opening time.' He explained that the two lads with the van had brought the wrong carpet. The one in our front room was due at auction that week. It was in the catalogue – there was even a photograph of it.

We rolled it up, but how were we to tie it? We'd string but that wouldn't have held – and this was one meaty fucker. We needed rope and had no hope of getting any at that time in the morning. We'd just have to manage as best we could.

We got it into the lift, with a lot of kicking and pushing, squeezed in after it and went to the ground floor. It was six o'clock in the morning, still dark and cold, when we got it outside, hefted it on to our shoulders and set off through the streets of Paddington for the auction rooms. This thing had some weight. It was like a wet log except it would unroll, which a log doesn't. Every fifty or sixty yards we had to stop and roll it tight again. What a way to start the week.

We got to Queensway and were walking on the opposite side to Whiteley's towards the park. I assumed the street was empty, it being so early, but to my surprise I heard a female voice saying, 'Business?'

It was a prostitute trying to get one last punter – or, in this case, two last punters – in before sunrise. As the carpet was on my left shoulder I hadn't seen her in whatever shop doorway she was standing in.

What if a police car came up now? I thought. How would this look? Two men, a prostitute and a thousand-pound carpet they didn't own. It would be interesting trying to talk your way out of that.

In the end we got the rug back to Uncle Hugh, and he found us another second-hand carpet, which John cut and fitted.

31

Now I'd a place to live with some furniture and something half decent on the floor, I needed a job – and I needed love. Both came quickly. One day Vincent was at the job centre, enquiring about work in a hospital in Marylebone, when he spotted a vacancy for a window-cleaner at Madame Tussaud's. I applied and got the job. There were dozens of windows in the main building, plus an office block behind that I also had to do, so I was kept busy.

There were lots of pretty girls going through Tussaud's every day. I talked to some, and if they were up for it, so was I. Whenever I filled my boots I always thought about the lads in prison who weren't getting it and felt, in some strange way, as if I was making up for what they didn't have – a ludicrous way to think. You don't fill your boots on anyone's behalf but your own. But, then, I wasn't thinking right. Physically I was out of jail but mentally I was still banged up.

Then I met Beth and fell in love for the first time in my life. It was marvellous. She became pregnant, and on 5 January 1981 our daughter Natalie was born. We weren't living together. They were staying with Beth's mum.

Vincent and I did one or two short news interviews for the BBC about our case, which created interest. Then we were asked to do something more ambitious: to go back to 43 Third Avenue and do an interview with a crew.

At first I wasn't sure about that. Did I want to go back to my old home – the home I'd been yanked out of? I thought about it long and hard. In the end I decided that it was a good idea and would help our case, which we wanted reopened.

The day for the interview arrived. Vincent and I went into the house. The current occupants had been paid to stay away while we were there. As the TV crew unpacked, I sat on the settee in the front room with Vincent and waited. After a minute or two, I noticed it was in the same place as we'd had ours. I thought that was a bit odd. It didn't have to go there: the front room was big enough for it to go in a number of positions. Then I realized that the armchairs, the coffee table and the TV were all exactly where ours had been, and at the same angles.

This was the room, I thought, where Dad would take off his watch, lay it on the coffee table, nod off, and I would put it on. This was where I had played and sometimes drew. This was where, now and again, I showed Dad my work. It was where we'd had Christmases and birthdays when we'd lived here as a family.

The afternoon light slanted through the window. I looked at each piece of furniture and as I did I heard talking, laughing, people coming and going. I began to feel cold. It occurred to me that if I shut my eyes I would see the people I could hear. One part of me wanted to. Another didn't. You can't re-enter the past, no matter how much you want to, and if you think you can, your mind's playing tricks.

I stood up and marched outside. One of the crew followed me.

'I can't do it,' I said. 'No way. I can't sit in that house another minute.'

We came back the following day and did the interview in the street.

Vincent had got married and left our flat, taking the cooker with him. I was alone there. Living by myself was hard. I was plagued by anger and resentment. I'd been banged away for something I hadn't done – none of us had done – then kicked out of jail and come home to nothing because Mum and Dad were still away. Nobody seemed to give a toss about all that had happened except our relatives, Aunt Teasy, Uncle Bill (when he was alive), Aunt Mary and Uncle Hugh in Belfast, Uncle Hugh and Aunt Kitty in Paddington, and some family friends. And as far as the police were concerned, I was still a guilty bastard.

If you'd asked me then, I doubt I could have put it as clearly as I have here but I know now that it was in there, swirling around, a horrible mixture of fury and resentment shot through with a

Patrick Maguire

determination not to let any of it show, to keep it bottled up because the last thing in the world I was going to do was let them – the system, the police, the courts, whoever – see that they'd got to me. If they'd known how I felt, that would have been their final victory. They'd have realized they'd broken me, and I couldn't have that. So I battened down the hatches, and pushed on with my life, tight-lipped on the outside, seething, raging and hurting inside.

This was the man with whom Beth and Natalie eventually moved in. We had fuck-all. But young love is marvellous. And the end of being alone was marvellous too.

It was Tuesday, 20 July 1982. Beth had taken Natalie on holiday with her mum, and I was at home painting the flat. I had the windows open. The sun shone down. It was a lovely summer's day. I worked steadily, slapping on paint, not thinking about anything, just enjoying the work, the transformation of the walls into clean, white surfaces, when I heard, from the centre of London, a kind of bang that I wasn't used to hearing. A bomb, I guessed, in which case the next thing I could expect was a visit from the police.

I had the radio on and I heard now that there had indeed been a bomb on South Carriage Road in Hyde Park. A detachment of the Blues and Royals on their way to the changing of the guard at Horseguards' Parade had been hit by a car bomb. Two bandsmen had been killed, seventeen spectators injured, and seven horses were either killed outright by the blast or had to be put down because of their injuries.

A couple of hours later there was another bang, this time from the north. On the news it was reported that while the bandsmen of the Royal Green Jackets were playing a selection from *Oliver*, a bomb had exploded under the bandstand on which they were performing in Regent's Park, killing six and injuring a further twenty-four. I heard later that the IRA had admitted responsibility. Well, now it was a certainty, I decided. The police would definitely be coming to see me.

As soon as I grasped this, a welter of horrible feelings followed. I was appalled by what had happened. Disgusted. Those were genuine feelings. But they didn't and wouldn't matter. My name had been blackened years earlier, and as far as the police were concerned, I was the same as the people who'd done this. But I hated the IRA. If they hadn't been fighting the mad lot on the other side, and the soldiers in between, we wouldn't have been nicked in the first place. None of it would have happened.

That doesn't mean I'm letting go of the rest of them. Oh, no. The police, the courts, the newspapers that covered our trial with their eyes closed, they were as much to blame. Each and every one of them had a part in it. And, unlike us, they'd got away with it. There had been no consequences for them. But there had for us.

A day or two after the bombings, Beth and Natalie were still away and I was still painting. There was a loud knock at the front door, and I knew it wasn't the postman. I opened it. There were ten plainclothes policemen on the doorstep.

'Bomb squad?' I said. 'I've been waiting for you.'

'What the fuck are you on about?' said a policeman with short legs. As he spoke first I assumed he was in charge. 'We're the burglary squad,' he went on, 'and you're nicked.'

'What for?'

'Burglary. What do you think? Didn't you hear? We're the burglary squad.'

'So you're not from the bomb squad?' I said.

'What is it with you and bombs?' said Short Legs. 'No, we're not.'

I decided to say no more about it. I stepped aside and they piled into the flat. One minute I was an IRA bomber and now I was a burglar – which I wasn't, at this time. So, what was new? As I knew only too well, the police could make you out to be whatever they wanted.

The squad pulled the flat apart while I stood in the front room with Short Legs.

'What are you looking for?' I asked.

'Things that don't belong to you.'

'I haven't fucking got anything. Look,' I said. This was true.

Beth and I had just a sofa, a small television in the corner, our bed and Natalie's cot.

'I think maybe you've got the wrong address,' I said. 'There's nothing here, really.'

'We haven't got the wrong address,' said Short Legs.

Now, I knew there was more than one family with the name Maguire in the area. After all, Maguire is a common Irish surname, and I knew the Maguires the burglary squad was looking for – they were friends of mine. But I didn't see why I should point them in the right direction. They could work it out for themselves, I decided, and then they could fuck off. Me, I was going to sit this one out.

'We've got your mum and dad down the Harrow Road police station,' Short Legs said, 'banged up in cells, so we know we've come to the right house. You're one of their sons.'

Now I had to put him right.

'No,' I said. 'You haven't got my mum and dad. My mum's in Durham prison, doing fourteen years, and my dad's in Gartree prison, also doing fourteen years. So I'll tell you again. You've come to the wrong flat.'

The penny dropped.

'Oh,' he said, 'you're one of them Maguires, the IRA and all that carry-on.'

Thank fuck for that, I thought. Now they can piss off and let me get back to the painting. But, no, it never works like that. Maybe it does in the movies but not in real life.

Short Legs asked about the court case. I hadn't cared for him from the moment he'd stepped into the flat and when he started on that I began to actively dislike him. I didn't want to make small talk about our case – I just wanted him to leave – so I declined to answer his questions, which annoyed him.

After a few minutes I thought, This can't go on much longer. The flat had been thoroughly turned over. There wasn't anywhere else to look. They must be going.

'All done?' Short Legs called.

'Yes,' I heard one policeman after another saying.

Thank fuck for that. I could hardly wait for them to go.

Then a policeman came in, hand outstretched with something on the palm.

'Gov, look what I've found,' he said, showing three bullets.

Short Legs took them in his hand. 'You're nicked now, all right,' he said. 'Where did these come from?'

'I got them down Portobello Market,' I said, which I had.

'Bollocks you did. Get him out of here and take him to the station.'

I was driven to Harrow Road police station. The same old bollocks followed, name, date of birth, and so on. Then I was brought by a policeman to a cell. He shoved me in, closed the door and locked it.

I looked around at the barred window and the narrow bed. I'd been in one of these often enough before and survived. Well, I could do it again. The only thing to do was lie down, close my eyes and get the facts straight in my mind.

Time passed. Food was offered but I said no. It would be rubbish and I reckoned that after a short chat I'd be out and home. It wasn't a big deal. I'd got them in the market like I'd said. Once I'd explained, I'd be out.

Finally, the door was unlocked. I was led to an interview room. There were two policemen. One was Short Legs; the other I hadn't seen before.

They gave their names. As I wasn't going to be sending either a Christmas card, I didn't make a note. The interview started. Short Legs did all the talking. The other watched. Presumably he was the good cop today and Short Legs the bad one.

'Where did they come from?'

'Portobello.'

'I'll ask you again, where did you get the three bullets from?'

'And I'll tell you again, from the Portobello Market.'

'They don't sell fucking live ammunition down a market. So tell us, where did you get them?'

'How many more times do I have to fucking say it? Down the Portobello Market.'

'Were they selling tanks as well that day?'

'I can't remember seeing any.'

'All right, you little shit, what stall did you buy them from? Who sold them to you? Were they black, white or what? Please, take your time and tell us.'

I didn't need to take my time. They had already given me more than enough of that when they'd put me in the cell and left me there. 'I didn't get them from a stall.'

'Oh, he didn't get them from a stall,' said Short Legs.

'I got them off this bloke who was sitting on a carpet just under the Westway. I wouldn't have seen him if I hadn't stood on his foot as I was walking by. After saying sorry and parting with one or two cigarettes, it was then that I saw what he had in front of him.'

'And what was that?' said Short Legs as he leant back in his chair, hands cupped behind his head.

'Three or four open shoeboxes set in their lids.'

'And what was inside these three or four shoeboxes?'

'Well, apart from the bullets there was all sorts – war medals, badges, cigarette cards, little toy cars, that kind of thing.'

'Were there no more bullets?'

'No, I think I got what was there.'

'We're going to send the bullets for testing,' said Short Legs. 'See if they match other ones used in crimes.'

'That won't get you anywhere. I bought them in the market, like I said.'

'What a load of bollocks, and you want us to believe it?'

'I don't give a fuck what you believe.'

'Oh, I think you will,' he said.

I was taken back to the cell and locked in. It wasn't hard to work out that I wasn't going anywhere now. More time passed. Then the door was unlocked and I was brought back to the interview room where I found the same two policemen waiting for me.

'Have you ever had a gun to go with the bullets?' said Short Legs.

'Did you find one?' I replied.

He was looking through some papers in a folder in front of

him, which he hadn't had during the first interview. Where had they come from? I wondered.

'So, what did he look like?'

'Who?'

'The bloke who sold the bullets to you – who do you think?'

'I can't remember.'

'Well, try.'

'All right,' I said. 'He had a beard, fuzzy hair, and he talked like a hippie.'

'How do you mean?'

'You know, "Yeah, yeah, cool, man, all right?" Like that.'

'You're full of shit, did you know that?' Short Legs opened the folder and looked at the paperwork inside. 'How long have your mum and dad left to do?'

'What the fuck has that got to do with anything?' I said.

'Are you all going back to Belfast when they get out?'

'Why would we want to go to Belfast?' I said. 'We don't come from fucking Belfast.'

He glanced at some notes, which lay in front of him on the table, then looked up again. 'Well, your mother and father do. And look at this! You were fucking born there. Isn't that right, Paddy?'

As a rule, I wouldn't normally have given them the time of day. But I wasn't going anywhere so I decided to go along with it. Also, it's good, now and then, to see how your enemies work, how they tick, how they try to work you out. And the way to do that is to talk to them.

'Right in the fucking middle of it, the Falls Road,' I said. 'Now, that bit of paper you've been reading, it should tell you that my parents left Belfast on the day they were married, came to London and never went back, except for the odd break, which was how I came to be born there. It just happened that way, an accident. But do tell me, what has any of this got to do with anything?'

'What was prison like?'

'Are you thinking of going?'

'It must have been hard, what with being an IRA bomber, English nick. Did you have a bad time?'

'No, I had a fucking great time, piece of piss. I could do it again on my head.'

'Well, you may get the chance to do just that.'

I didn't like the way he said it but I didn't let him see he'd stopped me in my tracks and given me something to think about. That would only have encouraged him.

'Take him away,' said Short Legs to a policeman at the door.

I was locked up and now my mind was racing. What was he talking about? 'Well, you may get the chance to do just that.' It wasn't as if they'd found an arms dump in my flat. It was only three bullets. 'Well, you may get the chance to do just that.' I couldn't fathom it. They couldn't send me back to prison for three bullets, could they?

The harder I thought, the worse I felt. Then I made a decision. There was no point in worrying about what he'd meant. I'd find out in due course and worrying wouldn't make it come any sooner. Also, I was starving. Why had I said I didn't want their food when they'd offered it earlier? Answer: because I hadn't thought I'd be there so long.

Well, that was a silly mistake, wasn't it?

I fell asleep, and was woken by the key going into the lock and the door swinging open. I was brought back to the same interview room where the same policemen were waiting.

'So, you won't tell us where or who you got the bullets from?' said Short Legs.

'I've told you what, where and how,' I said. 'Now, I really don't give a shit about this any more. Just do what you have to do.'

'Aylesbury prison.'

'What about it?'

'Do you remember on the day you got out you signed a piece of paper? A very important piece of paper, might I add.'

'I signed more than one that morning. What about it?'

'Well, you should have read them before putting your name on the dotted line. One was a Firearms Prohibition Licence, and it said you were banned for life from having anything to do with firearms, ammunition and anything else that goes fucking bang.

So, Paddy, you're in the shit-house now. You'll be going to court in the morning, first thing. And here's something for you to think about tonight. You're looking at five years in prison for this.'

What could I say? The only thing was the truth: that I wasn't going back to prison, not for anything. But I could hardly say so.

Early the next morning, in a wagon with its siren wailing and its blue light flashing, I was whizzed through the streets to Marylebone magistrates' court. I was kept in a holding cell for a while, then brought up to the dock. Charges were read and bail was mooted. I was all for that. I wanted out. The police opposed bail but the magistrate said I could have it if I could find someone to go bail for me. I made a phone call to my uncle Hugh, who came up. Bail was issued on condition that I handed in my passport and signed in once a week at Harrow Road police station until I went back to court.

We left the court and went to a café on Lisson Green. It smelt of coffee, tea and fried bacon.

'If the magistrate sends this up to the Crown Court,' I said, which might happen when I went back to the magistrates' court, 'and I'm found guilty, I'm looking at five years for breaking the terms of my FPL.'

Uncle Hugh said not to worry. It might not come to that.

Not to worry? I was looking at five years.

'If it goes to Crown Court, I'm off before it starts,' I said. 'I don't know how or where I'll go but I won't be hanging around.'

I continued in this vein for a while. Uncle Hugh listened to me but didn't say anything. That was smart. After that I settled a bit and he was able to talk sense into me. I should get expert advice, he said.

I found a solicitor who did legal aid. He thought I could beat this.

My first date at Marylebone magistrates' court came up. I got there early that morning – I'm always early. I found somewhere in the lobby to sit. Time passed. Where was my man? There was no sign of him. Any minute now I was sure I'd be called. How could I go into court alone?

'Mr Maguire?'

I stood up and saw a young woman with folders under her arm and a cup of coffee in her hand. She looked flustered and a bit dazed. 'Mr Maguire?' she said again.

'Patrick.'

'Hi, I'm Linda. Simon couldn't make it so I'm looking after you.' This wasn't good. 'Well, what do you know?' I said.

'Not a lot, really,' she said. 'I only got your file late last night and I haven't had time to look at it yet. Let's find a corner and see what it's all about. I can have my coffee at the same time.'

I thought she was a nice girl but what I was hearing had me worried. 'Look, Linda,' I said, 'has anyone at the office told you anything about me or filled you in?'

'No. Why?'

'Well, you'd better start reading while I drink your coffee.'

A look soon appeared on her face. A look that said, 'Ah, this is going to be awkward, isn't it?'

She glanced up from her papers.

'So what's the plan then?' I asked.

There was a long pause.

'I'll have to make a phone call, talk to someone at the office. I won't be long.'

'Patrick Maguire . . . Patrick Maguire.' The usher was calling us. Linda wouldn't be ringing the office. We had to go now.

I walked into the court and noticed two men with hard faces near the bench looking at me in a threatening way. I took the oath, and as I went into the dock one of the three magistrates ordered the court to be cleared. There was groaning. The place was full of people, some come to support their loved ones and others just to watch. They didn't understand. A court was open to the public, wasn't it? Why were they being told to go? I asked the same question myself.

The court was empty. The doors were closed. There was just me, Linda, the court officials, the magistrate, the policemen who'd be giving evidence against me, another solicitor, and the two men with the hard faces.

The proceedings got under way. Everyone had something to say, apart from those two men, who stared at me with their beady little eyes. I didn't deny having the bullets and said so when I was asked. I was reminded about the Firearms Prohibition Licence I'd signed on leaving HMP Aylesbury and of its terms. I said it had been just one more bit of paper to which I'd had to add my name in order to get out through the gate and no sooner had I signed it than I'd forgotten about it until I was in the interview room at Harrow Road police station with Short Legs and his mate.

I was told to go away and come back that afternoon when I would find out what was to happen. I took Linda to a café. She still hadn't put two and two together so I had to explain. I was a convicted terrorist: that was why there was all this commotion. I was Patrick Maguire, one of the Maguire Seven. Well, she'd heard of them. Who hadn't, in her business? Linda still wanted to make that phone call, but I told her not to worry about it. 'Let's see how it goes,' I said.

In the afternoon we returned to the empty court. I went into the dock.

A magistrate cleared his throat and started. He said I'd been a bad boy and reminded me again about the FPL. It was for life, he said. I was given a fine, told to be a good boy for two years, then directed to a side room where there were papers to sign.

I went to do the paperwork. One of the two men followed me.

'All right?' he said.

'Who are you?'

'Police,' was all he was prepared to say. Special Branch, I guessed.

'How's your mum?' he said.

'Doing fourteen fucking years for fuck-all. That's how's my mum is.'

'Take care,' he said, and glided away.

'Piss off!'

When I got home Beth and Natalie were there.

'I got a fine,' I said. I told her how much and how long I had to pay it. She didn't say anything.

32

There was a problem with the Madame Tussaud's job. My supervisor and I had never hit it off, and after I'd been there six months he told me I had to wear the uniform, company policy and all that bollocks. I'd had to wear a uniform in prison and I wasn't about to wear one at work now I was out. I went to the management, got him overruled. He was furious. We had a fantastic row. I put a chair through one of the staff-room windows, told him to stuff his job and walked. I loved the storming-out bit but it wasn't long before I was full of anxiety. I'd no new job to go to, no savings, a partner and daughter who needed feeding and clothing. I had to find a job pronto.

I saw an advertisement for a groundsman at the Paddington bowling club. That looked interesting, I thought. The work would be physical, outdoors, and as groundsmen worked alone, I wouldn't have anyone breathing down my neck.

I applied for the job. At the interview I told the head groundsman I had experience. I got the job. Now I had a problem. I had no experience. I hadn't a clue what I was supposed to do. I decided honesty was the best policy. I took the head groundsman aside and told him I'd fibbed at the interview because I needed the job desperately: I'd a young daughter at home to support. I hadn't any experience and I didn't know what to do.

I was right. Honesty was the best policy. Nothing more was said about my fib. He put me to work, and as I went along he showed me what to do. I loved the job, the open air, the independence, as I'd guessed I would before I'd applied.

Unfortunately, as the work side of my life was coming together, the domestic side was unravelling. It wasn't easy for Beth and me to live together. We tried but – and how many times have you heard this? – we were too young. Also I'd a few demons pushing around inside my head.

One evening I came in to find a bar in the far corner of the front room. It was black and silver with a mirrored counter. 'What the fuck is that?' I said.

'A bar,' said Beth.

'What did it cost?'

'One fifty.'

'One hundred and fifty quid?'

'Yeah.'

'Where did you get the money?'

'My mum.'

'You spent all that money on that? I don't believe it!'

'I thought you'd be pleased. I thought you'd like it.'

'We can't afford a bottle of brandy,' I said, 'or even a tin of lager, and you've bought a bar!'

I asked for a pay rise at the Paddington bowling club. They turned me down, so I left and went into business with Beth's brother, Ian, selling dodgy perfume around London's markets. It was Christmas 1983, and I was in Oxford Street, selling the stuff from a cardboard box. In the distance, coming through the crowds, I saw a big lump walking towards me, looking me right in the eyes. Oh, fuck, I thought. What's he want? Had I time to pack everything up and scarper? Not really. I'd have to butch it out.

The lump came right up to me. 'Hello, Pat,' he said.

He knew me. Who was he? I stood there, baffled. I didn't know him. I really didn't. Oh, yes, I did. He was one of the PE instructors at HMP Aylesbury.

I smiled.

'How are you getting on?' he said. 'Are you working? Are you keeping well?'

I said yes to everything. He said he was glad to see me, and glad I was doing well. He was in London for the rugby, he said, and he'd better get a move on. He said goodbye and went on his way.

For the rest of the day it was all there, swirling around in my head, the smell, the noise, the atmosphere of HMP Aylesbury. I might have been out for a few years but it could have been minutes, it was so vivid.

*   *   *

Christmas and New Year were over and we were into 1984. One day Ian came to me. 'We've finished with the shitty perfume,' he said. 'It's cigarettes now. Get us a van and I'll show you what I mean.'

I stole one and we set off together.

'What we need to find,' he said, 'are tobacconists, off-licences or sweet shops, anywhere with fags, but they've got to have dwellings above them and they've got to be empty.'

'Why?'

'You'll see.'

After a few minutes I spotted a shop that sold fags with a flat above. 'What about that?' I said.

We parked, went to the side door that gave access to the flat and rang the bell. No answer. We peeked through the letterbox. The floor inside was piled with dusty letters and circulars.

'Nice one,' said Ian.

We drove off and he explained: 'We break in later and go to the back of the flat. We cut the carpet, pull up some floorboards and kick the shit out of the ceiling below. Then we'll have a look through the joists and I bet we'll find – well, nine times out of ten you do – that we're looking at the storeroom and it's packed with fags.'

We went back, broke in and smashed through the ceiling. Bingo.

I jumped down and passed anything that could be smoked up through the hole in the ceiling. We bagged it up and hauled it out to the van. Then we left. No one had seen us.

The next day we asked around quietly and got the name of a shopkeeper who might take what we had, no questions asked. We went to see him. Was he interested? Yes, he was. He paid us cash, good money.

After that Ian and I knocked off dozens of shops, tobacconists and off-licences. It was the start of a new career.

I'd been out with Ian all day, flogging fags to dodgy shopkeepers, and it was early evening when I got back to my tower block. I took the lift to the top and walked down the corridor to my front door. I inserted the key and went in. The place was silent. Funny.

Normally Beth would be talking or Natalie playing and there'd be the sound of the television, but there was absolute silence.

'Hello? Beth?' I called. 'Natalie? Anybody home?'

I let the front door close behind me and walked down the hall. Perhaps they'd gone to the shops. Perhaps there'd be a note. I turned a corner. I could see the lounge in front of me. This was where Natalie normally was at this time if she wasn't having her bath, and Beth was usually in the kitchen, which was off the lounge to the right. But they weren't there this evening, I knew that now. I looked around. Natalie's toys, Beth's ironing pile, everything connected with them was gone.

I went back to the bedroom. Empty. I looked into Natalie's room. Empty. They hadn't gone to the shops. They'd gone for good. We hadn't been getting on, no doubt about that, and I'd tried to talk to Beth but she wouldn't listen – or even look at me. But I'd never thought I'd come home, find her and Natalie gone, the flat empty. She'd never hinted that this might be the outcome of our difficulties, so I was bewildered.

I went back to the kitchen, where the phone was, and dialled Beth's mum. I'd always got on with her, nice lady, always made me welcome whenever I was in her house, as did her boyfriend, her two sisters and her two brothers. Even the dog liked me. She answered.

'This is Patrick,' I said.

'Yes,' she said. Something in her voice, a sort of wariness, told me instantly. I'd guessed right.

'Is Beth there?'

'Yes.'

'Can I talk to her, please?'

Beth came on. Her voice was wary too. I asked a couple of questions and got a couple of curt answers. It was as I'd suspected. She'd taken Natalie and moved back in with her mum. We were finished. If I wanted to see Natalie, that was okay, I could come over to her mum's.

I put the phone down. Now I wanted my mum or my dad but I couldn't have either of them because they were still in prison. I resented that – Beth had a parent she could run to and I didn't. Fortunately I had Vincent, John and Anne-Marie.

A couple of days later Vincent came to see me. 'Listen,' he said, 'you've been through worse, and you've lost much more.'

He was right, though it took me a while to see it.

It came into my head that I wanted to see the gnomes that had given me so much pleasure as a boy. I went back to Portobello and walked up the market, passing the stalls, just as I had when Mum had taken Vincent, John and me out shopping. I found the flats and they hadn't changed, but the fencing was gone. There was no need for it now because the gnomes, the stone rabbits, the tortoise and the windmill were gone too.

I'd been stopped in the street, scooped up and brought to the Harrow Road police station. I was in a holding cell, standing in the middle of the floor, a policeman in the doorway. We were keeping a close eye on one another. The policeman was about five eight, my height.

'You know what?' he said, coming forward. 'You should be banged up, you and all the others, and you should never fucking get out. And you know why? You're fucking scumbags. And you know what should happen to scumbags like you? You know what I'd like to do with you? I wouldn't string you up. That would be too good for you. I'd like to cut your fucking head off.'

'Why don't you close the door a bit?' I said. 'Then it'll just be me and you in here, and we'll see how good you are, you little wanker.'

He sprang forward and delivered a blow to my gut that knocked all the wind out of me. I bent forward, holding my belly, steeling myself for the blow to my head that I was sure would follow. But instead, out of the corner of my eye, I saw that he'd turned and was about to head out of the door.

I couldn't have him hitting me and running away. I sprang forward and grabbed his neck. Down we tumbled to the cold cell floor, me first, him on top. He tried to get up, kicking wildly, but I wasn't letting go until I'd got my breath back.

In the passage outside, a policeman passed with someone for the cell beside mine and saw what was happening. Oh, no. Reinforcements.

I heard the door of the next cell slam. This is it, I thought. He'll be in to help his mate now. I was at a disadvantage on the floor but luckily I had enough air left in me to stand up, I thought.

I let go of the little policeman and tried to get to my feet but he held me down.

When the other policeman came in, the little policeman let go of me and got to his feet. Then the kicking started. I put my chin down, covered my head with my arms and rolled up into the tightest ball I could make. That done, there was nothing else to do but make certain my head didn't get in the way of their boots and wait until it finished.

I went to Beth's mum's to see Natalie. Beth made it clear that she didn't want me there and only allowed me in for Natalie's sake. She's angry, I thought. I was angry too, but as I was still hoping for a reconciliation I'd made a decision: I'd say nothing. I'd even decided to keep the bar, much as I wanted to throw it out. I reckoned that if she came home and found it wasn't in the lounge she'd go straight back to her mum's.

I continued to visit Natalie and, as time passed, Beth's attitude got harder. Eventually I got the point. There would be no reconciliation. She wasn't coming back. That being so, I decided I'd make our break official. At the end of my next visit I said, 'Can I have the keys to the flat, please, Beth?'

'Have you lost yours?' she said.

'No, but if you're not coming back you don't need them.'

'I'm not coming back to you but I'm going back to the flat,' she said, as she handed them over.

I went to Beth's mum. 'I can't do this any more,' I said. 'It's too much for me. I'm not coming back to see Natalie.'

Apart from Sam, who didn't really count, Beth was my first real girlfriend after prison, and my first love. I had accepted we were finished, but that didn't mean I was over it. I was deeply wounded.

I went home, dragged the bar to the lift, took it to the ground floor and heaved it into the communal dustbins.

Not long afterwards, Beth tried to get the council to evict me so that she could move in. She failed.

Then I heard she'd taken up with someone else. If she'd managed that so soon after she'd finished with me she couldn't have felt for me as I had for her.

And I wasn't bothered by the news. I was over her. Fantastic.

33

I rang Bob. We had stayed friends even though I hadn't stolen any cars for him in a long while.

'How are you, mate?'

'I'm up for it,' I said.

Bob promised to keep his ear to the ground and called me a few weeks later. 'I've a couple of mates,' he said, 'who're looking for a driver.'

I knew what that meant.

'I've given them your name,' he said, 'and I've put in a good word for you, but that doesn't mean you've got to do it if you don't want to. I can't say fairer than that, can I?' He brought me to meet Derek and Victor in a pub, introduced us and left.

They were a couple of years older than me and quite different from each other. Derek did the talking and I hit it off with him immediately. Victor said little but when he spoke he was loud. He had a hard look about him too, the kind kids on street corners put on. He didn't impress me.

After a couple of beers I asked where the toilet was. As I stood at the urinal I wondered what the fuck I was doing.

'You all right?'

It was the talkative one, Derek. He'd followed me in.

'You want some of this?'

He waved a small bag of speed.

I wasn't going to say no. I took a dab on the spot and got a rush straight away. Fucking great. And that was it. I decided, I was in.

It was still dark when the alarm clock went.

I got dressed and drove the car I'd got to the pick-up spot. Derek and Victor got out of the car they were waiting in. We were going on our first job together. One carried a holdall containing, I knew, a sawn-off shotgun and a revolver.

Derek and Victor got into my car.

I drove them to a building and dropped them off outside, then parked.

As I waited I adjusted the mirror so I could see the door to the building they'd gone into. I turned the car radio on. I heard a mad DJ talking bollocks and knew that soon mad music would be playing. I didn't want that. I was shitting myself. I needed something to calm me down.

I twiddled the dial until I heard something classical, then checked the mirror. No sign of them. Come on, I thought. What are you doing in there? Just get it over with and get the fuck out.

I checked the mirror again and again and again . . .

Suddenly I heard doors opening – my car's doors. Jesus Christ, what was this? I was about to jump out and make off when I realized. It was Derek and Victor. Somehow I'd missed them.

'All right, Paddy, away we go,' said Derek from the front passenger seat.

I pressed the accelerator down and we shot off.

'Fucking hell,' said Victor, in the back.

'Slow down, son,' said Derek. 'We want to get away but not attract attention. Take your time.'

'Yeah, and turn that fucking shit on the radio off.'

Derek turned in his seat. 'Whose car is this?' he said.

'It's not fucking his,' said Victor.

'He nicked it so it is his,' said Derek. 'Now shut up and have a smoke, you tart.' He faced forward again. 'Do you like this music?' he said.

'Yeah,' I said.

'Well, that's all right. You want to listen to it, you can. But it's shit, mate!'

Victor skinned up. The joint went backwards and forwards between them and it became very quiet in the car, just the music, the engine under the bonnet and, far away, the wheels on the road.

I dropped them off and parked. Then I got the tube home.

A few days later I went to meet them in a pub. They were going to pay me. As I went towards the table where they were sitting I expected Derek to say something. To my surprise it was Victor. 'Look who it fucking is,' he shouted, smiling. 'It's our old fucking friend. How fucking are you, mate? What do you want to fucking drink?'

He might have been off-hand at first but now he'd taken to me in a big way. It was as if we were old mates. He loved me.

Over the following year or two, as well as driving Derek and Victor, I did the odd day of furniture removals. I broke into shops and off-licences, stole the fags and sold them on. I got involved in some bigger cigarette jobs, nicking lorries loaded with them. I only did the driving but there were too many people involved in those operations for my liking. I didn't know the others very well and the money had to be split too many ways so I stopped that. I liked small teams because the fewer there were the less was said, and when the proceeds were divided there was more to go round.

Then Victor and Derek got into drugs. I'd nothing against it morally, it just wasn't for me. So the work with them tailed off. Also, I'd met someone and I'd an idea that if this was going to be a runner I'd have to drop this kind of serious work I'd been doing.

Dad was due for release in February 1984, after ten years served and with four years' remission, but Mum had another year to do. Though they'd had the same tariff, he'd done a year on remand while she hadn't, so he had a year less to serve. He had asked the Home Office if Mum could be released at the same time as him but they refused. Then he asked if he could stay in prison another year. Again the Home Office refused. He would be released in February 1984, and Mum would follow a year later.

On the day of his release I stayed at home waiting for the phone to ring, guessing that when the call came it would be from a pub. I was looking forward to seeing Dad but things had stopped being real for me years before. I wanted to be a small boy again, the one who had run around the house with Dad's watch on his arm, who waited for Dad to wake up so he could give it to him, who sat at his feet drawing while he slept off his beer on the settee, who waited outside the front door with Dad's tool bag for the lovely car that would take us to one of his private jobs. But I'd had to say goodbye to all that and to him. Time had passed. I had become a man with much behind him, not all of it good, and a father too. And now I had made a life in which I was so wrapped up that no one and nothing could touch me.

The call came. It was Vincent. 'There's someone here wants to talk to you,' he said.

There was a burst of pub chatter, then I heard Dad say, 'All right, son?'

'All right, Dad. Welcome home,' I said. It was the only thing that I could think to say even though home had gone years before, along with everything else.

He asked if I was coming down to the pub. I wasn't a big drinker at the time, and he told me that if I wasn't up to it, he'd see me later.

'Oh, no, I'm on my way,' I said.

The pub was crowded and there was Dad in the middle of it all. He was always a private person, a quiet man, never one for the jamboree, but he'd known a lot of people would want to say hello. He was in good physical shape – well, with no drink for ten years, of course he was. But when I looked into his face, I saw a troubled man. Vincent, John and Anne-Marie were there, the first time the five of us had been under the same roof for several years, but Mum was still away and that ate Dad up.

After an hour or two, I decided I was going. 'Dad, here's some money,' I said, pushing the notes I'd brought for him into his hand.

He didn't give them back but he didn't put them into his pocket either. He just held them. 'Are you sure?' he said. 'Do you have enough?'

'I have enough,' I said. 'I'll see you later.'

For a couple of months he lived with Uncle Hugh, sleeping on the Z-Bed I'd used. Then he moved in with John and Maxine and Anne-Marie, who were sharing a house. That lasted a fortnight until he moved into a bedsit. Then the council gave him a three-bedroom flat on a first floor, which wouldn't please Mum when she eventually came out: she wanted to be on the ground floor with a garden like she'd had at forty-three. But it was all that was offered so he took it. I went to see him quite often and helped him to get settled in.

These encounters were always strange – at least for me. I didn't know this man. I knew he was my dad, but the last time I was so close to him, without a table between us, or bars on the windows, or screws standing around, watching and listening to every word we said, I'd been just a boy. The only thing we had in common now was prison, and I wanted nothing more to do with that part of my life. When I'd walked out of Aylesbury, I'd put prison to the back of my mind, determined not to think about it ever again. That was the plan, at any rate.

I wanted to connect with earlier times. I wanted to ask Dad all sorts of things, mostly about himself, who he was, what he'd done in his life before we all got nicked, but because we were strangers – or I felt he was a stranger to me – I couldn't. And because of the distance between us, I didn't even bring the watch over. Funnily enough, he never asked about it. I should have taken it round and said, 'Here, Dad, remember this?' then told him that every time I looked at it, I was reminded of when he had given it to me in that cell below the Old Bailey. I should have said, 'I bet you never thought you'd give it to me like that. I bet you always thought you'd hand it over on my twenty-first birthday or when you bought me my first beer, didn't you?'

I should have said other things too, about that watch. I should have said that sometimes I got it out to look at it and thought of him looking at it as, years earlier, he'd left the house for work, and later, looking at it in the pub, having been asked if he'd like another pint and knowing that he should go home, that Mum would be waiting for him with his dinner, and saying, 'oh all right, one more pint then.'

But I didn't know how to approach him. Also, I didn't want to upset him. He had been through hell. One moment, he'd been the head of a household, and the next he wasn't. His wife and children were taken away and there was nothing he could do about it but watch. And Mum was still away. He was visiting her, of course, but when he said goodbye, knowing she would go back to her cell, it broke his heart. His own sentence hadn't ended even though he was free, and it wouldn't until she came out.

Mum was released from HMP Cookham Wood on 22 February 1985. Dad and Aunt Mary went to meet her. I don't know why I didn't go, but I saw her on the news that morning, coming through the prison gates: ITN and the BBC had been waiting for her. So had RTÉ, the Irish state broadcasting company. They had a car waiting to take her to London and interviewed her on the way.

When Mum arrived at Dad's place, John, Anne-Marie and I were there to meet her. She looked well, and she was happy to see us. We talked for hours, and even when Mum and Anne-Marie were making something for everyone to eat we didn't stop talking.

That afternoon RTÉ had arranged a press conference in a London hotel, which we all went to. That was where Mum first met Robert Kee, the writer and journalist who would do so much to highlight our case in his book, *Trial and Error: The Maguires, the Guildford Pub Bombings and British Justice*, published the following year.

That night, we sat down and had dinner together, which we hadn't done as a family for a very long time. The next day, Mum and Dad were flown to Dublin for more interviews with RTÉ. Afterwards they went to Belfast to see Mum's dad who had been very ill. He'd told a priest many times that he'd live to see Mum a free woman again and so he did.

A fortnight later he died.

When Mum came out she moved in with Dad. They lived together a long time until she got a flat immediately across the road from Dad's. After that she went over to see him every day, often with his dinner.

It was good to have Mum back, and it wasn't long before she made her new flat a home. I loved going round there for Sunday dinner, with everyone there. But as it had been with Dad, so it was with Mum. I hadn't grown up with her so there was a gap between us and, try as I might, I couldn't close it. She wanted to do so much for me, as any mother would – buy me clothes that she didn't have the money for, and do my washing. Even though I had my own flat, she was always telling me to bring my laundry for her to do. I never did.

When it came time to do up my flat again, a big job, I stayed at Mum's. She loved it. She had her little boy back. When the place was ready for me to move back, I waited until she had gone to bingo one night with her mates, then wrote a note and moved out. It was cowardly but I couldn't face telling her I was going back home. At heart I'm a loner. I don't know if it's because of what happened or I'm like that by nature, but it gets in the way of my life. That I do know.

34

It was when Mum came out that the campaign to clear our names began. We talked to newspapers, television, radio and anyone else who would take notice, because for years no one had. Meetings were held around the country to bring our cause to the country's attention.

We were at the Mansion House in Dublin, Mum, Vincent and I, to talk about our case. Mum was already out before the crowd; Vincent and I were waiting to go on. I was revved up, dead keen. Vincent wasn't quite so cheerful. 'How is it you can just go out there and do it?' he said. 'Don't you get nervous?'

'I love it,' I said, 'every bit of it. For years no one would listen to us. For years they wouldn't even give us the time of day, so any chance I get, I give it to them.'

On another day Dad was with Mum at the BBC, at White City. They were in a green room, waiting to go on. 'Help yourself,' said the assistant, pointing to the fridge, which contained just alcohol. Dad did as he was told, with predictable results. After that Mum and I did the talking.

The campaigning went on for years. TV crews came and went, passing each other in the hallway, the phone was always ringing, and the answering machine was full of missed calls. One afternoon I went round to Mum's with a mate, and found Cardinal Hume, who had taken an interest in our case, having tea in the front room. The campaign took over our lives but we could hardly complain. If we were going to prove we were innocent, it had to be done.

The girl I'd met was called Lorna and we fell in love. On 23 September 1987 our first son, Patrick, was born. From the off I stayed at her place but I kept on my old flat and went back there when I needed to be alone, which was quite often.

I bumped into Stan again. He was now a totter: he went on to building sites or into empty houses or rummaged through builders' skips and took anything he could, mostly lead, copper and stainless steel, which he then sold on to a scrap-metal dealer. 'Listen,' he said, 'I've got a proposition.'

'Go on,' I said.

'Mine's a two-man job but I've fallen out with my mate. Do you want to come in with me?'

It sounded like my kind of set up. 'All right,' I said.

That wasn't a good enough answer for Stan. Did I know exactly what I was getting myself into? he asked. 'If – no, *when* we're nicked, Patrick, the police will come down on us like a ton of shit because they don't like me and they fucking hate you.' Was I ready for that? he wanted to know.

I had to be, I said. When I ran into the police, it was always ugly. A lot of policemen, especially those from the Harrow Road police station, hated the Maguires for what they thought we'd done. 'I can take it,' I said, 'but what about you? You'll get it in the neck too. "What are you doing working with that bastard Maguire?" and all that.'

He shrugged. 'I can handle it,' he said. 'I'll just tell anyone who tries that to piss off.'

As the police in west London and the Harrow Road knew us too well, Stan and I did most of our work outside London or in other parts of the city where the police didn't know us. We would meet in the morning and drive around in his flatbed pickup looking for disused factories or offices. Once we were in, we'd haul out any chairs, desks or filing cabinets and sell them. Then we'd go back, rip out any metal and sell that for scrap.

One day we found a likely building on a main road and went in. It was divided into offices, and they were all furnished. Perfect. We parked at the front – dodgy, but there wasn't anywhere else to go – and started to carry out the furniture. After a bit a security guard appeared. The building was on his round and he'd come to check it.

'All right, lads?' he said.

'All right,' Stan said.

'What you up to, then?'

The key was to play it cool. We had to look like we were meant to be doing what we were doing.

'We're clearing out the furniture and taking it to the new building,' said Stan.

Good answer, I thought.

'I don't know anything about that,' said the guard. 'Who are you working for?'

I'd seen some headed notepaper in the building. I could get us out of this, I thought. 'I've got a letter in my coat inside,' I said. 'It says who we are and that we've to do this job. Hang on and I'll fetch it.'

I hadn't noticed any pens lying about so I got a Biro out of the cab, went in, wrote a load of bollocks on a sheet of notepaper, and came back. 'Here we are,' I said.

The guard glanced at it and went off, leaving us to get on.

A few months later we broke into a factory that had been used for industrial catering and found a kitchen full of six-ring cookers, stainless-steel worktops and double steel sinks. We'd been in kitchens like that before and we had a good contact who would take all the equipment, polish it up and sell it as new. We piled the stuff on to the truck and drove to his shop. He came out and looked the stuff over. 'Eight hundred quid,' he said. It was a much higher offer than we'd expected and we weren't going to haggle. He put his hand into his pocket, pulled out a wad of money, counted it out and put it into my hand. 'Drive round the back,' he said, 'and drop it off.'

He disappeared inside to open up and I got back into the cab.

'Right,' said Stan, checking the rear-view mirror. He knew where to go. We'd been here before.

'Stan,' I said.

'What?'

'He's only gone and given me eight hundred quid,' I said. Normally he'd only part with his money once we'd everything in the backyard.

'Fuck off,' said Stan.

I showed him the handful of notes.

'Is it all there, the full eight hundred?' he asked.

'Yes,' I said. I'd counted it.

Stan put the truck in gear and away we flew, along the side-street where we had parked and on to a main road.

Later, another bloke took it off us for eight hundred.

The abandoned hotel didn't have much in the way of security but the location was a bastard. The building was on a main road with a police-car pound on the other side. A high wooden fence topped with barbed wire surrounded the grounds. We could make a hole in it but the perimeter was in full view of either a council estate, some private houses or some shops. And even if we got through and inside, the building itself was a problem. The factories and offices where we habitually worked were close to the ground and had lots of ways in and out. This hotel had fifteen floors. If we were at the top ripping the bollocks out of it, we'd never hear the police coming in on the ground floor, and if we did hear them and made a run for it, there were only a couple of exits.

We passed the hotel often and like so many other totters we knew we thought, 'If only . . . Then one day we thought, Fuck it! With the yellow hard hats on that we always wore, and crowbars concealed, we went through the estate at the back, hoping that if someone saw us, they wouldn't phone the police. We found an opening in the fence – made by local kids, we guessed – and got in. Close up the hotel looked much bigger than it had before.

We opened a door and went into the basement. At some time it had been flooded: pools of water lay about and I could smell mould. Taking our time, we went up to the foyer on the ground floor, which was at street level, then up to the first floor. Here, there were forty rooms, six bathrooms and as many little kitchens. On the floor above, it was the same story, and so on, up to the top, a ton of furniture and metal fittings. We'd hit the totters' jackpot.

'We'll make a start tomorrow,' Stan said.

I agreed.

'I need a shit,' said Stan.

He hurried through a door to my right. Immediately a door to my left opened and a huge Indian man came out. 'What are you doing here?' he asked quietly.

'I'm waiting for my mate, who is now standing behind you,' I said.

Stan had either had the quickest shit he'd ever had or, hearing something, he'd put it off and come out.

'Who are you, and what are you doing here?' said Stan.

'I'm security,' the man said. He was employed by the hotel's owners, both Indians like himself, he explained.

We told him we wanted to clear the building and offered him thirty quid for every day we were there. He bought it, then told us that any time we saw a Rolls-Royce parked outside, we shouldn't come in. The owner, whose car it was, and his partner popped in once or twice a week but they never stayed long.

'Thanks for that,' said Stan. 'We'll be back in the morning and make a start.'

'You have forgotten my thirty pounds for today,' said the man.

'Fuck off, we haven't started yet,' said Stan. 'You'll get paid from tomorrow.'

We came back the next day and paid him as we'd promised. He was from Calcutta and he told us he'd send the money to his family in India. There was so much stuff in the hotel that we were at the job seven days a week and brought in two mates to help, with dustbins to carry away the tap fittings. When the owners dropped by we hid out the back. We gutted every room, with the exception of one bedsit on the top floor where we found a young soldier on the run. He hadn't eaten for days, he said, so we gave him some money.

The trickiest part was getting the industrial kitchen stuff out of the basement. It took the best part of a month to dismantle it and the only way to get it out was through the hotel's loading bay, which faced the entrance to the police-car pound. We got away with that because we looked the part.

It was early morning and we were south of the river when we found the empty factory. We removed the large padlock on the main door using a bolt-cutter, substituted our own and went off for breakfast. We always had a meal before we started in case we were nicked.

When we returned to the factory, we went in and secured the door by piling furniture against it. We didn't want it flapping in the wind and alerting anyone passing to our presence. Also, if anyone tried to come in they would make a lot of noise and we'd be able to get away.

We moved down a corridor, passed a small office and arrived on the factory floor. The place was full of furniture, the kind you see in an Argos catalogue. We had a quick scout about to see if this was where it was made. It wasn't. This was just a store.

Now for the dangerous part: we opened the iron shutter in the loading bay. Then, in full view, we loaded the back of the pickup. That done, we drove to the nearest Argos and picked up a catalogue, which gave us an idea of prices. Several second-hand furniture shops in Kilburn High Road took a load, and when they couldn't take any more, we went elsewhere. After three days we stopped, leaving more behind than we'd taken. We'd made good money and didn't want to push our luck.

The building had a restaurant at the bottom, offices above and flats at the top. Only the restaurant was in use. The rest was empty. We went up the fire escape, opened a back door with a crowbar and got into the offices. The walls were panelled in lovely old wood and the floors were parquet. The flats upstairs had more of the same. We'd had wooden floors and fittings, including door frames and skirting before, and decided we'd take these, but not today because the staff in the restaurant would hear us. We made a start with the antique door fittings, stripping out handles, push-plates, kick-plates and hinges. If we were surprised we could scarper with them.

After we'd done the office, I went for a piss. In the toilet I saw a big lead pipe in the corner. I knew it went right up to the top of the building, and that was a lot of lead. I got my hand behind it and pulled. The idea was to break it there and at the base.

Stan popped his head in. 'I think that's the main water supply to the building,' he said, meaning, 'That's not a good idea.' At that moment the pipe broke and water gushed out with such force it knocked me down.

I scrambled up, soaked, and ran. We grabbed our bag of door fittings, legged it to the van, laughing, and drove away past the building. The restaurant was in darkness, customers and staff standing in the street, water cascading through the open door and across the pavement. 'I told you it was the main supply', said Stan.

Despite the previous day's soaking, the next afternoon I found myself inside a factory washroom, doing it all over again. The washroom was on the ground floor and looked out on to other factories and offices. Several heavy copper pipes hung from the ceiling. I was standing on a tiled window ledge that ran the full length of the room above the hand-basins, trying to pull one down. The panes in the windows were frosted with wire going through them, so no one outside could see me working.

Stan came in. 'You're not doing it right,' he said.

I jumped down. 'You have a go, then.'

He got up and yanked at the copper. I lit a cigarette and watched, throwing the occasional unhelpful comment at him. Then, as if by magic, he was lying on his back outside, gazing up at the sky.

'Not a word. Not a fucking word,' he said.

'Bollocks,' I told him, laughing. 'This story's going in the local paper, you wanker.'

People who had been working in other buildings nearby and had heard the racket were staring at us. One or two called over, wondering what was going on. I didn't know what to say – that Stan had been ripping out a copper pipe and fallen through the window? – but was saved having to reply because Stan got up, went to the truck, got out the tape and measured the frame.

A face appeared at the empty window. 'Is your mate all right?'

'Yeah, he's fine,' I said.

Then Stan appeared, this time with a sheet of wood cut to size, which he fitted over the window he'd fallen through.

We found a set of steps and went back to the copper piping and for the rest of the day I took the piss out of him.

Both Stan and I had worked as removal men and handled some fine pieces of antique furniture. In that way we'd learnt a bit, and with books and telly we'd learnt a bit more, so, when we got into a 1920s swimming baths, we had some idea of the value of what we found.

Besides the actual pool, there were twenty bathrooms and in each a bath with its own mixer taps, and large showerheads, all in the twenties style and made of gun-metal. There was also an ornate iron banister with a brass handrail that went up the three floors, masses of brass carpet rods, door frames, skirting, wood panelling and some beautiful tiles.

It took a fortnight to get all that out and away to antiques dealers of our acquaintance. Then we set to work ripping out the copper piping. We cut it out and hauled it away for scrap.

Finally, all that was left was a length of stainless-steel piping that ran along the side of the pool. We hired an oxyacetylene cutter and got to work. Neither of us had used one before so it was trial and error at first, but soon we had the hang of it and were cutting the pipe into short lengths. At some point we heard a fire engine but thought nothing of it until ten firemen were standing beside us.

A passer-by had seen smoke – which we had made with all the cutting – and dialled 999.

'There's no fire,' said Stan. 'It's just us, working. Sorry about that.'

The firemen left. We finished and cleared off.

We had our eye on a big milk depot. We had a look at it a number of times, to see the layout and decide on the best time to go in. During the day, too much was going on outside, but we couldn't leave it until the middle of the night either. If it was too quiet, we might be heard going in and out. We needed the noise of cars, restaurants, bars, shops and people to cover us: early evening was the best time for this. Also, the whole place was well lit. We wouldn't need torches. A couple of security guards patrolled the yard now and then, but they did more talking than looking. Providing we kept to the back, where they didn't go, we'd be all right.

We cut our way through three wire fences to get to our goal – the place where the pallets were dumped. These beauties were like the wooden ones you'd see in a builder's yard, but they were made of aluminium and there were lots of them. We carried them, one at a time, through the holes in the fences, and loaded them on to the truck, covered them with a tarpaulin, drove away and put them into one of our lock-ups. We could have been at it all night and taken the lot, but we settled for five trips.

The following day we drove a load to a scrapyard we used regularly. The owner came out to have a look, lifted the edge of the tarpaulin and went red. 'I could be closed down for taking those,' he said, which was true. 'Get the fuck out of my yard.'

We went for breakfast and made a list of all the scrap-dealers we knew, then spent a day driving from one to the next. Eventually we found a bloke who took all five loads.

One evening we were driving home with not much when we passed an old factory with for-sale signs nailed to the walls. The downside was that there were houses and other buildings around it that weren't for sale: they were full of people. But as that hadn't stopped us before – we'd always brazened it out – we parked and had a look. At the far end of the building, just above the entrance, we saw a faded handpainted sign on the brickwork, which said that alcoholic liquors, whisky and gin, were made there. It was an abandoned distillery, so there was a good chance that it would be full of copper.

We got back into the truck, and drove round the perimeter walls, looking for signs that someone might be inside. Finding none, we parked in front of the gates, got out the bolt-cutters and went to the gate. I had a look at the lock and knew we wouldn't be cutting this one off. It was a new type that I hadn't come across before: once it was locked, there wasn't much for the bolt-cutter to get hold of. However, neither of us was one to give up, so we came up with a plan. We would reverse the truck into the gate. That would do the job – if it didn't smash the truck.

Stan pulled the truck well forward (so much so I thought for a moment he was going home) while I stood to the side – as you do when someone's reversing. It was important to look the part. Then, without warning, he put his foot down and reversed, hitting the gates right in the middle, where the lock was. They flew open, banged the walls, then bounced back to whack the sides of our pickup. We'd done it.

We drove around the site, looking in windows and checking loading bays. It was empty, all right, and it was ours. But it was too late to start now. We'd come back in the morning. We drove to the gates and as we didn't have a padlock of our own I closed them with some copper wire.

On the way home, both of us happy as Larry, we heard police cars behind us. Other drivers were pulling over and we did likewise. We didn't want to hold up the police. The police cars came closer. Suddenly they were stopping – one in front of the truck, another at the side and the third at the back. Someone had seen us ram the gates and phoned them.

What had we been doing? the police wanted to know.

'Oh, I was reversing up,' said Stan, 'and my mate here was guiding me, only I didn't hear him shout, "Stop," and I went into the gates.'

'So why did you drive around the site?'

'After he went through the gates I wrote a note saying how sorry we was, giving our details and saying we'd pay,' I said, 'and then we had to drive around until we found a door I could shove it under, which I did.'

This was on-the-spot bullshit at its best. Did we get away with it? Too right we did. But we couldn't go back, no matter how much money there was to be made. We'd got away with it once and we wouldn't push our luck.

We were in Brighton and we were hungry. The streets were jammed with parked cars and the only space we could find was a disabled spot. We decided to risk it, pulled over and went to a café for breakfast. When we got back the truck was gone. The local police had towed it away. We paid the fine – we knew we'd get our money back and more – and by midday we were at work, and came home with more than a stick of rock.

The next few months continued pretty well. We were stopped now and then by the police but we didn't have any real aggravation. Then, one day, a police car pulled us over and searched the van. We had nothing but we knew they were on to us.

The stops and searches grew more frequent. Then, one morning, we were in a café having breakfast before we went to work. A police car pulled up and parked outside. We could see the policemen and they could see us.

We finished our breakfast, drank our tea and paid. As we sauntered towards the door the police got out of their car.

'Morning,' said Stan.

The policemen nodded.

'You've been very considerate,' said Stan, 'waiting till we'd finished breakfast. There's nothing worse than being nicked on an empty stomach. In the station all you get to eat is shit.'

We were taken to the station, held for a few hours and released without charge.

35

It was a summer's morning, dry with plenty of sun. I was waiting for Stan in his front room, drinking tea and eating toast that his wife, Liz, had made, while I watched the television. Stan came in – it had been worth the wait, he was wearing Liz's pink dressing gown – and at that moment the local news caught our attention. Just down the road from where he lived there'd been a fire in two adjacent houses that were divided into flats.

We had to look lively. We weren't the only ones watching the news that morning. We rushed to the local hardware shop and picked up two padlocks to replace the ones we'd have to break to gain entry. Then we went round, broke off the padlocks that were on the doors and put on the ones we'd bought. After that we left. If the police turned up the property would look secure.

When we got back, there was no sign of the police. We opened one of the padlocks – we looked like the real workmen, in our yellow hats and carrying our own keys – and went in. We found ourselves in a hallway. Water dripped from the ceiling and ran down the walls. The floor under our feet was waterlogged and there was a strong smell of scorching. It was dark, too, because all of the windows and the glass in the front door were coated thickly with soot. We turned on our torches.

In the first room, we saw several pieces of burned furniture and a Georgian fireplace. We searched the rest of the house and the one next door, and found fourteen more just like it.

Fireplaces, we knew, could be a bugger. You could spend hours trying to prise one off the wall, sweating like a pig, only for it to break apart as it came away.

This time we were lucky. We got every one.

We sold them for a small fortune.

The factory looked empty when we broke in. All the furnishings, plant and merchandise were gone, except for ten large wooden containers in the loading bay, which turned out to be full of marble slabs. They were beautiful but they looked heavy. We'd have to carry them out together, one slab at a time – assuming we could move them. The work would be back-breaking and it would take an age. Still, if we wanted the marble, and we did, that was the only way.

Before we got stuck in, we decided to nose around a bit more. Lo and behold, what should we find, neatly parked in another part of the factory, but a fork-lift truck with the keys in it. We'd have those slabs on the back of our pickup in no time with this. There was only one thing. Neither of us knew how to drive a fork-lift. We tossed a coin. Stan would go first. Then it would be my turn. Whoever was the handiest would do the work.

Stan started up the fork-lift and set off for the loading bay, banging into doors and walls as he went. I followed on foot. Then it was my turn. I sort of looked as if I'd done it before as I got the prongs under a slab and shifted it up and down.

Stan lifted the shutters and backed up the pickup as close as he could. The factory was on an industrial estate and all the other units were working. The less people saw of me the better.

I got two containers on to the flatbed, which was all the truck would take. We locked the shutters and drove to a marble outlet to find out the going rates. Then it was off to the man who had bought the fireplaces. He took some, and wanted more. Then a bloke who fitted kitchens and bathrooms wanted as much as we could give him. Over the following week we hauled away six more containers. Then, disaster: the battery on the fork-lift went flat with two full crates remaining. Did we leave them? Did we fuck!

We asked the lad who was driving the fork-lift at the factory next door if he'd mind helping us with the last two. We paid him well and he promised not to mention what he'd done.

A few weeks later we went back, stripped out all the metal we could find and sold it for scrap.

We went on doing the scrap but now we were always on the lookout for fireplaces. You got so much for them. Stan had contacts in the building trade and got a tip-off from the workers on a site in Kensington. We put on our yellow hard hats and went in at five in the morning. The fireplaces were stacked against a wall and covered with tarpaulins. We loaded them up and drove away.

A dealer paid us in cash. We divided the money between us, quite a tidy sum each.

'Well,' said Stan, pocketing his cut, 'no need to push ourselves quite so hard for a bit.'

'No,' I agreed.

'Of course,' he said, 'this doesn't mean we won't be working at all.'

'Of course not,' I said.

'We'll just go easy.'

We went on working, having a day off here and there, and going on the piss. The police would stop us from time to time, hoping to find something wrong with the tyres, lights or indicators so they could nick us, but they didn't have much luck. We looked after the van well: it was our meals-on-wheels, it put food on the table.

Then came a summer's day when the sky was blue and a breeze filled the cab. We were sitting at traffic lights near Cromwell Road, West Kensington.

Suddenly, bang, ten or fifteen of them, all in plain clothes, were getting out of their motors and circling us. 'Come on, you two, out, now,' a policeman shouted.

The doors were opened. We were dragged out.

'What the fuck's going on?' said Stan.

'We're the Fireplace Squad,' said a policeman, taking the piss.

'Well, you're not getting any fireplaces today, you wankers,' I said.

I found out later that we'd been seen going into empty buildings in our bright yellow hats and this was the culmination of 'Operation Hard Hat'.

We were pulled over to a brick wall.

'Hands against the wall, open your legs,' a policeman shouted.

We were spreadeagled and they searched us. Then they searched the van. They didn't find any fireplaces, just bits of copper and lead. It didn't matter to them that they hadn't got what they wanted. They nicked us anyway.

We were put into the back of a police van and told not to talk to one another. Then a policeman got in with us. They didn't want us making up a story. But it was a bit late for that. We both knew what to say if it came to it. In our game you always had your story agreed in advance.

We were taken to Kensington police station. Inside, a sergeant was in charge of processing. I had to give him my name, date of birth, the usual old bollocks. Then came the best question of all: 'Have you ever been in trouble with the police before?' Fuck off, I thought. You know I have.

Once the paperwork was done the sergeant told a policeman to take me away. I was led down a corridor, past several steel doors with slits. The policeman told me to stop beside a steel door, which he opened. I was told to step inside.

It was a holding cell, with a concrete sleeping platform, a plastic-covered mattress and a stainless-steel toilet. It smelt of stale sweat, dirty feet, pee and cabbage, all very familiar.

The door closed, the key turned. Given the line of work I was in, this was inevitable. It came with the job. I felt a bit pissed off at being back in a cell, of course, but this wasn't the first time I'd been in one since prison: I'd been in plenty, so this wasn't traumatic for me and it wasn't terrifying. This I could handle.

So, what would would happen now? Well, it would be a long, boring day. At some point we'd be interviewed and charged. At some later point we'd go before the magistrate. It wasn't a serious offence, so we'd get bail. We'd go back to court in a few months' time, plead guilty probably and cop a fine. That was it. Theoretically, prison was possible, but I couldn't imagine we'd be sent away for a few bits of lead and copper. Everything would be all right. I was sure of it.

I stretched out on the mattress and kept an eye on the door.

Time passed. A policeman lifted the flap and looked in at me. I could only see his eyes. 'Your mate has told us everything so you might as well do the same,' he said.

'He wouldn't tell you the time of day, so piss off,' I said.

He slammed the flap.

Later, I was taken to an interview room. I sat on one side of a table and two policemen sat on the other. One showed me some photographs, all featuring Stan and me, dressed like Bob the Builder. There was one of me hanging from a crowbar, trying to open a door, another of Stan coming out of a house with bits of copper and lead.

'What do you know about fireplaces?' he said.

There wasn't one photograph showing either of us carrying a fireplace so I reckoned we were in the clear. 'Nothing,' I said.

'I don't believe you. I think you know a lot about fireplaces.'

'I know nothing,' I said.

'I don't believe you,' he said. 'You know a lot about them. You know you do.'

'I live in a flat at the top of a tower block,' I said. 'I don't have any use for a fireplace. The flat has no chimneys. I don't know anything about them.'

'Rubbish,' he said. 'You and your friend, in your yellow hats, have been seen going into empty buildings and carrying stuff out, including fireplaces.'

We were charged with burglary, and later that year we went to court. During the preliminaries, the clerk asked what I pleaded. I said I was no burglar. The empty buildings I'd allegedly been seen going into often didn't have doors or windows and some didn't even have roofs. How could that be burglary? A dwelling had to be involved if it was burglary.

I was told by the wig to answer correctly.

I said, 'Not guilty.' Stan said the same.

We were put into a holding cell, and had a visit from our brief. He told us that the wig wasn't happy.

'Fuck him,' I said, 'I'm not over the moon myself.'

The brief didn't look pleased to hear this. He said if we stuck to pleading not guilty and were found guilty, we'd go to prison. On the other hand, if we pleaded guilty we'd get a fine. We pleaded guilty.

At dinnertime they let us out for an hour. The court wasn't far from Harrods, so we went there. It was the first time I'd ever been inside. We went to the café on the top floor. Whoever had decided on the price of a cup of tea and a cheese sandwich should have been in court with us. We were robbed.

Back in the court, we were fined and told to be good boys for two years.

The next day we went back to work.

36

It was 19 October 1989. Early in the morning, Stan and I drove to Aylesbury, a town where I'd spent some time but I couldn't say I knew well. We stopped outside the prison. The officers were going into work. We gave one or two a mouthful. Then we went to an abandoned factory, broke in, opened up the shutters to a loading bay, drove in and parked the van in such a way that we could drop lead from the roof on to the flatbed.

When it began to get dark, we came off the roof, closed the van, which was loaded with lead, and drove away. There was no radio so we could hear only the engine under the bonnet.

We arrived at Stan's place. As he pulled up to the kerb his wife came out and hurried towards us. From her face, I saw she had something important to tell us.

Stan wound down his window.

'You didn't hear?' she said.

'Hear what?' said Stan.

Earlier in the day, at the Old Bailey, the Guildford Four had had their sentences quashed. They hadn't done it. It was official.

I went round to Mum's flat. She wasn't alone: there were reporters with her. The news came on. We stopped talking. The first item concerned the release of the Guildford Four. The appeal court, said a voice on the television, had taken half an hour to overturn the convictions for murder of four alleged terrorists found guilty of pub bombings in 1975 and sentenced to life imprisonment. The convictions of the Guildford Four had been based on police lies and fabricated confessions. Gerard Conlon, aged thirty-five, Carole Richardson, aged thirty-two, and Patrick Armstrong, aged thirty-nine, were freed at once after serving fourteen years for a crime they had not committed. The conviction of Paul Hill, the fourth defendant, was also quashed and he had been flown to Belfast, pending a hearing on his conviction for the murder of Brian Shaw, a British soldier. He was expected to be released the next day. A judicial inquiry had been ordered into the case. Allegations that senior detectives had tampered with and even concocted confessions had come to light in May, during enquiries by the Avon and Somerset Police. The court's decision had implications for members of the Maguire family, relations of Conlon, convicted after he had named them as bombmakers.

One of the reporters at Mum's said that an inquiry into our case was bound to follow. It had to. The Guildford Four's convictions and ours were tangled up together. Now that theirs were unravelling so would ours.

Later I went back to my flat. I went out on to the balcony and lit a cigarette, as I often did at night. London stretched away to the south, car headlamps moving slowly along roads, dark buildings and others with lights on inside.

Stan and I went on going out to work and making our money as we always had. Then we did a job that we only just got away with. Had we been caught we would have gone to prison. A couple of days later Stan told me we couldn't work together any more.

'What the fuck are you on about?' I said.

'Look,' he said, 'you were on TV last night, and you're in all the newspapers. Things are starting to look up for you and the family now. You can't fuck it up. If you get caught it won't look good.'

I was furious but I knew he was right. And Stan wasn't the only one thinking this. Dad, who'd always known I'd been at it, had been on at me too. 'I don't want to know what you're up to,' he'd said to me recently, 'but whatever it is, it stops now.'

'All right,' I said to Stan.

The next time I was to do any work it would be painting and decorating, but that was years away.

I was in a pub, and a bloke was looking at me, smiling. It seemed that he knew me and something about his face was familiar. I knew it. I just couldn't put a name to it.

He was coming towards me. Yeah, definitely, I knew him, I thought.

'Hello,' he said. 'TK.'

'Oh, my God, Tony Kinsella,' I said. 'Of course.' I'd met him on my first day at secondary school. We'd a few drinks and started talking about school.

'They never told me where you'd gone when you were sentenced,' he said. 'At first I thought you were sick, having a few days off school. I only found out what really happened much later. I was gutted. What was that about?'

What could I tell him? It made no more sense to me than it did to him. I felt sad, too, because seeing him now made me realize that here was something else I'd missed out on after I was sent away – being friends with TK and planning bank robberies. Now I had to ask: had his interest blossomed into a career? He shook his head.

'What about you?' he asked.

I couldn't sleep so I went to my doctor. He gave me tablets. They worked for a bit, then stopped. I went back. He gave me something else. They worked for a bit, then stopped. This went on and on.

'Right,' said the doctor, one day. 'I think you should talk to someone about what happened.'

The past was like a rock attached to me with a chain. I dragged it behind me but I didn't think about it. I knew it was there, oh, yes, but unless someone asked me a direct question about what had happened, I managed not to think about it, which suited me fine. Now, with what my doctor was suggesting, I wouldn't only be dragging it behind me, which was bad enough, I'd have to talk about it.

Fuck that, I thought. Forward was the direction I wanted to be going, not back. I said this to him.

'You're not sleeping,' he said, 'and not sleeping is probably connected to it, yes?'

'Yes.'

'We've tried tablets and they don't work, but you're still looking for help. Well, this is what's being offered. It's all that's being offered.'

He fixed an appointment for me at the psychiatric unit in St Mary's Hospital, Praed Street. On the day I went along, feeling nervous, and spoke to a woman called Kate Doyle. She knew of the Maguires, so we were halfway there before we'd started.

After that I saw Kate once a month and eventually once a week. At first I did a lot of listening. Then I started talking. At the end of one meeting she asked me, as I was leaving, to try to write down any thoughts I had, anything that came into my mind. 'I don't even write a list when I go to the shops,' I said, 'so I don't think I'll be doing that.'

To my surprise, a few days later I began to write, and found I couldn't stop. I wrote about what had happened to me and the family, I wrote about things I'd not thought about for years and some I'd not thought about at all until now.

After a few days' scribbling, I realized I needed a proper place to do this work. I decided to turn a bedroom into my study. I trundled in a couple of big gas heaters and laid some bits of wood between them. This was my desk and there I would sit, writing down everything that came into my head for six, even eight, hours at a time. This was a big surprise to me. I'd never been very good at sitting in one place and doing one thing for hour after hour.

At no time, as I scribbled away, did I think I was writing a book. Yes, I had a story to tell but who would want to read it – let alone buy it? I was writing it for me and my three children, hoping it would help them to understand their father.

I think Vincent was the first to read it. 'There's a book here, you know,' he said.

I gave what I'd written to Steve, a good friend. 'Where's the rest?' he said, when he'd finished.

'That's all I've done.'

'Well, get on with it,' he said.

One day Mum came up to the flat and saw the improvised trestle. 'If you're going to write,' she said, 'I'll get you a good desk.' And she did.

I also gave what I'd written to Kate. I had to. She'd commissioned it, hadn't she? She took it away and read it; when she gave it back she said she was pleased with what I had done.

On 26 June 1991 our convictions for having handled explosives were quashed by the Court of Appeal.

I was booked to do a radio show late that evening called *The Mix* for young people. They sent a car, as they do, I got in, and off we went.

'You're in a band,' said the driver, 'right? What kind of music do you play?'

It turned out he thought the Maguire Seven was a pop group. I wish.

Cardinal Basil Hume asked me to write something about my times in Lourdes for the *Catholic Herald*. This is what I wrote:

Lourdes

I knew two things about Lourdes. One was that a young girl called Bernadette had seen 'a beautiful lady' there, and the other thing I knew was that sick people went there. It never crossed my mind that I would go there myself.

My mum had been several times and had told me all about it, but I know how hard it is to try and explain to others who have not been just how beautiful it is, and what you feel when there.

Mid-1990, I was at the Archbishop's house, having tea, or was it a glass of beer? Anyway, I was with the Cardinal, who I had got to know over the years. He asked me would I like to go to Lourdes with him and lots of young people on a YAP [Young Adults Pilgrimage]. He told me what it was all about, but I had made up my mind long before he was finished.

You see, when I was a young boy of fourteen I was sent to prison for four years for something I didn't do or even understand. Other members of my family were sent to prison too.

For the first two weeks I was locked up, on my own, for twenty-three hours a day in the prison hospital. I cried day and night, and asked God, 'Why are you letting this happen? Where are you now?'

I just couldn't work it out. I had been to church every Sunday, and Sunday school. All right, I didn't always want to go, but I did. So where was he when I needed him?

I got through prison, with all its ups and downs. I got out after three years. There was no family waiting for me outside the prison gates, they still had many years to do.

That's when my sentence really started – when I got out. I got up to all sorts of things, some good but most of them bad. You name it, I did it, or was going to anyway.

I did find myself going to church over the years. I would ask God why my life was like this and why I did the things I did. It looked like God had no time for me, so I just got on with it. That was why I said no to the Cardinal when he asked me to go to Lourdes.

Some time later, out of the blue, my mum received a telephone call from the Archbishop's house. She was told that there was still a seat on one of the coaches going to Lourdes if Patrick would like to go for a week. As it happened, that week was one, like so many, that I was really down with depression, which I have suffered with for so many years. So I thought a week away was just what I needed. I didn't care where I was going, the only thing that was going through my mind was to get away from it all.

Three days later, I made my way to the Archbishop's house. When I arrived, there were so many young people, about three hundred, all going to Lourdes. How happy they all looked. I had never witnessed so many young people who looked so happy all at the one time.

I didn't know anyone other than the Cardinal, who welcomed me with a big smile and told me how good it was that I was going. After Mass we got on to our coaches, there were five of them in all, and off we went.

The question of whether I was doing the right thing in going did cross my mind, but it was too late now.

I sat next to a girl who was a prison welfare officer in Wandsworth prison, so we had one or two things to talk about.

The journey to Lourdes was hard, but so is the journey through life, and the reward I would get at the end of the week made it worth it.

The first things that really caught my eye were the Pyrenees, which I could see as we got near to our hotel. The beauty and peace that I felt just looking out through the window of the coach is something that I will always remember. We on the coach had become a community, as one.

When we got to the hotel and I had put my bags away, I went for a walk around the streets. I found myself at the Grotto. It was then that I knew I had been called. Mum had even said to me after getting the telephone call from the Archbishop's house, 'When you are called to Lourdes you go.'

She was right.

Being with lots of people I didn't know was not a new experience for me. I had been in that situation many times before. I must admit that they knew who I was or were familiar with my name. That was down to TV and newspapers.

We were on the go all the time throughout most of the week, so much to do – going to church every day, singing, talking, group meetings.

The group meetings were made up of eight people and a group leader. We could talk about all sorts of things. At some time in the week we got an opportunity to give our views to the Cardinal and the priests.

We also saw a film on the story of Bernadette. When I saw it, I couldn't believe how much we had in common. Throughout the week I found myself talking to people about my life. At first it was about the case – the Maguire Seven. Then I began to talk about the things that I had done over the years, the good and the not so good. I had so much to say. It was the first time in my life that I was being positive about what had happened to me. All the things that I had gone through were coming to light just by talking to other people.

I remember one girl who sat down next to me. She started to tell me all about her life, things she had never told anyone. When she had finished, she couldn't believe that she had said so much.

She asked me why I had come to Lourdes and I told her, 'Maybe just to listen to you.'

Many people told me, throughout the week, that what I had to say had helped them with their own lives. Just to see and hear me, knowing what I had been through as a boy, and a man, gave them hope in their lives. I don't go to church, only now and then, but I do say my prayers and talk to God.

It was in Lourdes that I more or less came to terms with what had happened to me, no longer blaming God – you know, why did you let this happen to me?

When I was there, I realized that maybe God had chosen me and my family to go through this, but he also gave us the strength to see it through. Lourdes was a very spiritual place. I felt it.

I have two children by different women. I lost touch with eleven-year-old Natalie, and her mother, but I hope to see her when she is older.

I have a four-year-old son, Patrick 'the third', who I see regularly and I'm looking forward to taking him to see Queens Park Rangers this year.

For four years now I have been saying three words which I hadn't used at all for a long time, 'I love you'. I tell him all the time, and he tells me. It's really nice.

I still find life hard, even as I write this. I see a therapist at St Mary's Hospital, Paddington, once a week. It's helping me.

Also I know that God is there, and that helps me through the bad times. When I came back from Lourdes, I started to write my book, which I have now been doing for over a year. There is so much to write that at times it seems like another cross that God has put on me. But with his strength I will finish it.

After my second visit to Lourdes I gave some talks, at different places. That helps me, but most of all I hope it helps others.

Experience is not what happens to a man, but what a man does with it. All I ask of myself is to be more positive with the things that happen to me to help others.

As for the world – more food, more love and peace to live as one. I look forward to going to Lourdes again this year, if only to be with God.

Catholic Herald, 17 January 1992

My meetings with Kate ended. She was moving on. I could have carried on seeing someone else, but that would have meant starting all over again with someone else, and I couldn't be doing with that.

I said to myself I would go on writing but then, like so many good things I've started, I stopped it, just like that, overnight. It was years before I went back to it.

37

On Saturday, 20 March 1993, the IRA laid two bombs that exploded at lunchtime in a shopping centre in Warrington, Cheshire. Shrapnel ripped through crowds doing last-minute Mother's Day shopping, killing four-year-old Jonathan Ball, injuring nearly fifty, who included twelve-year-old Tim Parry; he died later. On the Sunday, the IRA issued a statement in Dublin saying that it regretted the 'tragic consequences' of the blasts, and accusing the police of failing to react to telephone warnings.

On the Monday or Tuesday, I was listening to *The Jimmy Young Show* on Radio 2 and heard Young say he would be talking to a housewife from Dublin, a Mrs Susan McHugh, who'd set up a peace organization that was holding a meeting that evening at Trinity College to protest against the IRA and what they'd done at Warrington. I phoned the show and said that I'd be there if I could.

A bit later someone from the show phoned back. A listener would pay for my ticket. I went straight to Heathrow and checked in. As I headed for the plane I was stopped by a policeman and taken to an interview room.

'Where are you going?' he asked. He was a plainclothes detective.

'To Dublin.'

'For how long?'

'I should be back tonight.'

Actually, I hadn't thought about it until now, but I didn't have a change of clothes so returning later seemed likely. Nor did I have a passport but at least I knew you didn't need one to travel between Britain and Ireland.

'But you don't know for sure you'll be back tonight?' he said.

'I should be back tonight.'

'Why are you going to Dublin?'

'To take part in a peace meeting.'

'Do you know a lot about that then, Northern Ireland and the Troubles?'

I noticed he was writing in a notebook.

'Not a lot,' I said, 'but we all want peace.'

'So who else will be at the meeting tonight? And what part will you play in it?'

'I really don't know. I'm just going to give my support.'

I didn't want to be talking to him in the first place, but I told him about *The Jimmy Young Show*, the Warrington bomb, Susan McHugh's organization, and the well-wisher who had bought me my ticket, in the hope that this would move things along.

'Where is the meeting taking place that you're going to Dublin to attend?'

'I think it's at Trinity College.'

'You think. You don't know?'

'Well, that's where I'll go when I get there. Trinity.'

'And who is going to meet you?'

'I don't know.'

This wasn't going well, I thought. The plainclothes detective looked at the notebook he had been writing in, and said, 'Right. Let's see what we have here. You're going to Dublin. That much we do know. Someone off the radio, who you don't know, paid for your ticket, you have no ID, you have no bag, you're not too sure where the meeting to which you're going will take place, what part you will have in it, or who will be there. There's no one at the other end to meet you that you know of for sure, and you don't really know when you'll be back. This is far from good enough for me to let you go, I'm afraid.'

'Hold on. Are you telling me I can't leave my own country? You'd better go and have a word with someone, because if I don't get on that plane I'll phone *The Jimmy Young Show* tomorrow and we'll see what they have to say about this.'

He went off. I sat in the room. Time passed, thirty minutes at least. He came back. 'You can go,' he said quietly, almost apologetically.

I made my flight, got to Dublin and found a taxi outside Arrivals. 'Trinity College,' I said to the driver.

I got into the back. Off we went. After a moment or two I

noticed the driver looking at me in the rear-view mirror. 'How's your mother?' he said.

'Very well, thanks.'

It turned out he knew everything, my name, why I'd come – it had been on the radio. When we got to Trinity, he wouldn't take the fare.

I went in, not knowing who or what I was looking for. It didn't matter: they found me. After that, microphones, journalists, a hall with about a thousand people, Susan speaking, a couple of others speaking, and then it was me, out there in front of everyone. I told them that my family were also victims of the IRA. 'If it wasn't for the IRA,' I said, 'I would not have had to spend the last twenty years trying to prove my innocence. However, that said, it was the British legal system that failed my family and me.

'There are many things to make you angry, if you're young,' I said, 'like unemployment and poverty, and many young people are living in fear. But they should not allow their anger to be used for evil things. They should try to use the energy arising from that anger for good things, for positive things.

'We have to have hope. I held on to hope during the years when I was in prison and later when I was trying to clear my name. Without hope, what future is there for anyone?'

I sat down next to the man I had been next to all night. He was middle-aged, big-framed, grey-haired. 'Sorry,' he said. 'I've been sitting next to you and didn't know it was you until you started speaking.'

'That's all right,' I said. 'But I know who you are.' I had seen him on television. It was Gordon Wilson, whose daughter had died after the IRA bomb at the war memorial in Enniskillen. 'Pleased to meet you, sir.' We shook hands.

I found a bed that night, and flew back the next day. I got off the plane and started the long trek along various corridors to Arrivals. On the way I passed a policeman eyeballing everyone from the Dublin plane. He singled me out and brought me to an interview room. 'Any ID?'

'No.'

'Name, date of birth?'

I told him.

He went off and was not long in coming back. 'Born in Belfast?'

'Yes.'

'Are you visiting?'

'Visiting what?'

'The UK?'

'Do I sound like I'm a visitor?' I said. 'Doesn't my London accent tell you something? Look, mate, I had all this bollocks on the way out. Go and sort it out, will you? I want to go home.'

He went away. I waited.

He came back.

'Sorry about that, sir,' he said. 'You can carry on. Enjoy your stay in the UK.'

I said nothing, just hurried from the room, anxious to get home before I was deported.

On Sunday, 18 April 1993, I was at the Lord Elgin in Maida Vale, just across the road from the Underground station. My mate Terry was drinking pints and I was on halves.

When we left, Terry got into a taxi and I set off for home on foot. I passed a car with a policeman in uniform behind the wheel and a woman in uniform beside him. She wasn't bad-looking. She called me over. Well, nothing ventured, nothing gained. I ambled over. 'All right?' I said.

She asked me what I'd been doing, where I was going. It was innocent chit-chat.

A police van appeared in the distance, siren blaring, light flashing.

They're in a hurry, I thought.

We carried on talking.

The van hurtled towards us. I expected it would pass us but, to my surprise, it stopped. The doors opened and policemen piled out. 'Oi, you,' I heard.

They hadn't been heading off somewhere else, I realized. They'd been heading here, for me, and the policewoman had kept me talking until they arrived.

I was cuffed, dragged across the pavement and thrown into the back of the van. Two or three jumped in after me, the doors closed and it started, the kicking, slapping, punching and shouting. They always shouted when they hit: it was as if they needed to get themselves worked up so they could do the damage.

I was a cunt. So were all the Maguires. I shouldn't be out, running around like I was. I should still be inside for what I'd done. And that's where all the Maguires belonged, behind bars, and that's where they should stay, for ever and fucking ever, behind bars, because of what they'd done, the bombs they'd made, and the innocent people they'd killed in Guildford with their fucking bombs. The Maguires were fucking IRA scumbags and if the British legal system had any fucking sense, and wasn't run by a bunch of fucking liberals, we'd have been fucking strung up long ago and now we'd be lying rotting in the fucking ground.

I was taken to Harrow Road where I was charged with being drunk and disorderly and assaulting police officers.

Magistrates took just five minutes yesterday to acquit Patrick Maguire, one of the Maguire Seven, of charges of assaulting a police officer, after hearing allegations that police had launched an attack on him.

Mr Maguire – who was only thirteen when he became the victim of one of Britain's gravest miscarriages of justice – told Marylebone magistrates in central London yesterday that he had been manhandled into the back of a police van, kicked, punched and stamped upon by several officers.

His counsel, Nigel Lambert, claimed, 'It was no coincidence that the police had chosen to arrest Mr Maguire last April on the eve of the Old Bailey trial of Surrey officers accused of conspiring to pervert the course of justice in the trial of the Guildford pub bombing to which the Maguires were wrongly linked. 'You may think the story in the press would have sat nicely alongside that of the officers in the trial,' he said.

The evidence of the four police officers from Harrow Road police station in north-west London was inconsistent and contradictory. 'Sadly, we have to say there are grave doubts about the evidence they have given,' he said.

The prosecution had claimed that Mr Maguire, with a glass of beer in his hand, had staggered into the path of a marked police van. When two officers from the van went to remove the glass, he became abusive and violent, and elbowed and punched a sergeant in the face.

But Mr Maguire and his friend, Terry Meade, told the court that when they left the Lord Elgin together, Mr Maguire was neither drunk nor carrying a glass.

Mr Meade got into a taxi and Mr Maguire started walking home. As he passed an unmarked police car he said he was called over by a police officer. Then a police van came 'flying up the road, blue lights flashing' and about five or six officers got out, handcuffed him and bundled him into the back of the van.

In the van he said he was kicked and stamped upon as he lay on the floor. He admitted kicking out when officers refused to let him up from the floor. 'It was in self-defence,' he said. 'I wanted to sit up, not lie on the floor like a dog.'

Stephen French, who was walking his dog, told the court that he heard screaming and shouting and, looking in the van, saw Mr Maguire lying face down with about four officers sitting on benches on either side with their feet on his body. He said other officers were outside the van.

After the hearing Mr Maguire claimed the incident was part of a series of harassments he had suffered from Metropolitan Police since he had been wrongly arrested for running an IRA bomb factory. 'These officers treated me as officers have always treated me. I feel I am still paying the price of being a Maguire, even though we have been completely vindicated.'

Independent, 21 September 1993

All this had to stop. With my solicitor I went to the Harrow Road police station to see the man in charge. We met in his office. My solicitor explained that the incident outside the Lord Elgin was not the first, just the most recent, in a long line of such incidents since I had left jail. In all these incidents, he said, I had been abused and sometimes assaulted by policemen from the Harrow Road station who believed that I and my family were guilty of horrible crimes and had got off lightly.

'Your client is no angel,' said the policeman.

'What's that got to do with anything?' said the solicitor. He repeated what had happened. I had come out of the pub. A police-woman had called me over to her unmarked car and had started talking to me. I had been set upon. I hadn't done anything.

'All right,' said the policeman. 'You tell your client to behave and I'll tell my boys to behave.'

38

On Boxing Day 1993, *In the Name of the Father* was premiered in Ireland. This film claimed to tell the story of the relationship between Gerard Conlon and his father, Giuseppe, until Giuseppe's death in prison. My family and I had heard that the film was being made though the film-makers had never approached us. Our lawyer had seen the script and some amendments had been made regarding the portrayal of us but when we heard what was in the film after it had been screened we began to worry. The film was scheduled for release in Britain early in 1994, and because we were so anxious it was arranged for Mum and Dad and me, our solicitor Alastair Logan, and Carole Richardson and her lawyer to see it with the director, Jim Sheridan.

It was a good film except where it was untrue. I said to Jim Sheridan after the screening, 'that film you made, *My Left Foot*, that was good but I think you must have written this one with your right foot.' Given the untruths, we felt we had to issue a statement:

Statement by Patrick and Anne Maguire and family

We have been subjected to considerable pressure from the Media to respond to the film *In the Name of the Father*. We have only very recently been able to see the film. We were not consulted about the making of the film by the makers of the film because they were told by Gerard Conlon that we would be hostile to it. We would never hinder anyone who wished to make an honest and truthful account of our case. There is no feud between our family and the Conlon family. We believe that the assertion that there is a feud is a publicity tactic employed by those who wish to attack the film.

We are impressed by the artistic merits of the film, which dramatically depicts parts of the history of the miscarriages of justice in our case and that of the Guildford Four. We are concerned with the accuracy of a film in depicting events with which we were connected. Our concerns have been characterized as 'sour grapes' because this was not a film about our family. We have never solicited such a film. All we have ever asked of anyone is that they tell the truth. When we see untruths about us and our case we correct them. We have been doing so since 1974. If in seeking to ensure that the truth is told about us and the miscarriage of justice in our case we are perceived to be acting contrary to the 'spirit' in which the film is made then we have an apology to make.

We understand that the makers of this film assert that the film is 'faction', meaning it is a mixture of fact and fiction. Only those who have a knowledge of these cases would know what is fact and what is fiction. In the absence of any qualification by the makers the viewer may assume that this film is a documentary account. Documentaries represent real events. The film's audience may leave the cinema believing that what they saw is fact. Much of the detail in this film is fiction.

Our trial is depicted as having taken place jointly with that of the Guildford Four, and the film conveys the impression that we were tried jointly on the same enterprise. That is completely untrue. Also untrue is the depiction in the film of Paul Hill and Gerard Conlon eating a meal at our house on their arrival in England. Anne Maguire met Gerard Conlon and Paul Hill in October 1974, some two weeks after the Guildford bombings had occurred, at a public social function. That was the first and only time she had met Paul Hill before her arrest. None of the other members of our family ever met him before his arrest. Gerard Conlon had stayed at our house previously when he had been in England in 1973 but was no longer welcome there, as he knew in 1974, because of his behaviour. We therefore had no idea that Gerard was in the country in 1974 until Anne saw him at the function.

The suggestion that Gerard Conlon signed a blank statement form into which Anne's name was put by the police is also untrue. He made two long statements both of which were written by himself. Moreover, the Conlon family never sent any food parcels to us.

The case against us was factually and evidentially completely different from that of the Guildford Four. Mrs Peirce did not become involved until 1988, eight years after Giuseppe's death, when she commenced representing Gerard Conlon. We do not owe the quashing of the conviction to her.

The evidence of police perjury and fabrication, which secured the quashing of the convictions of the Guildford Four, and thus the re-examination of our case, was found by the Avon and Somerset Police in the papers of the Surrey Police. The evidence which secured the quashing of our convictions was discovered during and after Sir John May's inquiry. Our debt of gratitude is owed to a large number of people for their belief in us and for their support and hard work over many years to achieve justice in our case and that of the Guildford Four – people like Robert Kee, Yorkshire Television, Ros Franey, Grant McKee, Cardinal Basil Hume and his deputation, Sir John May and his inquiry team and those in the Police Service and the media who were prepared to look for the truth beyond the lies and the prejudice. None of these are mentioned in the film. Nor are the victims of the bombings.

The film is a dramatic interpretation of events and should not be regarded as a factual account of them. We are concerned to ensure that the truth about us and our case is not allowed to become a casualty. We regard the truth as our defence against those who would seek to malign us. We have always told the truth and will continue to do so.

On 27 December 1993, Lorna gave birth to our second son, Billy. Some time in the summer of 1994, when Billy was around six months old, I was at Lorna's house, seeing her and the kids. I was now living in my flat most of the time but I saw them often.

'Why don't you take Billy out?' said Lorna. 'Give him some fresh air.'

I put him in his pram and trundled him outside. Lying there on his back, he could see me pulling faces and the clear blue sky behind. I headed for Paddington Rec, where I'd played football when I was at primary school. It wasn't far from where the children lived with their mother. I pushed the pram through the gateway and set off along one of the paths. In the park people were lying on the grass in the sun, or sitting on benches, or walking around like me. Then a police patrol car appeared. In my childhood the police couldn't drive into the park but now they could. I wondered if they were going to stop me with the baby.

I watched the car, having a pretty good idea of what would happen. I was right. It stopped ahead. Two policemen got out and waited for me. I knew the driver, the older of the two: I had run into him and his mates many times over the years. The other I'd never seen before. I drew level.

'Maguire, what you got in the pram?' said the older one.

'Fuck me,' I said. 'Are they giving them stripes away?' The last time I'd seen him he had been an ordinary constable.

'I said, what you got in that pram?'

'What do you fucking think I've got in it?' I said.

'Still got the big mouth, then?'

'Look, is this going to take long?' I said. 'Just do what you've got to do and then fuck off, will you?'

'You might have bombs in there,' said the sergeant. 'Can't have you walking about with bombs.'

The other policeman screwed up his face. The sergeant saw he wasn't following. 'This is one of the Maguires,' he said. 'The whole family got caught making bombs for the IRA.' He looked at me. 'You got banged up, didn't you? Your mum, your dad, all of you. Isn't that right? You're all out now, but you ask me, you got off lightly. You should still be in fucking prison, doing life, or sent back to that shit-hole you all came from, fucking Belfast.'

'How long did you do?' said the other policeman, now he was up to speed.

I looked at him. I bet you weren't even born when I was nicked, I thought. 'Piss off,' I said.

'This baby yours?'

Some questions don't deserve an answer and this was one of them, so I stared at the sergeant and said nothing.

'You can be nicked for your language, you know,' said the younger one, who hadn't liked me telling him to piss off.

'Why don't you ask your sergeant what's going to happen now?' I said.

'What's his name?' The sergeant pointed at the pram.

'Maguire,' I said. 'Do you want to take his photo and prints?'

'No, there's plenty of time. Don't worry about that.'

They went back to their car and drove away.

* * *

It was Friday, late and very cold when I left the pub. I'd had a skinful and I was looking forward to getting home, and going to bed. I set off down the street, walking quickly. It was residential, just houses and cars parked along the kerbs. Now I was out in the open air and moving along the pavement at a lick, my head was clearing.

Suddenly, from out of nowhere, two white lads appeared and walked along beside me, one on either side, matching me step for step. One was short and stocky; he wore a baseball cap. The other was tall and very thin. His hood was pulled up over his head.

The skinny one said something, I didn't hear what, but there was no mistaking that it hadn't been friendly. I turned towards him. 'What was that?'

He lunged with his head at me and caught the top of my skull. Dong. Down he went, out cold.

I looked at him on the pavement. Was I going to hit him? I decided that would only bring him round. I crouched down and started to pull his mouth apart. It was the only thing I could think of. That was when I felt a heavy blow in the middle of my back.

I stood up and turned. The one in the baseball hat had a knife in his right hand with my blood on it. He won't do that again, not tonight anyway, I thought, and laid into him, blow after blow after blow, shouting that I was going to stick his fucking knife right up his arse.

The people in the houses nearby heard all the commotion and naturally wanted to know what was going on. Suddenly I became aware that they were on their doorsteps or looking out of their windows. They were staring at me and I knew I looked like the bad guy, especially as I'd picked up the knife. It was time to scarper.

I turned and ran, dumping the knife as I went. I didn't stop until I got to my front door. I went inside and got my things off. There was a hole in my coat and in the clothes underneath. The knife had had to go through so many layers that it had used up most of itself by the time it had got to me. There was a wound but it didn't look much. Thank goodness I didn't need to go to hospital and sit about in A & E for hours.

For the next week or two, my back was sore (it still plays up to this day), but not as sore as my assailants must have been.

So, who were they? Some were sure it was the police. After the last incident outside the Lord Elgin, they'd promised to be good so they couldn't hammer me any more. Maybe they'd put the two lads up to it. I have no idea, although I wouldn't put it past them. Those lads were certainly after me. I'd never seen them before so I couldn't identify them, and their interest was not in robbing but hurting me. It might have been a set-up, but I don't know for sure and I never will.

I was in a pub with Dad. It was nearly chucking-out time. 'What do you want, Dad?' I said.

'I'll have a wee brandy.'

I was expecting this. He always went on to the brandy at the end of the night. 'Do you want anything in it?' I said.

'Yeah, another brandy,' he said, in his sharp, pointed way. In his eyes, to add anything to brandy was a crime. Brandy was drunk straight.

I went to the counter. 'Two brandies, please.' The publican brought them to me in balloon glasses. I paid, put ice into mine and carried them back to the table. 'There you are, Dad,' I said. 'Your brandy.'

I sat down and played with my glass. I made the ice hit the sides. From the corner of my eye I saw him watching but he didn't say anything. I'd have to try harder. I lifted the glass and then, turning my head slightly towards him, took a slow sip, making sure there was lots of ice action. Come on, Dad. Shake your head or something. But he stayed absolutely still, and his face was blank.

We finished the round but there was time, just, for one more. It was Dad's shout. 'Do you want the same again?' he said.

'Yeah, please, Dad.'

He padded off to the counter, ordered, paid and carried back two glasses. 'There you are,' he said, and put one in front of me. Then he sat down.

I looked at my drink, then at him. 'You forgot the ice,' I said.

389

'Are you going to drink it or play with it?'
I drank the brandy and from then on I did without the ice.

Every day or two the thought would pop into my head: Mum and
Dad are going to die. Once the thought was out, I couldn't banish
it. Instead, I would have to see the whole funeral in my mind's
eye until the coffin went into the ground. Then I'd be free of it
for a day or two but the thought would come back and I'd play
the scene again. This went on for years.

Eventually I decided I wouldn't go to Mum or Dad's funeral.
I'd lost them once before and never really got them back. I wanted
no part in losing them again, which was what their funerals would
mean for me.

'Dad, is it all right if I don't go to your funeral?' I said to him
one afternoon.

'Do what you like,' he said.

I ran the idea past Mum one Sunday afternoon just after dinner
when everyone in the family, except Dad, was there.

'Do you mind if I don't turn up on your "big day"?' I said.

'Yes, I do, and you will be there,' said Mum. And that was that.

39

In 1993 Mum and I went to Chicago, just after Mum's book came
out, to appear on the Oprah Winfrey show.

In 1996, the Association in the Defence of the Wrongly
Convicted invited Mum and me to Canada. I couldn't make it but
I went the following year on my own to highlight our case and to
appear with other victims before a Canadian Royal Commission
on miscarriages of justice. The association's director at the time
was Rubin 'Hurricane' Carter, who was wrongly convicted in 1966
of three murders, and spent almost twenty years in prison until
he was cleared in 1985. He was a world-class boxer and, in 1993,
received an honorary championship title belt from the World

Boxing Council. Bob Dylan's song 'The Hurricane' is about him and when I asked him what he thought of it he said, 'Nice words, but you can't dance to it.'

It was 1 August 2002 and I was standing with Lorna, Patrick and Billy outside her flat. We were waiting for a cab to take us to the airport. We were off to Spain for a holiday.

It was early morning, the sky was a lovely rich blue and it was very warm. The two boys were running around. I felt like running around with them. I thought, If only we could count on the English weather being like this we could have gone to the Isle of Wight. I'd always loved it ever since I went there on a school trip in my last year at Queens Park Primary.

Lorna suggested I take the boys to say goodbye to their granddad.

'They can go on their own,' I said, and called them over. 'Run round to Granddad and say goodbye,' I said. 'Tell him I'll get him some tobacco in Spain and I love him.'

My sons ran off and came back. Then Mum appeared with Anne-Marie and her two girls, Le-Anne and Zoe. 'You have a good time,' said Anne-Marie, 'and I'll see you in Spain on the thirteenth.'

My sister, her partner Terry and her children were due to arrive at our hotel in Spain the day we were leaving. We would overlap for a few hours.

Two weeks elapsed, and on 13 August my sister's party turned up. The children piled into the pool and the grown-ups watched, had breakfast and drank beer.

Later, Le-Anne went to phone my mother to let her know they had arrived.

'Terry,' I said, 'do you want to come with me? I've got to get some tobacco for Dad.'

'I'd love to,' he said.

We'd have to have a drink, of course, when we bought the tobacco though naturally this wasn't mentioned.

Terry and I were about to head off when Le-Anne came back. I could tell from her face that something was up. 'You've to ring Uncle Vincent,' she said. He'd answered the phone at Mum's, she explained. 'I didn't speak to Nan but I could hear her crying in the background.'

I went to a phone booth in the lobby. Le-Anne had told me the code and that was all I had in my mind, a long, complicated number. I dialled.

Vincent answered. 'Dad's dead,' he said calmly.

I dropped the phone and opened the cubicle door. Anne-Marie was there. I stepped out, pushed her into the box and closed the door.

I watched through the glass as she put the phone to her ear, listened and started to cry.

We flew home together and went to Mum's, where everyone else was gathered. Mum held me in her arms as I cried and then I found out what had happened.

That morning John, who was staying with Dad, noticed he wasn't up, which was odd because Dad had always been an early riser. John had gone out for milk and a newspaper, thinking Dad would be about when he got back, but he wasn't. John went into Dad's bedroom. 'It was as if he was asleep,' he said. 'He was lying on his side, his hands together, one on top of the other and tucked under the pillows, and with a slight smile on his face. He's asleep and I don't want to wake him, I thought, but at the same time, deep down, I knew he was dead from the coldness in the room.'

Dad had died of a heart attack.

The day of the funeral, 22 August, was warm and sunny. When I arrived at Mum's, the mourners were congregating outside. I shook hands with some, then went inside. I was surprised to see Dad's open coffin in the front room. I began to cry and went back outside. Vincent followed me. 'Are you all right?' he said. 'Do you want to have a look at Dad?'

'No, I can't,' I said.

'All right, mate, you do what you want,' said Vincent. 'He looks well, though.'

Vincent, John, Terry and I carried Dad's coffin down Carlton Vale, where others were waiting to take over. I was crying so hard

I wouldn't or couldn't let go. We walked on to the Kilburn Park Road roundabout, where we transferred the coffin to a hearse. As we turned off the main road and headed up the narrow road that led to the church, the Immaculate Heart of Mary, Kilburn – Mum goes there every day of the week – we saw a huge number of people waiting, friends and neighbours, of course, but also Colonel Brian O'Reilly, who had come on behalf of the Irish president, Mary McAleese, Noel Kilkenny, a representative of the Irish embassy, Father Gerry Kivlehan of the Irish Societies and a piper who played 'Oh Flower of Scotland', which Dad had always liked.

We took the coffin inside and laid it before the altar. I got Dad's watch out of my pocket and I laid it on the lid. I wanted him to have it back, if only for a moment, and wished I'd done it when he was alive.

The funeral Mass was said by Father Reg, a priest I'd met at Lourdes in 1990 and with whom I'd stayed in touch. Then he said the last rites at the graveside. Then we scattered the first handfuls of earth over the top and it was over. I stopped crying and Father Reg gave me back the watch.

'Dad.' It was Billy. 'That watch.' He had never seen it before. 'Can I put it on?'

My first thought was, No, you can't have it, Billy. You'll only lose it. Then I thought, To hell with that. What if my dad had said no to me? 'There you are,' I said, and handed it to him.

He slipped it up to the top of his arm, then walked around the graveyard, showing it to anyone who would look.

Everyone went back to the Carlton, which had been Dad's local, for a drink, then I went on a pilgrimage with a mate to one or two other pubs Dad had used, ending up in the Lancer. The proprietor, Anne, an old friend of Mum's, was behind the bar. 'Can I have a brandy, please?' I said.

We started to reminisce.

'You were a right little fucker, you know,' she said.

I nodded. I'd been with her son when I'd set fire to the factory in Beethoven Street. 'You're right,' I said.

I walked back to the Carlton. Mum had put a framed photograph of Dad on the table where he liked to sit and, next to it, a pint with a glass of brandy.

I went to the bar. I'd get him another. 'Brandy,' I said.

The glass appeared. I reached for the ice bucket, then thought better of it.

It was a Friday. I met my mates down the pub. They were on pints. I wasn't a pints man: a cold bottle or two of beer did me. We all got pissed; they were more pissed than me. After closing we hit a club and tore the arse off it.

The next morning I felt groggy, tired and a bit hung-over. I knew I'd stay in on Saturday night. That was how I was. I only went drinking at weekends, never in the week, and it was always one night or the other, Friday or Saturday, never both. For some reason I preferred Friday.

At the end of that Friday night, as we were coming home, someone had said something about meeting up the following weekend. Was I up for that? I didn't know. I might be or I might not. I could go weeks, even months, without stepping inside a pub and not think anything of it. Then I'd decide to meet the mates: we'd have a beer and make a night of it. We'd have a few more nights after that and then I'd stop again. That was my pattern. I liked going out but not all the time, only now and then.

It was another evening in the pub. I'd had two bottles of beer. I was in the toilet. A mate offered a line of cocaine. I'd had it before. Loved it. 'All right,' I said. I took it. It stung my nose and then, a second later, the fuzzy feeling from the beer vanished and my head was clear. This was more than all right. It was magic.

I started taking cocaine when I went to the pub with my mates at weekends. Then I started visiting the pub on weekdays and taking it then, too.

Suddenly, from having been an occasional weekend drinker, I was in the pub almost every day, and I had a coke habit as well. Worse, I started having walks in the early hours when I was out of my nut and hot-wiring cars I fancied, or, if I found a car with the keys in the ignition, driving it away. Once I hopped into a minicab while the driver was helping a passenger with her bags. The driver jumped on to the bonnet, so I had to reverse and go forward to throw him off. All these cars I just drove about and then parked a few streets from my block. And if this wasn't bad enough, I also had the idea, lurking at the back of my head that maybe I'd go back to stealing cars too. I was still in touch with the lads.

It was evening. I phoned the dealer and arranged for some cocaine to be sent over to my flat. When I got in I took a beer out of the fridge – it was full of beer: it always was now I was drinking and snorting heavily. The runner arrived. I took delivery and paid. I finished my first beer, had three or four more, then a few glasses of red wine. Then I got the brandy down from the cupboard where it lived and poured some. I opened the wrap, cut myself a line, rolled a banknote and snorted it. I drank and snorted for a while, then saw how late it was. I had to get to bed, I thought, or I'd never get up in the morning.

I got under the covers and waited for sleep. I heard something. It was – oh, God, it was a key. It was a key at the end of a corridor, wasn't it? Yes. It was a screw's key, on his belt, jangling as he walked. He was whistling, too, but I couldn't hear him clearly. How could I? I was hearing him through the wall of my cell in Aylesbury, and I was curled up, in the dark, under the blankets, and I'd a great hard pain in my belly.

I couldn't be doing with this, I decided. I couldn't be lying on my own thinking I was back in jail. Oh, no. This really wouldn't do.

I got up, had another line, drank another glass of brandy, felt better, went back to bed and lay down. A moment passed and it started again. I heard the key and I could smell the pee in the piss pot. Mixed up with this were thoughts of the present. Should I go back to crime? I'd hardly seen Mum lately. I ought to see the family. But they'd be worried if they saw me, the state I was in. Course they would. Best to keep away, state I was in. Still seeing the boys, my sons, yes, now and again, just popping my head round the door of the house where they lived with their mother, saying hello, then running away. Did they notice how I'd changed? Hoped not.

I wanted to be a good dad, I really did. I wanted them to have a father. I always had. But was I really a good father? Frankly, if I thought I was, I was fooling myself. Yeah, I was, wasn't I? Absolutely. I had to face up to it. I had to look the facts in the eye, fair and square. And it wasn't very impressive, was it? No. It wasn't pretty, was it? No. I was absent, I was rubbish, and I was crap. I was a waste of space, really, when all was said and done. I was no good to anyone. I'd hit the nail on the head. Bull's eye. So what was I going to do? There was only one answer.

Piss off. Check out. Who'd notice? No one. Who'd care? No one. I didn't contribute anything. I hadn't done anything. And they'd all be better off, wouldn't they? Relieved too, not to have me mooching around, miserable all the time, dragging them down with me. They'd be better off, family, everyone, without me. So I should check out now. Get it over and done with.

But maybe my boys wouldn't be better off? Maybe they wanted me? It was hard to tell. Oh, hell, everything was fucked. I couldn't think any more. I couldn't see straight any more. I couldn't judge any more. Everything was ruined. Days, weeks, months, years of my life gone, vanished, and nothing to show except all this pain, indecision and misery . . .

I woke up. It was daylight. I felt terrible. My mouth was dry. My head hurt. My eyes hurt. My nose ached. My throat was sore. I couldn't go on like this. It was killing me. It had to stop. I wasn't having another night like that. Thinking those thoughts, feeling so awful, was a recipe for disaster, so it was.

I got up and went to the bathroom. I had a shower. I felt better. I strolled into the living room. I noticed the empty wrap on the table, a few little white crumbs. I wetted my forefinger, picked them up and rubbed them on my gum. I got the sour cocaine taste . . .

Well, maybe one more wrap and then I'd stop. Yeah, I really would stop then. Yeah, one more, the last, and I'd know when I was having it that it was the last. Then I'd knock the drinking and the cocaine on the head. That sounded like a good plan. I could do that.

Where was my mobile? I had the dealer's number. I'd give him a call now.

40

It was Wednesday, 28 January 2004. I was in my front room on the settee, kitchen one side of me, empty beer bottles on the worktop, the big window overlooking London, Big Ben and the Thames on the other.

In front of me was the coffee table. I saw a glass with some brandy in the bottom, the bottle beside it, and an open wrap with a little mound of cocaine. I'd kept this back the night before to get me going in the morning.

I saw the credit card. I saw the banknote. All I had to do was cut a line with the card, roll the banknote and snort. That was what I'd come to do. That was what I was there for. But what was this? Was I crying? Fuck, I was! I was crying. Fuck, Jesus, there were great hot wet tears pouring out of my eyes and running down my cheeks.

Christ, this was all I needed. I got up. I walked into the hall, up to the front door and back. Crying? I couldn't be doing with crying. When was the last time I'd cried? Dad's funeral, wasn't it? But I'd got over it then, hadn't I? Yeah, too right I had. Well, I had to get over this. Right now. This couldn't go on. I had to snap out of it. This was bollocks. This was fucking madness. I couldn't walk around blubbing. It had to stop.

'Come on, Patrick,' I said out loud, 'you've got to snap out of this.'

The tears flowed on and I paced from one end of my flat to the other, backwards and forwards, backwards and forwards, and as I went up and down, my face got hotter and wetter and redder and the back of my throat got sorer and sorer, just like it had when I cried as a child.

So how was I feeling? I asked myself. Since I was crying like this, I had to be feeling something.

I wasn't sad, I noticed, or unhappy. I just felt completely knackered. I was tired, but tired like I hadn't ever felt in my life before. I'd had as much as I could handle of being in my flat at the top of the tower block, drinking and snorting, going to bed alone and lying under the covers in the dark, remembering everything, feeling miserable and sometimes thinking of ending it all, being in the earth and rotting away, never having to think about any of this ever again, ever, ever again.

So what should I do? Ring Mum? 'Hello, I'm having a breakdown Mum.'

She'd be heartbroken, I didn't doubt that.

I couldn't do it.

It would have to be Father Reg. We were still in touch.

I rang him.

'Get in a cab,' he said, 'and come down now.'

I went down to the street and hailed a cab. I got in and off we went. The driver was talking. I couldn't follow what he was saying, but he was talking a lot. I knew that. He was talking and talking, talking and talking. Was he on something? Seemed like it.

I looked out of the window. I saw the street sliding by. He was still talking. Jesus, he could talk for England, this one. Maybe I should tell him to pull over. I could get out and walk, couldn't I? Anything was better than this, wasn't it? It wasn't that far to Parsons Green, was it? Or if I didn't fancy going to Reg's, I wasn't far from home, was I? I could just turn round and retrace my steps. I could go up to my flat. I could give it a clean. It needed a clean. I could sort myself out, couldn't I? I should at least try.

Oh, God, should I stop or go on? Go to Father Reg or go home? Why couldn't I decide? Why didn't I know what I wanted to do? Why wasn't I the master of my life any more?

The cab pulled up. The driver reached round and opened the door. 'Here we are, mate.'

I got out. I paid.

'Have a good day,' said the driver, as they do.

I walked up the path to Reg's front door. I pressed the bell. I heard his footsteps. I'd been here before so I recognized them. The door opened. There was Reg. He looked at me. What's he looking at? I didn't like that look. It was a worried look. An anxious look. Yeah, well, I needed a haircut and a shave. I knew that. I'd lost weight and my clothes weren't the cleanest. I probably looked like I'd been living on the streets, I thought suddenly.

'Come in,' said Reg. He walked me down the hall and into his study. The door closed behind me and it started, words and tears tumbling out together. I was a mess, I said. Everything had fallen apart. I was at the end of my tether and I couldn't go on like this any more. I needed help.

Reg told me he'd get me help. I wasn't to worry. What was my doctor's number? Vincent's? I had the mobile, thank God. I called out the numbers. He wrote them down. He gave me a cup of tea and made me sit down to drink it. He had to make some telephone calls. Did I understand? I said I did.

He left me in his study, sitting on a chair, holding the cup and saucer. The walls were lined with shelves and the shelves were packed with books. He's read all these books, I thought, and then I thought, But I've hardly read any books, have I?

I put down the cup, got up and went to the shelf. A book had caught my eye and I got it down. It was called *The Broken Body: A Journey to Wholeness* by Jean Vanier. I flicked through it, reading a sentence here and a sentence there. And as I did, in some other part of my head, the cogs were turning. Reg was on to my brother, wasn't he? Probably. And what was Vincent going to make of this? What would everyone else think once they all knew? That I'd let them down. Wasn't that what they'd think? By cracking up like this, by letting myself fall to bits like I had, I'd let them down. The thought was horrible and I felt sick and knotted inside. Oh, Jesus, how was I going to get through this?

I was in another cab. Reg was with me. We went north, to Maida Vale and my doctor's. I'd wanted to tell someone so much for so long but I couldn't, and now I was about to get my chance. I could talk to a proper professional, who'd understand why I was crying, what was going on inside my head, and who would know how to make me better. But when I got out of the waiting room and into the surgery, it wasn't my doctor sitting in the chair. He was away on holiday.

I talked a bit. The replacement doctor wanted to give me some tablets and send me home.

'Can I use your phone?' said Reg.

'Certainly,' said the doctor.

Reg phoned the Priory and told them to get a bed ready. 'When was the last time you'd something hot to eat?' said Reg.

I couldn't remember.

We went into a café near Maida Vale Underground station. Then Vincent came in his black cab – he's a taxi driver – with John, and we all went to my bank and got some money. I had received compensation for the wrongful arrest and imprisonment. Then we went south, crossed the Thames and drove into Barnes. There were stretches of muddy grass, trees with no leaves, then suddenly, a very sharp corner, and a tree, photos of a man with curly hair, burning candles and fresh flowers, some sort of memorial.

'What was that?' I asked.

'That's where Marc Bolan died,' said Vincent. Trust a cabbie to know. 'He was sitting in the front passenger seat and his car hit the tree.'

The T-Rex singer. We'd played his records, hadn't we, at the youth club? I'd loved them. I'd wanted to be him, hadn't I? Strange, thinking that when so much else was going on in my head.

We came off Queens Ride, passed Rosslyn Park RUFC, and turned left into Priory Lane. I saw the hospital's walls and, in the grounds, the long bare branches of trees, which reached up towards the sky. We came to the entrance, with the sign, white letters on black, 'The Priory Hospital' and turned in. Immediately inside, a security guard sat in a small shed and an avenue curved ahead, trees and shrubs lining one side with parking bays below, a green space with benches scattered around its well-kept surface. At the end there was a large, stately building with many windows. It looked a bit like a castle.

We drove up to the entrance, two glass doors smack in the middle, arches and large plants at either side.

There was the door. Once I went in, I'd be admitted and that would be that: I would be a patient at the Priory, the place people went – and for which they paid – when they'd had a breakdown, or had a habit that was killing them. Once I was inside, everyone would know I'd had a breakdown and had a habit. What would my family make of that? And my children? They would have to be told something. Thinking of them started me crying again.

Reg said he would take care of everything. He would break the news. I wasn't to worry about anything.

I had reached the point of no return. We were there. It was going to happen. End of.

Reg went in to sort things out. A few minutes later I was sitting in a room with a woman doctor, words and tears gushing.

There was some paperwork and then I was taken along winding corridors to a room on the ground floor overlooking the open green space at the front of the building. The room was big, with a high ceiling and large windows. It was furnished with a bed, a wardrobe, a chest of drawers, a desk and some chairs. There was an en-suite bathroom.

I went outside and sat in the garden with Reg and my brothers. There was an outdoor table-tennis table. It was a lovely day and we talked. They hugged me before they left, and Vincent promised he'd get some clothes from the flat and drop them in for me next time he was passing.

After they'd gone I was shown around. Here were the telephones. Here was the dining room. Here was the front door. Once it closed at night, that was it until morning. Here was the shop. Here were the rooms for group therapy. Here were the doctors' rooms. Here was the kitchenette if you wanted to make a cup of tea. Here was the art room, which was open all the time, my guide explained. Everyone was welcome to come in and have a go at painting, drawing, modelling, even pottery.

It was a large room, its walls covered with a collage, a worktop running round the edge strewn with paints, brushes, coloured pencils, Magic Markers, thin sticks of pastel, cupboards below with drawers so full of paper they wouldn't shut, a radio in the corner tuned to Classic FM and, in the middle, light-grey tables with about a dozen matching chairs and patients chatting as they worked.

If I'd had somewhere like this at Quintin Kynaston, or at HMP Aylesbury, I'd have been happy. But now, all these years later, I didn't want to come and get stuck in, which was a funny thing to feel, considering how much I'd loved art when I was younger.

Art was a good way, my guide said, for patients to meet up and do something together. Perhaps I might like to have a go.

Maybe, I said, to be polite. It looked nice but, really, it wasn't for me. It was all the patients sitting around talking. I could barely handle my own company, let alone other people's.

The tour over, I went to my room for a while, then walked back to the garden to smoke. There were people sitting on benches and one or two smiled or nodded as I passed. A different time, a different place, I'd have sat and talked. I like talking to people I don't know. But today I was in no mood to talk to anyone. I smiled, I nodded. That was it. I smoked my fag and went back to my room.

I lay down. I fancied a snooze but nothing happened. I went and found a member of staff. Could I have something to help me sleep? Absolutely. I took the tablet and went out like a light.

41

I felt someone jiggling my shoulder and calling my name. I opened my eyes and saw a doctor in a white coat. 'You've been asleep,' he said.

'How long for?'

'Hours,' he said.

He gave me a medical and asked me some questions. 'I'm going to put you on a twenty-eight-day programme for drink and drug addiction,' he said.

'Bollocks to that,' I said. 'I don't need a programme to sort me out, any programme.'

'Oh, yes, you do,' he said. 'The drink and the cocaine together, taken in the quantities you've been having, very nearly killed you, and if you'd carried on the way you were going, they would have killed you.'

This was still bollocks, I thought. 'Look,' I said, 'give me a week, and by the end I'll be clear. But if I go cold turkey, well, I'll go on the fucking programme.'

I went to bed. I woke at three in the morning. Where the fuck was I? Then I remembered. Well, bollocks to this, I thought. I'm not staying here. I need to get home.

I went off to find someone. The place was quiet, everyone was asleep, but eventually, in the staff room, I found the doctor who'd examined me having a cup of tea.

'Oi, mate,' I said. 'Can you get us a cab? I need to get home.'

'No you don't,' he said. 'You need to stay here and get better.'

'Oh, yes, I do,' I said. 'I need to get out of this shit-hole and get back to my flat.'

The doctor offered various reasons why I couldn't. I knocked them all flat. I had to go home, now, and would he get me a cab, please, for fuck's sake?

'No,' he said. 'I can't do that. There aren't any cabs.'

'What? No cabs?'

Didn't I realize it was snowing heavily and all the roads were blocked?

'No, bollocks, really?'

I went into the garden. He was right. A thick white layer covered the ground and crunched under my feet. I looked up. I saw a few flakes floating above me and then, behind, the night sky, pink and purple from the lights of London.

When had I last seen snow like this in the city? I was eight or nine, I thought. I was in church, midnight Mass, smell of stone, incense and polish. I came down the aisle and went out through the big double doors and on to the steps. I heard the snow under my feet, sounding as it does when it's tamped down. Snowflakes were swirling around me.

Thirty-five years later, it was still as good. A flake landed on my face. It had no weight. It was the cold, like a tiny pinch, that told me it was there. It was exceptionally quiet too because the snow had muffled all sounds.

I went back in, feeling calmer. I didn't need a cab. Anyway, I wasn't going to get one, was I? No.

The doctor gave me a glass of water and a tablet to go with it. 'That will help you sleep,' he said, 'and in the morning, if you feel the same way, you can go home.'

I went back to my room, got into my bed and went straight to sleep. When I woke up, the thought of going home was no longer there. I knew this was the right place to be.

I got up and went to the dining room, which had big windows down one side. The sky was very blue. I got two boiled eggs, toast and tea, and sat at a table by myself. I tapped the first egg and a cap of shell came away. A lad appeared and sat down opposite. 'Morning,' he said. 'I'm Hubert. Would you like me to get you an egg cup?'

I hadn't got one. 'No, I'm fine, thanks,' I said.

He offered his hand. It was the size of a shovel and the rest of him was just as big.

'Pleased to meet you. I'm Patrick,' I said.

We shook hands and talked. I took to him from the off. Big as he was, he had a gentle way with him that came over when he spoke. He was posh. He'd been to public school and was now the editor of a glossy magazine. His family home was open to the public in the week, while at the weekends his parents had fishing and shooting parties. If I ever wanted to try either, I'd be welcome, he added, which was nice as I'd never done any fishing or shooting before.

After breakfast he told me he had been in the Priory for some time and would be leaving soon, but he'd be coming back as an outpatient. He promised he'd look in and have a yarn whenever he was up, and I knew as he said it that I *would* see him and already, not a day into my stay at the Priory, I had a friend.

The Priory supplied me with a booklet. I read it. It told me about the various programmes on offer. There were two kinds: group therapy and one-on-one therapy. I had never been in a group and talked about myself to others and listened to others talking about themselves. That was completely new territory.

I knew something about one-on-ones of course. I'd had many over the years with psychiatric nurses at St Mary's Hospital in Paddington and Kate Doyle.

But I didn't fancy either option. I couldn't see myself talking about everything in public, while the one-on-ones I'd had in the past had sometimes left me feeling suicidal.

The booklet said everything was optional. Patients were supposed to find what they needed in their own time and their own way.

That was fine by me. I would lie low and wait to see how I felt. I saw the doctors, of course, and I was diagnosed with bipolar affective disorder, post-traumatic stress disorder and attention deficit disorder syndrome. I stayed quiet, mooched around, made friends with a couple of other patients, played the odd game of table tennis, slept, ate and took my medication. There was lots of it: I had blue and green, red and yellow pills and every day I downed them like a kid necking a tube of Smarties.

Initially, nothing changed, but then I began to feel better, and then, wow, a whole lot better again. Suddenly I was like a new man. Now I was flying, the doctors got suspicious. Was I taking cocaine on top of my medication? (I wonder what that would have been like. I bet I wouldn't be writing about it, if I had been.) No, of course I wasn't. I'd gone there to get better, not to go back to feeling how I'd felt before I came in. How could they think I was that stupid? They took a blood sample and sent it away for testing. The result was negative. I wasn't taking anything except the prescribed medication. After that I kept the tests up. I wanted them to be sure about me and that was the only way to do it.

Next thing, out of the blue I was reading, anything I could get my hands on: first I read newspapers, lots of them, then I moved on to books. I read and I read and I couldn't stop.

Then I felt the stirrings of a new craving to draw, which I'd not done seriously since I left Aylesbury. Yes, when my daughter was born, and later, after my sons were born, I'd done the odd cartoon, but that was the height of it. I hadn't done any serious art for twenty-five years.

It was evening now and I'd been waiting for this all day. I slipped along to the art-room door, opened it quietly and went in. The room smelt of acrylic paint, fixer and, vaguely, of wet clay.

I found a drawer with big sheets of white paper, then grabbed a handful of charcoal, light and brittle, wrapped it in kitchen roll and put it carefully into my trouser pocket where the sticks wouldn't snap.

I carried the swag back to my room and hid it in the bottom of the wardrobe. I didn't have to nick these materials, I could have asked for them, but I didn't want anyone to know what I was going to do, not that I had any idea what it was I was going to do. All I knew was that whatever I did, it had to be a secret, at least at the start.

The next day I kept my green floral curtains drawn: I'd been doing that a lot. I went out for my meals and when I was out I said hello to the patients I knew and made small talk. Once I'd eaten I hurried back to my room and lay on my bed with the lights off. I wanted to be in the dark, away from everything. I lay there while hundreds of thoughts tumbled and twisted inside my head, so many and all moving so fast that I couldn't single one out and follow it. I could only let them wash through me until I got so exhausted I fell asleep.

About a week had gone by since I raided the art room, a week given over to letting thoughts surge round my head, and now I was ready.

I got a sheet of paper and the charcoal out of the cupboard. I laid the paper on the floor, put the charcoal to my right and unfolded the kitchen roll so I could reach for a stick when I needed to.

I still hadn't any solid ideas as to what I would do but I knew one thing: I wasn't going to be drawing fucking cartoons. I picked up a stick of charcoal and looked at the clean, fresh sheet of paper laid out in front of me for a long time, rubbing the stick between my fingers as I waited. Then it came. There was no thought, only the certainty that it was inside and ready to come out, what I wanted to do. All I had to do now was draw.

I attacked the paper like a madman with a knife, only my weapon was a bit of burnt wood. I made my marks quickly, without thinking. The feelings just flowed straight from my head, down my arm to my hand and out, through the charcoal, on to the paper. It happened very fast and in no time I was moving on to another sheet of paper, then another and another. Then I ran out.

'Fuck it.'

I opened the art-room door. The patients sitting at the island of tables stopped and looked up at the figure in the doorway with charcoal-stained hands and black smudges on his face. A second passed and everyone went back to work, with the exception of the lady who took the class. She got up and asked me if she could help me. 'Yes. Do you have any large sheets of white paper I could have?'

'I'll have a look. Come in.'

I took two steps forward. I caught a glimpse of myself in the mirror over the sink. Oh, no, I didn't look that good. One or two people at the tables glanced up. I smiled my most reassuring smile. It said, 'No, I'm not bonkers and I'm sorry I'm so dirty. I'll be having a shower soon, though, promise.'

The lady was at one of the cupboards searching for paper. She stood up, closed the doors and went to the next. She couldn't find what she was looking for there, either, so she went on to the third. No luck again: so she tried the fourth, the fifth and the sixth, until she'd searched in every single cupboard. Now she was walking towards me.

I was still smiling my really-I'm-not-a-lunatic smile.

'I'm sorry,' she said, 'but we seem to have run out. I don't understand. There was some here last week. I saw it. And now it's gone, but I don't remember handing any out.'

I nodded. That was odd. Yes, very odd. Well, actually, not odd. She'd had some paper until I'd swiped it.

'I must order some more,' she said.

If I'd come and asked, I thought, as I should have, she'd have ordered more, wouldn't she? She wouldn't be turning me away empty-handed now. There was a lesson there, I thought.

'Would you like to join in with the class? Are you interested in painting or drawing?'

'I'm interested in both,' I said, 'but I won't come in just now. Maybe another time. Could I have some paper, any paper, and some charcoal, though?'

She went to a cupboard and came back with a bundle of sheets half the size of the ones in my room and a handful of charcoal.

I thanked her and said goodbye, went back to my room, spread a sheet on the floor, and started drawing again. When that sheet was full, I started on another. I went on until, once again, I had run out of paper.

This was starting to piss me off. I couldn't go back to the art room again, could I? No. The teacher would ask what I was doing with all her paper and I didn't want anyone to know about this. Not yet, anyway. So what was I going to do?

Then I remembered the lining paper I'd covered my walls with when I'd decorated my flat. If it was good enough to be pasted up it was good enough to draw on.

I found a member of staff and told him I was going to Putney. I'd been there with Reg a couple of weeks before to buy some clothes and I guessed it was probably the closest place to the Priory that I'd find a hardware shop. This would be my first time out alone, though, since I'd been there. Could I handle it? I was sure I could.

I signed out on a mild spring morning and caught the bus. I sat on the top deck and stared out. I saw people and cars, shops and pavements. Everything seemed vivid and a bit weird, not quite familiar, as everything does when you've been away for a bit. I'd felt much the same when I'd first come out of jail.

I got out on Putney High Street, found a café, drank a coffee and watched the world streaming past. Compared to the Priory, where everyone moved at a hospital pace, all sedate and slow, and where you could stop and do nothing whenever you wanted, everyone and everything in Putney High Street was moving all the time. It was faintly alarming, as was the thought of what lay ahead. I had never really liked shopping and had only ever done it when I had to. Local shops, where I knew people, I could manage, but when I got inside anything bigger, I always got anxious and wanted to leave as soon as possible.

I finished my coffee and set off. I found a hardware shop at the end of a side-street. It was small, old-fashioned, just the sort of place I could handle. I went in and bought ten rolls of the same heavy lining paper I'd used in my flat, each ten metres long, which gave me over a hundred metres of paper on which to draw. I also bought a Stanley knife to cut it up. I wasn't going to run out in a hurry now, oh, no.

The rolls were bagged and I set off. Back on the street, heading for my stop, I noticed an art shop on the other side, directly across from where I was. A bus nearly ran me over when I stepped off the pavement, so I went down to the traffic lights to cross.

I entered the shop by pushing the door with my bags. I pushed so hard with these makeshift battering rams that it banged on the wall and echoed through the shop. The young girl behind the till got a fright and put up her hands as if she was about to be robbed.

'Can I leave my bags at the side of the counter?' I said, in my politest voice. That would put her at her ease, I thought, bound to.

She nodded.

Well, maybe not.

I'd always loved pet shops. I'd discovered bookshops later and fallen in love with them too; the people who work in bookshops are just so nice. They can't help you enough when you ask, and they're so quiet as they look for that book. Libraries, incidentally, I had always hated: they're a graveyard for books. Now I was in my third great love: the art shop.

I wandered along the shelves, picking up this, then that, wondering what it was or what you did with it, putting it back, then peering into cabinets, which all looked like works of art, the way they were set out, row upon row of coloured pencils in one, pens and inks in another, tubes of oil paint in a third, big and fat, shiny and gorgeous.

A few minutes passed, me peering and thinking, and then I was stopped in my tracks by a thought that came out of nowhere. Should I be in here? Did I have the right? I didn't know what I was doing, did I? Not really. I just had a head full of ideas and I'd scribbled some down. I hoped to get some more down. But this was a place for another kind of person, wasn't it? This was for those who knew what they wanted to do. This was for those who knew what they wanted to do *and* how to do it. I couldn't even tell what half the things on display were for, or how to use them.

This wasn't where I belonged. I should go to WH Smith's or Woolworth's. They were where I'd always gone in the past and they were where I should stick to. Those were the shops for someone like me when I needed pencils or paper. I didn't belong here.

I was about to turn and retrace my steps to the bags I'd left, when I heard a voice, young, male. 'Can I help?'

It was a young man who worked there.

'Do you have any charcoal?' I said. What a question to ask. I was in a fucking art shop. Of course they'd have charcoal.

'Follow me.'

He led me to the far end of the shop and there it was, charcoal, lots of it, in different makes and different sizes, boxed and loose, the only constant being it was all black.

I knew better than to make out I knew about something when I didn't – I could never get away with it, and I certainly wasn't going to try here. 'What else do I need if I'm working with charcoal?' I said.

He found me a bottle of fixer and a fixer-blower, some lovely coloured charcoals to go with the black sticks I selected, some pencils and a book on working with charcoal. He also offered me some paper and I showed him one of my rolls of liner. Now there was paper, I said, and it wasn't a fraction of the price of the paper he was offering.

I left the art shop, called at a newsagent's, picked up cigarettes and Blu-tack, then caught the bus back to the Priory.

I signed myself back in and went to work. I sprayed all the work I'd done so far with fixer to stop the charcoal smudging and stuck it up on the walls of my room with Blu-tack.

Then I lay down, with the smell of fixer in the air, and fell asleep. When I woke up I had to turn the light on. I went to the dining room for something to eat, then began to cut the lining paper into workable lengths with the Stanley knife. I got fourteen sheets from the first roll. I laid three out and began to draw, moving freely from one sheet to another. As I worked, I knew I couldn't stop. I had the devil on my back and until he was drawn out he wouldn't let me go.

I fixed the new works and stuck them up, had a quick fag and went back to work. My mind was racing and when I got the charcoal between my fingers and the end on to the paper it poured out. They weren't pictures of things I'd seen exactly – though they were often made up of recognizable forms – but pictures of what I had felt and was feeling still. They were all very deep, and even I could tell that they were depressing to look at, but I didn't think their darkness mattered. Yes, the situations depicted might be gloomy or horrible but the drawings themselves couldn't be bad, not considering the feelings I had when I was making them, which were feelings of release I'd never known before. They couldn't be bad if they made me feel like that, could they?

I'd seen Hubert a few times when he was in as an outpatient at the start of my time at the Priory, and we'd nattered on the phone, but I hadn't seen him for a while and I wondered where he was. I went and found a doctor.

'I haven't heard from Hubert,' I said. 'What's happened to him, do you know?'

'Overdose,' said the doctor, 'but whether it was an accident or not, no one knows.'

I felt full to the brim with sadness. He was only in his thirties and a nice lad. I wrote a letter to his mum and dad – Lord and Lady So-and-so – telling them how sorry I was for their loss, and how glad I was to have met their son.

I found some plasterboard in a skip at the back of the Priory and used my Stanley knife to cut out a single piece on which to rest my paper when I was working. I powered on until I ran out of charcoal. I took the bus to Putney High Street again and went back to the art shop. Besides charcoal, I bought boxes of pastels and dozens of coloured felt-tip pens, as well as lots of sketch pads, A4 and smaller.

Back in my room I emptied everything on to my bed. 'What the fuck have I bought this lot for?' For the next while, I went on working in charcoal, black and white, and then one day, without thinking about it, I added colour, using the pastels, to the charcoal drawing I was working on. It wasn't much, just a touch, but it was a start. By the end of the week I was working primarily in pastel, adding just a bit of black here and there, sometimes none.

Next thing I stopped one of the Priory's maintenance men. 'Could I borrow a set of steps?'

'No problem,' he said. 'Keep them as long as you want.'

Back in my room, I set up the steps by my window, climbed up and unhooked the heavy curtains I'd kept closed since I'd arrived. The light flooded in from outside and that felt good.

My brothers had fetched my stereo from my flat. I got it out of its box and set it up. Then, with Classic FM thumping away, I stuck sheets I'd got from the linen cupboard over the bottom half of the windows with drawing pins from the art class. The light flooding in was now tinged white.

Then I got back to work and, with the music from the radio flowing through me, I moved my crayons or charcoal like a conductor moving his baton in front of a symphony orchestra. I went on drawing in colour, occasionally in charcoal, and keeping two or three works going simultaneously, hopping from one to another whenever I fancied a change. I had acquired a couple of big art folders from someone who'd left: one for the black drawings, the other for the coloured ones.

Then, one day, I decided I'd finished with the lining paper and I'd work only in the sketch pads. I got a small one, an A6, and filled the first page with black lines, then coloured in the spaces.

This was the hard part, if there was one: what colours to use and where to put them. It would take me hours to decide but I got a lot out of it. The colours gave me hope, and the pictures themselves made me smile, and as I worked on, I got faster and then I didn't have to think at all because it was just happening. Whatever was in my head was flowing down my arm and into my hand and on to the page.

As soon as one pad was full, I would go on to the next, and start doing the same thing all over again. Then I got so fast I'd be doing more than a pad at a time. In one sitting I got through five pads, that's 250 pages, and every page filled with outlines, which were coloured in.

When the A6 pads ran out I moved on to the bigger pads, which had fewer pages. The drawing mania took a lot out of me, both mentally and physically, but it gave me a sense of purpose and a belief that I could make work of some value. For the first time in a long while, life looked a lot better than I could remember – since I was a child in fact.

42

One morning I decided I'd had enough and I was going home. I got as far as the local newsagent's, bought some cigarettes and went back.

On 10 March 2004, I woke up and I knew that today I would be off. I can't remember what made me want to leave, only that I knew I wanted to. Whether I'd only make the local newsagent's and turn round or go through with it I didn't know.

I got up and walked out. I went to the bus stop. Was I doing the right thing? I could go back. It wasn't too late. No one would know I'd gone, would they? I saw the bus in the distance, coming towards me. It was the right thing to do. I'd finished. I'd had enough. I missed my sons, didn't I? I did. I'd see them, wouldn't I? Course I would. And we'd do things together. We'd go to QPR, see the home games together. We'd all got season tickets and my brothers had been taking them while I'd been at the Priory. It would be lovely to see them again. The bus rolled up. There was the door. Was I going or staying? I stepped on. That wasn't so hard, was it?

I got out in Putney, went into the Underground station and caught a District Line train. The carriage was empty. The train crossed the Thames and rumbled northwards through streets of houses made of yellow and red London brick. At Earls Court the carriage filled up. I got out at Bayswater and bought a sandwich in Marks & Spencer, which I ate as I walked up Porchester Road.

It started to rain. I walked on, letting it fall on me – I'd always loved being out in the rain – as I skirted the Westway. Then, in the distance, on a small bastion of land between the Grand Union Canal and the Harrow Road, I saw my tower block looming. I was nearly home. I'd made it.

I went into an off-licence, bought two six-packs of Budweiser and then, when I was back in the street, I rang the dealer.

Half an hour later I was in my flat, drinking a cold beer, when the bell rang. I went to the door. As expected, it was the man with my wraps of cocaine. Nice one. I made some more calls and arranged for some company. I didn't want to be alone. No way. I was going to party.

It was 17 March 2004. I had been at home for a week. I had not seen my children. I was in the lounge and Vincent was with me. 'You went to the Priory,' he said. 'You stayed two months. You made progress. And then what did you do? You left. You didn't tell anyone you were going, you just came back here to your flat and you started all over again, staying up all night, drinking, partying, not looking after yourself, doing all the things that made you ill in the first place. You have to stop this now. You have to go back. You can have your old room. I'll drive you there now in my cab.'

'No,' I said. 'I got here under my own steam. You just bring me to Bayswater Underground, and I'll do the rest. I'll get myself to the Priory.'

'Promise?'

'Promise.'

He took me to Bayswater and saw me down to the platform. I

caught the District Line train going south, got out at East Putney and caught the bus back to the Priory. I walked up the curving drive and in through the glass front doors.

There was a bit of paperwork and then a drugs test. I failed and was told off in a Priory sort of way. I went down to the basement. All my things were in boxes. I carried them back to my room and unpacked.

During my first two months, I hadn't attended any programme. Now I was back, though, the staff felt I should try so I went to my first group session. I sat in a circle with ten or so other patients and we told our stories. I found it hard, and it left me feeling sad. I went to one or two more, but then I packed it in. Not for me, I thought, any more than yoga or t'ai chi, both of which I'd tried once. I reckoned I got more benefit talking over a bowl of corn flakes at breakfast or out in the garden when I was having a smoke.

I'd been back a couple of weeks and now it was Sunday lunchtime. I was in a crowded pizzeria in Putney, to which Father Reg had brought me, with my boys and their mum. I'd not seen my children since I'd started at the Priory, though we had spoken on the telephone. They were curious. What was up with Dad? Why was he away? I didn't go into detail. I just told them I wasn't well, I was getting help and I'd be home soon.

It was decided I could leave the Priory but Father Reg was worried that if I went home I'd go back to my old ways. I'd be better off somewhere else, he thought. I went out with Vincent to look at flats. We saw several but I chose the second we viewed, an unfurnished two-bed off Fulham Palace Road, because a spiral staircase connected the front room to the first bedroom.

I moved in on 29 April 2004. I had broken with the past. I had made a new start. I spent my days quietly. I would go to the market on Fulham Broadway and stroll around. I would look at the stalls, buy my shopping, and have a coffee. I would go to Fulham Palace Gardens, just up the road from the flat. I would take my camera and a sketch pad.

I would walk round the park then cross the river Thames by Putney Bridge and walk along the other side, stopping now and then to take a photograph or to sketch something that had caught my eye. I would go back to the flat and work my sketches into drawings.

I would go out for lunch with Father Reg.

From time to time I would go back to the Priory. I would see my doctor there. I would tell him how I was getting on and I would get a fresh prescription for my medication. I would also meet up with people I'd got to know in there.

I would go to see my children and other members of my family. To begin with I liked that. Then I noticed that after each visit I felt dreadful on the journey back to Fulham, knowing I was going to be on my own again. I'd felt exactly the same loneliness in prison after a visit, walking back to my cell.

Halfway through the third month I closed all the curtains in the flat, shutting out the world, and didn't open them again. I turned off the phone. I only went out when I really needed to and then just to the little shop at the top of the street. I unplugged the television and the stereo. I stopped eating. I just lay, day after day, on the settee or on my bed, my mind flying, all kinds of thoughts coming and going, never staying long enough for me to work out what they were about. It was draining, mentally and physically. I started to cry again. I cried for hours. I cried for days. I didn't understand. I was taking my medication. I was staying away from Paddington. Why was this happening? What was I doing living in Fulham? I no longer knew myself.

Then came a Sunday morning. John appeared. He helped me pack everything and brought me home to my flat at the top of the tower block in Paddington. It was good to be back in my familiar place.

43

In January 2005 I heard that Giuseppe and Gerard Conlon were to get an apology from Tony Blair in a private ceremony at the Palace of Westminster. How come they were getting one and not us? We'd been campaigning for years. Peter Stanford, once the editor of the *Catholic Herald* – he'd done a lot for our campaign in the past – rang 10 Downing Street. He said the prime minister might be about to make a mistake in apologizing only to the Conlons. He should include the Maguires. It was agreed that he would do so.

It was the night before we were due at the Palace of Westminster. I was very down. It looked as if I wouldn't make it, not that I cared one way or the other.

After it got dark I began to write down what I would say the next day. Once I had that done, I knew I must go.

On 9 February we went to the House of Commons, Mum, Vincent, John, Anne-Marie and I. Journalists were outside, waiting to hear what we had to say.

When it was my turn to speak, this was what I told them: 'In January 2004, I ended up in the Priory Hospital. I was diagnosed as having bipolar affective disorder, post-traumatic stress disorder, and attention deficit disorder. After that diagnosis, I went on to medication for the various conditions, about twenty pills a day, and I have been told I will be on most of them for the rest of my life. And I'm still having difficulty sleeping.

'I suffered as a child as a result of wrongful imprisonment for handling nitroglycerine. As a result of that, my children suffered too. Because of what happened, their father was not the man he would have liked to be. And to them I would like to say sorry.'

We moved inside the Palace of Westminster.

The night before, I had decided that it was time to let go of my hatred for Gerry Conlon. For a long time, I had been very angry with him for having volunteered our names to the police. For a long time I would have killed him without thinking twice had I bumped into him – or so I believed. However, now I'd come to realize he wasn't the only one to blame for what had happened – there'd been many others – and he'd been a victim too. For these reasons I'd decided I'd talk to him, which I hadn't done since he told the police we were bombmakers. I would do it not for my peace of mind but for his. I hadn't told my family I was going to do this.

As we moved along a corridor, I saw him. I walked towards him with my hand out so he would not misunderstand my intentions. Then it was done, and it was good, and more followed. He spoke to Mum too and she spoke to him.

For me, that was the best part of the day. The apology from Tony Blair, which came a bit later, didn't mean much to me. First, Dad wasn't with us. Second, it was just politics. Third, it was thirty years too late.

When he was talking to us the prime minister said, 'Sorry it took so long,' and that help would be given. A couple of years later I decided to take him up on his offer and wrote looking for help with my Priory bill. These are the replies:

3-1-2007

Dear Mr Maguire

I am writing on behalf of the Prime Minister to thank you for your letter of 14 December. Mr Blair was sorry to learn of your ongoing difficulties.

The Prime Minister has asked me to arrange for a Minister in the Home Office to reply to you direct.

Yours sincerely

E. Adams

8-1-07

Dear Mr Maguire

Thank you for your further letter . . . addressed to the Prime Minister, regarding reimbursement of the costs of your treatment in the Priory Hospital, which you attribute to your wrongful conviction. Your letter has been passed to me to reply [to] as I have responsibility for this area of the law.

You refer to my letter of 5 December, which I sent in response to your earlier one to the Prime Minister. I am sorry if you feel that I did not address the point at issue.

However, I believe that I did so and that your request for financial assistance amounts to a claim for further compensation in respect of your wrongful conviction. The fact is, however, that you were paid compensation for your wrongful conviction, which you accepted in full and final settlement of your claim. As I said in my earlier letter, the compensation scheme must have finality. It is the case with civil damages generally that there may be difficulty in estimating future and contingent losses and that subsequent circumstances may demonstrate an award to have been too little or too much. However, it is also the case generally with civil damages that awards made and accepted in full and final settlement are made on a once and for all basis. Therefore any costs incurred by you in connection with your treatment attributable to the miscarriage of justice should have been met from the compensation paid to you.

Once again, I recognize that this will be a very disappointing reply to you in view of the continuing difficulties you have encountered since your conviction was quashed. I am, as is the Prime Minister, sympathetic to the difficulties that you have faced and we would not in any way wish to underestimate the impact that the wrongful conviction has had on you. I have, however, had to consider your request, amounting to a request for additional compensation, within the terms of the compensation scheme. I do not judge that there are sufficient exceptional grounds to go outside the general policy of not re-opening claims for compensation once a full and final settlement has been accepted by the applicant.

Yours

Gerry Sutcliffe

AFTERWORD

Until I was thirteen my life was great. Mum and Dad were very much there; so were my two brothers and sister. Family life was full and rich, and there was much love. Like all families we had our downs as well as our ups but I was happy. I'm sure of that. The world looked good. I'm sure of that too. At times, I was a little devil. What child isn't? As Dad would say, 'If you can't hear the children playing, then they're up to no good,' and many a time I wasn't heard because I was up to no good. But it wouldn't have lasted, running around the streets with my mates, all the larks I got up to, because Dad would have made sure of that. And I was planning to join the British Army when I was sixteen.

On 3 March 1976 I was convicted. I knew I wasn't ready for prison and I knew I didn't want to go. But I'd no choice. I knew I didn't want to be with the people I was going to meet in prison. But I'd no choice. Off I went.

At the beginning prison was horrible. It was like a ton of bricks falling on my head. I was stricken.

Then I saw what I had to do to survive, and before you could say Bob's your uncle, I was swaggering around with the lads, never letting my guard down, never being myself, driving the screws mad any time I could. I wouldn't have chosen to be what I became, but it was sink or swim and I chose to swim.

I left prison bewildered. I couldn't believe that what had happened had happened, even though I knew it had. How could I forget? 'Did all of this really fucking happen to us?' I would ask myself.

I thought somehow that if I went on asking the question long enough and hard enough the answer would be, 'No,' and every-thing would be all right.

But it did happen. Mum and Dad were taken away from me when I was a child. At a time when I should have had them and their love, I did not. As a result I didn't grow from boy to man with them around, find my feet, make my way in the world and remain connected to them. I matured on my own in the strange world that is prison, and when I came back to the real world, I found I wasn't connected to it. I was solitary. I was on the edge of my family looking in, on the edge of society looking in, on the edge of everything looking in.

After I left prison there was only one thing I wanted and once Sam had shown me the way I couldn't be stopped. Then I met my daughter's mother. She moved out of her home, in which she had wanted for nothing, and into the top floor of a tower block with a baby. I was young. I wasn't ready. I had the smell of prison. There was so much I wanted to do but I didn't know what it was. I soon felt trapped. I went back to filling my boots.

Lorna, the mother of my boys, was living in her own flat, working and looking after herself without any help when I met her. I liked her self-sufficiency – she could cook, clean, iron and do everything, just like I could. Like other members of my family who have always been there for me, though each was going through their own grief, she has stood by me, and above all is a good mother. I ask no more from her.

When we had our first son, Patrick, we lived together. Now she wanted to do for me all the things I'd always done for myself. That was a problem and another was my distrust. My first relationship had failed: would this one turn out the same? I found it hard to commit, and after Billy was born, we fell into what has been the pattern ever since: she had the boys with her and I would visit them or they would visit me.

After Mum and Dad came out of jail I couldn't stop thinking about them getting married and coming to London to start a new life together, full of plans, dreams and hopes, like any couple, not knowing the Troubles were on their way, never thinking that, one day, the police would come knocking. That was the equivalent of a bomb going off in their lives – and all because other men had planted bombs in the name of freedom, men who were indifferent to the innocent who would suffer, whether they were killed by those bombs or be wrongly arrested for them. These thoughts tortured me. I found the unfairness of it all unbearable. They were just two ordinary people doing their best, and the family they'd created was destroyed.

My Patrick was six or seven and he was cuddling up to me on the settee. 'Dad,' he said.

'Yeah.' I knew something important had popped into his head and now he was going to tell me what it was.

'Can I be a giraffe?'

I looked at him, 'OK, you be a giraffe.' I meant it.

His mother had been listening and now, gently, she said, 'Don't be silly. Don't tell him he can be a giraffe.'

'If he wants to be a giraffe for a minute, an hour, or a day,' I said, 'he can be, because in the end he'll find out he can't be a giraffe.'

One day Mum told me both my boys were the spit of me, though both far better than I ever was at school, where they paid attention, plus they always did their homework. Following Mum's remark, when each reached thirteen I couldn't stop thinking that this was what I'd looked like when they'd come to the house that night. From here it was easy, just a hop and a skip really, to imagining what it must have been like for Mum and Dad: their first night in jail, and all their subsequent nights in jail, separated from their children and not knowing whether they were happy or sad. It must have been, as I saw, agony for them, and as time passed my sense of their suffering became almost unbearable and I think it broke my heart.

Over the years, though I had no contact with my daughter other than for a couple of years in her late teens, since when I haven't seen her though I want to, I saw my sons as much as I was able. Sometimes they would come to stay with me, bringing life, warmth and love into my home, often lifting me out of despair. But I have not been a full-time, full-on father. I have been a part-time, often absent father, and I wonder if I've inflicted on them what was inflicted on me – fatherlessness. The answer is yes. That's exactly what I did.

Likewise, I have not been a full-time, full-on brother but a part-time one unavailable to his sister and brothers when he retreated into his shell. Brotherlessness is another sin and when you add sonlessness you've got the three, the Trinity, I've been an absent father, a wayward brother and a troubled son.

My flat sits at the top of a tower block: it's white. I like to keep it pristine, clean and fresh. It gets a new coat of paint regularly. After its last repainting, Mum visited and after looking round she said, 'You don't have much furniture, son.' We were in the sitting room at the time.

'It's the minimalist look,' I replied.

'It looks like you've been burgled.'

The room had nothing but two sofas, a piece of bog-oak sculpture and my City & Guilds certificate (NVQ Level 2, Catering) that I got in HMP Aylesbury. 'I don't like a lot of things around me,' I said.

I hate clutter, I hate mess, and I hate stuff. I like clean, empty and ordered.

And where was the first space I lived that was clean, empty and ordered? Certainly not 43 Third Avenue. It was my cell, the third one down from the PO's office on G Wing, HMP Aylesbury. I know that I have re-created in my flat a space like that space where I lived between 1976 and 1979.

There is one huge difference, though: except for the one at the front I never lock my doors.

So, my flat is and is not a prison.

My flat is white and cell-like.

My flat has nothing to stop me moving from room to room.

It is a heaven, a place of retreat where I find peace.

It is a hell, where I am isolated and separated from everyone I know and want to be with.

Living on my own, I got into the habit of doing things on my own. In fact, I came to prefer doing things on my own. Then I had my breakdown since when, if anything, my solitariness –

which was one reason for my breakdown – has got worse. Since my breakdown I have stayed indoors as much as I can, and I only go out at night when fewer people are about. Even then, it takes me hours to gear myself up to it.

I like to tell myself that it's not the flat that's the problem. The flat is fine, I tell myself. The problem is its location. Yes, the skyline is wonderful. In the daytime I can see Big Ben, the London Eye and Buckingham Palace. At night I can see the lights of the City of London. That's wonderful.

What's not so wonderful is what's in the foreground. It's Paddington Green police station, and right below my flat the Harrow Road, with police cars and vans racing up and down, sirens wailing, lights flashing.

Sometimes I don't know whether I'm looking out at them or they're looking in at me. If the flat could be moved to the coast and I could look out at a grey sea with white-capped waves, I would be happy, I think, because I wouldn't see things that remind me of what happened and trigger memories that churn me up.

Of course, this idea of living by the sea is a fantasy. This is my lot: I live at the top of a tower block and the police station will never be out of view. There's nothing I can do about that, except manage it.

I have two regrets – first, that I've failed somewhat as a father. When my children were born I had a chance to take up where Mum and Dad stopped, to be to my children what my parents had been to me. I could blame my circumstances for the fact that I didn't, but I'm too old for that: I blame myself. That's all there is to be said. I hope they can understand and forgive me. Like it or not, I will always be their father and they'll always be my children and that can't be erased. Neither can what they have been for me: the light at the end of the tunnel.

My other great regret is that I've never bumped into any of the policemen who beat the shit out of me after the arrest or after I got out of prison. There have been many times when I have felt like walking into the Harrow Road police station with a pair of hand guns and letting them have it. But I don't hate the police in general, just the wankers who beat me when I was a boy, most of all, the Giant. If I ever bumped into him he might tell me he was only doing his job. He might ask me to try to understand. Like fuck I would. I'd hit him so hard he wouldn't know what year it was.

Over the years it's been said to me, usually by well-intentioned people, 'You can't miss what you never had.' They mean, 'You never had a family life, really, so stop complaining.' But I had something until the night of 3 December 1974. Since then, I have worked very hard to find memories of those days that I know are buried inside me. What I have, I feel, is a jigsaw puzzle, a faded picture on the lid, and the puzzle inside with several pieces missing. I have never been able to reconstruct what I had which has been frustrating.

I have been angry about what I could remember only too clearly. It's funny how the good vanishes while the bad hangs around. The product of those memories, the rage and hate those experiences produced, boiled away inside me for years.

Mum went through more than any of us but did so with dignity, without bitterness and, supported by her faith in God and the love of her family, she stood tall and forgave. She knew me well and saw straight into my heart, which was why she gave the same sensible advice several times over the years: 'If you carry this hate around with you,' she said, 'in the end you'll be the one who suffers.'

In my head I saw she was right, but my heart wouldn't let it go. I continued raging until two things happened: I had my breakdown and my sons wanted to know what had really happened all those years ago.

When I began to talk to them I realized that the fury had to go. For one thing it was killing me and for another I didn't want them to be infected by it. Whatever else I did, I mustn't let them see the world as their angry father had. I couldn't hide anything from them but I mustn't scorch them with my rage. So I reined it in, not completely but quite a bit, and I felt better.

Then I began to write this book and more anger went. During the writing of this book, some things in my life have improved. There's still a little fire burning inside me but now that this book is finished, I hope it will go out, quietly, one day.

FURTHER READING

Conlon, Gerry, *Proved Innocent: The Story of Gerry Conlon of the Guildford Four* (Hamish Hamilton, London, 1990)

Hill, Paul, with Bennett, Ronan, *Stolen Years: Before and After Guildford* (Doubleday, London, 1990)

Kee, Robert, *Trial and Error: The Maguires, the Guildford Pub Bombings and British Justice* (Hamish Hamilton, London, 1986)

Maguire, Anne, with Gallagher, Jim, *Why Me?: One Woman's Fight for Justice and Dignity* (HarperCollins, London, 1994)

McKee, Grant, and Franey, Ross, *Timebomb: Irish Bombers, English Justice and the Guildford Four* (Bloomsbury, London, 1988)

O'Connell, Michael, *Truth: The First Casualty* (Riverstone, Ireland, 1993)

Victory, Patrick, *Justice and Truth: The Guildford Four and Maguire Seven* (Sinclair-Stevenson, London, 2002)

ACKNOWLEDGEMENTS

We are taught from a very young age how important history is. The foundations that I've grown up on and now stand on have been built from my history. For many years this story was a heavy weight. Sometimes it got in the way of everyday life. Sometimes it knocked me down, though I was always able to get back on my feet again. I had the love and support of family and friends, and I knew the truth. Also, as I got older and stronger, I got better and better at putting it completely out of my mind. I got so good at this that it would only surface occasionally if there was a trigger like a song or a smell. Or if I was asked to talk about what had happened.

Writing this story, and looking back over my life, has made me realize how lucky I have been. I could have been born blind or deaf. I could have been a hungry child in Africa whose parents had died of AIDS. I could have been one of the 'unwanted children' of Romania, left in one of its orphanages. I could have been a child living in squalor and confusion in one of India's many densely populated and polluted cities, or a street kid in Brazil or Honduras, fighting to stay alive, his reward to fight another day.

Nearer to home, I could have come from a broken family, finding myself, like so many of our young people, living homeless on our city streets, maybe with a mental or physical illness, dependent on drugs, begging for food and money, sleeping in doorways, or in a cardboard box under a dark, noisy, pigeon-infested bridge. Or, like so many others who find themselves as I once did, innocent and in prison. Like Sam Hallam, a young teenager from Hoxton,

Patrick Maguire

London, who is serving life for the murder of another innocent young teenager, Essayas Kessahan, a crime I believe that Sam Hallam didn't do.

For the best part of my life I've been very angry because of what happened, and you can't fight without anger. What angers me most is that it happened to me in my own country, Great Britain. Tell me, what's so great about it when it does this to its own, and doesn't give a shit.

However, there is also another side to this story: the people I've met who came from all walks of life, and who listened and fought alongside us when others wouldn't. Without them, we wouldn't have proved so many wrong. There are far too many to mention and I would hate to leave anyone out. They know who they are, and I thank them.

With the injustices happening in the world, and all those being victimized too, as I write this, I know that I am indeed one of the luckier ones.

I want to end, finally, by acknowledging my gratitude to our solicitor, Alastair Logan, who worked tirelessly and eventually successfully to have our convictions for handling explosives quashed by the Court of Appeal. He is a great man.

Patrick Maguire

I would like to thank the following for their assistance in the writing of this book: Julian Broadhead, Maggie Brooks, Alastair Logan, Robert Kee, Anne Maguire, Vincent Maguire, Anne Scott, Jason Thompson, Graham Rawle, Noel Smith and Peter Stanford, as well as the editor of the *Independent* newspaper for permission to quote Heather Mills the home affairs correspondent's article of 21 September 1993. Hazel Orme prepared the manuscript for publication.

All mistakes of course are our own.

Carlo Gébler